VOICES

OF

POWER

THE ECCO COMPANIONS SERIES

VOICES
OF
POWER

World Leaders Speak

□   □   □

Edited by Henry Bienen

THE ECCO PRESS

Copyright © 1995 by Henry Bienen
All rights reserved
The Ecco Press
100 West Broad Street
Hopewell, NJ 08525
Published simultaneously in Canada by
Penguin Books Canada Ltd., Ontario
Printed in the United States of America
FIRST EDITION

Library of Congress Cataloging-in-Publication Data
Voices of power : world leaders speak / Henry Bienen, editor.
—1st ed.
    p.   cm.
  ISBN 0-88001-384-2 (cloth)
   1. Politcal leadership. 2. Power (Social sciences)
3. Legitimacy of governments. I. Bienen, Henry.
JC330.3.V65   1994
303.3'4—dc20   94-46164

The text of this book is set in Monotype Joanna

Page 407 constitutes a continuation of this page.

□   □   □

For three friends from whom I have learned a great deal.

To Angus Stewart Deaton, William Church Osborne Professor of Economics and Public Affairs at Princeton, who has broken new ground in development economics by pioneering in analytic techniques and data gathering. I wish that more social scientists shared his commitment to analytical rigor and to working on interesting problems.

To Jeremiah P. Ostriker, Charles A. Young Professor of Astronomy and Chair, Department of Astrophysics at Princeton, whose phenomenal breadth of interest and clarity of mind are the envy of his friends and whom I have known for over forty years.

To Robert Tucker, IBM Professor Emeritus of International Studies at Princeton, who taught me and generations of his students and colleagues about Russia, and about political leadership, and whose own prose has always set standards the rest of us cannot match.

CONTENTS

Presidents of the United States

INTRODUCTION

I have wanted to provide readers with leaders' own reflections on power and authority. Not all leaders have had interesting things to say about power, legitimacy, and leadership, at least publicly. The great texts have more often been written by political theorists and advisers than by leaders themselves. We are more likely to read Machiavelli's *Prince* on the getting and holding of power than we are Margaret Thatcher's recent memoirs. As I read through the memoirs of contemporary leaders, including many U.S. twentieth-century presidents, I am struck by how few had systematically written in an interesting way about power. American presidents have been more evocative when writing about their loss of power and their withdrawal from high office than when they discussed obtaining, wielding, and holding power and authority.

Of course, it is not expected that all American presidents will be professional political theorists or social scientists, as was Woodrow Wilson, or that they will be writers like Theodore Roosevelt before he became president. Most twentieth-century presidents are not outstanding stylists, although many of them have been prolific authors, most recently Richard Nixon. Few passages in President Nixon's writings grip readers the way Lincoln's Gettysburg Address has over the decades, even though Nixon's presidency was highly dramatic.

The failure of contemporary leaders in the United States to write explicitly about power and authority may be a function of the fact that some memoirs are little more than compilations from White House logs. Perhaps the flatness of presidential memoirs by Lyndon Johnson, Jimmy Carter, Dwight Eisenhower, and Richard Nixon is a function of writing for mass markets from the logs. Of course, there are many wonderful diaries by historical figures. Ulysses S. Grant wrote his memoirs under financial pressure as well as the pressures of serious illness and produced interesting work. Perhaps it is the nature of the reading public that has changed or of the men who became presidents.

The lack of exciting writing on power by leaders is not confined to American presidents. I decided not to use Margaret Thatcher's memoirs and the autobiographies by Benazir Bhutto because they tell us little directly about the leaders' understanding of power. These leaders surely have views on the subject but chose not to reveal them to us in accessible and interesting ways.

Some leaders, however, have taken writing seriously. Winston Churchill won a Nobel Prize in literature, although the selections below are taken mostly from his speeches and broadcasts. He took the spoken word seriously, too, and his words resound through history. Charles de Gaulle also cared about his writing. So did Mussolini and Hitler, who were very conscious of propaganda and the power of communication. Mussolini had been a serious journalist.

The writings of the Marxist leaders combine serious but often arid treatment of power and authority with sometimes earthy statements. Mao Tse-tung's speeches, collected in *Mao Tse-tung Unrehearsed*, are trenchant and pungent, but many of his writings on organization and his modifications of Marxist thought are tedious and ponderous. Similarly, some of Stalin's more provocative musings on history and the role of leaders are found in the interview with Emil Ludwig presented in this book, while Stalin's own attempts to be a serious theoretician are often heavy-handed.

In the Leninist tradition Mao and Stalin, like Lenin himself, were very conscious of the importance of organization, military power, and individual decisiveness in bringing about desired results. This tradition posed some dilemmas for Marxists, who felt it necessary to debate and to worry about the issues of individual will, voluntarism, and class consciousness, in bringing historical tendencies to fruition. Most Marxists who did not believe in the importance of individual decisiveness and of the power of organization to be a revolutionary force did not survive as leaders very long.

From the start of his mature career as a revolutionary, Lenin argued for organization and will as critical factors, albeit in the context of historical stages and tendencies, but he came to worry about perversions of historical evolution that were brought about by rampant bureaucracy and individual corruption. In other words, there could be the wrong kind of individual action and this would be consequential.

These themes also concerned Mao and Trotsky. The latter well appreciated Lenin's role in the successful Bolshevik Revolution of 1917 and he also understood Stalin's role in the distortion of this revolution. What he may not have understood was the logic of a system of undemocratic rule and single-party leadership that led to concentration of power in one person's hands.

Castro, too, has been concerned with voluntary action. For Castro, a revolutionary must not wait for society to be prepared for revolution or to be ripe for revolution. Rather, it is the revolutionary's example and his exemplary action that galvanize society. Castro's words were put into action by his compadre Che Guevara, but Castro's success in Cuba could not be duplicated by Guevara in Bolivia. Castro, like

Mussolini before him, was a leader in search of a movement. He found his in opposition to a decaying regime. Guevara died in Bolivia having failed to mobilize a peasant resistance.

The revolutionary as a man of action characterized non-Marxist leaders. The role of the individual leader was glorified by Mussolini and by Hitler, although in their writings and speeches the people and the nation are also invoked. The individual leader personifies the best of the nation and carries forward its work. This theme is invoked by Juan and Eva Perón. Marxists had to be careful with their analyses of the role of the individual in seizing, using, and holding power; typically, Stalin invoked Lenin's majesty and importance, to build his own cult of the personality. Mao insisted on his own contributions as a theorist of Marxism-Leninism rather than calling up his role as a man of action, although he may well have prized both roles.

Nationalist leaders such as Kenyatta and Nyerere, Nehru and Indira Gandhi, and Nasser invoke the nation and the anti-colonial struggle as a means of legitimating their own rule. Nehru and Indira Gandhi also reflected on Mahatma Gandhi, both to educate followers and to legitimate themselves. The adducing of earlier leaders for self-legitimation and self-justification is not peculiar to nationalist leaders. American presidents frequently recall their great predecessors, as do Marxist leaders.

Nationalist leaders frequently blend socialism and homilies on decent living, using Benjamin Franklinesque sermons on the virtues of hard work by the individual for the nation. American presidents have their own homilies: hard work and capitalism.

All invoke the people. Mahatma Gandhi is somewhat unusual in that he explicitly says that the people may be wonderful but the people can make mistakes.

Nationalist and totalitarian leaders, whether Marxist or not, insist on self-purification for the good of the nation. Democratic leaders do not use the language of self-purification. They do not claim to personify the people. In the war speeches of Churchill and Roosevelt, though, there is a clear sense that they are expressing, for a time, the sentiments of the people; there is an invocation of the virtues of free people and the specific virtues of a nation under siege. In de Gaulle, to an extent, mysticism reappears. Leadership is a burden, a calling; it involves renunciation. Its rewards are the esteem of one's fellows.

Theodore Roosevelt stresses what he calls "manly virtues" and the need for individuals to take action. A commitment to representative government can be seen in Wilson and Roosevelt as well as in later American leaders. But what characterizes democratic leaders is their sense that their power is transitory. They will leave when asked, and there are limits of law and custom on the extent of their power. Many of the selections in these pages provide democratic leaders' reflections on withdrawal from power and on the morality of power.

There are many different styles of leadership and types of leaders. This book, in which leaders speak to specific audiences as well as to masses of followers, is not about leadership per se.[1] No division is made between reformers and revolutionaries or transforming leaders and transacting or bargaining ones.

This book does not explore the different sources of legitimacy for leaders—whether these stem from the legal structures of particular societies or regimes or whether they inhere in the leader as a charismatic individual. It is about leaders' direct reflections on power; here leaders are revealing their views of power.

Most leaders have had an ability to persuade and to communicate. But Ronald Reagan, known as the "Great Communicator," was a leader who left little in writing to recommend his place here. Thus, I did not include him. There are leaders like Mu'ammar al-Gadhafi of Libya, who can make fiery speeches but may not be able to communicate their views for posterity. Others, like Ayatollah Khomeini, may require specific contexts in order to get a hearing from listeners and followers. Yet, Khomeini is certainly worth reading on power and authority for readers who are not Shiite Muslims or Iranians, because he challenges conventional western ideas about the sources of authority and power.

There is a huge literature on the power and charisma of individual leaders.[2] It is striking that for the inner core of followers most leaders are not charismatic. That is, they do not necessarily command fervent loyalty and devotion. If they do, it is from some followers only. Hitler may have commanded this kind of worship from some of his immediate followers, but there were attempts against his life during World War II and he was embroiled in factional politics from the start of his career and all through the 1930s. Mao and Stalin faced opposition from high-level leaders, as did Lenin.

Leaders' speeches and writings are often aimed at lower-echelon or intermediate-level leaders or they are aimed over the heads of other leaders, at mass followers. Hitler's *Mein Kampf* was aimed at forging and consolidating a following. So were Khomeini's lectures, which were widely distributed via tape cassettes.

Robert Tucker rightly tells us that so-called charismatic appeal appears to have little to do with great oratory or particular qualities of demeanor or personality, and more to do with the cogency of the diagnosis of a situation.[3] This appears to have been the case for Ayatollah Khomeini. He may have had a more powerful personal appeal for some western visitors who were struck by his appearance and often could not understand his language, than for Iranians, who may have been more persuaded by his opposition to the Shah's regime and the alternative he presented.

Deification of the leader often comes well after the rise to power, when the propaganda machines take over. The deification of Lenin was largely a creation of Stalin, who used it for his own purposes and created the Stalin cult in his lifetime. Khrushchev's consolidation of power was furthered by his attack on the Stalin cult in a speech presented in these pages. Gorbachev, as was characteristic of him in domestic politics, was at first balanced and careful in his own dealing with Stalin's history. The role of Mao's place in Chinese history remains a debated one among the Chinese leadership precisely because the debate is a charged political one, not one of historical argument alone.

Followers always see leaders within a context, and often one of social and personal distress.[4] The distress may be that of social and economic dislocation or upheaval. This upheaval frequently stems from war and defeat. War shapes events and leaders. We still evaluate Churchill, Franklin Roosevelt, de Gaulle, Wilson, Stalin, Lenin, and Trotsky as great war leaders. Their words call out to us from historical epochs but they seem to reach beyond the specific context in which they were uttered or written. This is true, of course, for Lincoln's great speeches, which continue to resonate through the ages. Perhaps this is what is meant by greatness of political speech. Other words that seemed so stirring at a particular time—for example, John F. Kennedy's inaugural address—face revisionist analysis when the times change. In the aftermath of Vietnam, Kennedy's call to bear any burden rings hollow for some readers.

I have not tried to delve into the psychological wellsprings to understand leaders or their own specific analyses.[5] Rather, I have edited some famous and some not-so-famous statements. A number of texts are well known; others may be little known. I did not strive to be comprehensive even within the twentieth century. Not all presidents are represented, and surely not all major twentieth-century leaders.

I chose mostly leaders who have held the highest office in their nations. Gandhi, who was in many ways a supreme but unofficial leader, is an exception. So is Trotsky, who was a coleader for a time with both Lenin and Stalin but who never achieved supreme leadership.

I did try for regional variation, but hardly systematically so. In the end, this book contains what I consider significant reflections on power by a range of twentieth-century leaders. I often found the most interesting passages in autobiographies or other writings accomplished before a leader assumed power. This was true for Hitler, Mussolini, and de Gaulle. Most presidents of the United States write their memoirs after leaving office or compile speeches and "The Wit and Wisdom of . . ." just as they are running for the presidency. Woodrow Wilson and Theodore Roosevelt were atypical in that they were prolific writers before they were presidents. Winston Churchill was unusual. He wrote great prose before he became prime minister, during the War, and after he left office he wrote biographies of other leaders. Indeed, he tells us before 1910 that he was a journalist during the Boer War, he married and, end of story, was going to live happily ever after.[6]

In the passages that follow, sometimes the words soar; sometimes they are flat and matter-of-fact. On occasion they are very personal reflections and almost prosaic in style and tone, but nonetheless they reveal each leader's understanding of power and authority.

NOTES

1. Among many studies, see Bryan D. Jones, ed., Leadership and Politics (Lawrence, Kansas: University of Kansas Press, 1989); Robert C. Tucker, Politics as Leadership (Columbia, Missouri: University of Missouri Press, 1981); Angus McIntyre, ed., Aging and Political Leadership (Albany: State University of New York Press, 1988).

2. For discussions of charismatic leadership, see Robert C. Tucker, "The Theory of Charismatic Leadership," Daedalus 97:3 (Summer, 1968, 731–756 and see this issue of Daedalus titled "Philosophers and Kings: Studies in Leadership"; Jean Lacouture, The Demigods: Charismatic Leadership in the Third World (New York: Alfred A. Knopf, 1970).

3. Robert C. Tucker, Politics as Leadership, p. 94.

4. Ibid.

5. For such analyses, see Harold Lasswell, Power and Personality (New York: W. W. Norton, 1976); Alexander and Juliette George, Woodrow Wilson and Colonel Hous: A Personality (New York: W. W. Norton, 1973); Erik Erikson, Gandhi's Truth: On the Origins of Militant Nonviolence (New York: W. W. Norton, 1969).

6. Winston Churchill, My Early Life: A Roving Commission (London: T. Butterworth, 1930).

TOTALITARIAN LEADERS

ADOLF HITLER

FULL NAME:

Adolf Hitler

BORN:

20 April 1889, Braunau am Imn, Austria

DIED:

30 April 1945, Berlin, Germany

Soldier and artist. Leader of the National Socialist (Nazi) Party of Germany from 1920 to 21. In prison for attempted putsch in 1923. Unsuccessful bid for presidency in 1932. Officially Chancellor of Germany from 30 January 1933. Führer (Leader) after 2 August 1934. Offices of Chancellor and President merged in 1934.

His writings include *Mein Kampf* (New York: Reynal and Hitchcock, 1941) and *The Speeches of Adolf Hitler, April 1922–August 1939*, Volumes I and II (London: Oxford University Press, 1942). Biographies include: Alan Bullock, *Hitler: A Study in Tyranny* (London: Oldhams Press, 1952) and Joachim Fest, *Hitler* (New York, Harcourt Brace Jovanovich, 1974).

Mein Kampf[*]

"General Political Considerations from My Time in Vienna"

It is my conviction today that a man should not take any active public part in politics before the age of thirty, except in cases of outstanding ability. He should not do so because up to that time the formation of a general platform takes place from which he examines the various political problems and defines his own final attitude toward them. The man who has now matured at least mentally may or should take part in the political guidance of the community only after reaching a fundamental view of life and, with it, a stability of his own way of looking at the individual current problems.

If this is not the case, he runs the risk that some day he will have to change his attitude toward vital questions, or, despite his better knowledge and belief, to uphold points of view that reason and conviction have long since rejected. The first case is very embarrassing for him, for now personally uncertain, he has no longer the right to expect that his followers have the same unshakable belief in him as before; such a reversal on the part of the leader brings uncertainty to his followers and frequently a certain feeling of embarrassment as regards those they have been fighting. But in the second case there may happen what we so frequently see today: in the same measure in which the leader no longer believes in what he said, his defense will be hollow and shallow, and he will be base in his choice of means. While he himself no longer thinks seriously of defending his political revelations (one does not die for something one does not believe in), the demands he makes of his followers become greater and more impudent, till finally he sacrifices what is left of the leader in order to end up as a "politician"; that means that kind of man whose only real conviction is to have no convictions, combined with impudent obtrusiveness and the brazen-faced artfulness of lying . . .

I restrained myself from appearing in public, though I believe that I have occupied myself with politics more than many others. I talked of what occupied my mind or attracted me only in the narrowest circle. This speaking within the most limited frame had many advantages; I learned less to "speak" than to gain an insight into the unbelievably primitive opinions and arguments of the people. Thus I trained myself for my own further education without losing time or ignoring opportunities. Nowhere in Germany was the opportunity for this so favorable as in Vienna at that time. . . .

[*] which was begun in 1924 when Hitler was imprisoned

Is it at all possible to make a wavering majority of people ever responsible?

Is not the very idea of all responsibility closely connected with the individual?

Is it practically possible to make the leading person of a government liable for actions, the development and execution of which are to be laid exclusively to the account of the will and the inclination of a large number of men?

Or must not the task of the leading statesman be seen in the birth of a creative idea or plan in itself, rather than in the ability to make the ingenuity of his plans understandable to a flock of sheep and empty-heads for the purpose of begging for their gracious consent?

Is this the criterion of a statesman that he masters the art of persuasion to the same extent as that of the diplomatic shrewdness in the choice of great lines of direction or decision?

Is the inability of a leader proved by the fact that he does not succeed in winning the majority of a crowd of people for a certain idea, dumped together by more or less fine accidents?

Has this crowd ever been able to grasp an idea before its success was proclaimed by its greatness?

Is not every ingenious deed in this world the visible protest of genius against the inertia of the masses?

But what is the statesman to do who does not succeed in winning, by flattery, the favor of this crowd for his plans?

Is he to buy it?

Or is he now, considering the stupidity of his fellow citizens, to give up the carrying-out of the tasks he recognizes as of vital importance, or is he to retire, or should he still remain?

Does not, in such a case, a real character find himself in an inextricable dilemma between knowledge and decency, or rather honest conviction?

Where is the border that separates duty toward the community from the obligations of personal honor?

Must not every real leader refuse to be degraded in such a way to the level of a political profiteer?

And must not, on the other hand, every profiteer feel himself called on to "make" politics, as it is not he who bears the ultimate responsibility, but rather some incomprehensible crowd?

Must not our parliamentary principle of the majority lead to the demolition of the idea of leadership as a whole?

Or does one believe that the progress of the world has originated in the brains of majorities and not in the head of an individual?

Or are we of the opinion that in the future we can do without this preliminary presumption of human culture?

Does it not, on the contrary, appear more necessary today than ever before?

The parliamentary principle of decision by majority, by denying the authority of the person and placing in its stead the number of the crowd in question, sins against the aristocratic basic idea of Nature, whose opinion of aristocracy, however, need in no way be represented by the present-day decadence of our Upper Ten Thousand. . . .

The easier the responsibility of the individual leader is, the more will the number of those grow who, even with the most wretched dimensions, will feel called upon to put their immortal energies at the disposal of the nation. Yes, they can hardly await their turn; lined up in a long queue, they count the number of those waiting ahead of them with sorrowful regret, and they figure out the hour when in all human probability their turn will come. Therefore, they long for every change in the office they aspire to, and are grateful for every scandal that thins out the ranks ahead of them. . . .

For let it be said to all knights of the pen and to all the political dandies, especially of today: the greatest changes in this world have never yet been brought about by a goose-quill!

No, the pen has always been reserved to motivate these changes theoretically.

But the power that set the greatest historical avalanches of political and religious nature sliding was, from the beginning of time, the magic force of the spoken word alone.

The great masses of a nation will always and only succumb to the force of the spoken word. But all great movements are movements of the people, are volcanic eruptions of human passions and spiritual sensations, stirred either by the cruel Goddess of Misery or by the torch of the word thrown into the masses, and are not the lemonade-like outpourings of aestheticizing literati and drawing-room heroes.

Only a storm of burning passion can turn people's destinies, but only he who harbors passion in himself can arouse passion.

Passion alone will give to him, who is chosen by her, the words that, like beats of a hammer, are able to open the doors to the heart of a people.

He to whom passion is denied and whose mouth remains closed is not chosen by Heaven as the prophet of its will.

Therefore, may every writer remain by his inkwell in order to work "theoretically" if his brains and ability are sufficient for this; such writers are neither born nor chosen to become leaders.

Every movement with great aims has anxiously to watch that it may not lose connection with the great masses.

It has to examine every question primarily from this point of view and to make decisions in this direction.

Further, it has to avoid everything that could diminish or even weaken its ability to influence the masses; perhaps not for "demagogic" reasons, no, but because of the simple realization that without the enormous power of the masses of a people no great idea, no matter how sublime and lofty it may appear, is realizable. . . .

"The World War"

Only in the eternally regular use of force lies the preliminary condition for success. This perseverance is only and always the result of a certain spiritual conviction alone. All force that does not spring from a firm spiritual foundation will be hesitating and uncertain. It lacks the stability that can only rest in a fanatical view of life. It is the outcome of the energy of the moment and the brutal determination of a single individual, but therefore it is subjected to the change of the personality and its nature and strength.

But to this something else must be added:

Every view of life, be it more of a political or of a religious nature (sometimes the borderline between them can be ascertained only with difficulty), fights less for the negative destruction of the adversary's world of ideas, and more for the positive carrying-out of its own doctrine. Therefore, its fight is less a defense than an attack. Even as regards the definiteness of its goal, it has an advantage, as this goal represents the victory of its own idea, while the other way round it is difficult to decide when the negative aim of the destruction of the enemy's doctrine may be considered as completed and assured. For this reason alone the attack on a view of life will be more carefully planned and also more powerful than the defense of such a doctrine; as here, too, the decision is due to the attack and not to the defense. But the fight against a spiritual power by means of force is only a defense as long as the sword itself does not appear as the supporter, propagator, and announcer of a new spiritual doctrine. . . .

"View of Life and Party"

. . . Therefore I saw my own task especially in extracting from the abundant and unshaped material of a general view of life and in molding into more or less dogmatic forms those nuclear ideas which in their clear demarcation are suitable for bringing together those people who take their allegiance to this. In other words: *The National Socialist German Workers' Party takes over, out of the basic trend of thoughts of a general concep-*

tion of life, the essential features, and out of these, with consideration of practical reality, of time and of the existing human material as well as of its weaknesses, a political creed that now, in turn, by the tightly organizing integration of great human masses, made possible by this, creates the presumption for the victorious fighting through of this view of life.

"View of Life and Organization"

. . . Thus all inventions are the result of the creative ability of some person. All these persons themselves, whether willingly or unwillingly, are more or less great benefactors to all men. Later on their activity gives to millions, even billions of human beings aids for alleviating the execution of their struggle for life.

If in the origin of the present material culture we see always individual persons as inventors who supplement one another mutually and who build upon one another, the same is the case with the exercise and the execution of the things thought up and discovered by the inventors. For also all procedures of production, according to their origin, have in turn to be identified with inventions and thus to be considered dependent on the individual. Also the purely theoretical work of thinking, which in individual instances cannot even be measured but which is nevertheless the presumption for all further material inventions, appears again as the exclusive produce of the individual person. Not the masses invent and not the majority organizes or thinks, but all in all only the individual, the person. . . .

. . . Thereby it is not necessary that each individual who fights for this view of life have full insight into, and exact knowledge of, the ultimate ideas and trends of thought of the movement's leader. Rather it is necessary that one make clear to him only a few but very great viewpoints and that the essential basic lines are unforgettably branded in his memory, so that he is completely imbued with the conviction that the victory of his movement and its doctrine is necessary. The individual soldier, too, is not initiated into the thought development of higher strategy. As he is trained by strict discipline and a fanatical conviction of the right and the force of his cause and for complete devotion to it, so must be trained the individual adherent of a movement of great scope, great future, and greatest intentions.

As useless as an army would be the individual soldiers of which would all be generals, and be it only by their education and knowledge, just as useless would be a political movement as representation of a view of life if it were only the reservoir of "intellectual" people. No, it needs the primitive soldier too, as otherwise inner discipline cannot be achieved. . . .

"The Strong Man Is Mightiest Alone"

... It is certain that also here, by virtue of a natural order, the strongest man is chosen for fulfilling the great mission; but the realization that this *one* man is the one who is exclusively called upon usually dawns upon the others very late. On the contrary, they *all* look upon themselves as *having equal rights* and as *being called upon* for the solution of this task, and their contemporaries usually are least able to distinguish who of them—because solely capable of the highest achievements—solely deserves their support.

Thus in the course of centuries, frequently even within one and the same period, various men appear, they found movements in order to fight for objectives—at least so they assert—are the same or are felt by the great masses to be the same. The people itself harbors vague wishes and has general convictions, without, however, being able to see perfectly clearly about the very nature of the objective, or of its own wish, or even about the possibilities of realizing them.

The tragedy lies in the fact that those men aim at the same goal by quite different ways, without knowing one another, and that therefore, in the purest faith in their own mission, they consider themselves obliged to go their own way without considering the others. . . .

"Propaganda and Organization"

. . . Great *theorists* are only in the rarest cases great *organizers*, as the greatness of the *theorist* and the *program-maker* lies primarily in the *recognition* and in the *establishment of abstractly correct laws*, while the *organizer* has to be primarily a *psychologist*. He has to take man as he is, and for this reason he must know him. He must not overevaluate him just as he must not underestimate him in the mass. On the contrary, he must try to take account of the weakness and of the bestiality equally, so that, all factors considered, he will create a formation, which as a living organism is filled with the strongest and most constant force, and is thus suitable for carrying an idea and paving its way to success.

But still more rarely is a great theorist a great leader. More usually this will be the agitator, something that many people, who consider a question from the purely scientific viewpoint, do not like to hear; yet this is understandable. An agitator who shows the ability of imparting an idea to the great masses must be a psychologist, even though he were only a demagogue. In that case he will still be better suited to be a leader than the theorist who is an alien to the people and to the world. *For to lead means: to be able to move masses.* . . .

The Speeches of Adolf Hitler

*Speech on "The Morass of Parliament or
the Fight for Freedom," 4 May 1923*

The German people has to meet demands that are greater than the whole of its national wealth. These demands must therefore have a quite definite purpose that lies beyond purely economic considerations. France does not desire reparations, she desires the annihilation of Germany: it means for her the fulfillment of a very old dream—the hegemony of France over Europe. . . .

And that fact determines the lines on which alone the reconstruction of Germany is possible. First of all the question of the self-defense of the nation must be solved: and that is primarily not a technical question: it is a question of the spirit, of the will. And it will not be solved until the German people understands that one can conduct politics only when one has the support of power—and again power. . . .

But in the end the fire of German youth will conquer: Youth will have to support the state, which it creates for itself. . . . What can save Germany is the dictatorship of the national will and of the national resolution.

And if it be asked: "Is there a fitting personality to act as leader?"— it is not our task to look for such a person. He is either given by Heaven or he is not given. Our task is to fashion the sword for his use when he appears. Our task is to give to the dictator when he comes a people that is ripe for him. German people, awake! It draws near today!

*Reply to Otto Strasser's conception that the idea
must be the starting point, 21 May 1930*

In his conversation with Hitler on 21 May 1930 Otto Strasser was expounding his conception that the idea must ever be the starting-point: it controls the conscience and is the court of highest instance before which man must justify his action. Ideas are eternal, and we men are but the body in which the word becomes flesh. Leaders and subordinates are all alike servants of the idea. To this Hitler replied: This is all bombastic nonsense: . . . it boils down to this, that you would give to every member of the Party the right to decide on the idea—even to decide whether the leader is true to the so-called idea or not. That is democracy at its worst and there is no place with us for any such view. With us the leader and the idea are one, and every member of the Party has to do what the leader orders. The leader incorporates the idea and alone knows its ultimate goal.

Our organization is built up on discipline, and I have no wish to see this organization broken up by a few swollen-headed *littérateurs*. You yourself were a soldier. . . . I ask you: are you prepared to submit to this discipline or not?

Speech at Detmold on 15 January 1936, commemorating the successful Landtag election in Lippe of 15 January 1933

Time has proved that we were right. We saw the battle through and from it we have drawn a lesson for the future. There may yet be difficulties at some time in the future. But you do not know me yet— not by a long way. I see here my people, and I see history, and I recognize its teachings. I have trained up the whole movement in accordance with my ideals. Our opponents do not understand this, but I cannot help them. National Socialism governs in accordance with its ideals, and these the others must accept. We have no thought of giving up our ideals and adopting different aims. There is yet one more lesson for the future to be drawn from the election campaign of that time: the movement was then controlled by a single will, which swept everyone along with it. What should we have come to in Germany, if there had been not one movement, but thirty-six or forty-five? A leadership worthy of the name must have the courage to make its will the will of the nation—or else abdicate. There is only one central power, and it confers authority and sovereignty.

Speech to Nuremberg Parteitag, September 1933

. . . Thus were formed those communities that created the essential features of human organization through the welding together of different races. And this organization always demands the subjection of the will and the activity of many under the will and the energy of a single individual. As men come to discover the astonishing results of this concentration of their capacity and labor-force they begin to recognize not merely the expediency but also the necessity of such action. And thus it is that a great and significant Aryan civilization did not arise where Aryans alone were living in racial purity, but always where they formed a vital association with races otherwise constituted, an association founded not on mixture of blood but on the basis of an organic community of purpose. And what was at first undoubtedly felt by the conquered as bitter compulsion later became in spite of this even for them a blessing. Unconsciously in the master-people there grew up ever more clearly and vitally a recognition of the ethical demand that their supremacy must be no arbitrary rule but must be controlled by a noble reasonableness. The capacity to subdue others was not given to them by Providence in order to make the subjects feel that the lordship of their conqueror was a meaningless tyranny, a mere oppression: that capacity was given that through the union of the conqueror's genius with the strength of the conquered they might create for both alike an existence that because it was useful was not degrading to man. . . .

Speech at the Führertagung held in June 1933

The people that understands best how to set every fellow countryman in the place for which he is in a way born will produce the greatest achievement in the life of peoples. Germany has not in the political sphere produced a hierarchy of leaders, though this has been done in almost all other spheres. This is due to the fact that in the last century political leadership was more and more entrusted to a class that had arisen from purely economic successes. Political capacity is essentially a gift for organization and thus is clearly distinguished from the capacity needed in the economic sphere. . . . The state in the present century has been governed almost exclusively on the maxims with which one conducts a limited liability company and thus necessarily the people has become hostile to this kind of leadership. What was needed was the building up of a school of practical life that should stand open to all those who felt themselves called to the political struggle . . . Just as a magnet draws from a composite mass only the steel chips so should a movement directed exclusively toward political struggle draw to itself only those natures that are called to political leadership.

It is now the task of the National Socialist movement to build up organically a political leadership parallel with the leadership in cultural and economic life. To lead a nation that longs for clear and capable political leadership can always only be the task of a leading minority. He who puts in the foreground this conception of an organic selection of leaders is thinking historically. When we acted in this way we were not keeping in view merely the present: our aim was that posterity should be forced to admit that the men of our day had created foundations that would guarantee for centuries the life of successive generations. And that, too, our generation owes to its dead. We could not be content with half-measures that could not justify themselves before the judgment-seat of history; we had to perform our task completely. There is only one tolerance that we can practice—that toward the eternal life of our people: the parties could not be tolerated. Our task is to build up in Germany a hierarchy of political leadership that can be fitted into the fundamental laws of the nation's life. If we give the leadership to those who have a natural right to lead, then we shall fulfill a law alike of the highest reason and of the highest justice. The German Revolution will not be complete until the whole German people has been fashioned anew, until it has been organized anew and has been reconstructed.

Our aim is to draw from the midst of the people a class of leaders that shall be hard as steel. When in this way the people has been rightly trained through its political leadership, then the social spirit will come to its own, for he who thinks only in terms of economics will never be able to think and act truly socially.

Campaign speech for the presidency of the Reich against Hindenburg in 1932

In my will you will find one day that I ask that nothing may be put upon my tombstone save my name, Adolf Hitler. My title I create for myself with my name and my individuality: I ask titles from none: I receive no titles as a gift. Even Herr von Hindenburg cannot give me a title. What can a title mean for me, what meaning can the words Chancellor of the Reich have for me? My great rival, President von Hindenburg, is eighty-five years old and I am forty-three and I feel in excellent health. I am convinced that nothing will happen to me, for I know the greatness of the task for which Providence has chosen me. Before I am eighty-five years old Herr von Hindenburg will long ago have ceased to be.

Speech in Berlin on 8 April 1933

I can say with pride, comrades of the SA. and SS., that if the whole German people now was possessed of the spirit that is in us and in you, then Germany would be indestructible. Even without arms, Germany would represent an unheard-of strength through this inner will tempered like steel. It is true that this equality that is realized in you was realized only at the cost of that freedom of which others spoke. We have, too, adopted the principle of leadership, the conception of authority. That was a heavy sacrifice at a time when the whole people was running after the illusion of democracy and parliamentarianism, when millions believed that the majority was the source of a right decision. It was at this time that we began resolutely to build up an organization in which there was not one dictator but ten thousand. When our opponents say: "It is easy for you: you are a dictator"—we answer them, "No, gentlemen, you are wrong; there is no single dictator, but ten thousand, each in his own place." And even the highest authority in the hierarchy has itself only one wish, never to transgress against the supreme authority to which it, too, is responsible. We have in our movement developed this loyalty in following the leader, this blind obedience of which all the others know nothing and which gave to us the power to surmount everything.

Proclamation issued on New Year's Day 1934

The year 1933 had to bring the decision. For thirteen years as a National Socialist and as your leader I have with the utmost fanaticism maintained the thesis that the word "capitulation" must never find a place in our dictionary. It is always better to be destroyed in honor than voluntarily to submit to the foe. And only he who is determined to hold the field to the last man can hope in the end to come successfully to his rights. It was in this frame of mind that we had fought for thirteen years, and now in the fourteenth, although we had suffered very heavy sacrifices, already in the first month of the year we won once more a new great victory. The success of 15 January 1933 in Lippe-Detmold led to the final discouragement of our foes and thus introduced the greatest revolution that Germany had experienced for many centuries. . . . What has happened during the eleven months since 30 January 1933 is a change of such wonderful range and content that later generations will hardly be able to grasp it in the whole of its scope. . . .

The great life-task that I had set before myself was completed in barely six months! Marxism was destroyed and Communism laid in the dust. Fourteen years long have I preached the necessity of conquering this doctrine of madness and of destroying the organizations infected by it as the condition for the restoration of Germany. Marxism in Germany exists no longer. . . . National Socialism has remained the conqueror and it will never allow its foes to raise themselves again. For, my comrades, we have not forbidden to Marxism its organizations: we have taken from it the people. The army of the millions of German working men who had fallen victims to this madness has been led back into the community of the German people. The German working man is no longer an alien body in the German state: he is the force which sustains the German nation. And just as the Marxist foe of our people has been annihilated, so in the same way have the bourgeois parties been destroyed. The organizations of class-division, of class-hatred, and of class-war have on both sides been dissolved and swept away. And the state of these parties—it, too, exists no more.

Once for all parliamentary transactions with their corrupting intrigues have been brought to an end.

The National Socialist principle of the authority of the leadership has conquered parliamentary incompetence.

Thereby the conception of the value of personality has been secured in all its commanding significance: it is destined to form the foundation of our whole work of organization and reconstruction. At the same time we all clearly realize that the penetration of our public life by this new conception will take not merely a few months but will need an education lasting for decades and a continuous development.

Parallel with this victory over the party-state went the strengthening of the authority of the idea of the Reich. The elements responsible for continuous opposition, perpetual criticism, and unending carping— responsible even for the conscious sabotage to which the Reich was subjected—have either been overcome or destroyed. And this re-formation of the Reich gains its highest significance only through the formation of a real German nation. . . .

Speech delivered in Berlin on 1 May 1937

. . . We have not merely brought the unemployed back to be wage earners, but we have also increased the production of all the rest in order thereby to give a real foundation for their wages. That is the whole secret of German economic leadership and of German economic success! We have succeeded hitherto, and that success will continue in the future. I am further convinced that our people itself will continuously grow more healthy with this sober, clear, and decent political and economic leadership. I say "political leadership," for these successes are not due primarily to economics, but to the political leadership. Clever economists, one may presume, there are elsewhere, and I do not believe that German economists have grown clever only since the 30th of January 1933. If, before that date, there was no progress, that was because the political leadership and the formation of our people were at fault. The change is due to the National Socialist Party! And that change could be effected only by a movement that was not under obligations to one or another, that existed neither for employer nor for employee, not for the townsman and not for the farmer, neither for the middle classes nor for trade, but only for the German people and for this community bound together by our common destiny. This movement is subject to none, the servant of none, it belongs to no individual member of our people. It belongs to all and serves all! Its aim is to raise up a strong community, to govern with reason and with prudence in order thereby to give to all our fellow countrymen the necessities of life.

Let no man say that since these tasks are solved nothing remains to be done. Life constrains every generation to wage its own struggle for this life. But what centuries have built up in prejudices and unreason that cannot in four years be destroyed so as to leave no trace behind. The task cannot be accomplished once for all. But the will to be quit of the past, that we have and with this will we shall never capitulate!

And I think you will admit that we have no superficial conception of our task. In these four years we have created order; we have taken care that the man who is not prepared to act decently shall not in the last resort pocket the salary, but that the millions of the honest hard-working masses in town and country shall be able to come to their own. We in Germany have really broken with a world of prejudices. I leave myself out of account. I, too, am a child of this people; I do not trace my line from any castle: I come from the workshop. Neither was I a general: I was simply a soldier, as were millions of others. It is something wonderful that amongst us an unknown from the army of the millions of the German people—of workers and of soldiers—could rise to be the head of the Reich and of the nation. By my side stand Germans from all walks of life who today are amongst the leaders of the nation: men who once were workers on the land are now governing German states in the name of the Reich, former metal-workers are governors of German shires (Gauleiter) and so on. It is true that men who came from the bourgeoisie and former aristocrats have their place in this movement. But to us it matters nothing whence they come if only they can work to the profit of our people. That is the decisive test. We have not broken down classes in order to set new ones in their place: we have broken down classes to make way for the German people as a whole. Our action has been consistent. We have removed the animosity that some strata in our society felt for the handworker: we have introduced compulsory labor service. If one realizes that he who was once the young son of the bourgeoisie now shoulders the spade and in marsh and quarry takes his share of toil like any other, then, my fellow countrymen, you see our education at work, that education which is in the interest of all. But our education also trains men to respect intellectual achievement: we bring one to respect the spade, another to respect the compass or the pen. All now are but German fellow countrymen and it is their achievement that determines their value.

If a man is a genius, then assuredly I shall not employ him all his days in digging potatoes, but set him in another post. That, in the last resort, is the task of our community of people. For what is the meaning of Socialism and democracy? Can there by anything finer than an organization that draws from the people its most capable personalities and places them in positions of leadership? Is it not wonderful for every humble mother amongst our people and for every father to know that perhaps their boy may become anything—God knows what!—if only he has the necessary talent? . . .

Speech to Nuremberg Parteitag in 1939

. . . The idea of self-protection, and therefore of the duty of military service, finds its expression and support in the organization of the army; the National Socialist idea finds its home in the organization of the Party. The Party represents the political outlook, the political conscience, the political will. The task of the Party is thus in the first place to secure in all spheres of life a leadership of the people that corresponds with its Weltanschauung, and, secondly, to bring this political outlook into a permanent system that may secure its supremacy for all time. The Party has received the historic commission to study "the inner political substance of our people," to learn alike its strong and its weak points, and from the knowledge thus gained to fix and determine in all spheres of life the great aims of the nation's action, to bring public life into harmony with the duties that result from this inner disposition of the people, and this it must do with confidence and without hesitation: it must not be moved by those who question the justification for its action. In the fact of its historically incontestable existence lies its duty so to act, in the success of its work the subsequently established justification. And as a matter of experience history refuses this justification only to him who was either too weak to stand the test or too incapable and therefore unfit for the task. In the long run God's favor will be given only to him who deserves it. He who speaks and acts in the name of a people created by the Almighty continues to act under this commission so long as he does not sin against the substance and the future of the work of the Creator that has been placed in his hand. Therefore it is good that the conquest of power is always bound up with hard fighting. For what was won only with difficulty is in general also defended with courage. And the more stable the government of states is, the greater is the profit for the people!

The Party has to see to it that an organization is created through which the leadership may be permanently recruited: and this organization must have a stable *weltanschaulich* basis. Therefore to secure this end it must educate *all* Germans into the *Weltanschauung* of the National Socialists and the best National Socialists must become members of the Party, and the best members of the Party must assume the leadership of the state. From this duty of securing for the Party in the future supremacy in the state and from the duty to educate the people in service of the state there results the clear delimitation of the functions of the Party and the state:

The function of the state is the continuance of the administration, as it has in the course of history arisen and developed, of the state-organizations within the framework of and by means of the laws.

The function of the Party is

1. The building up of its own internal organization so as to create a stable, self-renewing, permanent cell of National Socialist teaching.
2. The education of the entire people in the meaning of the conceptions of this idea.
3. The introduction of those who have been so trained into the state to serve either as leaders or as followers. . . .

Speech delivered at the celebration of the tenth anniversary of the Parteitag at Weimar, 3 July 1936

May the German nation never forget that the hardiness (*Härte*) of a people is not tested when its leadership can point to visible successes but rather in hours of apparent failures. As long as a leadership is blessed by good fortune, every weakling can profess his loyalty. Only in the hours when good fortune seems to hide her face are the really valuable men declared. Only then will loyalty turn the scale. May the German people in the future retain these virtues! Then with these principles which have been tried in the past, with these fundamental beliefs of our movement, it will march into a great future! Today, together with my thanksgiving, there is but one petition I would address to the Almighty: that He would bless our people in our movement. For this is my most sacred conviction: so long as the National Socialist movement stands firm and strong in Germany, so long will Germany be strong and firm. And if ever this movement should decline, then will Germany, too, once more decline.

Speech to the Old Guard of the Movement in the Hofbräuhaus in Munich, 24 February 1934

The "hierarchy of leadership" would give to the political development of Germany stability and security: then Germany would no longer fall victim to evilly disposed speculators and to self-seeking interests. . . . It was in this hall in the early days that we National Socialists proclaimed: "With the spirit we wish to win the nation, but we wish also to subdue with the fist anyone who dares through terrorism to do violence to the spirit. . . ." It is our wish for the future to be nothing else than the people's delegates and so to fashion our lives that we can take our stand as decent and honorable men before the eyes of every German. It is essential that the movement should ever keep in view, year by year, this profession of faith, for only so will the association of the leadership with the whole German people be permanently secured: it is in this association that there lies the firmest guarantee for the future. . . . Years ago we said: "Our task is the conquest of power in Germany"; today we say: "The task of the movement is the conquest of the German for the power of this state."

Proclamation at the opening of the Party Congress in Nuremberg on 6 September 1938

To many who look back over the years that lie behind us, the path of the National Socialist movement and the rise of the Reich may seem dreamlike and unreal. One day, perhaps, men will speak of the miracle that Providence wrought for us. But however it came about, in the beginning of this miracle stood faith—faith in the eternal German people!

If once, as an unknown soldier of the World War, I entered on the path that led me to the head of the nation and that today brings me before you once again, I owe the courage to make that audacious decision solely to my own faith in the worth of my people. I feel that I must say here today that it was fortunate for me that in the years of my youth and during my time as a soldier I had the opportunity of learning to know only the people, for it alone gave me faith, and the memory of it has sustained me through all difficulties and mishaps.

If at that time, instead of my knowledge of the people, I had had the knowledge that came to me later of its intellectual leaders and especially of its bourgeois political leaders, their social ethic, and their public and private failings, I, too, perhaps should have felt doubts of the German people and its future. But what bore me up in those bitter days and weeks of collapse was not my knowledge of the political and military leaders of Germany or of the intellectual classes (Schichten), so far as personalities were concerned: it was my knowledge of the German rifleman, my knowledge of the German frontline soldier, my knowledge of those massed millions of German workmen and peasants from which this steel-hard core of the German people was made. . . . For on this point there can be no doubt. The human and moral worth of the leadership of the nation in those days did not even approximately correspond to the worth of those whom it led. Ninety-nine percent of the bravery and courage lay with the riflemen, and with them alone. Barely 1 percent could be claimed by the leadership of the Reich and the people.

But I formed the decision to build up for the Reich a new leadership, which should be characterized by just those fundamental qualities that we expect from the people itself, and that we found they possessed a thousandfold. In November 1918, and long before that, a ruling class of society had proved itself incapable of leadership. The problem to be solved, then, stood out clear as day before my eyes. A new organization of leadership must be built up. Every thought of rescuing the nation again through its old organizations meant the belief that, against all laws of reason and experience, proved weakness would suddenly and by chance be capable of changing into a new force. For more than four years this German people furnished proof of its inner worth such as history had never given before. Unflinchingly regiments lined up and shed their blood. Batteries kept on firing to the end. Officers and men of the fleet, grasping their tattered colors, went down into the deep with songs of German faith upon their lips. And in contrast with this gallant demonstration of endless heroism stood the devastating cowardice of the leaders of the Reich and nation. While for more than four years a front of heroes was proving its worth in efforts a thousand times repeated, not once did the leadership at home find the strength for a decision of equal magnitude and boldness. Bravery—it was all on the side of the riflemen, while all the cowardice was concentrated in the organized political leadership of the nation. Any attempt to set Germany on her feet again could in such circumstances succeed only if this political ruling class were rooted out and destroyed. For this purpose the way to a new principle of selecting the leaders must be found. But with this vanished all possibility of wishing to mold the future history of Germany in the framework of the old parties, and with their help. During those nights when I resolved finally to become a politician, the future of the German world of parties was also decided. . . .

Address to leaders of the National Socialist Democratic Party, 9 September 1938

. . . You will all among yourselves have the consciousness of how strong we are in this community. And especially at a time when there are clouds in the firmament I feel myself doubly fortunate to know that about me are those millions of the guard of fanatic National Socialists whose ranks none can break, whose spirit draws from you its inspiration, whose leaders you are!

Just as in the long years of the struggle for power in Germany I could always blindly rely on you so—I know it—today can Germany, can I rely on you!

You have been tested and hardened in these long years, you have yourselves learned by experience what strength dwells in a community that is indissolubly bound together, that carries in its heart an unwavering faith and is determined that it will capitulate to no one.

So it is that you today make it easy for me to be Germany's leader.

All those who for fifteen years reckoned upon the collapse of our movement, they have been disappointed. From every distress, from every danger, the movement emerged the stronger! And all those who today hope for a weakening of Germany will suffer just the same disappointment!

When I speak to you thus, then in you I see not the 140,000 political leaders who stand before me but you who are the German nation! A people is not more and not less than its leadership. But our leadership must be good—that we promise to the German people. . . .

References

Hitler, Adolf, *Mein Kampf* (New York: Reynal and Hitchcock, 1941).

Hitler, Adolf, *The Speeches of Adolf Hitler*, *April 1922–August 1939*, Volumes I and II (London: Oxford University Press, 1942).

BENITO MUSSOLINI

FULL NAME:

Benito Mussolini (Il Duce)

BORN:

29 July 1883, Predappio, Italy

DIED:

28 April 1945, near Dogo, Italy

Soldier, journalist, and schoolmaster. Early socialist and anti-nationalist with arrest record. Leader of the Fascist Party from 1920. Italian Premier from 1922 to 1943.

His writings include: Benito Mussolini, *The Doctrine of Fascism*, translated by E. Cope (Florence: Vallachi, 1937); and *My Autobiography* (London: Hutchinson & Co., Limited, 1928). Biographies in English include: Laura Fermi, *Mussolini* (Chicago: University of Chicago Press, 1961), Dennis Mack Smith, *Mussolini's Roman Empire* (New York: Viking Press, 1976), and Christopher Hibbert, *Benito Mussolini, A Biography* (London: Longmans, 1962).

Excerpts from My Autobiography

. . . During my life, I believe, neither my school friends, my war friends, nor my political friends ever had the slightest influence upon me. I have listened always with intense interest to their words, their suggestions, and sometimes to their advice, but I am sure that whenever I took an extreme decision I have obeyed only the firm commandment of will and conscience that came from within.

I do not believe in the supposed influence of books. I do not believe in the influence that comes from perusing books about the lives and characters of men.

For myself, I have used only one big book.

For myself, I have had only one great teacher.

The book is life lived.

The teacher is day-by-day experience.

The reality of experience is far more eloquent than all the theories and philosophies on all the tongues and on all the shelves.

I have never, with closed eyes, accepted the thoughts of others when they were estimating events and realities, either in the normal course of things or when the situation appeared exceptional. I have searched, to be sure with a spirit of analysis, the whole ancient and modern history of my country. I have drawn parallels because I wanted to explore to the depths on the basis of historical fact the profound sources of our national life and of our character, and to compare our capacities with those of other peoples.

For my supreme aim I have had the public interest. If I spoke of life I did not speak of a concept of my own life, my family life, or that of my friends. I spoke and thought and conceived of the whole Italian life taken as a synthesis—as an expression of a whole people. . . .

In the cycle of time again a dramatic period had come that was making it possible for Italy by the weight of its army to deal as an equal with the leading nations of the world.

That was our chance. I wanted to seize it. It became my one thought of intensity.

The World War began on 28 July 1914. Within sixty days I severed my official connection with the Socialist Party. I had already ceased to be editor of the *Avanti*.

I felt lighter, fresher. I was free! I was better prepared to fight my battles than when I was bound by the dogmas of any political organization. But I understood that I could not use with efficient strength my convictions if I was without that modern weapon, capable of all possibilities, ready to arm and to help, good for offense and defense—the newspaper.

I needed a daily paper. I hungered for one. I gathered together a few of my political friends who had followed me in the last hard struggle and we held a "War Council." When money alone is concerned I am anything but a wizard. When it is a question of means or of capital to start a project, or how to finance a newspaper, I grasp only the abstract side, the political value, and the spiritual essence of the thing. To me money is detestable; what it may do is sometimes beautiful and sometimes noble. . . .

I cannot try to narrate in one chapter all the events of the War on the Italian front. It is impossible. The War molded me; I was forced into its dramatic unfolding in the circumscribed viewpoint of a mere soldier of the War. I will tell what touched me most as a soldier and indirectly as a political man.

I made up my mind to be the best soldier possible from the very day that I wore again the glorious gray-green uniform of the regiment of Bersaglieri—the best shock troops of Italy, in which regiment I had already served during the time of my compulsory military service. I wanted to be a soldier, obedient, faithful to discipline, stretching myself with all my might to the fulfillment of my duty.

In this I feel that I succeeded. My political position brought me plenty of offers of privileges and sheltered places! I turned them down.

I wanted to create the impression of a complete and rigid consistence with an ideal. This was not a scheming on my part for personal gain; it was a deep need in my nature of what I believed, and I still hold on to—as my life's dedication—namely, that once a man sets up to be the expounder of an ideal or of a new school of thought he must consistently and intensively live daily life and fight battles for the doctrines that he teaches—at any cost until victory—to the end! . . .

I felt that we were left without any cohesive force, any suggestive heroism, any remembrance, any political philosophy, sufficient to overcome and stop the factors of dissolution. . . .

We suffered the humiliation of seeing the banners of our glorious regiments returned to their homes without being saluted, without that warm cheer of sympathy owed to those who return from victorious war. Now, again, it appeared to me and to my friends as if there was in everybody an instinct to finish the game of the war not with the idea of real victory, but with content that he had lost as little as possible. Ears and spirits were ready to listen to words of peace, of humanity, of brotherhood among the nations. At night before sleep came I used to meditate and realize that we had no dam to stop this general decay of faith, this renunciation of the interests and destiny of a victorious nation. The sense of destruction penetrated very quickly and deeply the spirit of all classes. Certainly the central government was no dike to prevent the flood of weakness.

Politicians and philosophers; profiteers and losers, for at least many had lost their illusions; sharks trying to save themselves; promoters of the War trying to be pardoned; demagogues seeking popularity; spies and instigators of trouble waiting for the price of their treason; agents paid by foreign money; in a few months threw the nation into an awful spiritual crisis. I saw before me with awe the gathering dusk of our end as a nation and a people.

With my heart in tumult and with a deep sense of bitterness corroding my soul, I could smell the danger. Some audacious men were with me—not many. My action was at first tied to the urgent duty to fight against one important and dark treason. Some Italians, blinded and having lost their memories, were led on by some complicity and selfish desires among the Allies. . . .

I was snatched up in this fight against the returning beasts of decadence. I was for our sacred rights to our own territories, therefore I had to neglect in a degree the petty internal political life that was floundering in bewilderment and wallowing in disorder. . . .

What a grave moment! An action of a handful of us on the public square was not sufficient; there were so many different fronts where one had to fight! We, who were to defend Italy from within, had to create one more unbreakable unity of strength, a common denominator of all the old pro-war partisans and loyalists—of all those that felt, like myself, desperately Italian. Then it was that I decided, after days and nights of reflection, to make a call through the medium of my newspaper for a full stop in the stumbling career toward chaos. . . .

Those who came to the meeting for the constitution of the Italian Fascisti of Combat used few words. They did not exhaust themselves by laying out dreams. Their aim seemed clear and straight-lined—it was to defend the victory at any price, to maintain intact the sacred memory of the dead and the admiration not only for those who fell and for the families of those who were dead, but for the mutilated, for the invalids, for all those who had fought. The prevalent note, however, was of anti-Socialist character and, as a political aspiration, it was hoped a new Italy would be created that would know how to value the victory and to fight with all its strength against treason and corruption, against decay within and intrigue and avarice from without.

There are some who profess not to understand what Fascimo had as its intent, and some who believe that it grew without a gardener. I was certain at the time that it was necessary to fix, without any possibility of equivocation, the essential brand of the new movement. . . .

Finally, we talked of organization—the organization that would be adapted to the new movement. I did not favor any bureaucratic, cut-and-dried organization. . . .

In the midst of general hardships and of cowardice, of grumbling of impotents, of the vaporings of dull critics, I, almost alone, had the courage to write that the state's employees, if they were right in view of the feebleness of the government, were wrong, in any case, toward the nation. To inflict upon a people the mortification of an ill-advised strike, to trample upon the rights of the whole, meant to lead men from modern civil life back again to tribal conflict. . . .

"If a revolution," said I, "has to take place, it is necessary to make one typically Italian, on the magnificent dimensions of the ideas of Mazzini and with the spirit of Carlo Pisacane!"

I had already, clear and strong, in my mind the concept of complete rebellion against the decrepit old state that did not know itself how to die. . . .

Believing with all my being that it was necessary to stop the flood of decadence in our foreign policy, I began to use our Fascisti organization and the *Popolo d'Italia*. I tried to raise some dikes. It was difficult to hold back the dirty water. There was a tendency to go toward Communism whatever the cost. The power of Lenin—I admit it—had assumed the character of potency only paralleled in mythology. The Russian dictator domineered the masses. He enchanted the masses. He charmed them as if they were hypnotized birdlings. Only some time afterwards the news of the dreadful Russian famine as well as the information furnished by our mission that had gone to Russia to study Bolshevism, opened the eyes of the crowd to the falsity of the Russian paradise mirage. Enthusiasm ebbed away little by little. Finally, Lenin remained only as a kind of banner and catchword for our political dabblers. . . .

It was necessary to beat the violent adversary on the battlefield of violence.

As if a revelation had come to me I realized that Italy would be saved by one historic agency—in an imperfect world sometimes inevitable still—righteous force.

Our democracy of yesterday had died; its testament had been read; it had bequeathed us naught but chaos.

* * *

Ignorance was still astride of the workmen and peasant masses. It was useless to attempt to blaze a trail by fine words, by sermons from chairs. It was necessary to give timely, genial recognition to chivalrous violence. The only straight road was to beat the violent forces of evil on the very ground they had chosen.

With us were elements who knew what war meant. From them was born the organization of Italian Bundles of Fight. Many also volunteered from our universities; they were students touched by the inspiration of idealism, who quit their studies to run to our call.

We knew that we must win this war too, throw into yesterday the period of cowardice and treachery. It was necessary to make our way by violence, by sacrifice, by blood; it was necessary to establish an order and a discipline wanted by the masses, but impossible to obtain through milk-and-water propaganda and by words, words, and more words, and parliamentary and journalistic sham battles.

We began our period of rescue and resurrection. Dead there were—but on the horizon all eyes saw the dawn of Italian rebirth. . . .

Oh, many had meditated upon my funeral. And yet love is stronger than hatred. I always felt a power over events and over men. . . .

. . . I wanted with all my desire to strip from our Party the personal character that the Fascist movement had assumed because of the stamp of my will. But the more I wished to give the Party an autonomous organization, and the more I tried, the more I received the conviction from the evidence of the facts—that the Party could not have existed and lived, and could not be triumphant, except under my command, my guidance, my support, and my spurs.

The meeting in Rome gave a deep insight into the fundamental strength of Fascism, but especially to me it was a revelation of my personal strength. . . .

I was preparing then every minute the details of the conquest of Rome and of power. I was certainly not moved by any mirage of personal power, nor by any other allurement, nor by a desire for egotistical political domination.

I have always had a vision of life that was altruistic. I have groped in the dark of theories, but I groped not to relieve myself, but to bring something to others. I have fought, but not for my advantage, indirect or immediate. I have aimed for the supreme advantage of my nation. I wanted finally that Fascism should rule Italy for her glory and her good fortune. . . .

The march on Rome could have set tragic fires. It might have spilled much blood if it had followed the example of ancient and modern revolutions. This was for me a moment in which it was more necessary than ever to examine the field with calm serenity and with cold reason to compare the near and far results of our daring action turned toward definite aims.

I could have proclaimed a dictatorship, I could have formed a dictatorial ministry composed solely of Fascisti on the type of the Directory that was formed in France at the time of the Convention. The Fascist revolution, however, had its unique characteristics; it had no antecedent in history. It was different from any other revolution also in its capacity to reenter, with deliberate will, legally established traditions and forms. For that reason also the mobilization I knew should last only the shortest time. . . .

My presence redoubled the great enthusiasm. I read in the eyes of those young men the divine smile of triumph of an ideal. With such elements I would have been inspired to challenge, if need be, not only the base Italian ruling class, but enemies of any sort and race.

In Rome there was waiting for me an indescribable welcome. I did not want any delay. Even before making contacts with my political friends I motored to the Quirinal. I wore a black shirt. I was introduced without formalities to the presence of His Majesty the King. The Stefani agency and the great newspapers of the world gave stilted or speculative details about this interview. I will limit myself, for obvious reasons of reserve, to declare that the conference was characterized by great cordiality. I concealed no plans, nor did I fail to make plain my ideas of how to rule Italy. I obtained the sovereign's approbation. I took up lodgings at the Savoy Hotel and began to work. First I made agreements with the general command of the army to bring a militia into Rome and file them off in proper formation in a review by the king. I gave detailed and precise orders. One hundred thousand Black Shirts paraded in perfect order before the sovereign. They brought to him the homage of Fascist Italy!

I was then triumphant and in Rome! I killed at once all unnecessary demonstrations in my honor. I gave orders that not a single parade should take place without the permission of the General Fascist Command. It was necessary to give to everybody, from the first moment, a stern and rigid sense of discipline in line with the regime that I had conceived. . . .

* * *

My revolutionary method and the power of the Black Shirts had brought me to a tremendous responsibility of power. My task, as I have pointed out, was neither simple nor easy; it required a large vision, it gathered continually more and more duties.

An existence wholly new began for me. To speak about it makes it necessary for me to abandon the usual form of autobiographic style. I must consider the organic whole of my governmental activity. From now on my life identifies itself almost exclusively with thousands of acts of government. Individuality disappears. Instead, the person expresses. I sometimes feel only measures and acts of concrete character, these do not concern a single person; they concern the multitudes, they concern and permeate an entire people. So one's whole life is lost in the whole.

Certainly I know that I took the direction of the government when the central power of the state was sinking to the bottom. . . .

It was necessary to recognize all civil life, without forgetting the organic problem of a watchful force. It was necessary to give order to political economy, to the schools, to our military strength. It was necessary to abolish double functions, to reduce bureaucracy, to improve public services. It was necessary to hold back the corroding and erosion of criticism developed by the remnants of old political parties. I had to fight the external attacks. I had to refine and improve Fascism. I had to divide and floor the enemies. I saw the vision that I must in every respect work to improve and give tonic to all the manners and customs of Italian political life. . . .

I had to keep Fascism from internal crises, often provoked by intrigue and trickery. I succeeded in this by being always inexorably against those who thought they could create disturbances and frictions in the Party itself. Fascism is a unit; it cannot have varying tendencies and trends, as it cannot have two leaders on any one level of organization. There is a hierarchy; the foundation is the Black Shirts and on the summit the chief, who is only one.

That is one of the first causes of my strength; all the dissolutions in our political parties were always born not from ideal reasons, but from personal ambitions, from false preconceptions or from corruption, or from mysterious, oblique, and hidden forces, which I could always identify as the work of our Italian Masonry. I took account of all this. I resolved not to yield a hairsbreadth. When the more urgent legislative problems were settled by Parliament I decided to dissolve the Chamber, and after having obtained extension of full powers, I announced elections for 6 April 1924. . . .

* * *

When one sees the building of the new structures, when hammers and concrete-mixers flash and turn, the occasion is not one in which to ask the superintendent his opinion about the plays of George Bernard Shaw, or to expect the architect to babble discursively on the subject of his preferences between the mountains and the seashore as summer playgrounds.

It is absurd to suppose that I and my life can be separated from that which I have been doing and am doing. The creation of the Fascist state and the passing of the hungry moments from sunrise to the deep profundity of night with its promise of another dawn avaricious for new labors cannot be picked apart. I am lockstitched into this fabric. It and myself are woven into one. Other men may find romance in the fluttering of the leaves on a bough; to me, whatever I might have been, destiny and myself have made me one whose eyes, ears, all senses, all thoughts, all time, all energy must be directed at the trunk of the tree of public life.

The poetry of my life has become the poetry of construction. The romance in my existence has become the romance of measures, policies, and the future of a state. These, to me, are redolent with drama.

So it is that I see as I look back over nearly six years of leadership the solution of problems, each of them a chapter in my life, a chapter in the life of my country. A chapter, long or short, simple or complex in history of the advance and experimentation and pioneering of mankind.

I am not deeply concerned that I am misunderstood. It is more or less trivial that conspiracies go on to misinterpret and, indeed, to misrepresent in full, what I have sought and why I have sought it. After all, I have been too busy to hear the murmur of liars.

He who looks back over his shoulder toward those who lag and those who lie is a waster; it is because I cannot write my life—my daily life, my active life, my thinking life, and even my own peculiar emotional life—without recording the steps I have taken to renew Italy and find a new place for her in the general march of civilization, that I call up one after another the recollections of my recent battles with measures that submerge men, with policies that bury under their simplicity and weight everything else I might have lived.

Two fields of my will and action, of my thoughts, my conclusions stand out as I write and as I record my life itself.

I think of all of them in terms of utter simplicity, stripped of complex phrases. I have seen the futility of those who speak endless streams of words. These words are like armies enlisted forever to go away into the night, never to return from a campaign where the enemies are compromise with principle, cowardice, inaction, and idealism without realism.

There are those, no doubt, who regard me, or have once regarded me, as an enemy to the peace of the world. To them there is nothing to say unless to recommend to them my biography for careful reading. The record of facts is worth more than the accusation of fools.

Reference

Mussolini, Benito, *My Autobiography* (London: Hutchinson & Co., Limited, 1928).

VLADIMIR LENIN

FULL NAME:

Vladimir Ilyich (Ulyanov) Lenin

BORN:

22 April 1870, Simbirsk, Russia

DIED:

21 January 1924, Gorky, USSR

Formulator of Marxism-Leninism while in exile in Siberia and western Europe. Founder of the Russian Communist Party (Bolshevik) and leader of the Bolshevik Revolution of 1917. First head of Soviet state, 1917–1924.

His works include: Vladimir Lenin, *Collected Works of V.I. Lenin* (New York: International Publications, 1927–1945). Biographies include: Louis Fischer, *The Life of Lenin* (New York: Harper and Row, 1964), and David Shub, *A Biography of Lenin* (Garden City, NY: Doubleday, 1948).

The Lenin Anthology

"What Is to Be Done?" 1901–1902

. . . You intellectuals can acquire this knowledge, and it is your duty to bring it to us in a hundred- and a thousandfold greater measure than you have done up to now; and you must bring it to us, not only in the form of discussions, pamphlets, and articles (which very often—pardon our frankness—are rather dull), but precisely in the form of vivid *exposures* of what our government and our governing classes are doing at this very moment in all spheres of life. Devote more zeal to carrying out this duty and *talk less about "raising the activity of the working masses."* We are far more active than you think, and think more about raising *your own* activity, gentlemen! . . .

* * *

We have seen that the conduct of the broadest political agitation and, consequently, of all-sided political exposures is an absolutely necessary and a *paramount* task of our activity, if this activity is to be truly Social-Democratic. However, we arrived at this conclusion *solely* on the grounds of the pressing needs of the working class for political knowledge and political training. But such a presentation of the question is too narrow, for it ignores the general democratic tasks of Social-Democracy, in particular of present-day Russian Social-Democracy. In order to explain the point more concretely we shall approach the subject from an aspect that is "nearest" to the Economist, namely, from the practical aspect. "Everyone agrees" that it is necessary to develop the political consciousness of the working class. The question is, *how* is that to be done and what is required to do it? The economic struggle merely "impels" the workers to realize the government's attitude toward the working class. Consequently, *however much we may try to* "lend the economic struggle itself a political character," *we shall never be able to* develop the political consciousness of the workers (to the level of Social-Democratic political consciousness) by keeping within the framework of the economic struggle, for *that framework is too narrow.* The Martynov formula has some value for us, not because it illustrates Martynov's aptitude for confusing things, but because it pointedly expresses the basic error that all the Economists commit, namely, their conviction that it is possible to develop the class political consciousness of the workers *from within,* so to speak, from their economic struggle, i.e., by making this struggle the exclusive (or, at least, the main) starting point, by making it the exclusive (or, at least, the main) basis. Such a view is radically wrong. Piqued by our polemics against them, the Economists refuse to ponder deeply over the origins of these disagreements, with the result that we simply cannot understand one another. It is as if we spoke in different tongues.

Class political consciousness can be brought to the workers *only from without*, that is, only from outside the economic struggle, from outside the sphere of relations between workers and employers. The sphere from which alone it is possible to obtain this knowledge is the sphere of relationships of *all* classes and strata to the state and the government, the sphere of the interrelations between *all* classes. For that reason, the reply to the question as to what must be done to bring political knowledge to the workers cannot be merely the answer with which, in the majority of cases, the practical workers, especially those inclined toward Economism, mostly content themselves, namely: "To go among the workers." To bring political knowledge to the *workers* the Social-Democrats must *go among all classes of the population;* they must dispatch units of their army *in all directions.*

We deliberately select this blunt formula, we deliberately express ourselves in this sharply simplified manner, not because we desire to indulge in paradoxes, but in order to "impel" the Economists to a realization of their tasks that they unpardonably ignore, to suggest to them strongly the difference between trade-unionist and Social-Democratic politics, which they refuse to understand. We therefore beg the reader not to get wrought up, but to hear us patiently to the end. . . .

"The Dual Power," 1917

The basic question of every revolution is that of state power. Unless this question is understood, there can be no intelligent participation in the revolution, not to speak of guidance of the revolution.

The highly remarkable feature of our revolution is that it has brought about a *dual power.* This fact must be grasped first and foremost: unless it is understood, we cannot advance. We must know how to supplement and amend old "formulas," for example, those of Bolshevism, for while they have been found to be correct on the whole, their concrete realization *has turned out to be* different. *Nobody* previously thought, or could have thought, of a dual power.

What is this dual power? Alongside the Provisional Government, the government of the bourgeoisie, *another government* has arisen, so far weak and incipient, but undoubtedly a government that actually exists and is growing—the Soviets of Workers' and Soldiers' Deputies.

What is the class composition of this other government? It consists of the proletariat and the peasants (in soldiers' uniforms). What is the political nature of this government? It is a revolutionary dictatorship, i.e., a power directly based on revolutionary seizure, on the direct initiative of the people from below, and *not on a law* enacted by a centralized state power. It is an entirely different kind of power from the one that generally exists in the parliamentary bourgeois-democratic republics of the usual type still prevailing in the advanced countries of Europe and America. This circumstance is often overlooked, often not given enough thought, yet it is the crux of the matter. This power is of *the same type* as the Paris Commune of 1871. The fundamental characteristics of this type are: (1) the source of power is not a law previously discussed and enacted by parliament, but the direct initiative of the people from below, in their local areas—direct "seizure," to use a current expression; (2) the replacement of the police and the army, which are institutions divorced from the people and set against the people, by the direct arming of the whole people; order in the state under such a power is maintained by the armed workers and peasants *themselves*, by the armed people *themselves*; (3) officialdom, the bureaucracy, is either similarly replaced by the direct rule of the people themselves or at least placed under special control; they not only become elected officials, but are also *subject to recall* at the people's first demand; they are reduced to the position of simple agents; from a privileged group holding "jobs" remunerated on a high, bourgeois scale, they become workers of a special "arm of the service," whose remuneration *does not exceed* the ordinary pay of a competent worker.

This, and this *alone*, constitutes the *essence* of the Paris Commune as a special type of state. This essence has been forgotten or perverted by the Plekhanovs (downright chauvinists who have betrayed Marxism), the Kautskys (the men of the "Center," i.e., those who vacillate between chauvinism and Marxism), and generally by all those Social-Democrats, Socialist-Revolutionaries, etc., etc., who now rule the roost. . . .

To become a power the class-conscious workers must win the majority to their side. *As long as* no violence is used against the people there is no other road to power. We are not Blanquists, we do not stand for the seizure of power by a minority. We are Marxists, we stand for proletarian class struggle against petit-bourgeois intoxication, against chauvinism-defensism, phrasemongering and dependence on the bourgeoisie.

Let us create a proletarian Communist Party, its elements have already been created by the best adherents of Bolshevism; let us rally our ranks for proletarian class work; and larger and larger numbers from among the proletarians, from among the *poorest* peasants will range themselves on our side. For *actual experience* will from day to day shatter the petit-bourgeois illusions of those "Social-Democrats," the Chkheidzes, Tseretelis, Steklovs and others, the "Socialist-Revolutionaries," the petit bourgeois of an even purer water, and so on and so forth.

The bourgeoisie stands for the undivided power of the bourgeoisie.

The class-conscious workers stand for the undivided power of the Soviets of Workers', Agricultural Laborers', Peasants', and Soldiers' Deputies—for undivided power made possible not by adventurist acts, but by *clarifying* proletarian minds, by *emancipating* them from the influence of the bourgeoisie.

The petit bourgeoisie—"Social-Democrats," Socialist-Revolutionaries, etc., etc.—vacillate and, thereby, *hinder* this clarification and emancipation.

This is the actual, the *class* alignment of forces that determines our tasks.

"Fright at the Fall of the Old and the Fight for the New," 1918

The capitalists and their supporters, witting and unwitting, are thinking, saying, and writing: "The Bolsheviks have now been in power for two months, but instead of a socialist paradise we find the hell of chaos, civil war, and even greater dislocation."

We reply: the Bolsheviks have been in power for only two months, but a tremendous step toward socialism has already been made. This is not evident only to those who do not wish to see or are unable to analyze the chain of historical events. They refuse to see that in a matter of weeks the undemocratic institutions in the army, the countryside, and industry have been almost completely destroyed. There is no other way—there can be no other way—to socialism save through such destruction. They refuse to see that in a few weeks, the lying imperialist foreign policy, which dragged out the war and covered up plunder and seizure through secret treaties, has been replaced by a truly revolutionary-democratic policy working for a really democratic peace, a policy that has already produced such a great practical success as the armistice and has increased the propaganda power of our revolution a hundredfold. They refuse to see that workers' control and the nationalization of the banks are being put into practice, and these are the first steps toward socialism.

Those tyrannized by capitalist routine, shocked by the thundering crash of the old world, and the blast, rumble, and "chaos" (apparent chaos) as the age-old structures of tsarism and the bourgeoisie break up and cave in cannot see the historical prospects; nor can those who are scared by the class struggle at its highest pitch when it turns into civil war, the only war that is legitimate, just and sacred—not in the clerical but in the human sense—the sacred war of the oppressed to overthrow the oppressors and liberate the working people from all oppression. Actually all these tyrannized, shocked, and scared bourgeois, petit bourgeois, and "those in the service of the bourgeoisie" are frequently guided, without realizing it, by that old, absurd, sentimental, and vulgar intellectualist idea of "introducing socialism," which they have acquired from hearsay and scraps of socialist theory, repeating the distortions of this theory produced by ignoramuses and half-scholars, and attributing to us Marxists the idea, and even the plan, to "introduce" socialism.

To us Marxists these notions, to say nothing of the plans, are alien. We have always known, said, and emphasized that socialism cannot be "introduced," that it takes shape in the course of the most intense, the most acute class struggle—which reaches heights of frenzy and desperation—and civil war; we have always said that a long period of "birth-pangs" lies between capitalism and socialism; that violence is always the midwife of the old society; that a special state (that is, a special system of organized coercion of a definite class) corresponds to the transitional period between the bourgeois and the socialist society, namely, the dictatorship of the proletariat. What dictatorship implies and means is a state of simmering war, a state of military measures of struggle against the enemies of the proletarian power. The Commune was a dictatorship of the proletariat, and Marx and Engels reproached it for what they considered to be one of the causes of its downfall, namely, that the Commune had not used its armed force with sufficient vigor to suppress the resistance of the exploiters.

These intellectualist howls about the suppression of capitalist resistance are actually nothing but an echo of the old "conciliation," to put it in a "genteel" manner. Putting it with proletarian bluntness, this means: continued kowtowing to the moneybags is what lies behind the howls against the present working-class coercion now being applied (unfortunately, with insufficient pressure or vigor) against the bourgeoisie, the saboteurs, and counter-revolutionaries. The kind Peshekhonov, one of the conciliating ministers, proclaimed in June 1917: "The resistance of the capitalists has been broken." This kind soul had no inkling of the fact that their resistance must really be broken, and it will be broken, and that the scientific name for this breaking-up operation is dictatorship of the proletariat; that an entire historical period is marked by the suppression of capitalist resistance, and, consequently, by systematic application of *coercion* to an entire class (the bourgeoisie) and its accomplices.

The grasping, malicious, frenzied filthy avidity of the moneybags, the cowed servility of their hangers-on is the true social source of the present wail raised by the spineless intellectuals—from those of *Rech* to those of *Novaya Zhizn*—against violence on the part of the proletariat and the revolutionary peasants. Such is the objective meaning of their howls, their pathetic speeches, their clownish cries of "freedom" (freedom for the capitalists to oppress the people), etc. They would be "prepared" to recognize socialism, if mankind could jump straight into it in one spectacular leap, without any of the friction, the struggles, the exploiters' gnashing of teeth, or their diverse attempts to preserve the old order, or smuggle it back through the window, without the revolutionary proletariat responding to each attempt in a violent manner. These spineless hangers-on of the bourgeoisie with intellectualist pretensions are quite "prepared" to wade into the water provided they do not get their feet wet.

The drooping intellectuals are terrified when the bourgeoisie and the civil servants, employees, doctors, engineers, etc., who have grown accustomed to serving the bourgeoisie, go to extremes in their resistance. They tremble and utter even shriller cries about the need for a return to "conciliation." Like all true friends of the oppressed class, we can only derive satisfaction from the exploiters' extreme measures of resistance, because we do not expect the proletariat to mature for power in an atmosphere of cajoling and persuasion, in a school of mealy sermons or didactic declamations, but in the school of life and struggle. To become the ruling class and defeat the bourgeoisie for good the proletariat must be *schooled*, because the skill this implies does not come ready-made. The proletariat must do its learning in the struggle, and stubborn, desperate struggle in earnest is the only real teacher. The greater the extremes of the exploiters' resistance, the more vigorously, firmly, ruthlessly, and successfully will they be suppressed by the exploited. The more varied the exploiters' attempts to uphold the old, the sooner will the proletariat learn to ferret out its enemies from their last nook and corner, to pull up the roots of their domination, and cut the very ground that could (and had to) breed wage-slavery, mass poverty, and the profiteering and effrontery of the moneybags.

The strength of the proletariat and the peasantry allied to it grows with the resistance of the bourgeoisie and its retainers. As their enemies, the exploiters, step up their resistance, the exploited mature and gain in strength; they grow and learn and cast out the "old Adam" of wage-slavery. Victory will be on the side of the exploited, for on their side is life, numerical strength, the strength of the mass, the strength of the inexhaustible sources of all that is selfless, dedicated, and honest, all that is surging forward and awakening to the building of the new, all the vast reserves of energy and talent latent in the so-called "common people," the workers and peasants. Victory will be theirs.

"How to Organize Competition," 1918

Bourgeois authors have been filling mountains of paper with praises of competition, private enterprise, and all the other magnificent virtues and blessings of the capitalists and of the capitalist system. Socialists have been accused of refusing to understand the importance of these virtues, and of ignoring "human nature." As a matter of fact, however, capitalism long ago replaced small, independent commodity production, under which competition could develop enterprise, energy, and bold initiative to any *considerable* extent, with large and very large-scale factory production, joint-stock companies, syndicates, and other monopolies. Under *such* capitalism, competition means the incredibly brutal suppression of the enterprise, energy, and bold initiative of the *masses* of the population, of its overwhelming majority, of ninety-nine out of every hundred toilers; it also means that competition is replaced by financial fraud, despotism, and servility on the upper rungs of the social ladder.

Far from extinguishing competition, socialism, on the contrary, for the first time creates the opportunity for employing it on a really *wide* and on a really *mass* scale, for actually drawing the majority of toilers into an arena of such labor in which they can display their abilities, develop their capacities, reveal their talents, of which there is an untapped spring among the people, and which capitalism crushed, suppressed, and strangled in thousands and millions.

Now that a socialist government is in power our task is to organize competition.

The hangers-on and spongers on the bourgeoisie described socialism as a uniform, routine, monotonous, and drab barrack system. The lackeys of the moneybags, the lickspittles of the exploiters—Messieurs the bourgeois intellectuals—used socialism as a bogey to "frighten" the people, who, precisely under capitalism, were doomed to penal servitude and the barracks, to arduous, monotonous toil, to a life of dire poverty and semi-starvation. The first step toward the emancipation of the people from this penal servitude is the confiscation of the landed estates, the introduction of workers' control and the nationalization of the factories and works, the compulsory organization of the whole population in consumers' cooperative societies, which are at the same time societies for the sale of products, and the state monopoly of the trade in grain and other necessities.

The great change from working in subjection to working for oneself, to labor planned and organized on a gigantic, national (and to a certain extent international, world) scale also requires—in addition to "*military*" measures for the suppression of the resistance of the exploiters—tremendous *organizational*, organizing effort on the part of the proletariat and the poor peasants. The organizational task is interwoven to form a single whole with the task of ruthlessly suppressing by military methods yesterday's slaveowners (capitalists) and their packs of lackeys—Messieurs the bourgeois intellectuals. Yesterday's slaveowners and their stooges, the intellectuals, say and think, "We have always been organizers and chiefs. We have commanded, and we want to continue doing so. We shall refuse to obey the 'common people,' the workers and peasants. We shall not submit to them. We shall convert knowledge into a weapon for the defense of the privileges of the moneybags and of the rule of capital over the people."

That is what the bourgeoisie and the bourgeois intellectuals say, think, and do. From the point of view of *self-interest* their behavior is comprehensible. The hangers-on and spongers on the feudal landlords—the priests, the scribes, the bureaucrats as Gogol depicted them, and the "intellectuals" who hated Belinsky—also found it "hard" to part with serfdom. But the cause of the exploiters and of their intellectual menials is hopeless. The workers and peasants are breaking their resistance—unfortunately, not yet firmly, resolutely, and ruthlessly enough—*and will break it*.

The workers and peasants are still "shy," they have not yet become accustomed to the idea that *they* are the *ruling* class now; they are not yet sufficiently resolute. The revolution could not *at one stroke* instill these qualities in millions and millions of people who all their lives had been compelled by hunger and want to work under the threat of the stick. But the strength, the virility, the invincibility of the Revolution of October 1917 lie exactly in the fact that it *awakens* these qualities, breaks down the old impediments, tears the obsolete shackles, and leads the toilers on to the road of *independent* creation of a new life.

Accounting and control—this is the *main* economic task of every Soviet of Workers', Soldiers', and Peasants' Deputies, of every consumers' society, of every union or committee of supplies, of every factory committee or organ of workers' control in general.

Accounting and control, *if* carried on by the Soviets of Workers', Soldiers', and Peasants' Deputies as the supreme state power, or on the instructions, on the authority, of this power—widespread, general, universal accounting and control, the accounting and control of the amount of labor performed and of the distribution of products—is the *essence* of the socialist transformation, once the political rule of the proletariat has been established and secured.

The accounting and control that is essential for the transition to socialism can be exercised only by the masses. The voluntary and conscientious cooperation, marked by revolutionary enthusiasm, of the masses of the workers and peasants in accounting and controlling *the rich, the crooks, the idlers, and the hooligans* can alone conquer these survivals of accursed capitalist society, these dregs of humanity, these hopelessly decayed and atrophied limbs, this contagion, this plague, this ulcer that socialism has inherited from capitalism.

Workers and peasants, toilers and exploited! The land, the banks, the factories and works have now become the possession of the whole of the people! You *yourselves* must set to work to take account of and control the production and the distribution of products—this, and this *alone* is the road to the victory of socialism, the only guarantee of its victory, the guarantee of victory over all exploitation, over all poverty and want! For there is enough bread, iron, timber, wool, cotton, and flax in Russia to satisfy the needs of all, provided only the *businesslike, practical* control over this distribution by the whole of the people is established, provided only we can defeat the enemies of the people: the rich and their hangers-on, and the rogues, the idlers, and the hooligans, *not only* in politics, but also in *everyday economic* life.

No mercy to these enemies of the people, the enemies of socialism, the enemies of the toilers! War to the bitter end on the rich and their hangers-on, the bourgeois intellectuals; war on the rogues, the idlers, and the hooligans! Both, the former and the latter, are of the same brood—the spawn of capitalism, the offspring of aristocratic and bourgeois society; the society in which a handful of men robbed and insulted the people; the society in which poverty and want forced thousands and thousands into the path of hooliganism, corruption, and roguery, and caused them to lose all semblance of human beings; the society which inevitably cultivated in the toiler the desire to escape exploitation even by means of deception, to maneuver out of it, to escape, if only for a moment, from loathsome toil, to procure at least a crust of bread by any possible means, at any cost, so as not to starve, so as to subdue the pangs of hunger suffered by himself and by his near ones.

The rich and the crooks are two sides of the same medal, they are the two principal categories of *parasites* that capitalism fostered; they are the principal enemies of socialism. These enemies must be placed under the special surveillance of the whole people; they must be ruthlessly punished for the slightest violation of the laws and regulations of socialist society. Any display of weakness, hesitation, or sentimentality in this respect would be an immense crime against socialism.

In order to render these parasites harmless to socialist society we must organize the accounting and control of the amount of labor performed, of production and distribution, to be exercised by the whole of the people, by millions and millions of workers and peasants, voluntarily, energetically, and with revolutionary enthusiasm. And in order to organize this accounting and control, which is fully within the ability of every honest, intelligent, and efficient worker and peasant, we must rouse their own organizing talent, the talent that comes from their midst; we must rouse among them—and organize on a national scale—competition in the sphere of organizational successes; the workers and peasants must be brought to see clearly the difference between the necessary advice of an educated man and the necessary control by the "common" worker and peasant of the slovenliness that is so usual among the "educated."

This slovenliness, this carelessness, untidiness, unpunctuality, nervous haste, the inclination to substitute discussion for action, talk for work, the inclination to undertake everything under the sun without finishing anything, is one of the characteristics of the "educated"; and this is not due to the fact that they are bad by nature, still less is it due to their evil will; it is due to all their habits of life, the conditions of their work, to fatigue, to the abnormal separation of mental from manual labor, and so on and so forth.

Among the mistakes, shortcomings, and omissions of our revolution a by no means unimportant place is occupied by the mistakes, etc., which are due to these deplorable—but at present inevitable—characteristics of the intellectuals in our midst, and to the lack of sufficient supervision by the workers over the organizational work of the intellectuals.

The workers and peasants are still "shy"; they must get rid of this shyness, and they certainly will get rid of it. We cannot dispense with the advice, the instruction of educated people, of intellectuals and specialists. Every sensible worker and peasant understands this perfectly well, and the intellectuals in our midst cannot complain of a lack of attention and comradely respect on the part of the workers and peasants. But advice and instruction is one thing, and the organization of practical accounting and control is another thing. Very often the intellectuals give excellent advice and instruction, but they prove to be ridiculously, absurdly, shamefully "unhandy" and incapable of carrying out this advice and instruction, of exercising practical control over the translation of words into deeds.

And in this very respect it is utterly impossible to dispense with the help and the *leading role* of the practical workers-organizers from among the "people," from among the workers and toiling peasants. "It is not the gods who make pots"—this is the truth that the workers and peasants should get well drilled into their minds. They must understand that the whole thing now is *practical work*; that the historical moment has arrived when theory is being transformed into practice, is vitalized by practice, corrected by practice, tested by practice; when the words of Marx, "Every step of real movement is more important than a dozen programs," become particularly true—every step in really curbing in practice, restricting, fully registering, and supervising the rich and the rogues is worth more than a dozen excellent arguments about socialism. For "theory, my friend, is gray, but green is the eternal tree of life."

Competition must be organized among the practical workers-organizers from the workers and peasants. Every attempt to establish stereotyped forms and to impose uniformity from above, as intellectuals are so inclined to do, must be combated. Stereotyped forms and uniformity imposed from above have nothing in common with democratic and socialist centralism. The unity of essentials, of fundamentals, of the substance, is not disturbed but ensured by *variety* in details, in specific local features, in methods of *approach*, in *methods* of exercising control, in *ways* of exterminating and rendering harmless the parasites (the rich and the crooks, slovenly and hysterical intellectuals, etc., etc.).

The Paris Commune gave a great example of how to combine initiative, independence, freedom of action, and vigor from below with voluntary centralism free from stereotyped forms. Our Soviets are following the same road. But they are still "shy," they have not yet got into their stride, have not yet "bitten into" their new, great, creative task of building the socialist system. The Soviets must set to work more boldly and display greater initiative. Every "commune," every factory, every village, every consumers' society, every committee of supply, must *compete* with its neighbors as a practical organizer of accounting and control of labor and distribution of products. The program of this accounting and control is simple, clear and intelligible to all; it is: everyone to have bread; everyone to have sound footwear and whole clothing; everyone to have warm dwellings; everyone to work conscientiously; not a single rogue (including those who shirk their work) should be allowed to be at liberty, but kept in prison, or serve his sentence of compulsory labor of the hardest kind; not a single rich man who violates the laws and regulations of socialism to be allowed to escape the fate of the crook, which should, in justice, be the fate of the rich man. "He who does not work, neither shall he eat"—this is the *practical* commandment of socialism. This is how things should be organized *practically.* These are the *practical* successes our "communes" and our worker- and peasant-organizers should be proud of. And this applies *particularly* to the organizers among the intellectuals (*particularly,* because they are *too much,* far *too much* in the habit of being proud of their general instructions and resolutions).

Thousands of practical forms and methods of accounting and controlling the rich, the rogues, and the idlers should be devised and put to a practical test by the communes themselves, by small units in town and country. Variety is a guarantee of vitality here, a pledge of success in achieving the single common aim—to cleanse the land of Russia of all sorts of harmful insects, of crook-fleas, of bedbugs—the rich, and so on and so forth. In one place, half a score of rich, a dozen crooks, half a dozen workers who shirk their work (in the hooligan manner in which many compositors in Petrograd, particularly in the party printing shops, shirk their work) will be put in prison. In another place, they will be put to cleaning latrines. In a third place, they will be provided with "yellow tickets" after they have served their time, so that all the people shall have them under surveillance, as *harmful* persons, until they reform. In a fourth place, one out of every ten idlers will be shot on the spot. In a fifth place, mixed methods may be adopted, and by probational release, for example, the rich, the bourgeois intellectuals, the crooks, and the hooligans who are corrigible will be given an opportunity to reform quickly. The more variety there will be, the better and richer will be our general experience, the more certain and rapid will be the success of socialism, and the easier will it be for practice to devise—for only practice can devise—the *best* methods and means of struggle.

In what commune, in what district of a large town, in what factory, and in what village are there *no* starving people, *no* unemployed, *no* idle rich, *no* scoundrelly lackeys of the bourgeoisie, saboteurs who call themselves intellectuals? Where has most been done to raise the productivity of labor, to build good new houses for the poor, to put the poor in the houses of the rich, to regularly provide a bottle of milk for every child of every poor family? It is on these points that *competition* should unfold itself between the communes, communities, producers-consumers' societies and associations, and Soviets of Workers', Soldiers', and Peasants' Deputies. This is the work in which *organizing talent* should reveal itself *in practice* and be promoted to work in the administration of the state. There is a great deal of this talent among the people. It is merely suppressed. It must be given an opportunity to display itself. It, *and it alone,* with the support of the masses, can save Russia and save the cause of socialism.

"Our Revolution," January 1923

I have lately been glancing through Sukhanov's notes on the revolution. What strikes one most is the pedantry of all our petit-bourgeois democrats and of all the heroes of the Second International. Apart from the fact that they are all extremely faint-hearted, that when it comes to the minutest deviation from the German model even the best of them fortify themselves with reservations—apart from this characteristic, which is common to all petit bourgeois democrats and has been abundantly manifested by them throughout the revolution, what strikes one is their slavish imitation of the past.

They all call themselves Marxists, but their conception of Marxism is impossibly pedantic. They have completely failed to understand what is decisive in Marxism, namely, its revolutionary dialectics. They have even absolutely failed to understand Marx's plain statements that in times of revolution the utmost flexibility is demanded, and have even failed to notice, for instance, the statements Marx made in his letters— I think it was in 1856—expressing the hope of combining a peasant war in Germany, which might create a revolutionary situation, with the working-class movement—they avoid even this plain statement and walk around and about it like a cat around a bowl of hot porridge.

Their conduct betrays them as cowardly reformists who are afraid to deviate from the bourgeoisie, let alone break with it, and at the same time they disguise their cowardice with the wildest rhetoric and braggartry. But what strikes one in all of them, even from the purely theoretical point of view, is their utter inability to grasp the following Marxist considerations: up to now they have seen capitalism and bourgeois democracy in western Europe follow a definite path of development, and cannot conceive that this path can be taken as a model only mutatis mutandis, only with certain amendments (quite insignificant from the standpoint of the general development of world history).

First—the revolution connected with the first imperialist world war. Such a revolution was bound to reveal new features, or variations, resulting from the war itself, for the world has never seen such a war in such a situation. We find that since the war the bourgeoisie of the wealthiest countries have to this day been unable to restore "normal" bourgeois relations. Yet our reformists—petit bourgeois who make a show of being revolutionaries—believed, and still believe, that normal bourgeois relations are the limit (thus far shalt thou go and no farther). And even their conception of "normal" is extremely stereotyped and narrow.

Secondly, they are complete strangers to the idea that while the development of world history as a whole follows general laws it is by no means precluded, but, on the contrary, presumed, that certain periods of development may display peculiarities in either the form or the sequence of this development. For instance, it does not even occur to them that because Russia stands on the borderline between the civilized countries and the countries that this war has for the first time definitely brought into the orbit of civilization—all the Oriental, non-European countries—she could and was, indeed, bound to reveal certain distinguishing features; although these, of course, are in keeping with the general line of world development, they distinguish her revolution from those that took place in the west European countries and introduce certain partial innovations as the revolution moves on to the countries of the East.

Infinitely stereotyped, for instance, is the argument they learned by rote during the development of west European Social-Democracy, namely, that we are not yet ripe for socialism, that, as certain "learned" gentlemen among them put it, the objective economic premises of socialism do not exist in our country. It does not occur to any of them to ask: but what about a people that found itself in a revolutionary situation such as that created during the first imperialist war? Might it not, influenced by the hopelessness of its situation, fling itself into a struggle that would offer it at least some chance of securing conditions for the further development of civilization that were somewhat unusual?

"The development of the productive forces of Russia has not attained the level that makes socialism possible." All the heroes of the Second International, including, of course, Sukhanov, beat the drums about this proposition in a thousand different keys, and think that it is the decisive criterion of our revolution.

But what if the situation, which drew Russia into the imperialist world war that involved every more or less influential west European country and made her a witness of the eve of the revolutions maturing or partly already begun in the East, gave rise to circumstances that put Russia and her development into a position that enabled us to achieve precisely that combination of a "peasant war" with the working-class movement suggested in 1856 by no less a Marxist than Marx himself as a possible prospect for Prussia?

What if the complete hopelessness of the situation, by stimulating the efforts of the workers and peasants tenfold, offered us the opportunity to create the fundamental requisites of civilization in a different way from that of the west European countries? Has that altered the general line of development of world history? Has that altered the basic relations between the basic classes of all the countries that are being, or have been, drawn into the general course of world history?

If a definite level of culture is required for the building of socialism (although nobody can say just what that definite "level of culture" is, for it differs in every west European country), why cannot we begin by first achieving the prerequisites for that definite level of culture in a revolutionary way, and then, with the aid of the workers' and peasants' government and the Soviet system, proceed to overtake the other nations?

You say that civilization is necessary for the building of socialism. Very good. But why could we not first create such prerequisites of civilization in our country as the expulsion of the landowners and the Russian capitalists, and then start moving toward socialism? Where, in what books, have you read that such variations of the customary historical sequence of events are impermissible or impossible?

Napoleon, I think, wrote: *"On s'engage et puis . . . on voit."* Rendered freely this means: "First engage in a serious battle and then see what happens." Well, we did first engage in a serious battle in October 1917, and then saw such details of development (from the standpoint of world history they were certainly details) as the Brest peace, the New Economic Policy, and so forth. And now there can be no doubt that in the main we have been victorious.

Our Sukhanovs, not to mention Social-Democrats still farther to the right, never even dream that revolutions cannot be made in any other way. Our European philistines never even dream that the subsequent revolutions in Oriental countries, which possess much vaster populations and a much vaster diversity of social conditions, will undoubtedly display even greater distinctions than the Russian revolution.

It need hardly be said that a textbook written on Kautskyan lines was a very useful thing in its day. But it is time, for all that, to abandon the idea that it foresaw all the forms of development of subsequent world history. It would be timely to say that those who think so are simply fools.

"Better Fewer, But Better," February 1923

In the matter of improving our state apparatus, the Workers' and Peasants' Inspection should not, in my opinion, either strive after quantity or hurry. We have so far been able to devote so little thought and attention to the efficiency of our state apparatus that it would now be quite legitimate if we took special care to secure its thorough organization, and concentrated in the Workers' and Peasants' Inspection a staff of workers really abreast of the times, i.e., not inferior to the best west European standards. For a socialist republic this condition is, of course, too modest. But our experience of the first five years has fairly crammed our heads with mistrust and skepticism. These qualities assert themselves involuntarily when, for example, we hear people dilating at too great length and too flippantly on "proletarian" culture. For a start, we should be satisfied with real bourgeois culture; for a start, we should be glad to dispense with the cruder types of pre-bourgeois culture, i.e., bureaucratic culture or serf culture, etc. In matters of culture, haste and sweeping measures are most harmful. Many of our young writers and Communists should get this well into their heads.

Thus, in the matter of our state apparatus we should now draw the conclusion from our past experience that it would be better to proceed more slowly.

Our state apparatus is so deplorable, not to say wretched, that we must first think very carefully how to combat its defects, bearing in mind that these defects are rooted in the past, which, although it has been overthrown, has not yet been overcome, has not yet reached the stage of a culture that has receded into the distant past. I say culture deliberately, because in these matters we can only regard as achieved what has become part and parcel of our culture, of our social life, our habits. We might say that the good in our social system has not been properly studied, understood, and taken to heart; it has been hastily grasped at; it has not been verified or tested, corroborated by experience, and not made durable, etc. Of course, it could not be otherwise in a revolutionary epoch, when development proceeded at such breakneck speed that in a matter of five years we passed from tsarism to the Soviet system.

It is time we did something about it. We must show sound skepticism for too rapid progress, for boastfulness, etc. We must give thought to testing the steps forward we proclaim every hour, take every minute and then prove every second that they are flimsy, superficial, and misunderstood. The most harmful thing here would be haste. The most harmful thing would be to rely on the assumption that we know at least something, or that we have any considerable number of elements necessary for the building of a really new state apparatus, one really worthy to be called socialist, Soviet, etc.

No, we are ridiculously deficient of such an apparatus, and even of the elements of it, and we must remember that we should not stint time on building it, and that it will take many, many years.

What elements have we for building this apparatus? Only two. First, the workers who are absorbed in the struggle for socialism. These elements are not sufficiently educated. They would like to build a better apparatus for us, but they do not know how. They cannot build one. They have not yet developed the culture required for this; and it is culture that is required. Nothing will be achieved in this by doing things in a rush, by assault, by vim or vigor, or in general, by any of the best human qualities. Secondly, we have elements of knowledge, education, and training, but they are ridiculously inadequate compared with all other countries.

Here we must not forget that we are too prone to compensate (or imagine that we can compensate) our lack of knowledge by zeal, haste, etc.

In order to renovate our state apparatus we must at all costs set out, first, to learn, secondly, to learn, and thirdly, to learn, and then see to it that learning shall not remain a dead letter, or a fashionable catch-phrase (and we should admit in all frankness that this happens very often with us), that learning shall really become part of our very being, that it shall actually and fully become a constituent element of our social life. In short, we must not make the demands that are made by bourgeois western Europe, but demands that are fit and proper for a country which has set out to develop into a socialist country.

The conclusions to be drawn from the above are the following: we must make the Workers' and Peasants' Inspection a really exemplary institution, an instrument to improve our state apparatus.

In order that it may attain the desired high level, we must follow the rule: "Measure your cloth seven times before you cut."

For this purpose, we must utilize the very best of what there is in our social system, and utilize it with the greatest caution, thoughtfulness, and knowledge, to build up the new People's Commissariat.

For this purpose, the best elements that we have in our social system—such as, first, the advanced workers, and, second, the really enlightened elements for whom we can vouch that they will not take the word for the deed, and will not utter a single word that goes against their conscience—should not shrink from admitting any difficulty and should not shrink from any struggle in order to achieve the object they have seriously set themselves.

We have been bustling for five years trying to improve our state apparatus, but it has been mere bustle, which has proved useless in these five years, or even futile, or even harmful. This bustle created the impression that we were doing something, but in effect it was only clogging up our institutions and our brains.

It is high time things were changed.

We must follow the rule: Better fewer, but better. We must follow the rule: Better get good human material in two or even three years than work in haste without hope of getting any at all.

I know that it will be hard to keep to this rule and apply it under our conditions. I know that the opposite rule will force its way through a thousand loopholes. I know that enormous resistance will have to be put up, that devilish persistence will be required, that in the first few years at least work in this field will be hellishly hard. Nevertheless, I am convinced that only by such effort shall we be able to achieve our aim; and that only by achieving this aim shall we create a republic that is really worthy of the name of Soviet, socialist, and so on and so forth.

Many readers probably thought that the figures I quoted by way of illustration in my first article were too small. I am sure that many calculations may be made to prove that they are. But I think that we must put one thing above all such and other calculations, i.e., our desire to obtain really exemplary quality.

I think that the time has at last come when we must work in real earnest to improve our state apparatus and in this there can scarcely be anything more harmful than haste. That is why I would sound a strong warning against inflating the figures. In my opinion, we should, on the contrary, be especially sparing with figures in this matter. Let us say frankly that the People's Commissariat of the Workers' and Peasants' Inspection does not at present enjoy the slightest authority. Everybody knows that no other institutions are worse organized than those of our Workers' and Peasants' Inspection, and that under present conditions nothing can be expected from this People's Commissariat. We must have this firmly fixed in our minds if we really want to create within a few years an institution that will, first, be an exemplary institution, secondly, win everybody's absolute confidence, and, thirdly, prove to all and sundry that we have really justified the work of such a highly placed institution as the Central Control Commission. In my opinion, we must immediately and irrevocably reject all general figures for the size of office staffs. We must select employees for the Workers' and Peasants' Inspection with particular care and only on the basis of the strictest test. Indeed, what is the use of establishing a People's Commissariat that carries on anyhow, that does not enjoy the slightest confidence, and whose word carries scarcely any weight? I think that our main object in launching the work of reconstruction that we now have in mind is to avoid all this.

The workers whom we are enlisting as members of the Central Control Commission must be irreproachable Communists, and I think that a great deal has yet to be done to teach them the methods and objects of their work. Furthermore, there must be a definite number of secretaries to assist in this work, who must be put to a triple test before they are appointed to their posts. Lastly, the officials whom in exceptional cases we shall accept directly as employees of the Workers' and Peasants' Inspection must conform to the following requirements:

First, they must be recommended by several Communists.

Second, they must pass a test for knowledge of our state apparatus.

Third, they must pass a test in the fundamentals of the theory of our state apparatus, in the fundamentals of management, office routine, etc.

Fourth, they must work in such close harmony with the members of the Central Control Commission and with their own secretariat that we could vouch for the work of the whole apparatus.

I know that these requirements are extraordinarily strict, and I am very much afraid that the majority of the "practical" workers in the Workers' and Peasants' Inspection will say that these requirements are impracticable, or will scoff at them. But I ask any of the present chiefs of the Workers' and Peasants' Inspection, or anyone associated with that body, whether they can honestly tell me the practical purpose of a People's Commissariat like the Workers' and Peasants' Inspection. I think this question will help them recover their sense of proportion. Either it is not worthwhile having another of the numerous reorganizations that we have had of this hopeless affair, the Workers' and Peasants' Inspection, or we must really set to work, by slow, difficult, and unusual methods, and by testing these methods over and over again, to create something really exemplary, something that will win the respect of all and sundry for its merits, and not only because of its rank and title.

If we do not arm ourselves with patience, if we do not devote several years to this task, we had better not tackle it at all.

In my opinion we ought to select a minimum number of the higher labor research institutes, etc., which we have baked so hastily, see whether they are organized properly, and allow them to continue working, but only in a way that conforms to the high standards of modern science and gives us all its benefits. If we do that it will not be utopian to hope that within a few years we shall have an institution that will be able to perform its functions, to work systematically and steadily on improving our state apparatus, an institution backed by the trust of the working class, of the Russian Communist Party, and the whole population of our Republic.

The spadework for this could be begun at once. If the People's Commissariat of the Workers' and Peasants' Inspection accepted the present plan of reorganization, it could now take preparatory steps and work methodically until the task is completed, without haste, and not hesitating to alter what has already been done.

Any halfhearted solution would be extremely harmful in this matter. A measure for the size of the staff of the Workers' and Peasants' Inspection based on any other consideration would, in fact, be based on the old bureaucratic considerations, on old prejudices, on what has already been condemned, universally ridiculed, etc. . . .

Let us hope that our new Workers' and Peasants' Inspection will abandon what the French call *pruderie*, which we may call ridiculous primness, or ridiculous swank, and which plays entirely into the hands of our Soviet and party bureaucracy. Let it be said in parentheses that we have bureaucrats in our party offices as well as in Soviet offices.

When I said above that we must study and study hard in institutes for the higher organization of labor, etc., I did not by any means imply "studying" in the schoolroom way, nor did I confine myself to the idea of studying only in the schoolroom way. I hope that not a single genuine revolutionary will suspect me of refusing, in this case, to understand "studies" to include resorting to some semi-humorous trick, cunning device, piece of trickery, or something of that sort. I know that in the staid and earnest states of western Europe such an idea would horrify people and that not a single decent official would even entertain it. I hope, however, that we have not yet become as bureaucratic as all that and that in our midst the discussion of this idea will give rise to nothing more than amusement.

Indeed, why not combine pleasure with utility? Why not resort to some humorous or semi-humorous trick to expose something ridiculous, something harmful, something semi-ridiculous, semi-harmful, etc.?

It seems to me that our Workers' and Peasants' Inspection will gain a great deal if it undertakes to examine these ideas, and that the list of cases in which our Central Control Commission and its colleagues in the Workers' and Peasants' Inspection achieved a few of their most brilliant victories will be enriched by not a few exploits of our future Workers' and Peasants' Inspection and Central Control Commission members in places not quite mentionable in prim and staid textbooks. . . .

Reference

Lenin, Vladimir Ilyich, *The Lenin Anthology*, edited by Robert C. Tucker (New York: W. W. Norton, 1975).

LEON TROTSKY

FULL NAME:

Leon (Lev Davidovich Bronstein) Trotsky

BORN:

7 November 1879, Yanovka, Kherson Province,
Russia

DIED:

20 August 1940, Loyoacán, near Mexico City

Revolutionary and military leader. In exile in 1905 to Siberia, then to Vienna and America. With Bolsheviks in 1917; Chairman of the Military Revolutionary Committee and later Commissar of Military Affairs. 1927 expulsion from Politburo and 1932 deportation from U.S.S.R. Assassination victim in Mexico in 1940.

Writings include: The Age of Permanent Revolution, edited by Isaac Deutscher (New York: Dell, 1964); Stalin (New York, Steen and Day, 1967); My Life (New York: Charles Scribner's Sons, 1930); and The History of the Russian Revolution (London: Victor Gollancz Ltd., 1934). Biographies include: Isaac Deutscher, The Prophet Armed: Trotsky 1879–1921 (New York: Oxford, 1963); Isaac Deutscher, The Prophet Outcast: Trotsky, 1929–1940 (New York: Oxford, 1963); and Max Eastman, Leon Trotsky, The Portrait of a Youth (New York: Greenberg, 1925).

Excerpts from My Life

... Of Zinoviev and Kamenev, Lenin writes, with an effect of casualness, that their capitulation in 1917 was "not an accident"; in other words, it is in their blood. Obviously such men cannot direct the revolution, but they should not be reproached for their pasts. Bukharin is not a Marxist but a scholastic; he is, however, a sympathetic person. Pyatakov is an able administrator, but a very bad politician. It is quite possible, however, that these two, Bukharin and Pyatakov, will still learn. The ablest is Trotsky; his defect is his excess of self-confidence. Stalin is rude, disloyal, and capable of abuse of the power that he derives from the party apparatus. Stalin should be removed to avoid a split. This is the substance of the "Will." It rounds out and clarifies the proposal that Lenin made me in our last conversation.

Lenin came to know Stalin really only after the October Revolution. He valued his firmness and his practical mind, which is three-quarters cunning. And yet, at every step, Lenin struck at Stalin's ignorance, at his very narrow political horizon, and his exceptional moral coarseness and unscrupulousness. Stalin was elected to the post of general secretary of the Party against the will of Lenin, who acquiesced only so long as he himself headed the Party. But after his first stroke, when he returned to work with his health undermined, Lenin applied himself to the entire problem of leadership. This accounts for the conversation with me. Hence, too, the Will. Its last lines were written on 4 January. After that, two more months passed during which the situation took definite shape. Lenin was now preparing not only to remove Stalin from his post of general secretary, but to disqualify him before the Party as well. On the question of monopoly of foreign trade, on the national question, on questions of the regime in the Party, of the worker-peasant inspection, and of the commission of control, he was systematically preparing to deliver at the Twelfth Congress a crushing blow at Stalin as personifying bureaucracy, the mutual shielding among officials, arbitrary rule, and general rudeness.

Would Lenin have been able to carry out the regrouping in the party direction that he planned? At that moment, he undoubtedly would. There had been several precedents for it, and one of them was quite fresh in mind and significant. In November 1922, while Lenin was still convalescent and living in the country, and while I was absent from Moscow, the Central Committee unanimously adopted a decision that dealt an irreparable blow at the monopoly of foreign trade. Both Lenin and I sounded the alarm, independently of each other, and then wrote to each other and coordinated our action. A few weeks later, the Central Committee revoked its decision as unanimously as it had adopted it. On 21 December, Lenin wrote triumphantly to me: "Comrade Trotsky, it seems that we have managed to capture the position without a single shot, by a mere maneuver. I suggest that we do not stop but press the attack." Our joint action against the Central Committee at the beginning of 1923 would without a shadow of a doubt have brought us victory. And what is more, I have no doubt that if I had come forward on the eve of the Twelfth Congress in the spirit of a "bloc of Lenin and Trotsky" against the Stalin bureaucracy, I should have been victorious even if Lenin had taken no direct part in the struggle. How solid the victory would have been is, of course, another question. To decide that, one must take into account a number of objective processes in the country, in the working class, and in the Party itself. That is a separate and large theme. Lenin's wife said in 1927 that if he had been alive he would probably have been doing time in a Stalin prison. I think she was right. For the thing that matters is not Stalin, but the forces that he expresses without even realizing it. In 1922–3, however, it was still possible to capture the commanding position by an open attack on the faction then rapidly being formed of National Socialist officials, of usurpers of the apparatus, of the unlawful heirs of October, of the epigones of Bolshevism. The chief obstacle was Lenin's condition. He was expected to rise again as he had after his first stroke and to take part in the Twelfth Congress as he had in the Eleventh. He himself hoped for this. The doctors spoke encouragingly, though with dwindling assurance. The idea of a "bloc of Lenin and Trotsky" against the apparatus-men and bureaucrats was at that time fully known only to Lenin and me, although the other members of the Politburo dimly suspected it. Lenin's letters on the national question and his Will remained unknown. Independent action on my part would have been interpreted, or, to be more exact, represented as my personal fight for Lenin's place in the Party and the state. The very thought of this made me shudder. I considered that it would have brought such a demoralization in our ranks that we would have had to pay too painful a price for it even in case of victory. In all plans and calculations, there remained the positive element of uncertainty— Lenin and his physical condition. Would he be able to state his own views? Would he still have time? Would the Party understand that it was a case of a fight by Lenin and Trotsky for the future of the revolution, and not a fight by Trotsky for the place held by Lenin, who was ill? Because of Lenin's exceptional position in the Party, the uncertainty of his personal condition became the uncertainty of the condition of the entire Party. The indefinite situation was being prolonged.

And the delay simply played into the hands of the epigones, since Stalin, as general secretary, became the majordomo of the apparatus for the entire period of the interregnum. . . .

Lenin's offensive was directed not only against Stalin personally, but against his entire staff, and, first of all, his assistants, Dzerzhinsky and Ordzhonikidze. Both of them are mentioned constantly in Lenin's correspondence on the Georgian question. Dzerzhinsky was a man of great and explosive passion. His energy was held at a high pitch by constant electric discharges. In every discussion, even of things of minor importance, he would fire up, his nostrils would quiver, his eyes would sparkle, and his voice would be so strained that often it would break. Yet, in spite of this high nervous tension, Dzerzhinsky had no apathetic intervals. He was always in that same state of tense mobilization. Lenin once compared him to a spirited thoroughbred. Dzerzhinsky fell in love, in a mad infatuation, with everything he did, and guarded his associates from criticism and interference with a passionate fanaticism that had no element of the personal in it, for he was completely dissolved in his work.

Dzerzhinsky had no opinion of his own. He never thought of himself as a politician, at least while Lenin was alive. On various occasions, he said to me: "I am not a bad revolutionary, perhaps, but I am no leader, statesman, or politician." This was not mere modesty; his self-appraisal was essentially right. In political matters, Dzerzhinsky always needed someone's immediate guidance. For many years he had followed Rosa Luxemburg and with her had gone through not only the struggle against Polish patriotism, but that against Bolshevism as well. In 1917 he joined the Bolsheviks. Lenin said to me with great joy, "No traces of the old fight are left." During the first two or three years, Dzerzhinsky was especially drawn to me. In his last years, he supported Stalin. In his economic work, he accomplished things through sheer temperament—appealing, urging, and lifting people off their feet by his own enthusiasm. He had no considered ideas about economic development. He shared all Stalin's errors and defended them with all the passion of which he was capable. He died practically on his feet, just after he had left the platform from which he had so passionately been denouncing the opposition.

Stalin's other ally, Ordzhonikidze, Lenin thought it necessary to expel from the Party because of his bureaucratic high-handedness in the Caucasus. I argued against it. Lenin answered me through his secretary: "At least for two years." How little could he imagine at that time that Ordzhonikidze would become head of the Control Commission that Lenin was planning to create to fight Stalin's bureaucracy, and that was to embody the conscience of the Party!

Aside from its general political aims, the campaign that Lenin opened had as its immediate object the creation of the best conditions for my work of direction, either side by side with him if he regained his health, or in his place if he succumbed to his illness. But the struggle, which was never carried out to its end, or even partway, had exactly the opposite result. Lenin managed only to *declare* war against Stalin and his allies, and even this was known only to those who were directly involved in it, and not to the Party as a whole. Stalin's faction—at that time it was still the faction of the trio—closed its ranks more tightly after the first warning. The indefinite situation continued. Stalin stood at the helm of the apparatus. Artificial selection was carried on there at a mad pace. The weaker the trio felt in matters of principle, the more they feared me—because they wanted to get rid of me—and the tighter they had to bolt all the screws and nuts in the state and party system. Much later, in 1925, Bukharin said to me, in answer to my criticism of the party oppression: "We have no democracy because we are afraid of you."

"Just you try to stop being afraid," I proffered by way of advice, "and let us work properly." But my advice was vain.

The year 1923 was the first year of the intense but still silent stifling and routing of the Bolshevist Party. Lenin was struggling with his terrible illness. The trio were struggling with the Party. The atmosphere was charged, and toward autumn the tension resolved itself into a "discussion" of the opposition. The second chapter of the revolution had begun—the fight against Trotskyism. In reality, it was a fight against the ideological legacy of Lenin. . . .

In the later struggle by Zinoviev and Kamenev against Stalin, the secrets of this period were disclosed by the members of the conspiracy themselves. For it was a real conspiracy. A secret political bureau of seven was formed; it comprised all the members of the official Politburo except me, and included also Kuibyshev, the present chairman of the Supreme Economic Council. All questions were decided in advance at that secret center, where the members were bound by mutual vows. They undertook not to engage in polemics against one another and at the same time to seek opportunities to attack me. There were similar centers in the local organizations, and they were connected with the Moscow "seven" by strict discipline. For communication, special codes were used. This was a well-organized illegal group within the Party, directed originally against one man. Responsible workers in the Party and state were systematically selected by the single criterion: Against Trotsky. During the prolonged "interregnum" created by Lenin's illness, this work was carried on tirelessly but still under cover, so that in the event of Lenin's recovery, the mined bridges could be preserved intact. The conspirators acted by hints. Candidates for posts were required to guess what was wanted of them. Those who "guessed" went up the ladder. In this war a special "careerism" was developed, which later on received unashamed the name of "anti-Trotskyism." Lenin's death freed the conspirators and allowed them to come out into the open. The process of personal selection descended a rung lower. It now became impossible to obtain a post as director of a plant, as secretary of a party local, as chairman of a rural executive committee, as bookkeeper or typist, unless one had proved one's anti-Trotskyism.

The members of the Party who raised their voices in protest against this conspiracy became the victims of treacherous attacks, made by reasons entirely remote and frequently invented. On the other hand, the morally unstable elements, who were being mercilessly driven out of the Party during the first five years, now squared themselves by a single hostile remark against Trotsky. From the end of 1923, the same work was carried on in all the parties of the Communist International; certain leaders were dethroned and others appointed in their stead solely on the basis of their attitude toward Trotsky. A strenuous artificial selection was being effected, a selection not of the best but of the most suitable. The general policy became one of a replacement of independent and gifted men by mediocrities who owed their posts entirely to the apparatus. It was as the supreme expression of the mediocrity of the apparatus that Stalin himself rose to his position.

* * *

I was often asked, and even now I still am asked: "How could you lose power?" In most instances, the question covers a naïve conception of letting some material object slip from one's hands, as if losing power were the same thing as losing a watch or a notebook. But as a matter of fact, when the revolutionaries who directed the seizure of power begin at a certain stage to lose it, whether peacefully or through catastrophe, the fact in itself signifies either a decline in the influence of certain ideas and moods in the governing revolutionary circles, or the decline of revolutionary mood in the masses themselves. Or it may be both at the same time. The leading groups of the Party that emerged from underground were inspired by the revolutionary tendencies that the leaders of the first period of the revolution were able to formulate clearly and to carry out completely and successfully in practice. It was exactly this that made them the leaders of the Party, and, through the Party, leaders of the working class, and, through the working class, leaders of the country. It was thus that certain individuals had concentrated power in their hands. But the ideas of the first period of the revolution were imperceptibly losing their influence in the consciousness of the party stratum that held the direct power over the country.

In the country itself, processes were shaping themselves that one may sum up under the general name of reaction. These extended, in varying degree, to the working class as well, including even its Party. The stratum that made up the apparatus of power developed its own independent aims and tried to subordinate the revolution to them. A division began to reveal itself between the leaders who expressed the historical line of the class and could see beyond the apparatus, and the apparatus itself—a huge, cumbrous, heterogeneous thing that easily sucked in the average Communist. At first this division was more psychological than political in character. Yesterday was still too fresh in mind, the slogans of October had not had time to vanish from the memory, and the authority of the leaders of the first period was still strong. But under cover of the traditional forms, a different psychology was developing. The international prospects were growing dim. The everyday routine was completely absorbing the people. New methods, instead of serving the old aims, were creating new ones and, most of all, a new psychology. In the eyes of many, the temporary situation began to seem the ultimate goal. A new type was being evolved.

In the final analysis, revolutionaries are made of the same social stuff as other people. But they must have had certain very different personal qualities to enable the historical process to separate them from the rest into a distinct group. Association with one another, theoretical work, the struggle under a definite banner, collective discipline, the hardening under the fire of danger, these things gradually shape the revolutionary type. It would be perfectly legitimate to speak of the psychological type of the Bolshevik in contrast, for example, to that of the Menshevik. An eye sufficiently experienced could tell a Bolshevik from a Menshevik even by his outward appearance, with only a slight percentage of error.

This doesn't mean, however, that a Bolshevik was always and in everything a Bolshevik. To absorb a certain philosophic outlook into one's flesh and blood, to make it dominate one's consciousness, and to coordinate with it one's sensory world is given not to everyone but to only a few. In the working masses, a substitute is found in the class instinct, which in critical periods attains a high degree of sensitiveness. But there are many revolutionaries in the Party and the state who come from the masses but have long since broken away from them, and who, because of their position, are placed in a separate and distinct class. Their class instinct has evaporated. On the other hand, they lack the theoretical stability and outlook to envisage the process in its entirety. Their psychology retains many unprotected surfaces, which, with the change of circumstances, expose them to the easy penetration of foreign and hostile ideological influences. In the days of the underground struggle, of the uprisings, and the civil war, people of this type were merely soldiers of the party. Their minds had only one string, and that sounded in harmony with the party tuning fork. But when the tension relaxed and the nomads of the revolutions passed on to settled living, the traits of the man in the street, the sympathies and tastes of self-satisfied officials, revived in them.

Quite frequently I heard isolated remarks of Kalinin, Voroshilov, Stalin, or Rykov with alarm. Where does this come from?—I asked myself—from what well does it gush? When I came to a meeting and found groups engaged in conversation, often they would stop when they saw me. There was nothing directed against me in those conversations, nothing opposed to the principles of the Party. But they showed an attitude of moral relaxation, of self-content and triviality. People began to feel an urge to pour out these new moods upon each other—moods in which the element of philistine gossip came to have a very prominent place. Heretofore they had realized the impropriety of this sort of thing not only in Lenin's or my presence but even with one another. On occasions when vulgarity showed itself—for example, on the part of Stalin—Lenin, without even lifting his head from his papers, would look around as if trying to find someone else who was repelled by the remark. In such cases, a swift glance, or an intonation in the voice was enough to reveal indisputably to both of us our solidarity in these psychological appraisals.

If I took no part in the amusements that were becoming more and more common in the lives of the new governing stratum, it was not for moral reasons, but because I hated to inflict such boredom on myself. The visiting at each other's homes, the assiduous attendance at the ballet, the drinking parties at which people who were absent were pulled to pieces, had no attraction for me. The new ruling group felt that I did not fit in with this way of living, and they did not even try to win me over. It was for this very reason that many group conversations would stop the moment I appeared, and those engaged in them would cut them short with a certain shamefacedness and a slight bitterness toward me. This was, if you like, a definite indication that I had begun to lose power.

I am here limiting myself to the psychological aspect of the matter, and disregarding its social basis, that is, the changes in the anatomy of the revolutionary society. In the final reckoning, it is, of course, these latter changes that decide. But in actual life it is their psychological

reflection that one encounters directly. The inner events were developing rather slowly, facilitating the molecular processes of the transformation of the upper stratum, and leaving no opening for contrasting
the two irreconcilable positions before the masses. One must add that
the new moods were for a long time, and still are, disguised by traditional formulas. This made it all the more difficult to determine how
far the process of metabolism had gone. The Thermidor conspiracy at
the end of the eighteenth century, prepared for by the preceding
course of the revolution, broke out with a single blow and assumed
the shape of a sanguinary finale. Our Thermidor was long drawn out.
The guillotine found its substitute—at least for a while—in intrigue.
The falsifying of the past, systematized on the conveyer plan, became
a weapon for the ideological rearming of the official Party. Lenin's illness and the expectation of his return to the leadership made the temporary situation indefinite, and it lasted, with an interval, for over two
years. If the revolution had been in the ascendancy, the delay would
have played into the hands of the opposition. But the revolution on
the international scale was suffering one defeat after another, and the
delay accordingly played into the hands of the national reformism by
automatically strengthening the Stalin bureaucracy against me and my
political friends.

The out-and-out philistine, ignorant, and simply stupid baiting of
the theory of permanent revolution grew from just these psychological sources. Gossiping over a bottle of wine or returning from the ballet, one smug official would say to another: "He can think of nothing
but permanent revolution." The accusations of unsociability, of individualism, of aristocratism, were closely connected with this particular mood. The sentiment of "Not all and always for the revolution, but
something for oneself as well," was translated as "Down with permanent revolution." The revolt against the exacting theoretical demands
of Marxism and the exacting political demands of the revolution gradually assumed, in the eyes of these people, the form of a struggle
against "Trotskyism." Under this banner, the liberation of the philistine in the Bolshevik was proceeding. It was because of this that I lost
power, and it was this that determined the form that this loss took.

I have said before that Lenin, from his deathbed, was preparing a
blow at Stalin and his allies, Dzerzhinsky and Ordzhonikidze. Lenin valued Dzerzhinsky highly. The estrangement began when Dzerzhinsky
realized that Lenin did not think him capable of directing economic
work. It was this that threw Dzerzhinsky into Stalin's arms, and then
Lenin decided to strike at him as one of Stalin's supports. As for
Ordzhonikidze, Lenin wanted to expel him from the Party for his ways
of a governor-general. Lenin's note promising the Georgian Bolsheviks

his full support against Stalin, Dzerzhinsky, and Ordzhonikidze was addressed to Mdivani. The fates of the four reveal most vividly the sweeping change in the Party engineered by the Stalin faction. After Lenin's death, Dzerzhinsky was put at the head of the Supreme Economic Council, that is, in charge of all state industries. Ordzhonikidze, who had been slated for expulsion, has been made the head of the Central Control Commission. Stalin not only has remained the general secretary, contrary to Lenin's wish, but has been given unheard-of powers by the apparatus. Finally, Budu Mdivani, whom Lenin supported against Stalin, is now in the Tobolsk prison. A similar "regrouping" has been effected in the entire directing personnel of the Party and in all the parties of the International, without exception. The epoch of the epigones is separated from that of Lenin not only by a gulf of ideas, but also by a sweeping overturn in the organization of the Party.

Stalin has been the chief instrument in carrying out this overturn. He is gifted with practicality, a strong will, and persistence in carrying out his aims. His political horizon is restricted, his theoretical equipment primitive. His work of compilation, The Foundations of Leninism, in which he made an attempt to pay tribute to the theoretical traditions of the Party, is full of sophomoric errors. His ignorance of foreign languages compels him to follow the political life of other countries at second hand. His mind is stubbornly empirical, and devoid of creative imagination. To the leading group of the Party (in the wide circles he was not known at all) he always seemed a man destined to play second and third fiddle. And the fact that today he is playing first is not so much a summing-up of the man as it is of this transitional period of political backsliding in the country. Helvetius said it long ago: "Every period has its great men, and if these are lacking, it invents them." Stalinism is above all else the automatic work of the impersonal apparatus on the decline of the revolution. . . .

On many sides it has been explained to me that my disbelief in democracy is my greatest sin. How many articles and even books have been written about this! But when I ask to be given a brief object lesson in democracy, there are no volunteers. The planet proves to be without a visa. Why should I believe that the much more important question—the trial between the rich and poor—will be decided with strict observance of the forms and rituals of democracy?

And has the revolutionary dictatorship produced the results expected of it?—I hear a question. It would be possible to answer it only by taking a reckoning of the experience of the October Revolution and trying to indicate its future prospects. An autobiography is no place for this, and I will try to answer the question in a special book on which I had already begun to work during my stay in Central Asia.

But I cannot end the story of my life without explaining, if only in a few lines, why I adhere so completely to my old path.

That which has happened in the memory of my generation, already mature or approaching old age, can be described schematically as follows: During several decades—the end of the last century and the beginning of the present—the European population was being severely disciplined by industry. All phases of social education were dominated by the principle of the productivity of labor. This yielded stupendous results and seemed to open up new possibilities to people. But actually it only led to war. It is true that through the war humanity has been able to convince itself, in the face of the crowings of anemic philosophy, that it is not degenerating after all; on the contrary, it is full of life, strength, bravery, enterprise. Through the same war, it realized its technical power with unprecedented force. It was as if a man, to prove that his pipes for breathing and swallowing were in order, had begun to cut his throat with a razor in front of a mirror.

After the end of the operations of 1914–18, it was declared that from now on the highest moral duty was to care for the wounds that had been the highest moral duty to inflict during the preceding four years. Industry and thrift were not only restored to their rights, but were put into the steel corsets of rationalization. The so-called "reconstruction" is directed by those same classes, parties, and even individuals who guided the destruction. Where a change of political regime has taken place, as in Germany, the men who play the leading roles in the direction of reconstruction are those who played second and third roles in guiding the destruction. That, strictly speaking, is the only change.

The war has swept away an entire generation, as if to create a break in the memory of peoples and to prevent the new generation from noticing too closely that it is actually engaged in repeating what has been done before, only on a higher historical rung, which implies more menacing consequences.

The working class of Russia, under the leadership of the Bolsheviks, made an attempt to effect a reconstruction of life that would exclude the possibility of humanity's going through these periodical fits of sheer insanity, and would lay the foundations of a higher culture. That was the sense of the October Revolution. To be sure, the problem it has set itself has not yet been solved. But in its very essence, this problem demands many decades. Moreover, the October Revolution should be considered as the starting-point of the newest history of humanity as a whole.

Toward the end of the Thirty Years' War, the German Reformation must have appeared the work of men who had broken out of a lunatic asylum. To a certain extent, it really was: European humanity broken out of the medieval monastery. Modern Germany, England, the United States, and the modern world in general would never have been possible without the Reformation with its countless victims. If victims are generally to be permitted—but whose permission could one ask?—it is certainly victims that move humanity forward.

The same can be said of the French Revolution. That narrow-minded, reactionary pedant, Taine, imagined that he was making a most profound discovery when he established the fact that a few years after the execution of Louis XVI, the French people were poorer and more unhappy than under the old regime. But the whole point of the matter is that such events as the great French Revolution cannot be viewed on the scale of "a few years." Without the great revolution, the entire new France would never have been possible, and Taine himself would still have been a clerk in the service of some contractor of the old regime instead of being able to blacken the revolution that opened a new career to him.

A still greater historical perspective is necessary to view the October Revolution. Only hopeless dullards can quote as evidence against it the fact that in twelve years it has not yet created general peace and prosperity. If one adopts the scale of the German Reformation and the French Revolution, representing two different stages in the evolution of bourgeois society, separated from each other by almost three centuries, one must express amazement at the fact that a backward and isolated Russia twelve years after the revolution has been able to ensure for the masses of the people a standard of living that is not lower than that existing on the eve of the war. That alone is a miracle of its kind. But of course the significance of the October Revolution does not lie in that. The revolution is an experiment in a new social regime, an experiment that will undergo many changes and will probably be remade anew from its very foundations. It will assume an entirely different character on the basis of the newest technical achievements. But after a few decades and centuries, the new social order will look back on the October Revolution as the bourgeois order does on the German Reformation or the French Revolution. This is clear, so incontestably clear, that even the professors of history will understand it, though only after many years.

And what of your personal fate?—I hear a question, in which curiosity is mixed with irony. Here I can add but little to what I have said in this book. I do not measure the historical process by the yardstick of one's personal fate. On the contrary, I appraise my fate objectively and live it subjectively, only as it is inextricably bound up with the course of social development.

Since my exile, I have more than once read musings in the newspapers on the subject of the "tragedy" that has befallen me. I know no *personal* tragedy. I know the change of two chapters of the revolution. One American paper that published an article of mine accompanied it with a profound note to the effect that in spite of the blows the author had suffered, he had, as evidenced by his article, preserved his clarity of reason. I can only express my astonishment at the philistine attempt to establish a connection between the power of reasoning and a government post, between mental balance and the present situation. I do not know, and I never have, of any such connection. In prison, with a book or a pen in my hand, I experienced the same sense of deep satisfaction that I did at the mass-meetings of the revolution. I felt the mechanics of power as an inescapable burden, rather than as a spiritual satisfaction. But it would perhaps be briefer to quote the good words of someone else.

On 26 January 1917, Rosa Luxemburg wrote to a woman friend from prison: "This losing oneself completely in the banalities of daily life is something that I generally cannot understand or endure. See, for example, how Goethe rose above material things with a calm superiority. Just think of what he had to live through: the great French Revolution, which at near range must have seemed a bloody and utterly aimless farce, and then from 1793 to 1815, a continuous sequence of wars. I do not demand that you write poetry as Goethe did, but his view of life, the universality of his interests, the inner harmony of the man, everyone can create for himself or at least strive for. And should you say that Goethe was not a political fighter, I maintain that it is precisely the fighter who must try to be above things, or else he will get his nose stuck in all sorts of rubbish—of course, in this case, I am thinking of a fighter in the grand style. . . . "

Brave words. I read them for the first time the other day and they immediately brought the figure of Rosa Luxemburg closer and made her dearer to me than ever before.

In his views, his character, his world outlook, Proudhon, that Robinson Crusoe of socialism, is alien to me. But Proudhon had the nature of a fighter, a spiritual disinterestedness, a capacity of despising official public opinion, and finally, the fire of a many-sided curiosity never extinguished. This enabled him to rise above his own life, with its ups and downs, as he did above all contemporaneous reality.

On 26 April 1852, Proudhon wrote to a friend from prison: "The movement is no doubt irregular and crooked, but the tendency is constant. What every government does in turn in favor of revolution becomes inviolable; what is attempted against it passes over like a cloud: I enjoy watching this spectacle, in which I understand every single picture; I observe these changes in the life of the world as if I had received their explanation from above; what oppresses others, elevates me more and more, inspires and fortifies me; how can you want me then to accuse destiny, to complain about people and curse them? Destiny—I laugh at it; and as for men, they are too ignorant, too enslaved for me to feel annoyed at them."

Despite their slight savor of ecclesiastical eloquence, those are fine words. I subscribe to them.

The History of the Russian Revolution

. . . Kamenev, in the argument we are discussing, comes to the defense of Lenin. All the epigones defend themselves under this imposing pseudonym. How could Lenin, he asks, have fought so passionately for an insurrection, if it was already nine-tenths accomplished! But Lenin himself wrote at the beginning of October: "It is quite possible that right now we might seize the power without an insurrection." In other words, Lenin postulated that the "silent" revolution had already taken place before the ninth of October, and moreover not by nine- but by ten-tenths. He understood, however, that this optimistic hypothesis could only be verified in action. For that reason Lenin said in the same letter: "If we cannot seize the power without an insurrection, then we must make an insurrection immediately." It was this question that was discussed on the tenth and sixteenth, and on other days.

The recent Soviet histories have completely erased from the October Revolution the extremely important and instructive chapter about the disagreements between Lenin and the Central Committee—both upon the basic matter of principle in which Lenin was right, and also upon those particular, but very important, questions upon which the Central Committee was right. According to the new doctrine, neither Lenin nor the Central Committee could make a mistake, and consequently there could have been no conflict between them. In those cases where it becomes impossible to deny that there was a disagreement, it is, in obedience to a general prescription, laid at the door of Trotsky.

The facts speak otherwise. Lenin insisted upon raising an insurrection in the days of the Democratic Conference. Not one member of the Central Committee supported him. A week later Lenin proposed to Smilga to organize an insurrectionary headquarters in Finland, and strike a blow at the government from that point with the sailors. Again ten days later he insisted that the Northern Congress become the staring-point of an insurrection. Nobody at the Congress supported this proposal. At the end of September Lenin considered the postponement of the insurrection for three weeks, until the Congress of Soviets, fatal. Nevertheless the insurrection, deferred to the eve of the Congress, was accomplished while the Congress was in session. Lenin proposed that the struggle begin in Moscow, assuming that there it would be resolved without a fight. As a matter of fact, the insurrection in Moscow, notwithstanding the preceding victory in Petrograd, lasted eight days and cost many victims.

Lenin was no automaton of infallible decisions. He was "only" a man of genius, and nothing human was alien to him, therein included the capacity to make mistakes. Lenin said this of the attitude of epigones to the great revolutionists: "After their deaths, attempts are made to convert them into harmless icons, to canonize them, so to speak, to render a certain homage to their names . . ." in order thus the more safely to betray them in action. The present epigones demand that Lenin be acknowledged infallible in order the more easily to extend the same dogma to themselves.

What characterized Lenin as a statesman was a combination of bold perspectives with a meticulous estimation of tiny facts and symptoms. Lenin's isolation did not prevent him from defining with incomparable penetration the fundamental stages and turns of the movement, but it deprived him of the possibility of making timely estimates of episodic factors and temporary changes. The political situation was in general so favorable to an insurrection as to admit several different possibilities of victory. If Lenin had been in Petrograd and had carried through at the beginning of October his decision in favor of an immediate insurrection without reference to the Congress of Soviets, he would undoubtedly have given the carrying out of his own plan a political setting that would have reduced its disadvantageous features to a minimum. But it is at least equally probable that he would himself in that case have come around to the plan actually carried out.

We have given in a separate chapter our estimate of the role of Lenin in the general strategy of the revolution. To point our idea in regard to Lenin's tactical proposals we will add that without Lenin's pressure, without his urgings, his suggestions, his variant plans, it would have been infinitely more difficult to get over onto the road toward insurrection. Had Lenin been in Smolny during the critical weeks, the general leadership of the insurrection—and that not only in Petrograd but Moscow—would have been on a considerably higher level. But Lenin as an "emigré" could not take the place of Lenin in Smolny. . . .

References

Trotsky, Leon, My Life (New York: Charles Scribner's Sons, 1930).

Trotsky, Leon, The History of the Russian Revolution (London: Victor Gollancz Ltd., 1934).

JOSEPH STALIN

FULL NAME:

Iosef Vissarionovich Dzhugashvili Stalin

BORN:

21 December 1879, Gori, Georgia

DIED:

5 March 1953, Kuntsevo, near Moscow

Seminarian turned revolutionary leader in Georgia and the Caucasus. General Secretary of the Communist Party from 1922 until his death in 1953. Responsible for Communist Party purges. Supreme Leader in 1930s. Commander in Chief of the Armed Forces of the Soviet Union.

His many works have been collected in: *Problems of Leninism (Voprosy Leninizma)* (Moscow: 1952); *Foundations of Leninism* (New York: International Publishers, 1932); *Works (Sochineniya)* (Moscow: 1951); *Marxism and the National Question* (New York: International Publishers, 1942); *The Essential Stalin, 1905–1952* (Garden City, NY: Anchor, 1972); and *Stalin's Kampf*, edited by M. R. Werner (New York: Howell, Soskin & Company, 1940). Among the numerous biographies of Stalin are: Isaac Deutscher, *Stalin, A Political Biography* (London: Oxford, 1946); Robert C. Tucker, *Stalin As Revolutionary, 1879–1926* (New York: W. W. Norton, 1973); and Milovan Djilas, *Conversations with Stalin* (New York: Harcourt, 1962).

Stalin's Kampf

Speech to the workers of Tiflis, 1926

I must, in all conscience, tell you, that I have not deserved half the eulogy that has been given me. It appears that I am one of the heroes, the director of the Communist Party of the Soviet Union, the head of the Communist International, a peerless knight and all sorts of other things. This is mere fantasy, and a perfectly useless exaggeration. That is the way one speaks at the grave of a revolutionary. But I am not preparing to die. Therefore I must give you a true picture of what I once was and say to whom I owe my present position in the Party. Comrade Arakel (Okuashvili) has said that he once considered himself as one of my masters and me as his pupil. That is absolutely correct. I have been and still am a pupil of the pioneer workmen of the Tiflis railway workshops. . . .

Allow me to revert to the past. I remember the year 1898, when for the first time the workers in the railway shops put me in charge of a club. I remember how, at Comrade Sturua's rooms, in the presence of Sylvester Djibladze (he was then also one of my teachers), of Zakro Chodrishvili, of George Chkheidze, of Mikha Bochorishvili, of Ninua, and other advanced workers of Tiflis, I learned practical work. In comparison with these men I was then a tyro.

Perhaps I had a little more booklearning than many of them. But in the practice of revolution I was certainly a beginner. Here, among these colleagues, I received my first baptism of fire in revolution. As you see, my first teachers were the workers of Tiflis. Allow me to express to them now the sincere gratitude of a comrade.

Then I remember the years 1905 to 1907, when at the desire of the Party I was thrown into the work at Baku. Two years of revolutionary work among the oil workers made me a practical fighter and a practical leader. In the society of the advanced sections of workers at Baku such as Vatsek, Saratovetz and others, on the one hand, and on the other in the stormy conflicts between the oil workers and the oil masters, I learned for the first time what the leadership of great masses of workmen really meant. I had my second baptism of fire in revolution. Then I became a journeyman of revolution. Let me now express my sincere gratitude as a comrade to my Baku teachers. . . .

I remember 1917, when by the decision of the Party, after prison and deportation, I was thrown into Leningrad. There, among the Russian workers, in close contact with the great educator of the proletariat throughout the world, Comrade Lenin, in the storm of the mighty struggle between the proletariat and the bourgeoisie, during the World War, I learned for the first time to understand what it meant to be one of the leaders of the great working-class Party. There, in the midst of Russian workmen, liberators of oppressed nations and fighters in the proletarian struggle in all countries and among all nations, I received my third baptism of fire in revolutionary warfare. There, in Russia, under Lenin's direction, I became a master-worker in revolution. Let me express to my Russian teachers my sincere gratitude as a comrade and bow my head before the memory of my master Lenin.

From apprentice at Tiflis, to journeyman at Baku, to master-worker in our revolution at Leningrad—such is the course of my apprenticeship to revolution, the true picture, honest and without exaggeration, of what I was and what I have become. . . .

I became a Marxist thanks so to speak to my social position—my father was a worker in a shoe-factory and my mother was also a working-woman—but also because I could hear the murmurs of revolt among the people who lived at the social level of my parents, finally on account of the rigorous intolerance and Jesuitical discipline so cruelly crushing me in the orthodox seminary where I passed some years. The atmosphere in which I lived was saturated with hatred against Tsarist oppression and I threw myself with all my heart into revolutionary activity.

Interview with Emil Ludwig, 13 December 1931

I joined the revolutionary movement at the age of fifteen, when I became connected with certain illegal groups of Russian Marxists in Transcaucasia. These groups exerted a great influence on me and instilled in me a taste for illegal Marxian literature. . . .

My parents were uneducated people, but they did not treat me badly by any means. It was different in the theological seminary of which I was then a student. In protest against the humiliating regime and the Jesuitical methods that prevailed in the seminary, I was ready to become, and eventually did become, a revolutionary, a believer in Marxism as the only genuinely revolutionary doctrine. . . .

[The Jesuits] are methodical and persevering in their work. But the basis of all their methods is spying, prying, peering into people's souls, to subject them to petty torment. What is there good in that? For instance, the spying in the boardinghouse. At nine o'clock the bell rings for morning tea, we go to the dining hall, and when we return we find that a search has been made and all our boxes have been turned inside out. What is there good in that?

Statement on Stalin's recollections of Lenin

I met Lenin for the first time in December 1905 at the Bolshevik Conference at Tammerfors, in Finland. I expected to see the mountain eagle of our Party a great man, not only politically but physically, for I had formed for myself a picture of Lenin as a giant, a fine figure of a man. What was my disappointment when I saw the most ordinary looking individual, below middle height, distinguished from ordinary mortals by nothing, literally nothing. A great man is permitted to be generally late at meetings so that those present may be apprehensive at his non-arrival, and so that before the great man's appearance there may be cries of "Hush—silence—he is coming." This ceremony seemed to me useful, for it creates respect. What was my disappointment to find that Lenin had arrived before the delegates and was carrying on the most ordinary conversation, with the most ordinary delegate, in a corner.

Interview with Emil Ludwig, 13 December 1931

Very few of those who remained in Russia were as closely associated with Russian affairs and with the working-class movement within the country as was Lenin, although he spent a long time abroad. Whenever I visited from abroad—in 1907, 1908, and 1912—I saw heaps of letters he had received from practical workers in Russia. Lenin always knew more than those who stayed in Russia. He always regarded his stay abroad as a burden.

Of course, there are in our Party and its leading bodies many more members who have never been abroad than former exiles, and of course they were able to bring more advantage to the revolution than those who were in exile. There are very few former exiles left in our Party [1931]. There are about 100 or 200 in all, among the two million members of the Party. Of the seventy members of the Central Committee not more than three or four lived in exile abroad.

As to knowledge of Europe and a study of Europe, of course, those who wished to study Europe had a better opportunity to do so while living in Europe. From that point of view, those of us who have not lived long abroad, lost something. But living abroad is not essential in order to study European economics, technology, the leading cadres of the working-class movement, literature—fiction and scientific literature. Other conditions being equal, it is of course easier to study Europe while living in Europe. But the disadvantage of those who have not lived long in Europe is not very great. On the contrary, I know many comrades who were twenty years abroad, lived somewhere in Charlottenburg or in the Latin Quarter, spent years sitting in cafés and consuming beer, and yet did not study Europe and failed to understand Europe.

As for myself, I am merely a pupil of Lenin, and my aim is to be a worthy pupil of his. The task to which I have devoted my life is to elevate another class—the working class. That task is, not to strengthen any national state, but to strengthen a socialist state—and that means an international state. Everything that contributes to strengthening the state helps to strengthen the international working class. If in my efforts to elevate the working class and strengthen the socialist state of that class, every step taken were not directed toward strengthening and improving the position of the working class, I should consider my life as purposeless. . . .

As to Lenin and Peter the Great, the latter was but a drop in the sea—Lenin was a whole ocean. . . . Marxism does not deny that prominent personalities play an important role, nor the fact that history is made by people. In The Poverty of Philosophy and in other works of Marx you will find it stated that it is people who make history. But, of course, people do not make history according to their own fancy or the prompting of their imagination. Every new generation encounters definite conditions already existing, ready-made, when that generation was born. And if great people are worth anything at all, it is only to the extent that they correctly understand these conditions and know how to alter them. If they fail to understand these conditions and try to change them according to their own fancies, they will put themselves in a quixotic position. So you will see that precisely according to Marx, people must not be contrasted to conditions. It is people who make history, but they make it only to the extent that they correctly understand the conditions they found ready-made, and to the extent that they know how to change those conditions. That, at least, is the way we Russian Bolsheviks understand Marx. And we have been studying Marx for a good many years. . . . Marxism never denied the role of heroes. On the contrary, it admits that they play a considerable role, with the provisos that I have just made. . . .

We Bolsheviks have always been interested in such figures as Bolotnikov, Razin, Pugachev, and so on. We regard the acts of these people as the reflection of the seething unrest of the oppressed classes and of the spontaneous revolt of the peasantry against the feudal yoke. We have always studied with interest the history of these first attempts at revolt on the part of the peasantry. But, of course, no analogy can be drawn between them and the Bolsheviks. Isolated peasant revolts, even when they are not of the bandit and unorganized character of that of Stenka Razin, cannot be successful. Peasant revolts can be successful only if they are combined with revolts of the workers. Only a combined revolt led by the working class has any chance of achieving its aim. Moreover, when we speak of Razin and Pugachev, it must never be forgotten that they were Tsarists: they were opposed to the landlords, but were in favor of a "good Tsar." That was their motto . . . no analogy with the Bolsheviks can be drawn here. . . .

Speech at Plenum of the Central Committee of the Communist Party, April 1929

What is the sharpening of the class struggle due to? It is due to the fact that the capitalist elements will not depart from the scene voluntarily; they resist, and will continue to resist socialism, for they see that the last days of their existence are approaching. And they are still in a position to resist, since, in spite of their relative decrease, absolutely, they still continue to increase; the petit bourgeoisie of town and country, as Lenin said, daily and hourly, throw up from their ranks capitalists and small capitalists, and these capitalist elements go to any length to preserve their existence.

There have yet been no cases in history when dying classes have voluntarily departed from the scene. There have been no cases in history when the dying bourgeoisie has not exerted all its remaining strength to preserve its existence. Whether our lower apparatus is good or bad, our advance, our offensive, will reduce the numbers of the capitalist elements and force them out of existence, and they, the dying classes, will resist at all costs.

This is the social basis for the sharpening of the class struggle. . . .

The dying classes resist, not because they have become stronger than we are, but because socialism is growing faster than they are, and they are becoming weaker than we. And because they are becoming weaker, they feel that their last days are approaching and are obliged to resist with every means and method in their power. . . .

The policy should be to arouse the working class and the exploited masses of the countryside, to increase their fighting capacity and develop their ability to mobilize for the fight against the capitalist elements of town and country, for the fight against the resisting class enemies. The Marxist-Leninist theory of the class struggle is valuable, among other reasons, for the very fact that it facilitates the mobilization of the working class against the enemies of the dictatorship of the proletariat.

Lectures at Sverdlov University, April 1924

The opportunists of the Second International have a series of theoretical dogmas which they always use as a starting point. Let us consider some of them.

First dogma: concerning the prerequisites for the seizure of power by the proletariat. The opportunists assert that the proletariat cannot and ought not to seize power if it does not itself constitute a majority in the country. No proofs are adduced, for this absurd thesis cannot be justified either theoretically or practically. Let us admit this for a moment, Lenin replies to these gentlemen of the Second International. But suppose an historic situation arises (war, agrarian crisis, etc.) in which the proletariat, a minority of the population, is able to rally around itself the vast majority of the working masses, why should it not seize power then? Why should it not profit by the favorable internal and international situation to pierce the front of capitalism and hasten the general climax? Did not Marx say, as far back as the 1850s, that the proletarian revolution in Germany would be in a "splendid" position if it could get the support of a "new edition, so to speak, of the Peasant War"? Does not everyone know that at that period the number of proletarians in Germany was relatively smaller than, for example, in the Russia of 1917? Has not the practical experience of the Russian proletarian revolution shown that this favorite dogma of the heroes of the Second International is devoid of all vital significance for the proletariat? Is it not obvious that the experience of the revolutionary mass struggle smashes this obsolete dogma?

Second dogma: The proletariat cannot retain power if it does not possess adequate, educated administrative cadres ready for and capable of organizing the administration of the country; first of all, these cadres must be trained under capitalist conditions and only afterwards must power be seized.

Well, suppose that is so, replies Lenin. But why not do it this way: first seize power, create favorable conditions for the development of the proletariat, and then advance with seven-league strides to raise the cultural level of the working masses and form numerous cadres of leaders and administrators recruited from among the workers? Has not Russian experience demonstrated that these working-class cadres of leaders are growing a hundred times more rapidly and thoroughly with the proletariat, in power than under the rule of capital? Is it not obvious that the experience of the revolutionary mass struggle ruthlessly refutes also this theoretical dogma of the opportunists? . . .

Does not the history of the revolutionary movement show that the parliamentary struggle is only a school, only an aid for the organization of the extra-parliamentary struggle of the proletariat, that under the capitalist system the essential questions of the labor movement are settled by force, by direct struggle, the general strike, the insurrection of the proletarian masses?

Interview with H. G. Wells, 23 July 1934

Of course the old system is breaking down, decaying. That is true. But it is also true that new efforts are being made by other methods, by every means, to protect, to save this dying system . . . the old world is breaking down. But it is [not] breaking down of its own accord. No, the substitution of one social system for another is a complicated and long revolutionary process. It is not simply a spontaneous process, but a struggle; it is a process connected with the clash of classes. Capitalism is decaying, but it must not be compared simply with a tree that has decayed to such an extent that it must fall to the ground of its own accord. No, revolution, the substitution of one social system for another, has always been a struggle, a painful and a cruel struggle, a life-and-death struggle. And every time the people of the new world came into power they had to defend themselves against the attempts of the old world to restore the old order by force; these people of the new world always had to be on the alert, always had to be ready to re-pel the attacks of the old world upon the new system.

The old social system is breaking down; but it is not breaking down of its own accord. Take Fascism, for example. Fascism is a reactionary force that is trying to preserve the old world by means of violence. What will you do with the Fascists? Argue with them? Try to convince them? But this will have no effect upon them at all. Communists do not in the least idealize the methods of violence. But they, the Communists, do not want to be taken by surprise, they cannot count on the old world voluntarily departing from the stage, they see that the old system is violently defending itself, and that is why the Communists say to the working class: Answer violence with violence; do all you can to prevent the old dying order from crushing you; do not permit it to put manacles on your hands, on the hands with which you will overthrow the old system. As you see, the Communists regard the substitution of one social system for another, not simply as a spon-taneous and peaceful process, but as a complicated, long, and violent process. Communists cannot ignore facts.

What about the October Revolution? Were there not plenty of peo-ple who knew that we alone, the Bolsheviks, were indicating the only correct way out? Was it not clear that Russian capitalism had decayed?

But you know how great was the resistance, how much blood had to be shed in order to defend the October Revolution from all its enemies, internal and external.

Or take France at the end of the eighteenth century. Long before 1789 it was clear to many how rotten the royal power, the feudal system was. But a popular insurrection, a clash of classes was not, could not be avoided. Why? Because the classes, which must abandon the stage of history, are the last to become convinced that their role is ended. It is impossible to convince them of this. They think that the fissures in the decaying edifice of the old order can be mended, that the tottering edifice of the old order can be repaired and saved. That is why dying classes take to arms and resort to every means to save their existence as a ruling class.

Was the great French Revolution a lawyers' revolution and not a popular revolution, which achieved victory by rousing vast masses of the people against feudalism and championed the interests of the Third Estate? And did the lawyers among the leaders of the great French Revolution act in accordance with the laws of the old order? Did they not introduce new, bourgeois-revolutionary laws?

The rich experience of history teaches that up to now not a single class has voluntarily made way for another class. There is no such precedent in world history. The Communists have learned this lesson of history. Communists would welcome the voluntary departure of the bourgeoisie. But such a turn of affairs is improbable; that is what experience teaches. That is why the Communists want to be prepared for the worst and call upon the working class to be vigilant, to be prepared for battle. Who wants a captain who lulls the vigilance of his army, a captain who does not understand that the enemy will not surrender, that he must be crushed? To be such a captain means deceiving, betraying the working class. That is why I think that what seems to you to be old-fashioned is in fact a measure of revolutionary expediency for the working class.

In order to achieve a great object, an important social object, there must be a main force, a bulwark, a revolutionary class. Next it is necessary to organize the assistance of an auxiliary force for this main force; in this case this auxiliary force is the Party, to which the best forces of the intelligentsia belong. . . . Were there not plenty of educated people on the side of the old order in England in the seventeenth century, in France at the end of the eighteenth century, and in Russia in the epoch of the October Revolution? The old order had in its service many highly educated people who defended the old order, who opposed the new order. Education is a weapon the effect of which is determined by the hands that wield it, by whom it is to be struck down. Of course, the proletariat, socialism, needs highly educated people. Clearly, simple-tons cannot help the proletariat to fight for socialism, to build a new so-ciety. I do not underestimate the role of the intelligentsia; on the con-trary, I emphasize it. The question is, however, which intelligentsia are we discussing? Because there are different kinds of intelligentsia. . . .

The main thing for the revolution is the existence of a social bul-wark. This bulwark of the revolution is the working class.

Second, an auxiliary force is required, that which the Communists call a Party. To the Party belong the intelligent workers and those ele-ments of the technical intelligentsia that are closely connected with the working class. The intelligentsia can be strong only if it combines with the working class. If it opposes the working class it becomes a cipher.

Third, political power is required as a lever for change. The new po-litical power creates the new laws, the new order, which is revolution-ary order.

I do not stand for any kind of order. I stand for order that corre-sponds to the interests of the working class. If, however, any of the laws of the old order can be utilized in the interests of the struggle for the new order, the old laws should be utilized.

Generally speaking, it must be said that of all the ruling classes, the ruling classes of England, both the aristocracy and the bourgeoisie, proved to be the cleverest, most flexible from the point of view of their class interests, from the point of view of maintaining their power. Take as an example, say, from modern history: the general strike in England in 1926. The first thing any other bourgeoisie would have done in the face of such an event, when the General Council of Trade Unions called for a strike, would have been to arrest the trade union leaders. The British bourgeoisie did not do that, and it acted cleverly from the point of view of its own interests. I cannot conceive of such a flexible strategy being employed by the bourgeoisie in the United States, Germany, or France. In order to maintain their rule, the ruling classes of Great Britain have never forsworn small concessions, reforms. But it would be a mistake to think that these reforms were revolutionary. . . .

Owing to pressure from below, the pressure of the masses, the bourgeoisie may sometimes concede certain partial reforms while re-maining on the basis of the existing social-economic system. Acting in this way, it calculates that these concessions are necessary in order to preserve its class rule. This is the essence of reform. Revolution, however, means the transference of power from one class to another. That is why it is impossible to describe any reform as revolution. That is why we cannot count on the change of social systems taking place as an imperceptible transition from one system to another by means of reforms, by the ruling class making concessions.

Besides, can we lose sight of the fact that in order to transform the world it is necessary to have *political power?* What can those, even with the best intentions in the world, do if they are unable to raise the question of seizing power, and do not possess power? At best they can help the class that takes power, but they cannot change the world themselves. This can only be done by a great class that will take the place of the capitalist class and become the sovereign master as the latter was before. This class is the working class. Of course, the assistance of the technical intelligentsia must be accepted; and the latter, in turn, must be assisted. But it must not be thought that the technical intelligentsia can play an independent historical role. The transformation of the world is a great, complicated, and painful process. For this task a great class is required. Big ships go on long voyages.

Interview with Foreign Workers' Delegations, 5 November 1927

The G.P.U. or the Cheka is a punitive organ of the Soviet government. It is more or less similar to the Committee of Public Safety which existed during the great French Revolution. It punishes primarily spies, plotters, terrorists, bandits, speculators, and forgers. It is something in the nature of a military political tribunal set up for the purpose of protecting the interests of the revolution from attacks on the part of the counter-revolutionary bourgeoisie and their agents.

This organ was created on the day after the October Revolution, after all kinds of plots, terrorist and spying organizations financed by Russian and foreign capitalists were discovered. This organ developed and became consolidated after a series of terrorist acts had been perpetrated against the leaders of the Soviet government, after the murder of Comrade Uritsky, member of the Revolutionary Committee of Leningrad (he was killed by a Socialist-Revolutionary), after the murder of Comrade Volodarsky, member of the Revolutionary Committee of Leningrad (he was also killed by a Socialist-Revolutionary), after the attempt on the life of Lenin (he was wounded by a member of the Socialist-Revolutionary Party). It must be admitted that the G.P.U. aimed at the enemies of the revolution without missing. By the way, this quality of the G.P.U. still holds good. It has been, ever since, the terror of the bourgeoisie, the indefatigable guard of the revolution, the unsheathed sword of the proletariat.

It is not surprising, therefore, that the bourgeoisie of all countries hate the G.P.U. All sorts of legends have been invented about the G.P.U.

The slander which has been circulated about the G.P.U. knows no bounds. And what does that mean? It means that the G.P.U. is properly defending the interests of the revolution. The sworn enemies of the revolution curse the G.P.U. Hence, it follows that the G.P.U. is doing the right thing.

But this is not how the workers regard the G.P.U. You go to the workers' districts and ask the workers what they think of it. You will find that they regard it with respect. Why? Because they see in it a loyal defender of the revolution.

I understand the hatred and distrust of the bourgeoisie for the G.P.U. I understand the various bourgeois tourists who, on coming to the U.S.S.R., inquire before anything else as to whether the G.P.U. still exists and whether the time has not yet come for its liquidation. This is comprehensible and not out of the ordinary. But I cannot understand some workers' delegates who, on coming to the U.S.S.R., ask with alarm as to whether many counter-revolutionaries have been punished by the G.P.U. and whether terrorists and plotters against the proletarian government will still be punished by it and is it not time yet for its dissolution. Why do some workers' delegates show such concern for the enemies of the proletarian revolution? How can it be explained? How can it be justified?

They advocate a maximum of leniency, they advise the dissolution of the G.P.U. . . . But can anyone guarantee that the capitalists of all countries will abandon the idea of organizing and financing counter-revolutionary plotters, terrorists, incendiaries, and bomb-throwers after the liquidation of the G.P.U.? To disarm the revolution without having any guarantees that the enemies of the revolution will be disarmed—would not that be folly, would not that be a crime against the working class? No, we do not want to repeat the errors of the Paris Communards. The Communards of Paris were too lenient in dealing with Versailles, for which Marx rightly reproved them at the time. They had to pay for their leniency, and when Thiers came to Paris, tens of thousands of workers were shot by the Versailles forces. Do the comrades think that the Russian bourgeoisie and nobility are less bloodthirsty than those of Versailles in France? We know, at any rate, how they behaved toward the workers when they occupied Siberia, the Ukraine, and the North Caucasus in alliance with the French and British, Japanese and American interventionists.

I do not mean to say by this that the internal situation of the country is such as makes it necessary to have punitive organs of the revolution. From the point of view of the internal situation, the revolution is so firm and unshakable that we could do without the G.P.U. But the trouble is that the enemies at home are not isolated individuals. They are connected in a thousand ways with the capitalists of all countries who support them by every means and in every way. We are a country surrounded by capitalist states. The internal enemies of our revolution are the agents of the capitalists of all countries. The capitalist states are the background and basis for the internal enemies of our revolution. In fighting against the enemies at home we fight the counter-revolutionary elements of all countries. Judge for yourselves whether under such conditions we can do without such punitive organs as the G.P.U.

No, we do not want to repeat the mistakes of the Paris Communards. The G.P.U. is necessary for the revolution and it will continue to live and strike terror into the hearts of the enemies of the proletariat.

Lectures at Sverdlov University, April 1924

I refrain from speaking of the fear of self-criticism that exists within the parties of the Second International; of their habit of hiding their mistakes, of glossing over thorny problems, of covering up their shortcomings by falsely pretending that all is well. This is what Lenin wrote about self-criticism in proletarian parties in "Left-Wing" Communism, An Infantile Disorder:

> The attitude of a political party toward its own mistakes is one of the most important and surest criteria of the seriousness of the party, and of how it fulfills in practice its obligations toward its class and toward the toiling masses. To admit a mistake openly, to disclose its reasons, to analyze the conditions that gave rise to it, to study attentively the means of correcting it—these are the signs of a serious party; this means the performance of its duties; this means educating and training the class, and, subsequently, the masses.

Some say that the exposure of its own mistakes and self-criticism are dangerous to the Party because the enemy may use this against the party of the proletariat. Lenin regarded such objections as frivolous and wholly incorrect. This is what he wrote on this point in 1904 in his pamphlet One Step Forward, Two Steps Backward, when our Party was still weak and insignificant:

> They (i.e., the opponents of the Marxists—J.S.) gloat and grimace over our controversies, and, of course, they will try to pick isolated passages from my pamphlet, which deals with the defects and shortcomings of our Party, and use them for their own ends. The Russian Marxists have already been sufficiently steeled in battle not to let themselves be disturbed by these pinpricks and to continue, in spite of them, with their work of self-criticism and of the ruthless exposure of their own shortcomings that will inevitably and certainly be overcome in the course of the growth of the working class movement. (Collected Works, Russian edition, Vol. VI, p. 161.)

Report to the Fourteenth Conference of the Russian Communist Party, Moscow, 9 May 1925

Self-criticism is a symptom of the strength and not of the weakness of our Party. Only a strong party, a party rooted in life, a party that is marching forward to victory, can indulge in so ruthless a criticism of its own shortcomings, as it has and always will indulge in before the whole people. A party that conceals the truth from the people, a party that fears light and criticism, is not a party, but a clique of frauds, doomed to failure. Messieurs the bourgeoisie judge us according to their own standards. They fear the light of day, and zealously conceal the truth from the people; they mask their deficiencies by a parade of ostensible well-being. And so they think that we Communists, too, must conceal the truth from the people. They fear the light, for to permit any serious self-criticism, any free criticism of their own shortcomings would be enough to shatter the whole edifice of the capitalist order to its foundations. And so they think that when we Communists indulge in self-criticism it is a sign that we are surrounded and hanging in the air, as it were. These worthy bourgeois and Social-Democrats judge us by their own standards. Only parties that are becoming things of the past, parties that are doomed to disappear, need dread light and criticism. But we are not afraid of either the one or the other; we are not afraid, for ours is a rising party, a party marching to victory.

Report to the Central Committee of the Communist Party at the Fifteenth Party Congress, 22 December 1927

. . . If we Bolshevists, who are ready to criticize all the world and, as Marx said, to storm the heavens, eschew self-criticism for the sake of the peace of mind of some of our comrades, is it not obvious that tremendous harm can result for our cause? Marx said that the proletarian revolution was distinct from all other revolutions also in the fact that it criticized itself and was strengthened through self-criticism. This is a very important remark by Marx. If we, champions of the proletarian revolution, close our eyes to our errors and settle matters in a familiar and convivial way by preserving silence as to our mutual mistakes and thus driving the festering ulcers into the interior of our party organism, who will finally correct our shortcomings? Is it not obvious that we shall then cease to be proletarian revolutionaries, that we shall probably go under if we countenance a growth of this "family and neighbor" system in the settlement of important matters? Is it not obvious that by eschewing an honest and direct self-criticism, an open and honest correction of our errors we are barring our way to progress, to the promotion of our cause, and to new successes of our great enterprise?

Our development is not uniform and all-comprehending. No, we have still classes among us, there are still contradictions in this country; we have a past, a present, and a future, between which there are great differences, so that we cannot progress easily and, so to speak, on the crests of the waves. Our progress must take the form of a struggle, by the development, recognition, and overcoming of those contrasts and differences. So long as there are classes in our midst we shall never be in position to say, "Now, thank God, all is in order!" This will never be the case among us. Here something is constantly dying, but it refuses to die without a struggle, it fights for its obsolete existence. At the same time other things are born, but they are not born quietly either; they struggle into the world, immediately defending their right to existence. The fight between the old and the new, the dying and the developing, is the very basis of our existence.

If we do not openly and honestly, as becomes Bolshevists, show up the faults and shortcomings in our work, we bar our own way to progress. But we desire to progress. And just because we desire to progress, we must look upon an honest revolutionary self-criticism as one of our foremost tasks. Otherwise no progress and no development can be attained. But just in this connection there is still much that calls for correction. Nay, worse than that; a certain success suffices to cause all shortcomings to be forgotten; conscience is appeased and vanity begins to assert itself. Two or three big achievements and all is self-satisfaction; two or three more and self-satisfaction knows no limits. But the faults remain and the shortcomings continue, the ulcers being driven into the interior of the party organism. . . .

A further shortcoming consists in the desire on the part of very many of our comrades to swim with the current, calmly and easily, without any prospects, without looking ahead, with something in the sense of a festive atmosphere on all hands, with solemn sessions day by day and the chance for every one of us in turn to become an honorary member of some select body or other. This irrepressible wish to see a holiday atmosphere on all sides, this craving for decorations, for all sorts of jubilees, with or without just reason, this wish to swim with the current as long as there is the possibility of swimming without looking to see whither it leads, all this goes to make up a shortcoming in our party life.

Have you ever seen men rowing honestly and with all their might but not looking whither the current was taking them? I have seen such rowers on the Yenisei. They were honest, untiring rowers. The misfortune is that they did not see and would not see that they might be dashed by the wave against the rocks, where disaster awaited them. The same thing is happening to some of our comrades. They row bravely without interruption, they skim lightly along, allowing the current to carry them, but they do not know whither they are going, nor do they want to know it. Work without any perspective, without rudder or tiller, that is what results from floating with the current. And the ultimate outcome is obvious. First they get mildewed, then they sink into the mire of the petit bourgeoisie, until finally they become thoroughly bourgeoisie. This is the path of absolute deterioration. . . .

Is there any sense or value in discussion? A discussion is sometimes quite indispensable and altogether useful. It is only a question as to what sort of a discussion it is. If it is carried on in a spirit of comradeship, within the limits of the Party, and if it sets itself the task of self-criticism and of a criticism of party shortcomings, if it thus advances our cause and makes our working class more capable of defending itself, such a discussion is necessary and useful. But there is another kind of discussion, which aims not at the improvement of our common cause but at its aggravation, not at strengthening the ties of our Party, but at loosening them. Such a discussion generally leads not to a more militant spirit among our workers, but rather to their disarmament. Such a discussion as this we do not want. . . .

Speech to the Functionaries of the Moscow Organization of the Communist Party, 13 April 1928

Finally, there is another circumstance which drives us to self-criticism. I mean the question of the masses and their leaders. Of late a peculiar relation has developed among us between the masses and their leaders. On the one hand, we can observe the development of a group of leaders whose authority is greater and greater and who are becoming almost inaccessible to the masses. On the other hand, the masses of the working class and of the workers in general advance too slowly, the result being that they come to look up to their leaders from below and often fear to criticize them. Naturally the fact that a group of leaders should have developed in this country, who have been set above the rest and enjoy a great measure of authority is in itself a great achievement for our Party. It is obvious that without the existence of such an authoritative group of leaders the control of a great realm is unthinkable. But the fact that in their rise, the leaders should have separated themselves from the masses, which are beginning to look up to them at a steep angle without venturing to criticize them—such a fact must needs entail a certain danger of estrangement of the leaders from the masses and the falling-off of the masses from their leaders. This danger may lead, again, to the leaders becoming puffed-up and considering themselves infallible. And what good can it do us if our leaders grow proud and begin looking down on the masses? It is obvious that the inevitable consequence would be the ruin of the Party. But we do not want to ruin the Party; we want to advance and to improve on our own achievements. And just for the purpose of progress and of improved relations between masses and leaders, the safety valve of self-criticism must be left constantly open, the members of the Soviets being enabled to criticize the shortcomings of their leaders, so that the latter may not become puffed-up and may not become estranged from the masses.

Article "Against Discrediting of the Slogan of Self-Criticism," London, 12 July 1928

Others again are of the opinion that self-criticism dispenses with the necessity of leaders; the horse may be given his head and "things allowed to take their course." This is no self-criticism, but an outrage. Self-criticism must not weaken leadership, but is on the contrary necessary to strengthen it, enabling a "paper" and little authoritative leadership to be transformed into a living and authoritative one.

There is still another sort of "self-criticism," one which leads to the disintegration of Party discipline, to the isolation of the Soviet authorities, to the weakening of our constructive work, to the breaking up of our economic cadres, to the disarmament of the working class, and to all the nonsense talked about "degeneration." It was only yesterday that the Trotskyist opposition called upon us to exercise such "self-criticism" as this. It is scarcely necessary to emphasize that the Party has nothing in common with this description of "self-criticism," and that it will employ every means to combat it.

Speech to the Central Committee of the Communist Party, October 1927

I am rude toward those who traitorously break their word, who split and destroy the Party. I have never concealed it and I do not conceal it now. Right from the first session of the Central Committee, after the Thirteenth Congress, I asked to be released from the obligations of the general secretaryship. The Congress itself examined the question.

Each delegation examined the question, and every delegation, including Trotsky, Kamenev, and Zinoviev, voted unanimously in favor of Stalin remaining at his post. What could I do then? Abandon my post? Such a thing is not in my character. . . . At the end of one year I again asked to be set free and I was again forced to remain at my post. What could I do then?

They complain of our arresting wreckers, men who have been expelled from the Party and who are carrying on anti-Soviet intrigues. Yes, we have arrested them and we shall arrest them so long as they undermine the Party and the Soviet power. . . . They say that such things are unknown in the history of the Party. This is not true. . . .

Interview with Emil Ludwig, 13 December 1931

No, under no conditions would our workers now tolerate the domination of one person. Individuals of greatest authority are reduced to nonentities as soon as they lose the confidence of the masses, and as soon as they lose contact with the masses. Plekhanov used to enjoy exceptional authority. And what happened? As soon as he began to commit political errors, the workers forgot him; they abandoned him and forgot him. Another instance: Trotsky. Trotsky also used to enjoy very great authority, although, of course, not as much as Plekhanov. What happened? As soon as he lost contact with the workers, he was forgotten. . . . They remember him sometimes—with bitterness. . . . As far as our class-conscious workers are concerned, they remember Trotsky with bitterness, with irritation, with hatred.

Speech to the Second Congress of Soviets, 26 January 1924

We Communists are people of a special mold. We are made of special material. We are those who comprise the army of the great proletarian strategist, the army of Lenin. There is nothing higher than the honor of belonging to this army. There is nothing higher than the title of member of the Party founded and led by Lenin. It is not given to all to be members of such a party. It is not given to all to withstand the stress and storm that accompanies membership in such a party. Sons of the working class, sons of poverty and struggle, sons of incredible deprivation and heroic effort—these are the ones who must first of all be members of such a party. That is why the Leninist Party, the Communist Party, at the same time calls itself the Party of the working class.

In departing from us, Comrade Lenin bequeathed to us the duty of holding aloft and guarding the purity of the great title of member of the Party. We vow to you, Comrade Lenin, that we will fulfill your bequest with honor.

Scores and hundreds of times in the course of centuries have the toilers tried to throw their oppressors off their backs and become masters of their own conditions. But every time, defeated and disgraced, they were compelled to retreat, their hearts burning with shame and degradation, anger and despair, and they turned their eyes to the unknown, to the heavens, where they hoped to find salvation. The chains of slavery remained intact, or else the old chains were exchanged for new ones equally burdensome and degrading. Only in our country have the oppressed and suppressed masses of toilers succeeded in throwing off the rule of the landlords and capitalists and in putting in its place the rule of the workers and peasants.

Now the whole world admits this, that this gigantic struggle was led by Lenin and his Party. The greatness of Lenin lies first of all in the fact that he, by creating the republic of Soviets, showed by deeds, to the oppressed masses of the whole world, that hope of salvation is not lost, that the rule of the landlords and capitalists will not last long, that the kingdom of labor can be created by the efforts of the toilers themselves, that the kingdom of labor must be created on earth and not in heaven. By that he inflamed the hearts of the workers and peasants of the whole world with the hope of liberation. This explains the fact that the name of Lenin has become a name most beloved to the toilers and the exploited masses.

In departing from us, Comrade Lenin bequeathed to us the duty of guarding and strengthening the dictatorship of the proletariat. We vow to you, Comrade Lenin, that we will spare no effort to fulfill also this bequest of yours with honor. . . .

Lenin never regarded the republic of Soviets as an end in itself. He always regarded it as a necessary link for strengthening the revolutionary movements in the lands of the West and the East, as a necessary link for facilitating the victory of the toilers of the whole world over capital. Lenin knew that only such an interpretation is the correct one, not only from the international point of view, but also from the point of view of preserving the republic of Soviets itself. Lenin knew that only in this way is it possible to inflame the hearts of the toilers of all countries for the decisive battles for emancipation. That is why this genius among the great leaders of the proletariat, on the very morrow of the establishment of the proletarian dictatorship, laid the foundation of the workers' International. That is why he never tired of expanding and consolidating the union of the toilers of the whole world, the Communist International.

In departing from us, Lenin bequeathed to us the duty of remaining loyal to the principles of the Communist International. We vow to you, Comrade Lenin, that we will not spare our lives to strengthen and expand the union of the toilers of the whole world—the Communist International.

Lectures at Sverdlov University, April 1924

The achievement and maintenance of the dictatorship of the proletariat are impossible without a party strong in its cohesion and iron discipline. But iron discipline in the Party is impossible without unity of will and without absolute and complete unity of action on the part of all members of the Party. This does not mean of course that the possibility of a conflict of opinion within the Party is thus excluded. On the contrary, iron discipline does not preclude but presupposes criticism and conflicts of opinion within the Party. Least of all does it mean that this discipline must be "blind" discipline. On the contrary, iron discipline does not preclude but presupposes conscious and voluntary submission, for only conscious discipline can be truly iron discipline. But after a discussion has been closed, after criticism has run its course and a decision has been made, unity of will and unity of action of all party members become indispensable conditions without which party unity and iron discipline in the Party are inconceivable.

> "In the present epoch of intensified civil war," says Lenin, "the Communist Party can discharge its duty only if it is organized with the highest degree of centralization, ruled by iron discipline bordering on military discipline, and if its Party center proves to be a potent authoritative body invested with broad powers and enjoying the general confidence of the Party members."

This is the position in regard to discipline in the Party in the period of struggle preceding the establishment of the dictatorship.

The same thing applies, but to a greater degree, to discipline in the Party after the establishment of the dictatorship.

It follows that the existence of factions is incompatible with Party unity and with its iron discipline. It need hardly be emphasized that the existence of factions leads to the creation of a number of centers, and the existence of a number of centers connotes the absence of a common center in the Party, a breach in the unity of will, the weakening and disintegration of discipline, the weakening and disintegration of the dictatorship. The parties of the Communist International, which organize their activities on the basis of the task of achieving and strengthening the dictatorship of the proletariat, cannot afford to be "liberal" or to permit the formation of factions. The Party is synonymous with unity of will, which leaves no room for any factionalism or division of authority in the Party.

Speech to the Fifteenth Conference of the Communist Party, November 1926

The opposition wants to know of what our practical differences consist? You want to know what the Party demands of you.

Very well, listen.

1.   The Party cannot and will not any longer tolerate it, that any time you are in the minority you go into the highways and byways and declare that there is a crisis in the Party and attack the Party. The Party will tolerate that no longer.

2.   The Party cannot and will not tolerate any longer that you, after you have lost hope of winning the majority of our Party, mobilize around yourselves all dissatisfied elements as material for a new Party. The Party cannot and will not tolerate this any longer.

3.   The Party cannot and will not tolerate that you slander the leading party apparatus and the regime in the Party, break the iron party discipline, and mobilize all the tendencies condemned by the Party under the flag of fractional freedom in order to form a new party. The Party will not tolerate that.

4.   We know that we are faced with great difficulties on the way of the building up of socialism. We see these difficulties and we have the possibility of overcoming them. We would welcome the assistance of the opposition in overcoming these difficulties. But the Party cannot and will not tolerate that you attempt to exploit these difficulties to worsen our situation, and to attack the Party.

5.   The Party understands better than all the oppositions together that the advance of the industrialization and the advance of socialism is only possible upon the condition of a permanent rise of the material and cultural situation of the working class. The Party is doing everything and will do everything to see to it that the material and cultural situation of the working class permanently improves. But the Party cannot and will not tolerate it that the material and cultural situation of the working-class demagogic demands for an immediate increase of wages from 30 to 40 percent although it very well knows that at the present moment industry is not in a position to stand such wage increases. Such demagogy has not the betterment of the situation of the working class as its aim, but the promotion of dissatisfac-

tion amongst the backward sections of the toilers against the Party and to organize it against the working class. The Party cannot and will not tolerate this.

6. The Party cannot and will not tolerate it that the opposition continues to undermine the basis of the alliance between the workers and the peasants by propagating the idea of raising the prices of industrial commodities and increasing the pressure of taxation upon the peasantry. That the opposition represents the relation between the proletariat and the peasantry not as a relation of economic cooperation but as a relation of the exploitation of the peasantry by the proletarian state. The Party cannot and will not tolerate this. . . .

These, comrades of the opposition, are our practical differences of opinion.

Report to the Central Committee of the Communist Party at the Fifteenth Party Congress, December 1927

All this talk about democracy! What is democracy within the Party? Democracy for whom? If democracy is understood to mean the right of a few intellectuals, severed from the actual revolution, to twaddle without limit and to have their own press organs, we need no such democracy, for that is the democracy of a tiny minority opposing the will of the tremendous majority.

Articles "The Elections in St. Petersburg," 12 January 1913, and "The Results of the Elections in the Workers' Curia of St. Petersburg," 24 October 1912

Trotsky has done all that is possible for us to have two rival newspapers, two rival platforms, two conferences that repudiate each other— and now this champion with the fake muscles himself is singing to us about unity!

This is no unity, but a game fit for a comedian.

. . . Despite his "heroic" efforts and "terrible threats" Trotsky proved in the end to be just a loud-mouthed champion with fake muscles, for after five years of "work" he did not succeed in uniting anybody but the Liquidators. New fuss—old affairs.

Trotsky . . . lumps everyone together, opponents and supporters of party organization alike, and, of course, he gets no unity whatever. . . . The practical experience of the movement shatters Trotsky's childish plan of uniting the un-unitable. . . .

Reply to Comrades on the Collective Farms, 3 April 1930

Success sometimes turns people's heads. It sometimes engenders excessive self-opinion and conceit. That may very easily happen to the representatives of a party that holds power, especially in the case of our Party, the strength and authority of which is almost immeasurable. Here, cases of Communist conceit, against which Lenin fought so fiercely, may very easily occur. Here, belief in the omnipotence of decrees, resolutions, and orders is quite possible. Here, there is a real danger of the revolutionary measures of the Party being transformed into empty, bureaucratic decreeing by individual representatives of the Party in this or that corner of our vast country. I have in mind not only local functionaries, but even certain Regional Committee members, and even certain members of the Central Committee. "Communist conceit," said Lenin, "means that an individual, who is a member of the Communist Party and has not yet been cleaned out of the Party, imagines that he can perform all his duties by Communist decrees. . . . "

The main thing in this matter is to have the courage to admit one's errors and to have the strength to correct them in the shortest possible time. The fear of admitting one's errors after the recent intoxication by successes, the fear of self-criticism, unwillingness to correct one's errors rapidly and decisively—that is the main difficulty. It is worthwhile mastering these difficulties; it is worthwhile casting aside swollen figures and bureaucratic maximalism; it is worthwhile switching our attention over to the tasks of organizational and economic construction of the collective farms, in order that not a trace of these errors shall remain. There is no reason whatsoever for doubting that, fundamentally, the Party has already mastered this alarming difficulty. Lenin said:

All revolutionary parties that have hitherto perished, perished from the fact that they got a swelled head, and were unable to see where their strength lay, *were afraid to speak of their own weaknesses*. But we shall not perish, because we are not afraid to speak of our weaknesses, and we shall learn how to overcome our weaknesses.

These words of Lenin must not be forgotten.

Speech "Dizziness from Success," March 1930

Everybody is talking of the successes achieved by the Soviet government in the sphere of the collective farm movement. Even our enemies are compelled to admit important successes. And indeed these successes are considerable.

It is a fact that by 20th February of the year 1930, half of the peasant farms of the U.S.S.R. had already been collectivized. That we *exceeded the Five-Year Plan by more than 100 percent. . . .*

What does all this show?

It shows that *a radical swing of the village toward socialism may already be regarded as guaranteed.*

There is no need to prove that these successes are of first-rate importance for the fate of our country, for the whole working class, in its capacity as the leading force of our country, and, finally, for the Party itself. Apart from the direct practical results, these successes are of tremendous significance for the internal life of the Party itself, for the education of our Party. They inspire our Party with a spirit of confidence and faith in its own power. They arm the working class with faith in the victory of our cause. They bring to our Party new millions of reserves.

Hence follows the task of our Party: to *consolidate* the successes already achieved and to *make systematic use of them* for further advances.

But successes also have their seamy side; especially when they are achieved with comparative "ease," "unexpectedly," so to speak. Such successes at times induce a spirit of conceit and pride: "We can do anything!" "That's easy!" People frequently are intoxicated by such successes, they become dizzy with success, they lose all sense of proportion, they lose the faculty of understanding realities, they reveal a tendency to overestimate their own strength and to underestimate the strength of the enemy; reckless attempts are made to settle all the problems of socialist construction "in a trice." There is no longer any concern for the *consolidation* of the successes achieved and for making *systematic use* of them for further advances. Why trouble about consolidating successes? We shall reach the complete victory of socialism "in a trice," anyhow, "We can do anything!" "That's easy!"

Hence follows the task of the Party: to conduct a determined struggle against this dangerous frame of mind, which is so harmful for the cause and to eradicate it from the Party.

Hence follows the task of our press: systematically to expose any such anti-Leninist frame of mind.

A few facts.

1.   The success of our collective farm policy is to be explained, among other things, by the fact that this policy is based on the collective farm movement being a *voluntary* one and on the *recognition of the diversity of conditions* existing in the various regions of the Soviet Union. Collective farms cannot be set up by force. To do so would be stupid and reactionary. The collective farm movement must lean on the active support of the basic masses of the peasantry. Forms of collective farm construction in the developed regions cannot be mechanically trans-

planted to the backward regions. To do so would be stupid and reactionary. Such a "policy" would discredit the idea of collectivization at one blow. In determining the speed and methods of building collective farms we must carefully take into account the diversity of conditions prevailing in the various regions of the Soviet Union. . . .

But what do we sometimes find taking place in practice? Can it be said that the voluntary principle and the principle of taking local peculiarities into account are not violated in a number of regions? No, unfortunately, that cannot be said. It is known, for example, that a number of the northern regions of the grain-importing belt, where favorable conditions for the immediate organization of collective farms are comparatively less than in the grain-bearing regions, not infrequently endeavor to *replace* the preparatory work for the organization of collective farms by bureaucratically decreeing the collective farm movement, by paper resolutions regarding the growth of collective farms, by the organization of collective farms, "on paper," farms, which in reality do not yet exist, but regarding the "existence" of which there is a pile of braggart resolutions. Or, let us take certain regions of Turkestan, where conditions favoring the immediate organization of collective farms are even less than in the northern oblasts of the grain-importing belt. We know that in a number of regions of Turkestan there have already been attempts to "overtake and surpass" the advanced regions of the Soviet Union by resorting to threats of applying military force, by threatening to deprive the peasants who do not yet wish to enter the collective farms of irrigation water and of manufactured goods.

What relation is there between this Sergeant Prishibeiev [a personage of one of Chekhov's tales, who introduces into private life the manners of the barracks and drill ground] "policy" and the policy of the Party, which is based on the voluntary principle and on a regard for local peculiarities in collective farm construction? It is obvious that they have nothing in common.

Who benefits by these distortions, this bureaucratic decreeing of the collective farm movement, this wretched threatening of the peasants? Nobody, but our enemies!

What may be the result of these distortions? The strengthening of our enemies and the discrediting of the collective farm movement idea. . . .

The question arises: who benefits by this stupid and harmful precipitancy? Irritating the peasant-collective-farm-member by "collectivizing" living premises, all the milch cattle, all the small livestock and the domestic poultry, when the grain problem *is still unsolved*, when the artel form of the collective farm is not yet *consolidated*—is it not obvious that such a "policy" can please and benefit only our sworn enemies? One such fiery "collectivizer" even went so far as to issue an instruction to the artel ordering "that within three days every single head of poultry in every household be registered," that special "commanders" be appointed to register and supervise, "to occupy the key positions in the artel," "to lead the fight for socialism, without quitting their posts," and—of course—to seize the whole artel by the throat. What do you call that—a policy of leading the collective farm, or a policy of *disintegrating and discrediting it?* I will not speak of those "revolutionaries"—save the mark—who *begin* the work of organizing an artel by removing the church bells. Just think of it—to remove the church bells, is not this r-r-revolutionary!

How could such blockheaded exercises in collectivization, such ludicrous attempts to lift oneself by one's own bootstraps, attempts the purpose of which is to ignore classes and the class struggle, but which in practice bring grist to the mill of our class enemies, occur in our midst? They could occur only because of the atmosphere of "easy" and "unexpected" successes that has prevailed on the front of collective farm construction. They could occur only as a result of the blockhead frame of mind prevailing in the ranks of a section of our Party: "We can do anything!" "That's easy!" They could occur only as a result of the fact that certain of our comrades became dizzy with success, and for a while lost clear-mindedness and sober vision.

In order to straighten out the line of our work in the sphere of building collective farms *we must put an end to this frame of mind.*

That is now one of the immediate tasks of the Party.

The art of leadership is a serious matter. One must not lag behind a movement, because to do so is to become isolated from the masses. But one must not rush ahead, for to rush ahead is to lose contact with the masses. He who wishes to lead a movement, and at the same time keep touch with the vast masses, must conduct a fight on two fronts—against those who lag behind and against those who rush on ahead.

Our Party is invincible because, while leading the movement, it knows how to maintain and multiply its contacts with the millions of the worker and peasant masses.

Stalin's Works

Interview with Emil Ludwig, 13 December 1931

Ludwig: I am extremely obliged to you for having found it possible to receive me. For over twenty years I have been studying the lives and deeds of outstanding historical personages. I believe I am a good judge of people, but on the other hand I know nothing about social-economic conditions.

Stalin: You are being modest.

Ludwig: No, that is really so, and for that very reason I shall put questions that may seem strange to you. Today, here in the Kremlin, I saw some relics of Peter the Great and the first question I should like to ask you is this: Do you think a parallel can be drawn between yourself and Peter the Great? Do you consider yourself a continuer of the work of Peter the Great?

Stalin: In no way whatever. Historical parallels are always risky. There is no sense in this one.

Ludwig: But after all, Peter the Great did a great deal to develop his country, to bring western culture to Russia.

Stalin: Yes, of course, Peter the Great did much to elevate the landlord class and develop the nascent merchant class. He did very much indeed to create and consolidate the national state of the landlords and merchants. It must be said also that the elevation of the landlord class, the assistance to the nascent merchant class, and the consolidation of the national state of these classes took place at the cost of the peasant serfs, who were bled white.

As for myself, I am just a pupil of Lenin's, and the aim of my life is to be a worthy pupil of his.

The task to which I have devoted my life is the elevation of a different class—the working class. That task is not the consolidation of some "national" state, but of a socialist state, and that means an international state; and everything that strengthens that state helps to strengthen the entire international working class. If every step I take in my endeavor to elevate the working class and strengthen the socialist state of this class were not directed toward strengthening and improving the position of the working class, I should consider my life purposeless.

So you see your parallel does not fit.

As regards Lenin and Peter the Great, the latter was but a drop in the sea, whereas Lenin was a whole ocean.

Ludwig: Marxism denies that the individual plays an outstanding role in history. Do you not see a contradiction between the materialist conception of history and the fact that, after all, you admit the outstanding role played by historical personages?

Stalin: No, there is no contradiction here. Marxism does not at all deny the role played by outstanding individuals or that history is made by people. In Marx's *The Poverty of Philosophy* and in other works of his you will find it stated that it is people who make history. But, of course, people do not make history according to the promptings of their imagination or as some fancy strikes them. Every new generation encounters definite conditions already existing, ready-made when that generation was born. And great people are worth anything at all only to the extent that they are able correctly to understand these conditions, to understand how to change them. If they fail to understand these conditions and want to alter them according to the promptings of their imagination, they will land themselves in the situation of Don Quixote. Thus it is precisely Marx's view that people must not be counterposed to conditions. It is people who make history, but they do so only to the extent that they correctly understand the conditions that they have found ready-made, and only to the extent that they understand how to change those conditions. That, at least, is how we Russian Bolsheviks understand Marx. And we have been studying Marx for a good many years.

Ludwig: Some thirty years ago, when I was at the university, many German professors who considered themselves adherents of the materialist conception of history taught us that Marxism denies the role of heroes, the role of heroic personalities in history.

Stalin: They were vulgarizers of Marxism. Marxism has never denied the role of heroes. On the contrary, it admits that they play a considerable role, but with the reservations I have just made.

Ludwig: Sixteen chairs are placed around the table at which we are seated. Abroad people know, on the one hand, that the U.S.S.R. is a country in which everything must be decided collectively, but they know, on the other hand, that everything is decided by individual persons. Who really does decide?

Stalin: No, individual persons cannot decide. Decisions of individuals are always, or nearly always, one-sided decisions. In every collegium, in every collective body, there are people whose opinion must be reckoned with. In every collegium, in every collective body, there are people who may express wrong opinions. From the experience of three revolutions we know that out of every hundred decisions taken by individual persons without being tested and corrected collectively, approximately ninety are one-sided.

In our leading body, the Central Committee of our Party, which directs all our Soviet and Party organizations, there are about seventy members. Among these seventy members of the Central Committee are our best industrial leaders, our best cooperative leaders, our best managers of supplies, our best military men, our best propagandists and agitators, our best experts on state farms, on collective farms, on individual peasant farms, our best experts on the nations constituting the Soviet Union and on national policy. In this Areopagus is concentrated the wisdom of our Party. Each has an opportunity of correcting anyone's individual opinion or proposal. Each has an opportunity of contributing his experience. If this were not the case, if decisions were taken by individual persons, there would be very serious mistakes in our work. But since each has an opportunity of correcting the mistakes of individual persons, and since we pay heed to such corrections, we arrive at decisions that are more or less correct.

Ludwig: Do you not think that among the Germans as a nation love of order is more highly developed than love of freedom?

Stalin: There was a time when people in Germany did indeed show great respect for the law. In 1907, when I happened to spend two or three months in Berlin, we Russian Bolsheviks often used to laugh at some of our German friends on account of their respect for the law. There was, for example, a story in circulation about an occasion when the Berlin Social-Democratic Executive fixed a definite day and hour for a demonstration that was to be attended by members of all the suburban organizations. A group of about two hundred from one of the suburbs arrived in the city punctually at the hour appointed, but failed to appear at the demonstration, the reason being that they had waited two hours on the station platform because the ticket collector at the exit had failed to make his appearance and there had been nobody to give their tickets to. It used to be said in jest that it took a Russian comrade to show the Germans a simple way out of their fix: to leave the platform without giving up their tickets. . . .

But is there anything like that in Germany now? Is there respect for the law in Germany today? What about the National Socialists, who one would think ought to be the first to stand guard over bourgeois legality? Do they not break the law, wreck workers' clubs, and assassinate workers with impunity?

I make no mention of the workers, who, it seems to me, long ago lost all respect for bourgeois legality.

Yes, the Germans have changed quite a bit lately.

Ludwig: Under what conditions is it possible to unite the working class finally and completely under the leadership of one party? Why is such a uniting of the working class possible only after the proletarian revolution, as the Communists maintain?

Stalin: Such a uniting of the working class around the Communist Party is most easily accomplished as the result of a victorious proletarian revolution. But it will undoubtedly be achieved in the main even before the revolution.

Ludwig: Does ambition stimulate or hinder a great historical figure in his activities?

Stalin: The part played by ambition differs under different conditions. Ambition may be a stimulus or a hindrance to the activities of a great historical figure. It all depends on circumstances. More often than not it is a hindrance.

Ludwig: Is the October Revolution in any sense the continuation and culmination of the great French Revolution?

Stalin: The October Revolution is neither the continuation nor the culmination of the great French Revolution. The purpose of the French Revolution was to abolish feudalism in order to establish capitalism. The purpose of the October Revolution, however, is to abolish capitalism in order to establish socialism.

References

Stalin, Josef, *Stalin's Kampf*, edited by W. R. Werner (New York: Howell, Soskin & Company, 1940).

Stalin, Josef, *Works (Sochineniya)* Volume 13, July 1930–January 1934 (Moscow: 1951).

MAO TSE-TUNG

BORN:

26 December 1893, Shao-shun, Hunan Province,
China

DIED:

9 September 1976, Beijing, China

An important Marxist theorist and prolific writer. Leader of the Chinese Communist Party from 1931. Leader in anti-Japanese War and revolutionary struggle against the Chiang Kai-shek regime. Chairman of the People's Republic of China from 1949 to 1959. Leader of the Communist Party until his death.

His works include: *Mao Tse-tung Unrehearsed*, edited by Stuart Schram (Harmondsworth, UK: Penguin, 1974); *Selected Military Writings* (Peking: Foreign Languages Press, 1966); *Selected Readings* (Peking: Foreign Languages Press, 1967); and *Selected Works* (London: Lawrence and Wishart, 1954). Biographies include: Richard H. Solomon, *Mao's Revolution and the Chinese Political Culture* (Berkeley: University of California Press, 1971); Richard Wilson, *Mao, the People's Emperor* (London: Hutchinson, 1979); and Pierre Ryckman (Simon Leys), *The Chairman's New Clothes: Mao and the Cultural Revolution* (London: Alison and Busby, 1977).

Mao Tse-tung Unrehearsed

Talk at the Chengtu Conference, 10 March 1958

. . . Having cleared away blind faith, we no longer have any spiritual burdens. Buddhas are made several times life-size in order to frighten people. When heroes and warriors appear on the stage they are made to look quite unlike ordinary people. Stalin was that kind of a person. The Chinese people had got so used to being slaves that they seemed to want to go on. When Chinese artists painted pictures of me together with Stalin, they always made me a little bit shorter, thus blindly knuckling under to the moral pressure exerted by the Soviet Union at that time. Marxism-Leninism looks at everyone on equal terms, and all people should be treated as equals. Khrushchev's complete demolition of Stalin at one blow was also a kind of pressure, and the majority of people within the Chinese Party did not agree with it. Others wished to submit to this pressure and do away with the cult of the individual. There are two kinds of cults of the individual. One is correct, such as that of Marx, Engels, Lenin, and the correct side of Stalin. These we ought to revere and continue to revere forever. It would not do not to revere them. As they held truth in their hands, why should we not revere them? We believe in truth; truth is the reflection of objective existence. A squad should revere its squad leader; it would be quite wrong not to. Then there is the incorrect kind of cult of the individual in which there is no analysis, simply blind obedience. This is not right. Opposition to the cult of the individual may also have one of two aims: one is opposition to an incorrect cult, and the other is opposition to reverence for others and a desire for reverence for oneself. The question at issue is not whether or not there should be a cult of the individual, but rather whether or not the individual concerned represents the truth. If he does, then he should be revered. If truth is not present, even collective leadership will be no good. Throughout its history, our Party has stressed the combination of the role of the individual with collective leadership. When Stalin was demolished some people applauded for their own personal reasons, that is to say because they wanted others to revere them. Some people opposed Lenin, saying that he was a dictator. Lenin's reply was straightforward: better that I should be a dictator than you! . . .

When Stalin was criticized in 1956, we were on the one hand happy, but on the other hand apprehensive. It was completely necessary to remove the lid, to break down blind faith, to release the pressure, and to emancipate thought. But we did not agree with demolishing him at one blow. They do not hang up his picture, but we do. In 1950 I argued with Stalin in Moscow for two months. On the questions of the Treaty of Mutual Assistance, the Chinese Eastern Railway, the joint-stock companies, and the border we adopted two attitudes: one was to argue when the other side made proposals we did not agree with, and the other was to accept their proposal if they absolutely insisted. This was out of consideration for the interests of socialism. Then there were the two "colonies," that is the North-East and Sinkiang, where people of any third country were not allowed to reside. Now this has been rescinded. After the criticism of Stalin, the victims of blind faith had their eyes opened a bit. In order that our comrades recognize that the old ancestor also had his faults, we should apply analysis to him, and not have blind faith in him. We should accept everything good in Soviet experience, and reject what is bad. Now we are a bit more skillful in this, and understand the Soviet Union a bit better, and understand ourselves. . . .

The Chinese revolution won victory by acting contrary to Stalin's will. The fake foreign devil [in Lu Hsün's *True Story of Ah Q*] "did not allow people to make revolution." But our Seventh Congress advocated going all out to mobilize the masses and to build up all available revolutionary forces in order to establish a new China. During the quarrel with Wang Ming from 1937 to August 1938, we put forward ten great policies, while Wang Ming produced sixty policies. If we had followed Wang Ming's, or in other words Stalin's, methods the Chinese revolution couldn't have succeeded. When our revolution succeeded, Stalin said it was a fake. We did not argue with him, and as soon as we fought the war to resist America and aid Korea, our revolution became a genuine one [in his eyes]. But when we brought out *On the Correct Handling of Contradictions among the People* we talked about this question but they didn't, and what's more they said we were going in for liberalism, so it seemed that we were not genuine again. When this report of ours was published, the *New York Times* printed it complete, and also carried an article that claimed that China was being "liberalized." It is quite natural for the bourgeoisie to clutch at straws when drowning. But bourgeois politicians are not altogether without discernment. For example when Dulles heard about our report he said he wanted to see it. Within a couple of weeks he had come up with a conclusion: China was bad through and through; the Soviet Union was a little better. But the Soviet Union couldn't see it, and sent us a memorandum because they feared we were moving to the right. When the Anti-Rightist Movement started, naturally our "liberalization" vanished.

In short, our basic line is universal truth, but details differ. This applies to each country and to each province. There is unity and there are also contradictions. The Soviet Union stresses unity, and doesn't talk about contradictions, especially the contradiction between the leaders and the led. . . .

Speech at the Lushan Conference, 23 July 1959

Now that you have said so much, let me say something, will you? I have taken sleeping pills three times, but I can't get to sleep.

These are the ideas I want to talk about. I have read the comrades' reports, speeches, and documents, and talked to a certain number of them. I feel they have two tendencies and I want to say a few words about them here. One is the tendency to be touchy—with these people it's very much a case of: "If you touch him he jumps." Wu Chih-hui used to say that Sun Fo jumped if anyone touched him. So some people feel the pressure; that is, they don't want others to say bad things about them. They don't want to hear bad things, only good things. I advise these comrades to listen. There are three kinds of words, and the mouth has two functions. A person has only one mouth and its duty is first, to eat, and secondly, to speak. Ears are for listening with. If someone wants to talk, what can you do about it? The trouble with some comrades is that they don't like listening to bad words. But good words and bad words are all words, and they should listen to both kinds. There are three kinds of words: one is correct, the second is basically correct, or not too correct, and the third is basically incorrect, or just plain incorrect. The two extremes are opposites: correct and incorrect are opposites. . . .

If you want others to stand firm, you must first stand firm yourself. If you want other people not to waver, you must not waver yourself: this is another lesson. As I see it these comrades are not rightists but middle-of-the-roaders. They are not leftists (i.e., leftists without quotation marks). I am talking about tendencies because there are some people who have run into difficulties. They have suffered broken heads and they are anxious. They were unable to stand firm; they wobbled into the middle of the road. The question is whether they are more inclined to the right of the middle or to the left of the middle. We must analyze this. They have gone the same way as those comrades who made mistakes in the second half of 1956 and the first half of 1957. They are not rightists, but they are on the verge of becoming rightists. They are still thirty kilometers away from the rightists. The rightists very much welcomed the trend of what they had to say and it would be surprising if they didn't. These comrades' brinkmanship is rather dangerous. If you don't believe me, wait and see what happens.

I am saying these things before a big audience. Some of what I say may hurt people. But if I remained silent now, this would not be in these comrades' interest.

To the subjects that I have raised might be added another one: the question of unity. But I will write a separate piece on it: "Raise the banner of unity, unity of the people, the nation, and the Party." I am not saying whether this is good or bad for these comrades. Even if it is harmful I must still talk about it. Our Party is a Marxist political party. Those on one side must listen; so must those on the other side. Both sides should listen. Didn't I say I wanted to speak? One should not only speak, but also listen to others. I have not been in a hurry to speak: I have toughened my scalp to endure it. Why don't I go on doing so? I have done it for twenty days already and it's nearly time for the conference to adjourn. . . .

Talk to the Leaders of the Center, 21 July 1966

I say to you all: youth is the great army of the great Cultural Revolution! It must be mobilized to the full.

After my return to Peking I felt very unhappy and desolate. Some colleges even had their gates shut. There were even some that suppressed the student movement. Who is it who suppressed the student movement? Only the Pei-yang Warlords. It is anti-Marxist for communists to fear the student movement. Some people talk daily about the mass line and serving the people, but instead they follow the bourgeois line and serve the bourgeoisie. The Central Committee of the Youth League should stand on the side of the student movement. But instead it stands on the side of suppression of the student movement. Who opposes the great Cultural Revolution? The American imperialists, the Soviet revisionists, the Japanese revisionists, and the reactionaries.

To use the excuse of distinguishing between "inner" and "outer" is to fear revolution. To cover over big-character posters that have been put up, such things cannot be allowed. This is a basic error of orientation. They must immediately change direction, and smash all the old conventions.

We believe in the masses. To become teachers of the masses we must first be the students of the masses. The present great Cultural Revolution is a heaven-and-earth-shaking event. Can we, dare we, cross the pass into socialism? This pass leads to the final destruction of classes, and the reduction of the three great differences.

To oppose, especially to oppose "authoritative" bourgeois ideology, is to destroy. Without this destruction, socialism cannot be established nor can we carry out first struggle, second criticism, third transformation. Sitting in offices listening to reports is no good. The only way is to rely on the masses, trust the masses, struggle to the end. We must be prepared for the revolution to be turned against us. The Party and government leadership and responsible party comrades should be prepared for this. If you now want to carry the revolution through to the end, you must discipline yourself, reform yourself in order to keep up with it. Otherwise you can only keep out of it.

There are some comrades who struggle fiercely against others, but cannot struggle with themselves. In this way, they will never be able to cross the pass.

It is up to you to lead the fire toward your own bodies, to fan the flames to make them burn. Do you dare to do this? Because it will burn your own heads.

The comrades replied thus: "We are prepared. If we're not up to it, we will resign our jobs. We live as Communist Party members and shall die as Communist Party members. It doesn't do to live a life of sofas and electric fans." [Chairman Mao said:]

It will not do to set rigid standards for the masses. When Peking University saw that the students were rising up, they tried to set standards. They euphemistically called it "returning to the right track." In fact it was "diverting to the wrong track."

There were some schools which labeled the students as counter-revolutionaries. *(Liaison officer Chang Yen went out and labeled twenty-nine people as counter-revolutionary.) [Chairman Mao said:]*

In this way you put the masses on the side of the opposition. You should not fear bad people. How many of them are there after all? The great majority of the student masses are good.

Someone raised the question of disturbances. What do we do in such cases about taking legal action? [Chairman Mao said:]

What are you afraid of? When bad people are involved you prove that they are bad. What do you fear about good people? You should replace the word "fear" by the word "dare." You must demonstrate once and for all whether or not the pass into socialism has been crossed. You must put politics in command, go among the masses and be at one with them, and carry on the great Proletarian Cultural Revolution even better.

Talk at an enlarged Central Work Conference, 30 January 1962

. . . It seems that some of our comrades still do not understand the democratic centralism that Marx and Lenin talked of. Some of these comrades are already veteran revolutionaries, with a "three-eight style" or some other style—anyway they have been party members for several decades, yet they still do not understand this question. They are afraid of the masses, afraid of the masses talking about them, afraid of the masses criticizing them. What sense does it make for Marxist-Leninists to be afraid of the masses? When they have made mistakes they don't talk about themselves, and they are afraid of the masses talking about them. The more frightened they are, the more haunted they become. I think one should not be afraid. What is there to be afraid of? Our attitude is to hold fast to the truth and be ready at any time to correct our mistakes. The question of right or wrong, correct or incorrect in our work has to do with the contradictions among the people. To resolve contradictions among the people we can't use curses or fists, still less guns or knives. We can only use the method of discussion, reasoning, criticism, and self-criticism. In short, we can only use democratic methods, the method of letting the masses speak out.

Both inside and outside the Party there must be a full democratic life, which means conscientiously putting democratic centralism into effect. We must conscientiously bring questions out into the open, and let the masses speak out. The result of their curses at worst will be that we are thrown out and cannot go on doing this kind of work—demoted or transferred. What is so impossible about that? Why should a person only go up and never go down? Why should one only work in one place and never be transferred to another? I think that demotion and transfer, whether it is justified or not, does good to people. They thereby strengthen their revolutionary will, are able to investigate and study a variety of new conditions, and increase their useful knowledge. I myself have had experience in this respect and gained a great deal of benefit. If you do not believe me, why not try it yourselves? . . .

I must point out that I am not advocating the indiscriminate wrong treatment of our cadres, our comrades, or anybody else, in the way in which the ancients detained Wen Wang, starved Confucius, exiled Ch'ü Yüan, or cut off Sun-tzu's kneecaps. I am not in favor of this way of doing things—I oppose it. What I am saying is that in every stage of mankind's history there have always been such cases of mishandling. In class societies such cases are numerous. Even in a socialist society such things cannot be entirely avoided either, whether it be in a period of leadership by a correct or an incorrect line. There is however one distinction: namely, that during a period of correct line of leadership, as soon as it has been discovered that things have been mishandled, people can be cleared and rehabilitated, apologies can be made to them, so that their minds can be set at rest and they can lift up their heads again. But during a time when leadership follows an incorrect line, this way of doing things becomes impossible. Then the only thing is for those who represent the correct line, at a suitable opportunity to use the methods of democratic centralism to take the initiative to set mistakes right. As for those who have themselves made mistakes, after their mistakes have been criticized by comrades and their cases have been appraised by the higher levels and they are given correct treatment, then if they are demoted or transferred one hardly need say that this demotion or transfer may be helpful to them in correcting their mistakes and gaining new knowledge.

Now there are some comrades who are afraid of the masses initiating discussion and putting forward ideas that differ with those of the leaders and leading organizations. As soon as problems are discussed they suppress the activism of the masses and do not allow others to speak out. This attitude is extremely evil. Democratic centralism is written into our party constitution and state constitution, but they don't apply it. Comrades, we are revolutionaries. If we have really committed mistakes of the kind that are harmful to the people's cause, then we should seek the opinions of the masses and of comrades and carry out a self-examination. This sort of self-examination should sometimes be repeated several times over. If once is not enough and people are not satisfied, then it should be done a second time. If they are still not satisfied, it should be done a third time until nobody has any more criticisms. Some provincial party committees have done this. Some provinces are taking more initiative and letting everyone talk. Those who started self-criticism earlier did so as early as 1959. The late-starters started self-criticism in 1961. Some provincial party committees were compelled to carry out self-examinations, such as Honan, Kansu, and Chinghai. According to some reports there are other provinces that are only now starting on self-criticism. It does not matter whether you take the initiative on the question of self-examination, or whether you are forced into it. It does not matter whether you do it earlier or later, provided you look squarely at your mistakes and are willing to admit them and correct them, and you are willing to let the masses criticize you—provided only that you adopt this kind of attitude you will be welcomed. . . .

Those of you who shirk responsibility or who are afraid of taking responsibility, who do not allow people to speak, who think you are tigers, and that nobody will dare to touch your arse, whoever has this attitude, ten out of ten of you will fail. People will talk anyway. You think that nobody will really dare to touch the arse of tigers like you? They damn well will!

Unless we fully promote people's democracy and inner-party democracy in our country, and unless we fully implement the system of proletarian democracy, it will be impossible to achieve a true proletarian centralism. Without a high degree of democracy, it is impossible to achieve a high degree of centralism, and without a high degree of centralism, it is impossible to establish a socialist economy. If our country does not establish a socialist economy, what kind of situation shall we be in? We shall become a country like Yugoslavia, which has actually become a bourgeois country; the dictatorship of the proletariat will be transformed into a bourgeois dictatorship, into a reactionary fascist type of dictatorship. This is a question which demands the utmost vigilance. I hope comrades will give a great deal of thought to it.

Without the system of democratic centralism, the proletarian dictatorship cannot be consolidated. To practice democracy among the people and to practice dictatorship over the enemies of the people, these two aspects are inseparable. When these two aspects are combined, this is then proletarian dictatorship, or it may be called people's democratic dictatorship. Our slogan is: "A people's democratic dictatorship, led by the proletariat, and based on the alliance of the workers and peasants." How does the proletariat exercise leadership? It leads through the Communist Party. The Communist Party is the vanguard of the proletariat. The proletariat unites with all classes and strata who approve of, support, and participate in the socialist revolution and socialist construction, and exercises dictatorship over the reactionary classes or the remnants thereof. In our country the system of exploitation of man by man has already been eliminated. The economic foundations of the landlord class and the bourgeoisie have been eliminated. The reactionary classes are now no longer as ferocious as hitherto. For example, they are no longer as ferocious as in 1949 when the People's Republic was founded, nor as ferocious as in 1957 when the right-wing bourgeoisie madly attacked us. Therefore we speak of them as the remnants of the reactionary classes. But we may on no account underestimate these remnants. We must continue to struggle against them. The reactionary classes that have been overthrown are still planning a comeback. In a socialist society, new bourgeois elements may still be produced. During the whole socialist stage there still exist classes and class struggle, and this class struggle is a protracted, complex, sometimes even violent affair. Our instruments of dictatorship should not be weakened; on the contrary they should be strengthened. Our security system is in the hands of comrades who follow the correct line. It is possible that the security departments in some places may be in the hands of bad people. There are also some comrades engaged on security work who do not rely on the masses or on the Party. In the work of purging counter-revolutionaries, they do not follow the line of purging them with the help of the masses under the leadership of the party committee. They rely solely on secret work, on so-called professional work. Professional work is necessary; it is absolutely necessary to use the methods of detection and trial to deal with counter-revolutionary elements, but the most important thing is to carry out the mass line under the leadership of the party committee. When we are concerned with dictatorship over the whole reactionary class, it is especially important to rely on the masses and the Party. To exercise dictatorship over the reactionary classes does not mean that we should totally eliminate all reactionary elements, but rather that we should eliminate the classes to which they belong. We should use appropriate methods to remold them and transform them into new men. Without a broad people's democracy, proletarian dictatorship cannot be consolidated and political power would be unstable. Without democracy, without the mobilization of the masses, without mass supervision, it will be impossible to exercise effective dictatorship over the reactionary and bad elements, and it will be impossible effectively to remold them. Thus they would continue to make trouble and might still stage a comeback. This problem demands vigilance, and I hope comrades will give a great deal of thought to this, too. . . .

Talk at the Report Meeting, 24 October 1966

The Chairman said: "What is there to be frightened of? Have you read the brief report by Li Hsüeh-feng [First Secretary of the Kiangsu Provincial Committee]? His two children ran off and when they came back they gave Li Hsüeh-feng a lecture. 'Why are you old leaders so frightened of the Red Guards? They haven't beat you up and yet you just won't examine yourself.' Wu Hsiu-ch'üan has four children and they all belong to different factions and lots of their schoolmates go to his home, sometimes ten or more at a time. When you have had more contact with them then you realize there is nothing to be afraid of; instead you think they are quite lovable. If one wants to educate others the educator should first be educated. You are not clearheaded and dare not face the Red Guards, nor speak the truth to the students; you act like officials and big shots. First of all you don't dare to see people and then you don't dare to speak. You have been making revolution for many decades, but the longer you do it the stupider you get. In the letter Shao-ch'i wrote to Chiang Wei-ch'ing, he criticized Chiang Wei-ch'ing and said that he was stupid, but is he himself any cleverer?"

The Chairman asked Liu Lan-t'ao: "When you have gone back, what do you have in mind to do?"

Liu replied: "I first want to go back and have a look."

The Chairman said: "When you speak you always mince your words."

Chairman Mao asked Premier Chou about the progress of the meeting. The Premier said: "It's almost finished. We will meet for another half-day tomorrow. As for the concrete problems, we can solve them according to basic principles when we get back."

Chairman Mao asked Li Ching-ch'üan: "How's Liao Chih-kao [First Secretary of the Szechuan Provincial Committee] getting on?"

Li replied: "In the beginning he wasn't very clear, but in the latter part of the meeting he was somewhat better."

The Chairman said: "What's all this about being consistently correct? You yourself did a bunk. You were frightened out of your wits and rushed off to stay in the military district. When you get back you must pull yourself together and work properly. It's bad to paste up big-character posters about Liu and Teng in the streets. Mustn't we allow people to make mistakes, allow people to make revolution, allow them to change? Let the Red Guards read *The True Story of Ah Q.*"

The Chairman said: "The meeting this time is somewhat better. At the last meeting it was all indoctrination and no progress. Moreover we had no experience. Now we have had two months' more experience. Altogether we have had less than five months' experience. The democratic revolution was carried on for twenty-eight years; we made many mistakes and many people died. The socialist revolution has been carried on for seventeen years, but the cultural revolution has only been carried on for five months. It will take at least five years to get some experience. One big-character poster, the Red Guards, the great exchange of revolutionary experience, and nobody—not even I—expected that all the provinces and cities would be thrown into confusion. The students also made some mistakes, but the mistakes were mainly made by us big shots."

The Chairman asked Li Hsien-nien: "How did your meeting go today?"

Li replied: "The Institute of Finance and Economics held an accusation meeting, and I wanted to make a self-examination, but they wouldn't let me speak."

The Chairman said: "You should go there again tomorrow and make your examination, otherwise people will say you have done a bunk."

Li said: "Tomorrow I have to go abroad."

The Chairman said: "You should also tell them that in the past it used to be San-niang who taught her son. Nowadays it's the son who teaches San-niang. I think you are a bit lacking in spirit.

"If they don't want to listen to your self-examination, you must still go ahead and make one. If they accuse you, you should admit your mistakes. The trouble was stirred up by the Center, the responsibility rests with the Center, but the regions also have some responsibility. What I'm responsible for is the division into first and second lines.

Why did we make this division into first and second lines? The first reason is that my health is not very good; the second was the lesson of the Soviet Union. Malenkov was not mature enough, and before Stalin died he had not wielded power. Every time he proposed a toast, he fawned and flattered. I wanted to establish their prestige before I died; I never imagined that things might move in the opposite direction."

Comrade T'ao Chu said: "Supreme power (ta ch'üan) has slipped from your hands."

The Chairman said: "This is because I deliberately relinquished it. Now, however, they have set up independent kingdoms; there are many things I have not been consulted about, such as the land problem, the Tientsin speeches, the cooperatives in Shansi, the rejection of investigation and study, the big fuss made of Wang Kuang-mei. All these things should really have been discussed at the Center before decisions were taken. Teng Hsiao-p'ing never came to consult me: from 1959 to the present he has never consulted me over anything at all. In 1962 suddenly the four vice-premiers, Li Fu-ch'un, T'an Chen-lin, Li Hsien-nien, and Po I-po, came to look me up in Nanking, and afterwards went to Tientsin. I immediately gave my approval, and the four went back again, but Teng Hsiao-p'ing never came. I was not satisfied with the Wuchang Conference; I could do nothing about the high targets. So I went to Peking to hold a conference, but although you had met for six days, you wouldn't let me hold mine even for a single day. It's not so bad that I am not allowed to complete my work, but I don't like being treated as a dead ancestor. . . ."

Mao Tse-tung

"On the Question of Stalin," Peking Review,
20 September 1963

In what position does Khrushchev, who participated in the leadership of the Party and the state during Stalin's period, place himself when he beats his breast, pounds the table, and shouts abuse of Stalin at the top of his voice? In the position of an accomplice to a "murderer" or a "bandit"? Or in the same position as a "fool" or an "idiot"? . . .

Editorial "On the Historical Experience of the Dictatorship of the Proletariat," People's Daily, *6 April 1956*

Some people consider that Stalin was wrong in everything. This is a grave misconception. Stalin was a great Marxist-Leninist, yet at the same time a Marxist-Leninist who committed several gross errors without realizing that they were errors. We should view Stalin from an historical standpoint, make a proper and all-around analysis to see where he was right and where he was wrong, and draw useful lessons therefrom. . . .

Both the things he did right and the things he did wrong were phenomena of the international Communist movement and bore the imprint of the times. Taken as a whole, the international Communist movement is only a little over a hundred years old, and it is only thirty-nine years since the victory of the October Revolution. Experience in many fields of revolutionary work is still inadequate. Great achievements have been made, but there are still shortcomings and mistakes. . . .

Selected Works of Mao Tse-tung

Resolution "On the Rectification of Incorrect Ideas in the Party," December 1929

. . . Subjectivism exists to a serious extent among certain Party members and this is very harmful in analytically studying a political situation and in guiding the work. Subjective analysis of a political situation and subjective guidance of work inevitably result either in opportunism or in adventurism. As to subjective criticism inside the Party, random talk not based on facts, or mutual suspicion, it often foments unprincipled conflicts and disrupts the party's organization.

Another point should be mentioned in connection with inner-party criticism, namely, that some comrades in their criticism do not pay attention to the major issues, but only to the minor ones. They do not understand that the main purpose of criticism is to point out political and organizational mistakes. As to personal defects, unless they are related to political and organization errors, one need not be so censorious as to place the comrades concerned in a quandary. Moreover, there is a great danger that, once such criticism develops, the attention of the Party may be entirely concentrated on trivial defects, and everybody may become timorous, punctiliously well-mannered, and forget the Party's political tasks.

The method of rectification: Chiefly to educate party members so as to raise their thought and their inner-party life to a political and scientific level. To achieve this end we must: (1) Teach party members to apply the Marxist-Leninist method in analyzing a political situation and appraising class forces in place of subjective analysis and appraisal.

(2) Direct the party members' attention to social and economic investigations and studies, to determine thereby the tactics of struggle and the methods of work, and make comrades understand that without the investigation of actual conditions they will fall into the abyss of fantasy and adventurism. (3) In inner-party criticism, guard against subjective, dogmatic, and vulgar tendencies: statements must be based on facts and criticisms must center around politics.

The individualist tendency in the Party in the Red Army assumes the following manifestations:

1. Vindictiveness. After being criticized inside the Party by a soldier comrade, to seek chances to retaliate on him outside the Party—beating or scolding is one way of retaliation. Retaliation is also sought inside the Party: you attack me at this meeting, so I shall retaliate by finding fault with you at the next. Such vindictiveness proceeds solely from placing personal considerations above the interests of the class and of the Party as a whole. Its target is not the enemy class but individuals in our own ranks. It is a corrosive that weakens the organization and its fighting capacity.

2. Cliquism. To care only about the interests of one's own small group and ignore general interests—although apparently not concerned with personal interests, this contains in reality individualism of an extremely narrow kind and likewise has an exceedingly corrosive and centrifugal effect. In the Red Army, cliquism has all along been rampant; although it has now become less serious as a result of criticism, its remnants still exist and further effort is needed to overcome it.

3. The mercenary view. Not to appreciate that one is a member of the Party and the Red Army, both of which are instruments for carrying out revolutionary tasks. Not to appreciate that one fulfills a responsible role in the revolution, but to think oneself only responsible to individual officers and not to the revolution. This passive mercenary view of revolution is also a manifestation of individualism. The mercenary view of revolution explains why there are so few people who are enthusiastic and active, and exert themselves unreservedly. If the mercenary view is not eliminated, the number of such people cannot be increased and the heavy burden of the revolution will always rest on the shoulders of a few, much to the detriment of the struggle.

4. Hedonism. In the Red Army there are also quite a few whose individualism finds expression in seeking pleasure. They constantly hope that the troops will march to the big cities. They want to go there not to work but to enjoy themselves. What they dislike most is to work in the Red areas where life is hard.

5. Passivity and inactivity. To become passive and stop working whenever things go against one's wishes. This is mainly due to lack of

education, although sometimes it is also due to the leadership's incorrect ways of handling matters, assigning work, or enforcing discipline.

6. The desire to leave the army. The number of people who ask for transfer from work in the Red Army to local work is on the increase. This is not entirely due to personal reasons but also to: (1) the material hardships of life in the Red Army; (2) the feeling of exhaustion after a long struggle; and (3) the leadership's incorrect ways of handling matters, assigning work, or enforcing discipline.

The methods of rectification: Chiefly to intensify education in order to rectify individualism ideologically. Next, to handle matters, assign work, and enforce discipline correctly. Furthermore, to take measures to improve the material life in the Red Army and utilize every available opportunity for rest and rehabilitation in order to ameliorate the material conditions. We must explain clearly in carrying out education that individualism is in its social source a reflection in the Party of petit-bourgeois and bourgeois ideologies. . . .

Selected Readings from the Works of Mao Tse-tung

Report on an investigation of the Peasant Movement in Hunan March 1927

During my recent visit to Hunan I made a first-hand investigation of conditions in the five counties of Hsiangtan, Hsianghsiang, Hengshan, Liling, and Changsha. In the thirty-two days from 4 January to 5 February, I called together fact-finding conferences in villages and county towns, which were attended by experienced peasants and by comrades working in the peasant movement, and I listened attentively to their reports and collected a great deal of material. Many of the hows and whys of the peasant movement were the exact opposite of what the gentry in Hankow and Changsha are saying. I saw and heard of many strange things of which I had hitherto been unaware. I believe the same is true of many other places, too. All talk directed against the peasant movement must be speedily set right. All the wrong measures taken by the revolutionary authorities concerning the peasant movement must be speedily changed. Only thus can the future of the revolution be benefited. For the present upsurge of the peasant movement is a colossal event. In a very short time, in China's central, southern, and northern provinces, several hundred million peasants will rise like a mighty storm, like a hurricane, a force so swift and violent that no power, however great, will be able to hold it back.

They will smash all the trammels that bind them and rush forward along the road to liberation. They will sweep all the imperialists, warlords, corrupt officials, local tyrants, and evil gentry into their graves. Every revolutionary party and every revolutionary comrade will be put to the test, to be accepted or rejected as they decide. There are three alternatives. To march at their head and lead them? To trail behind them, gesticulating and criticizing? Or to stand in their way and oppose them? Every Chinese is free to choose, but events will force you to make the choice quickly. . . .

Speech "Be Concerned with the Well-Being of the Masses, Pay Attention to Methods of Work," Second National Congress of Workers' and Peasants' Representatives, Juchin, Kiangsi Province, 27 January 1934

There are two questions which comrades have failed to stress during the discussion and which, I feel, should be dealt with.

The first concerns the well-being of the masses.

Our central task at present is to mobilize the broad masses to take part in the revolutionary war, overthrow imperialism and the Kuomintang by means of such war, spread the revolution throughout the country, and drive imperialism out of China. Anyone who does not attach enough importance to this central task is not a good revolutionary cadre. If our comrades really comprehend this task and understand that the revolution must at all costs be spread throughout the country, then they should in no way neglect or underestimate the question of the immediate interests, the well-being, of the broad masses. For the revolutionary war is a war of the masses; it can be waged only by mobilizing the masses and relying on them.

If we only mobilize the people to carry on the war and do nothing else, can we succeed in defeating the enemy? Of course not. If we want to win, we must do a great deal more. We must lead the peasants' struggle for land and distribute the land to them, heighten their labor enthusiasm and increase agricultural production, safeguard the interests of the workers, establish cooperatives, develop trade with outside areas, and solve the problems facing the masses—food, shelter and clothing, fuel, rice, cooking oil and salt, sickness and hygiene, and marriage. In short, all the practical problems in the masses' everyday life should claim our attention. If we attend to these problems, solve them, and satisfy the needs of the masses, we shall really become organizers of the well-being of the masses, and they will truly rally around us and give us their warm support. Comrades, will we then be able to arouse them to take part in the revolutionary war? Yes, indeed we will. . . .

We are the leaders and organizers of the revolutionary war as well as the leaders and organizers of the life of the masses. To organize the revolutionary war and to improve the life of the masses are our two major tasks. In this respect, we are faced with the serious problem of methods of work. It is not enough to set tasks, we must also solve the problem of the methods for carrying them out. If our task is to cross a river, we cannot cross it without a bridge or a boat. Unless the bridge or boat problem is solved, it is idle to speak of crossing the river. Unless the problem of method is solved, talk about the task is useless. Unless we pay attention to giving leadership to the work of expanding the Red Army and devote particular care to our methods, we will never succeed even though we recite the phrase "Expand the Red Army" a thousand times. Nor can we accomplish our tasks in any other field, for instance, in checking up on land distribution, or in economic construction, or culture and education, or our work in the new areas and the outlying districts, if all we do is to set the tasks without attending to the methods of carrying them out, without combatting bureaucratic methods of work and adopting practical and concrete ones, and without discarding commandist methods and adopting the method of patient persuasion. . . .

Report on "The Role of the Chinese Communist Party in the National War," Sixth Plenary Session of the Sixth Central Committee, October 1968

The Chinese Communist Party is a party leading a great revolutionary struggle in a nation several hundred million strong, and it cannot fulfill its historic task without a large number of leading cadres who combine ability with political integrity. In the last seventeen years our Party has trained a good many competent leaders, so that we have a framework of cadres in military, political, cultural, party, and mass work; all honor is due to the Party and to the nation for this achievement. But the present framework is not yet strong enough to support the vast edifice of our struggle, and it is still necessary to train capable people on a large scale. Many activists have come forward, and are continuing to come forward, in the great struggle of the Chinese people. We have the responsibility for organizing and training them and for taking good care and making proper use of them. Cadres are a decisive factor, once the political line is determined. Therefore, it is our fighting task to train large numbers of new cadres in a planned way.

Our concern should extend to non-party cadres as well as to party cadres. There are many capable people outside the Party whom we must not ignore. The duty of every Communist is to rid himself of aloofness and arrogance and to work well with non-party cadres, give them sincere help, have a warm, comradely attitude toward them, and enlist their initiative in the great cause of resisting Japan and reconstructing the nation.

We must know how to judge cadres. We must not confine our judgment to a short period or a single incident in a cadre's life, but should consider his life and work as a whole. This is the principal method of judging cadres.

We must know how to use cadres well. In the final analysis, leadership involves two main responsibilities: to work out ideas, and to use cadres well. Such things as drawing up plans, making decisions, and giving orders and directives, are all in the category of "working out ideas." To put the ideas into practice, we must weld the cadres together and encourage them to go into action; this comes into the category of "using the cadres well." Throughout our national history there have been two sharply contrasting lines on the subject of the use of cadres, one being to "appoint people on their merit," and the other to "appoint people by favoritism." The former is the honest and the latter the dishonest way. The criterion the Communist Party should apply in its cadres policy is whether or not a cadre is resolute in carrying out the party line, keeps to party discipline, has close ties with the masses, has the ability to find his bearings independently, and is active, hardworking, and unselfish. This is what "appointing people on their merit" means. The cadres policy of Chang Kuo-tao was the exact opposite. Following the line of "appointing people by favoritism," he gathered personal favorites around himself to form a small clique, and in the end he turned traitor to the Party and decamped. This is an important lesson for us. Taking warning from it and from similar historical lessons, the Central Committee and the leaders at all levels must make it their major responsibility to adhere to the honest and fair way in cadres policy and reject the dishonest and unfair way, and so consolidate the unity of the Party.

We must know how to take good care of cadres. There are several ways of doing so.

First, give them guidance. This means allowing them a free hand in their work so that they have the courage to assume responsibility and, at the same time, giving them timely instructions so that, guided by the Party's political line they are able to make full use of their initiative.

Second, raise their level. This means educating them by giving them the opportunity to study so that they can enhance their theoretical understanding and their working ability.

Third, check up on their work, and help them sum up their experience, carry forward their achievements, and correct their mistakes. To assign work without checking up and to take notice only when serious mistakes are made—that is not the way to take care of cadres.

Fourth, in general, use the method of persuasion with cadres who have made mistakes, and help them correct their mistakes. The method of struggle should be confined to those who make serious mistakes and nevertheless refuse to accept guidance. Here patience is essential. It is wrong lightly to label people "opportunists" or lightly to begin "waging struggles" against them.

Fifth, help them with their difficulties. When cadres are in difficulty as a result of illness, straitened means, or domestic or other troubles, we must be sure to give them as much care as possible.

This is how to take good care of cadres. . . .

"Some Questions Concerning Methods of Leadership," *1 June 1943*

1. There are two methods that we Communists must employ in whatever work we do. One is to combine the general with the particular; the other is to combine the leadership with the masses.

2. In any task, if no general and widespread call is issued, the broad masses cannot be mobilized for action. But if persons in leading positions confine themselves to a general call—if they do not personally, in some of the organizations, go deeply and concretely into the work called for, make a breakthrough at some single point, gain experience, and use this experience for guiding other units—then they will have no way of testing the correctness or of enriching the content of their general call, and there is the danger that nothing may come of it. In the rectification movement of 1942, for example, there were achievements wherever the method of combining the general call with particular and specific guidance was used, but there were no achievements wherever this method was not used. In the rectification movement of 1943, each bureau and sub-bureau of the Central Committee and each area and prefectural party committee, in addition to making a general call (a rectification plan for the whole year), must do the following things, gaining experience in the process. Select two or three units (but not too many) from the organization itself and from other organizations, schools, or army units in the vicinity. Make a thorough study of those units, acquire a detailed knowledge of the development of the rectification movement in them and a detailed knowledge of the political history, the ideological characteristics, the

zeal in study, and the strong and weak point in the work of some (again not too many) representative members of their personnel. Furthermore, give personal guidance to those in charge to find concrete solutions for the practical problems facing those units. The leaders in every organization, school, or army unit must do likewise, as each of these has a number of subordinate units. Moreover, this is the method by which the leaders combine leading and learning. No one in a leading position is competent to give general guidance to all the units unless he derives concrete experience from particular individuals and events in particular subordinate units. This method must be promoted everywhere so that leading cadres at all levels learn to apply it.

3. Experience in the 1942 rectification movement also proves it is essential for the success of the rectification that a leading group should be formed in each unit in the course of the movement, made up of a small number of activists and with the heads of the given unit as its nucleus, and that this leading group should link itself closely with the masses taking part in the movement. However active the leading group may be, its activity will amount to fruitless effort by a handful of people unless combined with the activity of the masses. On the other hand, if the masses alone are active without a strong leading group to organize their activity properly, such activity cannot be sustained for long, or carried forward in the right direction, or raised to a high level. The masses in any given place are generally composed of three parts, the relatively active, the intermediate, and the relatively backward. The leaders must therefore be skilled in uniting the small number of active elements aaround the leadership and must rely on them to raise the level of the intermediate elements and to win over the backward elements. A leading group that is genuinely united and is linked with the masses can gradually be formed only in the process of mass struggle, and not in isolation from it. In the process of a great struggle, the composition of the leading group in most cases should not and cannot remain entirely unchanged throughout the initial, middle, and final stages; the activists who come forward in the course of the struggle must constantly be promoted to replace those original members of the leading group who are inferior by comparison or who have degenerated. One fundamental reason why the work in many places and many organizations cannot be pushed ahead is the lack of a leading group that is united, linked with the masses, and kept constantly healthy. A school of a hundred people certainly cannot be run well if it does not have a leading group of several people, or a dozen or more, which is formed in accordance with the actual circumstances (and not thrown together artificially) and is composed of the most active, upright, and alert of the teachers, the other staff, and

the students. In every organization, school, army unit, factory, or village, whether large or small, we should give effect to the ninth of Stalin's twelve conditions for the bolshevization of the Party, namely, that on the establishment of a nucleus of leadership. The criteria for such a leading group should be the four that Dimitrov enumerated in his discussion of cadres policy—absolute devotion to the cause, contact with the masses, ability independently to find one's bearings, and observance of discipline. Whether in carrying out the central tasks— war, production, education (including rectification)—or in checking- up on work, examining the cadres' histories, or in other activities, it is necessary to adopt the method of linking the leading group with the masses, in addition to that of linking the general call with particular guidance.

4. In all the practical work of our Party, all correct leadership is necessarily "from the masses, to the masses." This means: take the ideas of the masses (scattered and unsystematic ideas) and concentrate them (through study turn them into concentrated and systematic ideas), then go to the masses and propagate and explain these ideas until the masses embrace them as their own, hold fast to them and translate them into action, and test the correctness of these ideas in such action. Then once again concentrate ideas from the masses and once again go to the masses so that the ideas are persevered in and carried through. And so on, over and over again in an endless spiral, with the ideas becoming more correct, more vital and richer each time. Such is the Marxist theory of knowledge.

5. The concept of a correct relationship between the leading group and the masses in an organization or in a struggle, the concept that correct ideas on the part of the leadership can only be "from the masses, to the masses," and the concept that the general call must be combined with particular guidance when the leadership's ideas are being put into practice—these concepts must be propagated every- where during the present rectification movement in order to correct the mistaken viewpoints among our cadres on these questions. Many comrades do not see the importance of, or are not good at, drawing together the activists to form a nucleus of leadership, and they do not see the importance of, or are not good at, linking this nucleus of lead- ership closely with the masses, and so their leadership becomes bu- reaucratic and divorced from the masses. Many comrades do not see the importance of, or are not good at, summing up the experience of mass struggles, but fancying themselves clever, are fond of voicing their subjectivist ideas, and so their ideas become empty and imprac- tical. Many comrades rest content with making a general call with re- gard to a task and do not see the importance of, or are not good at, fol-

lowing it up immediately with particular and concrete guidance, and so their call remains on their lips, or on paper or in the conference room, and their leadership becomes bureaucratic. In the present rectification movement we must correct these defects and learn to use the methods of combining the leadership with the masses and the general with the particular in our study, in the checkup on work and in the examination of cadres' histories; and we must also apply these methods in all our future work.

6. Take the ideas of the masses and concentrate them, then go to the masses, persevere in the ideas, and carry them through, so as to form correct ideas of leadership—such is the basic method of leadership. In the process of concentrating ideas and persevering in them, it is necessary to use the method of combining the general call with particular guidance, and this is a component part of the basic method. Formulate general ideas (general calls) out of the particular guidance given in a number of cases, and put them to the test in many different units (not only doing so yourself, but by telling others to do the same); then concentrate the new experience (sum it up) and draw up new directives for the guidance of the masses generally. Comrades should do this in the present rectification movement, and also in every other kind of work. Better leadership comes with greater skill in doing this.

7. In relaying to subordinate units any task (whether it concerns the revolutionary war, production, or education; the rectification movement, checkup on work, or the examination of cadres' histories; propaganda work, organizational work, or anti-espionage, or other work), a higher organization and its departments should in all cases go through the leader of the lower organization concerned so that he may assume responsibility; in this way both division of labor and unified centralized leadership are achieved. A department at a higher level should not go solely to its counterpart at the lower level (for instance, a higher department concerned with organization, propaganda, or anti-espionage should not go solely to the corresponding department at the lower level), leaving the person in overall charge of the lower organization (such as the secretary, the chairman, the director, or the school principal) in ignorance or without responsibility. Both the person in overall charge and the person with specific responsibility should be informed and given responsibility. This centralized method, combining division of labor with unified leadership, makes it possible, through the person with overall responsibility, to mobilize a large number of cadres—on occasion even an organization's entire personnel—to carry out a particular task, and thus to overcome shortages of cadres in individual departments and turn a good number of people into active cadres for the work in hand. This, too, is a way of

combining the leadership with the masses. Take, for instance, the examining of cadres' histories. If the job is done in isolation, if it is done only by the few people in the organization department in charge of such work, it certainly cannot be done well. But if it is done through the administrative head of a particular organization or school, who mobilizes many or even all of his staff, or many or even all of his students, to take part in the work, while at the same time the leading members of the organization department at the higher level give correct guidance, applying the principle of linking the leadership with the masses, then undoubtedly the task of examining the cadres' histories will be satisfactorily accomplished.

8. In any given place, there cannot be a number of central tasks at the same time. At any one time there can be only one central task, supplemented by other tasks of a second or third order of importance. Consequently, the person with overall responsibility in the locality must take into account the history and circumstances of the struggle there and put the different tasks in their proper order; he should not act upon each instruction as it comes from the higher organization without any planning of his own, and thereby create a multitude of "central tasks" and a state of confusion and disorder. Nor should a higher organization simultaneously assign many tasks to a lower organization without indicating their relative importance and urgency or without specifying which is central, for that will lead to confusion in the steps to be taken by the lower organizations in their work and thus no definite results will be achieved. It is part of the art of leadership to take the whole situation into account and plan accordingly in the light of the historical conditions and existing circumstances of each locality, decide correctly on the center of gravity and the sequence of the work for each period, steadfastly carry through the decision, and make sure that definite results are achieved. This is also a problem of method of leadership, and care must be taken to solve it when applying the principles of combining the leadership with the masses and the general with the particular.

9. Details concerning methods of leadership are not dealt with here; it is hoped that comrades in all localities will themselves do some hard thinking and give full play to their own creativeness on the basis of the principles here set forth. The harder the struggle, the greater the need for Communists to link their leadership closely with the demands of the vast masses, and to combine general calls closely with particular guidance, so as to smash the subjectivist and bureaucratic methods of leadership completely. All the leading comrades of our Party must at all times counterpose scientific, Marxist methods of leadership to subjectivist, bureaucratic methods of leadership and use

the former to overcome the latter. Subjectivists and bureaucrats do not understand the principles of combining the leadership with the masses and the general with the particular; they greatly impede the development of the work of the Party. To combat subjectivist and bureaucratic methods of leadership, we must promote scientific, Marxist methods of leadership both extensively and intensively.

On Revolution and War

"Win the Masses in Their Millions for the Anti-Japanese National United Front," May 1937

A great revolution requires a great party and many first-rate cadres to guide it. In China, with a population of 450 million, it is impossible to carry through our great revolution, which is unprecedented in history, if the leadership consists of a small, narrow group and if the party leaders and cadres are petty-minded, shortsighted, and incompetent. The Chinese Communist Party has been a large party for a long time and it is still large despite the losses during the period of reaction; it has many good leaders and cadres, but still not enough. Our party organizations must be extended all over the country and we must purposefully train tens of thousands of cadres and hundreds of first-rate leaders. They must be cadres and leaders versed in Marxism-Leninism, politically farsighted, competent in work, full of the spirit of self-sacrifice, capable of tackling problems on their own, steadfast in the midst of difficulties, and loyal and devoted in serving the nation, the class, and the Party. It is on these cadres and leaders that the Party relies for its links with the membership and the masses, and it is by relying on their firm leadership of the masses that the Party can succeed in defeating the enemy. Such cadres and leaders must be free from selfishness, from individualistic heroism, ostentation, sloth, passivity, and sectarian arrogance, and they must be selfless national and class heroes; such are the qualities and the style of work demanded of the members, cadres, and leaders of our Party. Such is the spiritual legacy handed down to us by the tens of thousands of members, the thousands of cadres, and the scores of first-rate leaders who have laid down their lives for the cause. Beyond any doubt, we ought to acquire these qualities, do still better in remolding ourselves, and raise ourselves to a higher revolutionary level. But even this is not enough; we must also regard it as our duty to discover many more new cadres and leaders in the Party and the country. Our revolution depends on cadres. As Stalin said, "Cadres decide everything."

"Methods of Work of Party Committees," March 1949

1. The secretary of a party committee must be good at being a "squad leader." A party committee has ten to twenty members; it is like a squad in the army, and the secretary is like the "squad leader." It is indeed not easy to lead this squad well. Each bureau or sub-bureau of the Central Committee now leads a vast area and shoulders very heavy responsibilities. To lead means not only to decide general and specific policies but also to devise correct methods of work. Even with correct general and specific policies, troubles may still arise if methods of work are neglected. To fulfill its task of exercising leadership, a party committee must rely on its "squad members" and enable them to play their parts to the full. To be a good "squad leader," the secretary should study hard and investigate thoroughly. A secretary or deputy secretary will find it difficult to direct his "squad" well if he does not take care to do propaganda and organizational work among his own "squad members," is not good at handling his relations with committee members, or does not study how to run meetings successfully. If the "squad members" do not march in step, they can never expect to lead tens of millions of people in fighting and construction. Of course, the relation between the secretary and the committee members is one in which the minority must obey the majority, so it is different from the relation between a squad leader and his men. Here we speak only by way of analogy.

2. Place problems on the table. This should be done not only by the "squad leader" but by the committee members, too. Do not talk behind people's backs. Whenever problems arise, call a meeting, place the problems on the table for discussion, make some decisions, and the problems will be solved. If problems exist and are not placed on the table, they will remain unsolved for a long time and even drag on for years. The "squad leader" and the committee members should be tolerant and understanding in their relations with each other. Nothing is more important than mutual tolerance, understanding, support, and friendship between the secretary and the committee members, between the Central Committee and its bureaus, and between the bureaus and the area party committees. In the past this point received little attention, but since the Seventh Party Congress much progress has been made in this respect and the ties of friendship and unity have been greatly strengthened. We should continue to pay constant attention to this point in the future.

3. "Exchange information." This means that members of a party committee should keep each other informed and exchange views on matters that have come to their attention. This is of great importance

in achieving a common language. Some fail to do so. . . . In the past some of our high-ranking cadres did not have a common language even on basic theoretical problems of Marxism-Leninism, because they had not studied enough. There is more of a common language in the Party today, but the problem has not yet been fully solved. For instance, in the land reform there is still some difference in the understanding of what is meant by "middle peasants" and "rich peasants."

4. Ask your subordinates about matters you don't understand or don't know, and do not lightly express your approval or disapproval. Some documents, after having been drafted, are withheld from circulation for a time because certain questions in them need to be clarified and it is necessary to consult the lower levels first. We should never pretend to know what we don't know, we should [as Confucius said] "not feel ashamed to ask and learn from people below," and we should listen carefully to the views of the cadres at the lower levels. Be a pupil before you become a teacher; learn from the cadres at the lower levels before you issue orders. In handling problems, this should be the practice of all bureaus of the Central Committee and party committees of the fronts, except in military emergencies or when the facts of the matter are already clear. To do this will not lower one's prestige, but can only raise it. Since our decisions incorporate the correct view of the cadres at the lower levels, the latter will naturally support them. What the cadres at the lower levels say may or may not be correct; we must analyze it. We must heed the correct views and act upon them. The reason why the leadership of the Central Committee is correct is chiefly that it synthesizes the material, reports, and corrects views coming from different localities. It would be difficult for the Central Committee to issue correct orders if the localities did not provide material and put forward opinions. Listen also to the mistaken views from below; it is wrong not to listen to them at all. Such views, however, are not to be acted upon but to be criticized.

5. Learn to "play the piano." In playing the piano all ten fingers are in motion; it won't do to move some fingers only and not others. But if all ten fingers press down at once, there is no melody. To produce good music, the ten fingers should move rhythmically and in coordination. A party committee should keep a firm grasp on its central task and at the same time, aaround the central task, it should unfold the work in other fields. At present, we have to take care of many fields; we must look after the work in all the areas, armed units, and departments, and not give all our attention to a few problems, to the exclusion of others. Wherever there is a problem, we must put our finger on it, and this is a method we must master. Some play the piano well and some badly, and there is a great difference in the melodies they

produce. Members of party committees must learn to "play the piano" well.

6. "Grasp firmly." That is to say, the party committee must not merely "grasp" but must "grasp firmly" its main tasks. One can get a grip on something only when it is grasped firmly, without the slightest slackening. Not to grasp firmly is not to grasp at all. Naturally, one cannot get a grip on something with an open hand. When the hand is clenched as if grasping something but is not clenched tightly, there is still no grip. Some of our comrades do grasp the main tasks, but their grasp is not firm and so they cannot make a success of their work. It will not do to have no grasp at all, nor will it do if the grasp is not firm.

7. "Have a head for figures." That is to say, we must attend to the quantitative aspect of a situation or problem and make a basic quantitative analysis. Every quality manifests itself in a certain quantity, and without quantity there can be no quality. To this day many of our comrades still do not understand that they must attend to the quantitative aspect of things—the basic statistics, the main percentages, and the quantitative limits that determine the qualities of things. They have no "figures" in their heads and as a result cannot help making mistakes. For instance, in carrying out the land reform it is essential to have such figures as the percentages of landlords, rich peasants, middle peasants, and poor peasants among the population and the amount of land owned by each group, because only on this basis can we formulate correct policies. Whom to call a rich peasant, whom a well-to-do middle peasant, and how much income derived from exploitation makes a person a rich peasant as distinct from a well-to-do middle peasant—in all these cases, too, the quantitative limits must be ascertained. In all mass movements we must make a basic investigation and analysis of the number of active supporters, opponents, and neutrals and must not decide problems subjectively and without basis.

8. "Notice to Reassure the Public." Notice of meetings should be given beforehand; this is like issuing a "Notice to Reassure the Public," so that everybody will know what is going to be discussed and what problems are to be solved and can make timely preparations. In some places, meetings of cadres are called without first preparing reports and draft resolutions, and only when people have arrived for the meeting are makeshifts improvised; this is just like the saying "Troops and horses have arrived, but food and fodder are not ready," and that is no good. Don't call a meeting in a hurry if the preparations are not completed.

9. "Fewer and better troops and simpler administration." Talks, speeches, articles, and resolutions should all be concise and to the point. Meetings also should not go on too long.

10. Pay attention to uniting and working with comrades who differ with you. This should be borne in mind both in the localities and in the army. It also applies to relations with people outside the Party. We have come together from every corner of the country and should be good at uniting in our work not only with comrades who hold the same views as we but also with those who hold different views. There are some among us who have made very serious mistakes; we should not be prejudiced against them but should be ready to work with them.

11. Guard against arrogance. For anyone in a leading position, this is a matter of principle and an important condition for maintaining unity. Even those who have made no serious mistakes and have achieved very great success in their work should not be arrogant. Celebration of the birthdays of party leaders is forbidden. Naming places, streets, and enterprises after party leaders is likewise forbidden. We must keep to our style of plain living and hard work and put a stop to flattery and exaggerated praise.

12. Draw two lines of distinction. First, between revolution and counterrevolution. . . . Secondly, within the revolutionary ranks, it is necessary to make a clear distinction between right and wrong, between achievements and shortcomings, and to make clear which of the two is primary and which secondary. For instance, do the achievements amount to 30 percent or to 70 percent of the whole? It will not do either to understate or to overstate. We must have a fundamental evaluation of a person's work and establish whether his achievements amount to 30 percent and his mistakes to 70 percent, or vice versa. If his achievements amount to 70 percent of the whole, then his work should in the main be approved. It would be entirely wrong to describe work in which the achievements are primary as work in which the mistakes are primary. In our approach to problems we must not forget to draw these two lines of distinction, between revolution and counterrevolution and between achievements and shortcomings. We shall be able to handle things well if we bear these two distinctions in mind; otherwise we shall confuse the nature of the problems. To draw these distinctions well, careful study and analysis are of course necessary. Our attitude toward every person and every matter should be one of analysis and study.

The members of the Politburo and I personally feel that only for using the above methods can party committees do their work well. In addition to conducting party congresses well, it is most important for the party committees at all levels to perform their work of leadership well. We must make efforts to study and perfect the methods of work so as to raise further the party committees' level of leadership.

"Some Questions Concerning Methods of Leadership," June 1943

1. There are two methods that we Communists must employ in whatever work we do. One is to combine the general with the particular; the other is to combine the leadership with the masses.

2. In any task, if no general and widespread call is issued, the broad masses cannot be mobilized for action. But if persons in leading positions confine themselves to a general call—if they do not personally, in some of the organizations, go deeply and concretely into the work called for, make a breakthrough at some single point, gain experience and use this experience for guiding other units—then they will have no way of testing the correctness or of enriching the content of their general call, and there is the danger that nothing may come of it. . . . Select two or three units (but not too many) from the organization itself and from other organizations, schools, or army units in the vicinity. Make a thorough study of those units, acquire a detailed knowledge of the development of the rectification movement in them and a detailed knowledge of the political history, the ideological characteristics, the zeal in study, and the strong and weak points in the work of some (again not too many) representative members of their personnel. Furthermore, give personal guidance to those in charge to find concrete solutions for the practical problems facing those units. . . .

3. Experience . . . proves it is essential for the success of the rectification that a leading group should be formed in each unit in the course of the movement, made up of a small number of activists and with the heads of the given unit as its nucleus, and that this leading group should link itself closely with the masses taking part in the movement. However active the leading group may be, its activity will amount to fruitless effort by a handful of people unless combined with the activity of the masses. On the other hand, if the masses alone are active without a strong leading group to organize their activity properly, such activity cannot be sustained for long, or carried forward in the right direction, or raised to a high level. The masses in any given place are generally composed of three parts, the relatively active, the intermediate, and the relatively backward. The leaders must therefore be skilled in uniting the small number of active elements aaround the leadership and must rely on them to raise the level of the intermediate elements and to win over the backward elements. A leading group that is genuinely united and linked with the masses can be formed only gradually in the process of mass struggle, and not in isolation from it. In the process of a great struggle, the composition of

the leading group in most cases should not and cannot remain entirely unchanged throughout the initial, middle, and final stages; the activists who come forward in the course of the struggle must constantly be promoted to replace those original members of the leading group who are inferior by comparison or who have degenerated. . . .

4. In all the practical work of our Party, all correct leadership is necessarily "from the masses to the masses." This means: take the ideas of the masses (scattered and unsystematic ideas) and concentrate them (through study turn them into concentrated and systematic ideas), then go to the masses and propagate and explain these ideas until the masses embrace them as their own, hold fast to them and translate them into action, and test the correctness of these ideas in such action. Then once again go to the masses so that the ideas are persevered in and carried through. . . .

5. The concept of a correct relationship between the leading group and the masses in an organization or in a struggle, the concept that correct ideas on the part of the leadership can only be "from the masses, to the masses," and the concept that the general call must be combined with particular guidance when the leadership's ideas are being put into practice—these concepts must be propagated everywhere during the present rectification movement in order to correct the mistaken viewpoints among our cadres on these questions. . . .

"Problems of War and Strategy," November 1938

. . . Every Communist must grasp the truth, "Political power grows out of the barrel of a gun." Our principle is that the party commands the gun, and the gun must never be allowed to command the Party. Yet, having guns, we can create Party organizations. . . . We can also create cadres, create schools, create culture, create mass movements. Everything in Yenan has been created by having guns. All things grow out of the barrel of a gun. According to the Marxist theory of the state, the army is the chief component of state power. Whoever wants to seize and retain state power must have a strong army. . . . The guns of the Russian Communist Party created socialism. We shall create a democratic republic. Experience in the class struggle in the era of imperialism teaches us that it is only by the power of the gun that the working class and the laboring masses can defeat the armed bourgeoisie and landlords; in this sense we may say that only with guns can the whole world be transformed. We are advocates of the abolition of war, we do not want war; but war can only be abolished through war, and in order to get rid of the gun it is necessary to take up the gun.

References

Mao Tse-tung, *Mao Tse-tung Unrehearsed; Talks and Letters 1956–1971*, edited by Stuart Schram (Harmondsworth, UK: Penguin Books, 1974).

Mao Tse-tung, *Mao Tse-tung*, edited by Stuart Schram (Harmondsworth, UK: Penguin, 1966).

Mao Tse-tung, *Selected Works of Mao Tse-tung* (London: Lawrence and Wishart, 1954).

Mao Tse-tung, *Selected Readings from the Works of Mao Tse-tung* (Peking: Foreign Languages Press, 1967).

Mao Tse-tung, *On Revolution and War*, edited by M. Rejaj (Garden City, NY: Doubleday Anchor, 1970).

JUAN PERÓN

FULL NAME:

Juan Domingo Perón

BORN:

8 October 1895, Buenos Aires Province, Argentina

DIED:

1 July 1974, Buenos Aires, Argentina

Army colonel who served as Secretary of Labor and Social Welfare, 1944, and Vice President and Minister of War, 1945. Founder and leader of the Perónist Movement. Elected President of Argentina, 1946, and reelected in 1951; overthrown and fled to Paraguay, 1955. On brief return to Argentina in 1972 and 1973, Perónist candidates captured the presidency and a majority in the legislature. President again in 1973–1974.

His writings are largely in Spanish and include: *Juan Domingo Perón, Filosofia Peronista* (Buenos Aires: Editorial; Freeland, 1973); *Juan Domingo Perón, Seleccion de sus escritos, conferencias y discursos* (Buenos Aires: Ediciones Sinteses, 1973); and *Juan Domingo Perón, The Voice of Perón* (Buenos Aires: 1950). Biographies include: Robert Alexander, *Juan Domingo Perón* (Boulder, CO: Westview Press, 1979).

The Voice of Perón

I have said, and I repeat, with the greatest of pride as an Argentine, that I represent a powerful government because I rule over many millions of Argentine hearts. This strength, my friends, which is given by the close relationship of the hearts of the people with the heart of their ruler, is a force which history shows has always been, all down the ages, absolutely invincible.

Speech at the First Party Meeting, Luna Park Stadium,
25 June 1949

We are aiming at politics of the people, of the great masses.

For us it is the people who must decide; for us it is the people who govern through their representatives. And for us it is for the people, and solely for the people, that we are obliged to work, because for that reason they have chosen us, and for that purpose they are paying us in our posts.

Speech on the work of the government, 20 August 1947

An overenthusiastic ruler is usually an unjust one, and justice, with prudence is innate in the born ruler. He should be tolerant, even with intolerance, without being weak, but able to act energetically when an attack is made against the State, or law and order, or the recognized authorities; but never when the attack is against his own person. He should get used to the injustice, calumny, and slander that others will use against him when they are unable to combat him with the weapons of truth.

Speech on the reform of the National Constitution,
27 January 1949

When it is obvious that popular belief, that has been accepted as irrefutable becomes a thing of the past, one must have the courage to admit it. Even though it is upheld by tradition, the law, or science, it should be declared obsolete as soon as the public conscience claims it to be so. To maintain a principle that has lost its virtuosity, is the same thing as to maintain what is fictitious.

With the proper reforms we hope to draw a thick veil over the subterfuges Argentines of our age have had to live through. We wish to bring to an end the reign of haziness and deception. We aim at achieving a worthy and true life for Argentina. But this can only become a reality if the constitution guarantees the lasting existence of genuine democracy.

Speech to Trade Union representatives, 24 February 1949

As one who governs I shall always listen to the will of the people and if they are mistaken it will be they who will suffer the consequences.

My moral obligation is to carry out, to the best of my ability, the will of the people.

I must execute intelligently that which the people desire. If the people say that they want this or that, it is my duty to satisfy them in such a way that everything is for the best. This much I have learned, it is not just an idea of mine; there are certain lessons that one never forgets.

Therefore we want the people to have the final word in politics but they are very many and it is not very easy to get to know their wishes.

It is necessary to be so organized that a ruler may know what his people want at any given moment.

Speech honoring Colonel Mercante at the Railway Union, 23 February 1948

Fortunately for Argentina, her people of the working class possess high moral integrity. On them rest the foundations of this struggle to save the Argentine people from the threatened return to an era of which we have very bitter memories. She will shape her own destiny. Only the people can save the people. Neither I, myself, nor good luck can save them; only by making sacrifices can they be saved: sacrifices made by the people in their work and self-denial.

Speech on constitutional reform, 27 January 1949

The revolutionary idea would not have been able to materialize along constitutional lines if it had not been able to withstand the criticism, the violent attacks, and even the strain on principles when they run up against the rocks that appear every day in the path of a ruler. The principles of the revolution would not have been able to be upheld if they had not been the true reflection of Argentine sentiments.

The guiding principles of our movement must have made a very deep impression on the national conscience for the people in the last elections to have consecrated them by giving us full power to make reforms.

Speech to the Meeting of the Railway Union, 29 July 1949

We are building cities, we are constructing gaspipe lines 1,800 kilometers long; we are building an aerodrome that may quite possibly be the largest and best-equipped in the world, and we are acquiring a merchant fleet that is already beginning to take its place among the most important on the high seas.

By this I mean to point out that I was not just being vainglorious three years ago when I took over the government and said that the country was sick and tired of little things, and I wanted to make it sick and tired of big things.

Speech at the First Party Meeting, Luna Park Stadium, 25 July 1949

The "caudillo" (name given to South American autocratic political leaders) improvises while the statesman makes plans and carries them out. The "caudillo" has no initiative, the statesman is creative. The "caudillo" is only concerned with measures that are applicable to the reigning circumstances, whereas the statesman plans for all time; the deeds of the "caudillo" die with him, but the statesman lives on in his handiwork. For that reason the "caudillo" has no guiding principles or clear-cut plan, while the statesman works methodically, defeating time and perpetuating himself in his own creations. "Caudillismo" is a trade, but statecraft is an art.

Speech to national legislators and political leaders of the Perónist Party, 18 June 1948

"Caudillismo" (tyrannical political leadership) must be substituted by the permanent organic state of the political masses, and that will be,

Gentlemen, the great triumph of our party, if we are able to impose this in the national life. If we are prepared to organize our party, the other political parties must do the same thing if they wish ever to come into power again. If tomorrow we are defeated by a party that was better organized than our own, I should feel intensely happy because nothing but good for the country could come from a well-organized party; on the other hand, many evils can be expected from men, however well-intentioned they may be, who govern with no definite plan of action. . . .

Our doctrine is a doctrine of moral purity, something humanizing and truly patriotic. So that there is no objection whatever to its dissemination throughout the schools, colleges, and universities, in short, everywhere. If it were an evil doctrine I should be the first to oppose it, but being as it is, nothing but good, we should aim at making it known everywhere and teaching it to every man and woman. Thus we shall ensure for ourselves the triumph of collective action. . . .

To guide the masses one must first instruct and educate them, which can be done at meetings or at lectures on politics, to be given in our centers, not to tell them to vote for us, or that they must do this or that so that Peter or James will be elected to represent them. No, we must speak to them of what their obligations are, because in our country there is much talk of rights and little of moral obligations. We must talk somewhat more about the obligations of each citizen toward his country and toward his fellow countrymen, and forget for a time their rights since we have mentioned them often enough.

Speech to the Legislative Assembly, 1 May 1948

I can say without undue boasting, that, used as I am to the strict discipline of the army, I adapted my mind to the new problems that arise out of the uneven rhythm of this postwar period, devising a well-balanced comprehensive plan to be carried out during the six years of my government. Its outlines and structure are well-known to all of you. I explained it to everyone; I used every means at my disposal to make it accessible to the masses, to those who were indifferent, to those who were prepared for it, and to the children in the schools.

Speech to the Legislative Assembly, 1 May 1949

It is always the people, in their great variety and discord, who bring great ideas to fruition. Without the warm sympathy of the people even the most beautiful creative ideas are relegated to the limbo of forgotten and neglected dreams. Only when the idea is embraced by the invigorating spirit of the people can it be transformed into action, and the action into accomplishment.

It was only the cooperation of the people that made it possible for the Emperor Octavio Augusto, when he saw his dreams had materialized, to put on record for posterity these famous words: "I received a Rome built of bricks and I give it back to you in marble."

The enterprise that we Argentines have embarked upon is not the exclusive work of one party, or set, or group. The doors are open to everybody, because in the history of the people who go forward there are no party colors or programs. There are opportunities even for those who have not yet realized that Argentina's hour has arrived.

The hour has really arrived and everyone must choose between continuing to live in a dim and shadowy manner or boldly taking the first step toward his own redemption. . . .

I have always believed that to be noble all human deeds must be inspired by an ideal. This is truer still in the case of a ruler who must have the incentive of a definite ideal to be able to carry out a governmental plan. Possibly private actions may stem from other motives. But if to govern well means to seek the means whereby to establish the public welfare, there is no doubt that the determination to achieve one's highest aims is not possible without the inducement of a definite vision of the end in view.

And my great ambition, as I have said over and over again, is for the aggrandizement of the Argentine nation.

Speech to the Meeting of Agriculturlists at Firmat, 3 April 1949

A policy like this shows that the object of the State in taking over the commercialization of the grain production is not to obtain substantial benefits from it. We have a far greater and nobler purpose, which is to establish the prices of farm and agricultural products on a remunerative level and to ensure the normal and continual development of this basic activity for the national economy.

Reference

Perón, Juan, *The Voice of Perón* (Buenos Aires: Subsecretaria de Información de la Presidencia de la Nacion Argentina, 1950).

EVA PERÓN

FULL NAME:
Eva Duarte de Perón, "Evita"

BORN:
7 May 1919, Los Toldos, Argentina

DIED:
26 July 1952, Buenos Aires, Argentina

Second wife of Juan Perón. Powerful unofficial leader during Perón's first term, 1946–1952. De facto Minister of Health and Labor. Formidable symbol even after her death.

Biography: Julie M. Taylor, *Eva Perón: The Myths of a Woman* (Chicago: University of Chicago Press, 1979).

Eva Perón: The Myths of a Woman

From Juan Perón, "Las memorias de Juan Perón,"
21 April 1970

One of the greatest forces of women in leadership is that they use the little means [*pequeños medios*] that are so powerful, something that we do not do because we are men. They take advantage of this, and one should see the strength they have! This must undoubtedly be a factor of strength that women offer us in politics, a factor of extraordinary strength.

Eva Perón is an instrument of my creation. I prepared her so that she would do what she did. I needed her in the sector of social work within my leadership. And her work was extraordinary . . . My life at her side formed part as well of the art of leadership. As a politician I am barely an amateur. The area in which I am a professional is in leadership. A leader must imitate nature, or God. If God came down every day to solve men's problems, we would already have lost our respect for Him and there would be no lack of some fool who would want to replace Him. For that reason, God works through Providence. That was the role which Eva filled: that of Providence.

From Otelo Borroni and Roberto Vaca, La Vida de Eva Perón,
volume 1, citing Eva Perón's words, 1970

Friends: The link of so many months with the microphone of LR$_3$ Radio Belgrano must necessarily have created in us by now the special relationship of friends. The fact is, we are friends, and we are such with that type of friendship that is generated by the shared enjoyment of something emotional and moving: The characters that I interpret on the air . . . What more can I say about myself that has not already been amply treated in the press? . . . in an almost child-like way I live and dream each of the characters that I act. I actually cry over my strange, fascinating destinies . . . With this fresh and sincere voice I would like to proclaim how loyal I am to all of you . . . it hurts me to think that I do not reach your hearts. . . . My greatest satisfaction—as a woman and as an actress—would be to offer my hand to all those who carry inside them the flame of faith in something or in someone and in those who harbor a hope: . . . Friends [*amigas*], I have closed another chapter of my confidences, and I hope that it has not reached you in vain, knowing that in Evita Duarte exists your best friend.

Eva Perón did not officially renounce the vice-presidential candidacy until 31 August. At eight o'clock that night she read the announcement, stating:

From announcement renouncing the vice-presidential candidacy, 31 August

I realized that I must not change my battle position the Perónist movement for any other place. . . . This decision comes from the most intimate part of my conscience and for that reason is totally free and has all the force of my definitive will. . . .

I do not have in these moments more than one ambition, a single and great personal ambition: that of me it shall be said . . . that there was at the side of Perón a woman who dedicated herself to carrying the hopes of the people to the President, and that the people affectionately called this woman "Evita." That is what I want to be. . . .

On 17 October I formulated my permanent vow, before my own conscience: to place myself entirely at the service of the descamisados, who are the humble and the workers. I had an almost infinite debt to pay to them [reference to the part played by the descamisados in demanding the release of Perón in 1945]. I believe I have done all that was in my power to fulfill that vow and to pay my debt.

Reference

Taylor, Julia M., Eva Perón: The Myths of a Woman (Chicago: University of Chicago Press, 1979).

FIDEL CASTRO

FULL NAME:

Fidel Castro Ruz

BORN:

13 May 1927, Mayari, Oriente Province, Cuba

Lawyer and revolutionary leader who unsuccessfully attacked Moncada Barracks in July 1953 and was imprisoned and exiled. After 1956 return to Cuba, he overthrew the Batista regime in 1959. Prime Minister in 1959. Commander in Chief of Cuban Armed Forces, 1959. President in 1976.

Castro's major works in English are: *Castro Speaks*, edited by Martin Kenner and James Petras (New York: Grove Press, 1969); *Revolutionary Struggle*, Volume I of *The Selected Works of Fidel Castro*, edited by Rolando E. Bonachea and Nelson R. Valdés (Cambridge: Cambridge University Press, 1972); and *History Will Absolve Me* (New York: Lyle Stuart, 1961). His works in Spanish include: *Presente y futuro de Cuba* (Mexico City: 1991); *Un encuentro con Fidel* (Montevideo: 1988); *Por el camino correcto: compilacion de textos (1988–1989)* (Havana: 1989). Studies of Castro include: Frank Mankiewicz and Kirby Jones, *With Fidel: A Portrait of Castro and Cuba* (Chicago: Playboy Press, 1975); Theodore Draper, *Castro's Revolution: Myths and Realities* (New York: Praeger, 1962); and Herbert Mathews, *Fidel Castro* (New York: Simon and Schuster, 1969).

Revolutionary Struggle 1947–1958

"History Will Absolve Me"

. . . In what country is the prosecutor living? Who told him that we promoted an uprising against the *constitutional powers of the state?* Two things come into view. First of all, the dictatorship oppressing the nation is not constitutional but has corrupted the legitimate constitution of the Republic. A legitimate constitution is that which emanates directly from a sovereign people. Further on I shall fully demonstrate this point, despite all the arguments to the contrary that the cowards and traitors have invested to justify the unjustifiable. Second, the article refers to *powers* in the plural, not singular, because it takes into consideration a republic ruled by a legislative power, an executive power, and a judicial power, which check and balance one another. We have incited a rebellion against a single illegitimate power that has usurped and concentrated in its hands the legislative and executive powers of the nation, thus destroying the whole system that the article of the Code we are analyzing precisely tried to protect. As to the independence of the judicial power after 10 March, I shall not say even a word, as I am in no mood for jokes. No matter how you stretch, shrink, or mend it, there is not a single comma of Article 148 applicable to the events of 26 July. Let us put it aside until such time as it may be applied to those who do incite an uprising against the Constitutional Powers of the State. I shall return later to the Code, in order to refresh the memory of the prosecutor on certain circumstances that, unfortunately, he has forgotten.

I warn you that I have just begun. If there remains in your heart a vestige of love for your country, for humanity, and for justice, then listen to me attentively. I know that I shall be silenced for many years. I know they will try to conceal the truth by every possible means. I know that there will be a conspiracy to force me into oblivion. But my voice will never be drowned; for it gathers strength within my breast when I feel most alone, and it will give my heart all the warmth that cowardly souls deny me.

I listened to the dictator on Monday, 26 July, from a shack in the mountains, when there were still eighteen of us under arms. Those who have not lived similar moments will never know the meaning of bitterness and scorn. Just as the long-cherished hopes of liberating our people came tumbling down, we saw the despot rise up over them more vicious and arrogant than ever. The flood of stupid, hateful, and repugnant lies and slanders that gushed from his mouth were only equal to the enormous flood of pure and youthful blood being spilled since the night before with his full knowledge, consent, complicity . . .

Honorable Magistrates: I am that humble citizen who one day, to no avail, presented himself before the courts to ask that the ambitious men who had violated the laws and destroyed our institutions be punished. And now, when it is I who am being accused of wanting to overthrow this illegal regime and reestablish the legitimate constitution of the Republic, I am held incommunicado for seventy-six days, not being allowed to speak to anyone, nor even to see my own son. I am taken across the city between high-caliber machine guns, and they finally bring me to this hospital to be judged secretly with all the severity of the law and to face a prosecutor who solemnly asks, with the Code in his hand, that I be sentenced to twenty-six years in prison.

You will reply that on the previous occasion the judges did not impart justice because they were prevented by force from doing so. Then, confess it: This time force again will oblige you to condemn me. The first time you could not punish the guilty; now you will have to punish the innocent—the maiden of justice twice raped by force.

How much charlatanry to justify the unjustifiable, to explain the unexplicable, and to reconcile the irreconcilable! And from there they have gone as far as to hold, as supreme reason, that might makes right. That is to say that, by hurling tanks and soldiers into the streets and taking the Presidential Palace, the Treasury Department, and other public buildings, and by aiming their weapons at the hearts of the people, they vested themselves with a lawful right to govern the people. The same argument was used by the Nazis when they occupied European nations and installed puppet governments.

I admit, because I so believe, that revolutions constitute a source of law. But the nocturnal, armed assault of 10 March can never be called a revolution. Commonly, as José Ingenieros [well-known Argentine writer and political philosopher] has said, the name *revolution* is usually given to those small disorders that dissatisfied groups provoke to take away political plums or economic advantages from the well fed, such revolutions always ending in a mere change of some men for others, in a new distribution of jobs and benefits. But that is not the criterion of the philosopher of history, nor can it be that of a cultured man. . . .

I have said all this mainly to have someone tell me whether such a political situation as the one we are facing can be termed a law-engendering revolution; whether it is legitimate or not to fight against it; and whether the courts of the Republic must be prostituted if citizens are sentenced to jail for fighting to free their country from infamy.

Cuba is suffering a cruel and ignominious despotism, and you well know that resistance to despotism is legitimate. This is a universally recognized principle, and our Constitution of 1940 consecrates it in paragraph 2 of Article 40: "Adequate resistance for the protection of previously guaranteed human rights is legitimate." But even if this right were not so consecrated in our fundamental law, it is presupposed that without this right the existence of a democratic collectivity cannot be conceived. The difference between a political and juridical constitution is established by Professor Infiesta in his book on constitutional law:

> At times constitutional principles are included in juridical constitutions, and even though they might not be so classified they would carry just the same force because of the people's consent. Such principles, for example, are those of majority rule and representation in our democracy.

The right to rebel against tyranny is one of those principles that, whether included or not in juridical constitutions, is always enforced in a democratic society. Bringing up this question before a court of justice is one of the most interesting problems of public law. Duguit [French revolutionary thinker and jurist, known as an authority on constitutional law] has said in his *Treatise on Constitutional Law* that "if the insurrection fails, there would be no tribunal that would dare to declare that there was no conspiracy or attempt against the security of the State on the garounds that the government was tyrannical and the intention to overthrow it was legitimate." But, notice that he did not say, "the tribunal should not," but that "there would be no tribunal that would dare. . . ." Speaking more clearly, we may say that there is no tribunal that would dare because there is not one with sufficient courage to do so under a tyrannical government. There is no alternative to the question; if this tribunal is a courageous one and complies with its duty, it will not dare to condemn me. . . .

A constitution, as we understand it, is the fundamental and supreme law of a nation; it defines the political structure and regulates the functioning of the organs of the state, placing a limit to its powers. It must be stable, enduring, and to a certain extent rigid. The statutes do not fill any of these requisites. They do confirm, when referring to the integration of the Republic and the principles of sovereignty, the following most shameless, cynical, and monstrous contradiction. Article 1 states, "Cuba is an independent and sovereign state, organized as a democratic Republic." Then Article 2 states, "The sovereignty resides in the people, from whom all powers are derived." But then comes Article 118, which says, "The President of the Republic shall be designated by the Council of Ministers." It is no longer the people who choose the president, but the cabinet. And who chooses the cabinet? Paragraph 13 of Article 120 reads, "The President should have the power to name and remove freely the ministers and to substitute them as the occasion demands." Who then elects whom? Is it not the classical problem of the chicken and the egg, which no one has solved yet?

One day eighteen adventurers met. The plan was to attack the Republic and get hold of its 350-million-dollar budget. Cloaked by treachery and in the shadows of the night, they achieved their purpose. "And now, what shall we do?" one of them said to the others, "You appoint me prime minister and then I will appoint you generals." When this was done, he looked aaround for twenty spineless flatterers and said to them, "I will appoint you all ministers and then you appoint me president." Thus, they appointed each other generals, ministers, president, and kept the Republic's Treasury for themselves.

It is not a question of someone usurping sovereignty once in order to appoint ministers, generals, and a new president; but rather that in some statutes one man should proclaim himself to have absolute sovereignty and also control of the life and death of every citizen as well as the very existence of the nation. Therefore, I hold it to be evident that the attitude of the Court of Constitutional and Social Guarantees is not only traitorous, vile, cowardly, and repugnant but also absurd! . . .

The right to rebel against despotism, Honorable magistrates, has been recognized since the most ancient times by men of all doctrines, ideas, and beliefs.

In the theocratic monarchies of remote antiquity, in China for instance, it was practically a constitutional principle that when an emperor governed blunderingly and despotically he was to be deposed and replaced with a virtuous prince.

The thinkers of ancient India encouraged active resistance to arbitrary authority. They justified revolution and often carried their theories into practice. One of India's spiritual guides said that "An opinion held by the majority is stronger than the king himself. A rope of many strands is strong enough to drag a lion."

The city-states of Greece and the Roman Republic not only accepted but praised the violent deaths of tyrants.

In the Middle Ages, John of Salisbury, in his work *The Book of a Statesman*, says that when a prince does not govern according to law and becomes a tyrant, his violent overthrow is legitimate and justified. He recommended that a dagger, not poison, be used against a tyrant.

St. Thomas Aquinas, in the *Summa Theologica*, rejected the doctrine of tyrannicide but nevertheless maintained the thesis that the tyrant should be deposed by the people.

Martin Luther proclaimed that when a ruler degenerates into a tyrant, violating the law, the subjects become free of all duty of obedience. His disciple, Philipp Melanchthon, maintains the right of resistance when the rulers become tyrants. Calvin, the most famous thinker of the Reformation from the point of view of political ideas, postulates that the people have the right to take up arms against any usurpation.

None other than Spanish Jesuit Juan Mariana during the period of Philip II in his book *De Rege et Regis Institution* affirms that when the ruler usurps power or when, once elected, he rules tyrannically, his assassination by a private citizen, by his own hand or availing himself of trickery, with the least disturbance possible, is legitimate.

The French writer François Hotman maintained that between the people and the government there exists a contract and that the people can rise in rebellion against the tyranny of the government when the latter violates that pact.

At the same time there appeared a widely read pamphlet entitled *Vindiciae Contra Tyrannos,* signed with the pseudonym of Stephanus Junius Brutus, which openly proclaimed that resistance to the government when it oppresses the people is legitimate and that it was the duty of honorable judges to lead the battle.

The Scotch reformers John Knox and John Poynet maintained the same point of view. The most important book of that movement, written by George Buchanan, says that if a ruler obtains power without the consent of the people or rules their destinies in an unjust and arbitrary manner, he has become a tyrant and can be overthrown, or killed as a last recourse. . . .

Already in 1649, John Milton was writing that political power resides in the people, who can name and dethrone kings and who have the duty to remove tyrants from the government.

John Locke, in his *Treatise on Government,* maintains that when the natural rights of man are violated, the people have the right and the duty to suppress or change the government. "The only remedy against force without authority is to oppose it with force."

Jean Jacques Rousseau eloquently states in his *Social Contract,*

When a people sees itself forced to obey, and obeys, it does well; as soon as it can shake off the yoke, and shakes it off, it does better, for it recovers freedom by the same right with which it was taken away. The strongest is never sufficiently strong to be the master forever if he does not transform force into right and obedience into duty. . . . Force is a physical power; I do not see how morality can be derived from its effects. To cede to force is an act of necessity, not of will; everything else is an act of prudence. In what sense can this be considered a duty?

To renounce freedom is to renounce the quality of being a man, the rights of humanity, including its duties. There is no possible reward for he who renounces all. Such renunciation is incompatible with man's nature, and to take away all freedom of self-determination is to take away all morality of the action. Finally, it is a vain and contradictory conviction to stipulate absolute authority for one side and unlimited obedience for the other.

Thomas Paine said that "A just man is more worthy of respect than a crowned ruffian."

Only reactionary writers, like that clergyman from Virginia, Jonathan Boucher, were opposed to this right of the people: "The right to revolt was a condemnable doctrine derived from Lucifer, the father of rebellion."

The Declaration of Independence of the Congress of Philadelphia, 4 July 1775, consecrated this right in a beautiful paragraph:

> We hold these truths to be self-evident; that all men are created equal; that they are endowed by their Creator with certain inalienable rights; that among these are Life, Liberty, and the Pursuit of Happiness. That to secure these rights, Governments are instituted among men, deriving their just powers from the consent of the governed, that whenever any form of government becomes destructive of these ends, it is the right of the people to alter or abolish it, and to institute new Government, laying its foundation on such principles and organizing its power in such form, as to them shall seem most likely to effect their safety and happiness.

The famous French Declaration of the Rights of Man bequeathed to coming generations the following principle:

> When the government violates the rights of the people, insurrection is for them the most sacred of rights and the most imperative of duties. . . . When one person seizes sovereignty, he should be condemned to death by free men.

I believe that I have sufficiently justified my point of view. They are stronger reasons than those which the Prosecutor brandished when requesting that I be sentenced to twenty-six years in jail. All of them favor men who fight for the freedom and happiness of the people; none of them favors those who oppress, debase, and pitilessly rob the people. That is why I have had to expound many reasons while the Prosecutor did not expound even one.

How was the Prosecutor to justify Batista's right to power, when he obtained it against the will of the people, violating by treason and by force the laws of the Republic? How was he to qualify as legitimate a regime of blood, oppression, and ignominy? How was he to call a government revolutionary, when it was composed of the most reactionary men, ideas, and methods of our public life? How was he to consider juridically valid the high treason of the court whose mission was to defend our constitution? By what right can he send to jail citizens who came to give their blood and their lives for the honor of their country? That would be a monstrous thing in the eyes of the nation and in the face of principles of true justice!

But we have one more reason on our side, a reason stronger than all the others: We are Cubans and to be a Cuban implies a duty; not to fulfill this duty is to commit a crime, to commit treason. We are proud of the history of our country. We learned it in school; as we grew up, we heard people speak of liberty, justice, rights. Early in life we were taught to look up to the deeds of our heroes and martyrs. The names Céspedes, Agramonte, Maceo, Gómez, and Martí were the first ones to be engraved in our minds. We were told that the titan Maceo had said that you do not beg for freedom, but that you win it with the edge of the sword. We were taught that for the education of the citizens in a free country, Martí had written in his *Edad de Oro*,

> The man who conforms to obeying unjust laws and permits the man who mistreats him to trample the country in which he was born is not an honest man. . . . In the world there must be a certain amount of honor, as there must be a certain amount of light. When there are many men without honor, there are always others who have in themselves the honor of many men. These are the ones who rebel with terrible force against those who rob the people of their right to be free, which is the same as robbing men of their honor. In those men there are thousands of men, a whole nation, human dignity itself.

We were taught that 10 October and 24 February are glorious dates of patriotic rejoicing because they were the dates on which the Cubans rebelled against the yoke of infamous tyrannies. We were taught to love and defend the beautiful flag of the lone star, and to sing every afternoon a hymn whose verses say that to live in chains is to live in disgrace and abject submission, and that to die for the fatherland is to live. We learned all that and we shall not ever forget it, even though today in our fatherland men are being killed and jailed for putting into practice the ideas they were taught from the cradle. We were born in a free country, which was left to us by our fathers, and we would rather the island sink into the sea than consent to be anyone's slave.

It looked as if the apostle Martí was going to die in the year of the centennial of his birth. It looked as if his memory would be extinguished forever, so great was the affront! But he lives. He has not died. His people are rebellious, his people are worthy, his people are faithful to his memory. Cubans have fallen defending his doctrines. Young men, in a magnificent gesture of reparation, have come to give their blood and to die at the side of his tomb so that he might continue to live in the hearts of his countrymen. Oh, Cuba, what would have become of you if you had let the memory of your apostle die!

I conclude my defense, but I shall not end it as all lawyers for the defense do, asking for acquittal of the defendant. I cannot ask for acquittal when my companions are already suffering in the ignominious prison on the Isle of Pines. Send me there that I may share their fate. It is conceivable that honest men should be dead or in prison when the president is a criminal and a thief!

To you, Your Honors, my sincere gratitude for having allowed me to express myself freely, without base coercion. I feel no rancor toward you. I recognize that in some aspects you have been humane, and I know that the presiding judge of this court, the man of unimpeachable backgaround that he is, cannot disguise his repugnance for the reigning state of things that forces him to dictate an unjust verdict. . . .

"Manifesto No. 1 to the People of Cuba," 8 August 1955

I live for my fatherland and for its true freedom, although I know that my life may not last long enough to enjoy the fruit of my labors and that this service must be given with the certainty and thought of receiving no reward for it.   —José Martí

My duties to the fatherland and to my convictions stand above all personal concerns; that is why I shall be free or shall perish for the redemption of my people.   —Antonio Maceo

Under this battle cry, which recalls past national rebellion, the Cuban revolutionary movement is today organized and prepared for its great task of redemption and justice.

By the express agreement of its leaders, I have been entrusted with the drafting of this first manifesto to the country and those which in the future will be published clandestinely.

In carrying out this mission, which duty imposes on me, I do not hesitate to assume the responsibility involved in signing these proclamations that will be a constant reminder to the people, an open call for revolution, and a frontal attack against the clique of criminals who trample the honor of the nation and rule its destiny counter to its history and the sovereign will of the people. And although at the present time I am absent from the soil of our nation and therefore outside the jurisdiction of the courts that issue the sentences ordered by the master, I did not hesitate to unmask the executioner when that court was judging me there, or from prison to accuse by name the dictator and his bloodthirsty generals of the Moncada Barracks' crimes in a manifesto dated 6 January 1954, or to reject amnesty with conditions attached, or again, when freed, to show the people evidence of the cruel and inhuman character of the Batista regime. What a cruel and inhuman apparatus Batista's regime has! I do not care what accusations they may make against me in the special courts! Cuba is my fatherland, and I shall never return to it or I shall return with the dignity I have pledged myself to. The bridges have been burned: Either we conquer the fatherland at any price so that we can live with dignity and honor, or we shall remain without one.

> The fatherland means something more than oppression, something more than a piece of land without freedom and without life. . . .
> (source unknown)

Stubborn fools are those who believe that a revolutionary movement can be measured by the millions available to it and not by the reason, idealism, determination, and honor of its fighters! "What matters," Martí said, "is not the number of weapons in one's hand, but the number of stars on one's forehead!" To those who ask us to abandon the revolutionary struggle and accept the crumbs of legality the regime offers, we answer, Why do you not ask Batista to abandon office first?

He is the only obstacle. It was he who used violence when all legal paths were open. He protects and safeguards the henchmen who murder and kill. He, only he, is the man who has provoked this situation of uncertainty, unrest, and ruin.

Why ask a people to renounce their rights instead of asking a lucky adventurer to abandon a power that does not belong to him? To those who impudently advise participation in partial elections as a national solution, we answer: Who is concerned with those elections? The discontent is found, not on the part of the politicians who seek posts, but in the people who seek justice. Those who believe that serious political, social, and economic problems can be solved by simply satisfying the appetites of a hundred or so miserable candidates for a few posts as mayors and representatives think very badly of Cuban citizens. What have petty politics given the country in the last fifty years? Speeches, sinecures, congas [Cuban dance. It has the connotation of irresponsibility], lies, compromises, deceit, betrayals, improper enrichment of a clique of rogues, empty talk, corruption, infamy. We do not view politics as the traditional politicians do. We are concerned not with personal benefit but with the benefit of the people whom we serve as missionaries of an ideal of redemption. Glory is worth more than triumph, and "there is only one glory for certain—that of a soul at peace with itself." Those electoral crumbs with which Batista buys his unimportant enemies should not be offered to us. The pride with which we put them aside is worth more than all of the electoral posts put together. . . .

The 26th of July Movement is formed without hatred for anyone. It is not a political party but a revolutionary movement. Its ranks are open to all Cubans who sincerely desire to see political democracy reestablished and social justice introduced in Cuba. Its leadership is collective and secret, formed by new men of strong will who are not accomplices of the past. Its structure is functional. Young and old, men and women, workers and peasants, students and professionals, can join its fighting groups, its youth cadres, its secret workers' cells, its women's organizations, its economic sections, and its undergaround distribution apparatus throughout the country, for not all can take up arms. There will never be sufficient weapons to equip each of those who wishes to give his life in the struggle, but each can participate to the extent that he can, contributing money, distributing proclamations, or leaving work in a gesture of solidarity and proletarian support when the revolutionary call to struggle comes. Above all, this must be a revolution of the people, with the blood of the people and the sweat of the people. . . .

Fidel Castro Speaks

"The Duty of a Revolutionary Is to Make the Revolution: The Second Declaration of Havana," 4 February 1962

. . . The duty of every revolutionary is to make the revolution. It is known that the revolution will triumph in America and throughout the world, but it is not for revolutionaries to sit in the doorways of their houses waiting for the corpse of imperialism to pass by. The role of Job doesn't suit a revolutionary. Each year that the liberation of America is speeded up will mean the lives of millions of children saved, millions of intelligences saved for culture, an infinite quantity of pain spared the people. Even if the Yankee imperialists prepare a bloody drama for America, they will not succeed in crushing the people's struggles, they will only arouse universal hatred against themselves. And such a drama will also mark the death of their greedy and carnivorous system. . . .

"Eulogy for Che Guevara," Plaza de la Revolución, 18 October 1967

Che was an incomparable soldier. Che was an incomparable leader. Che was, from a military point of view, extraordinarily courageous, extraordinarily aggressive. If, as a guerrilla, he had his Achilles' heel, it was this excessively aggressive quality, his absolute contempt for danger.

The enemy believes it can draw certain conclusions from his death. Che was a master of warfare! He was a virtuoso in the art of guerrilla struggle! And he showed that an infinite number of times. But he showed it especially in two extraordinary deeds. One of these was in the invasion, in which he led a column, a column pursued by thousands of enemy soldiers over flat and absolutely unknown terrain, carrying out—together with Camilo—an extraordinary military accomplishment. He also showed it in his lightning campaign in Las Villas Province, especially in the audacious attack on the city of Santa Clara, entering, with a column of barely three hundred men, a city defended by tanks, artillery, and several thousand infantry soldiers.

These two heroic deeds stamped him as an extraordinarily capable leader, as a master, as a virtuoso in the art of revolutionary war. However, now, after his heroic and glorious death, some attempt to deny the truth or value of his concepts, his guerrilla theories. '

The master may die—especially when he is a virtuoso in an art as dangerous as revolutionary struggle—but what will surely never die is the art to which he dedicated his life, the art to which he dedicated his intelligence.

What is so strange about the fact that this master died in combat? What is stranger is that he did not die in combat on one of the innumerable occasions when he risked his life during our revolutionary struggle. And many times it was necessary to take steps to keep him from losing his life in actions of minor significance.

And so it was in combat—in one of the many battles he fought— that he lost his life. We do not have sufficient evidence to enable us to make deductions about what circumstances preceded that combat, to imagine how far he may have acted in an excessively aggressive way, but—we repeat—if, as a guerrilla, he had an Achilles' heel, that Achilles' heel was his excessive daring, his complete contempt for danger.

And this is where we can hardly agree with him, since we consider that his life, his experience, his capacity as a seasoned leader, his prestige and everything his life signified were more valuable, incomparably more valuable than he himself, perhaps, believed.

His conduct may have been profoundly influenced by the idea that men have a relative value in history, the idea that causes are not defeated when men fall, that the powerful march of history cannot and will not be halted when leaders fall.

That that is true, there is no doubt about it. It shows his faith in men, his faith in ideas, his faith in examples. However—as I said a few days ago—with all our hearts we would have liked to see him as a forger of victories, to see victories forged under his leadership, since men of his experience, men of his caliber, of his really unique capacity, are not common.

We have a full understanding of the value of his example. We are absolutely convinced that many men will strive to live up to his example, that men like him will emerge from the heart of the people.

It is not easy to find a person with all the virtues that were combined in him. It is not easy for a person, spontaneously, to develop a personality like his. I would say that he is one of those men who are difficult to match and virtually impossible to surpass. But I would also say that the examples of men like him contribute to the appearance of men of the same ilk.

In Che, we not only admire the fighter, the man capable of performing great feats. And what he did, what he was doing, the very fact of his rising, with a handful of men, against the army of the ruling class—trained by Yankee advisers, sent in by Yankee imperialism, and backed by the oligarchies of all neighboring countries—in itself constitutes an extraordinary feat.

And if we search the pages of history it is likely that we will find no other case in which a leader with such a limited number of men has set about a task of such import, a case in which a leader with such a limited number of men has set out to fight against such large forces. Such proof of confidence in himself, such proof of confidence in the people, such proof of faith in men's capacity to fight, can be looked for in the pages of history—but the like of it will never be found.

And he fell.

The enemy believes it has defeated his ideas, his guerrilla concepts, his points of view on revolutionary armed struggle. And what they accomplished, by a stroke of luck, was to eliminate him physically; what they accomplished was to gain an accidental advantage that an enemy may gain in war. And we do not know to what degree that stroke of luck, that stroke of fortune, was helped along, in a battle like many others, by that characteristic of which we spoke before—his excessive aggressiveness, his absolute disdain for danger.

This also happened in our War of Independence. In a battle at Dos Rios they killed the Apostle of our Independence. In a battle at Punta Brava they killed Antonio Maceo, a veteran of hundreds of battles. Countless leaders, countless patriots of our War of Independence were killed in similar battles. And, nevertheless, that did not spell defeat for the Cuban cause.

The death of Che—as we said a few days ago—is a hard blow for the revolutionary movement, in that it deprives it, without a doubt, of its most experienced and able leader.

But those who are boasting of victory are mistaken. They are mistaken when they think that his death is the end of his ideas, the end of his tactics, the end of his guerrilla concepts, the end of his theses. For the man who fell, as a mortal man, as a man who faced bullets time and again, as a soldier, as a leader, is a thousand times more able than those who killed him by a stroke of luck.

However, how must revolutionaries face this serious setback? How must we face this loss? If Che had to express an opinion on this point, what would it be? He gave his opinion, he expressed that opinion quite clearly when he wrote in his message to the Latin American Conference of Solidarity that, if death surprised him anywhere, it would be welcome as long as his battle cry had reached a receptive ear and another hand stretched out to take up his rifle.

And his battle cry will reach not just one receptive ear, but millions of receptive ears! And not one hand but millions of hands will stretch out to take up arms!

New leaders will emerge. And the men—of the receptive ears and the outstretched hands—will need leaders who emerge from the ranks of the people, just as leaders have emerged in all revolutions.

Those hands will not have available a leader of Che's extraordinary experience and enormous ability. Those leaders will be formed in the process of struggle; those leaders will emerge from among the millions of receptive ears, from the millions of hands that will sooner or later stretch out to take up arms.

It isn't that we feel that his death will necessarily have immediate repercussions in the practical sphere of revolutionary struggle, that his death will necessarily have immediate repercussions in the practical sphere of development of the struggle. The fact is that when Che took up arms again he was not thinking of an immediate victory; he was not thinking of a speedy victory against the forces of the oligarchies and of imperialism. As an experienced fighter, he was prepared for a prolonged struggle of five, ten, fifteen, or twenty years if necessary. He was ready to fight for five, ten, fifteen, twenty years, or all his life if need be!

And within this time perspective, his death—or rather his example—will have tremendous repercussions. The force of that example will be invincible.

Those who cling to the idea of luck try in vain to deny his experience and his capacity as a leader. Che was an extraordinarily able military leader. But when we remember Che, when we think of Che, we do not think fundamentally of his military virtues. No! Warfare is a means and not an end; warfare is a tool of revolutionaries. The important thing is the revolution; the important thing is the revolutionary cause, revolutionary ideas, revolutionary objectives, revolutionary sentiments, revolutionary virtues!

And it is in that field, in the field of ideas, in the field of sentiments, in the field of revolutionary virtues, in the field of intelligence, that—apart from his military virtues—we feel the tremendous loss that his death means to the revolutionary movement.

Che has become a model of what men should be, not only for our people but also for people everywhere in Latin America. Che carried to its highest expression revolutionary stoicism, the revolutionary spirit of sacrifice, revolutionary combativeness, the revolutionary's spirit of work. Che brought the ideas of Marxism-Leninism to their freshest, purest, most revolutionary expression. No other man of our time has carried the spirit of proletarian internationalism to its highest possible level, as Che did.

And in the future, when an example of a proletarian internationalist is spoken of, when an example of a proletarian internationalist is sought, that example, high above any other, will be Che's example! National flags, prejudices, chauvinism, and egoism had disappeared from his mind and heart. And he was ready to shed his generous blood spontaneously and immediately, in behalf of any people, for the cause of any people!

And thus, his blood fell on our soil when he was wounded in several battles; and his blood was shed in Bolivia, for the redemption of the exploited and the oppressed. That blood was shed for the sake of all the exploited and all the oppressed; that blood was shed for all the peoples of America and for the people of Vietnam, because while fighting there in Bolivia, fighting against the oligarchies and imperialism, he knew that he was offering Vietnam the highest possible expression of his solidarity!

It is for this reason, comrades of the Revolution, that we must face the future with optimism. And in Che's example we will always find inspiration, inspiration in struggle, inspiration in tenacity, inspiration in intransigence toward the enemy, inspiration in internationalist sentiment!

Therefore, after tonight's impressive ceremony, after this incredible demonstration of multitudinous recognition—incredible for its magnitude, discipline, and spirit of devotion—that demonstrates that our people are a sensitive, grateful people who know how to honor the memory of the brave who die in combat, and that our people recognize those who serve them, that demonstrates the people's solidarity with the revolutionary struggle and how this people will raise aloft and maintain ever higher aloft their revolutionary banners and revolutionary principles—in these moments of remembrance let us lift our spirits with optimism in the future, with absolute optimism in the final victory of the peoples, and say to Che and to the heroes who fought and died with him: Ever onward to victory!

Patra o Muerte! Venceremos!

References

Castro, Fidel, *Revolutionary Struggle: 1947–1958*, Volume I of *The Selected Works of Fidel Castro*, edited by Rolando E. Bonachea and Nelson P. Valdés (Cambridge, MA: The MIT Press, 1972).

Castro, Fidel, *Fidel Castro Speaks*, edited by Martin Kenner and James Petras (New York: Grove Press, 1969).

AYATOLLAH KHOMEINI

FULL NAME:

Ayatollah (Ruholla Mussaui) Khomeini

BORN:

1900 in Khomein, Iran

DIED:

3 June, 1989, Teheran, Iran

Was exiled in 1964 after imprisonment. Became leader of the Iranian Revolution that overthrew the Shah in 1979. Religious and political leader who held no official government position but was supreme leader and became Fagih or religious guide as well with title of "ayatollah."

Books include many untranslated works in Farsi. His work has been translated by Hamid Algar in *Imam Khomeini, Islam and Revolution: Writings and Declarations* (London: FPI, 1985).

Books about him include: Marvin Zonis and Daniel Brumberg, *Khomeini, the Islamic Republic of Iran and the Arab World* (Cambridge: Center for Middle East Studies, Harvard University, 1987); Ervand Abrahmanian, *Khomeinism* (Berkeley: University of California Press, 1993).

Islam and the Revolution

Lecture given between 21 January and 8 February 1970

. . . "The *fuqaha* are the trustees of the prophets" is not that the *fuqaha* are trustees simply with respect to the giving of juridical opinions. For in fact the most important function of the prophets (peace be upon them all) is the establishment of a just social system through the implementation of laws and ordinances (which is naturally accompanied by the exposition and dissemination of the divine teachings and beliefs). This emerges clearly from the following Qur'anic verse: "Verily We have sent Our messengers with clear signs, and sent down with them the Book and the Balance, in order that men might live in equity" (57:25). The general purpose for the sending of prophets, then, is so that men's lives may be ordered and arranged on the basis of just social relations and true humanity may be established among men. This is possible only by establishing government and implementing laws, whether this is accomplished by the prophet himself, as was the case with the Most Noble Messenger (peace and blessings be upon him) or by the followers who come after him. . . .

Now God Almighty appointed the Most Noble Messenger (peace and blessings be upon him) head of the community and made it a duty for men to obey him: "Obey God and obey the Messenger and the holders of authority from among you" (4:59). The purpose for this was not so that we would accept and conform to whatever judgment the Prophet delivered. Conformity to the ordinances of religion is obedience to God; all activities that are conducted in accordance with divine ordinance, whether or not they are ritual worship, are a form of obedience to God. Following the Most Noble Messenger, then, is not conforming to divine ordinances; it is something else. Of course, obeying the Most Noble Messenger is, in a certain sense, to obey God; we obey the Prophet because God has commanded us to do so. But if, for example, the Prophet, in his capacity as leader and guide of Islamic society, orders everyone to join the army of Usama, so that no one has the right to hold back, it is the command of the Prophet, not the command of God. God has entrusted to him the task of government and command, and accordingly, in conformity with the interests of the Muslims, he arranges for the equipping and mobilization of the army, and appoints or dismisses governors and judges.

This being the case, the principle: "The *fuqaha* are the trustees of the prophets" means that all of the tasks entrusted to the prophets must also be fulfilled by the just *fuqaha* as a matter of duty. Justice, it is true, is a more comprehensive concept than trustworthiness, and it is possible that someone may be trustworthy with respect to financial affairs, but not just in a more general sense. However, those designated in the principle: "The *fuqaha* are the trustees of the prophets" are those who do not fail to observe any ordinances of the law and who are pure and unsullied, as is implied by the conditional statement: "as long as they do not concern themselves with the illicit desires, pleasures, and wealth of this world"—that is, as long as they do not sink into the morass of worldly ambition. If a *faqih* has as his aim the accumulation of worldly wealth, he is no longer just and cannot be the trustee of the Most Noble Messenger (upon whom be peace and blessings) and the executor of the ordinances of Islam. It is only the just *fuqaha* who may correctly implement the ordinances of Islam and firmly establish its institutions, executing the penal provisions of Islamic law and preserving the boundaries and territorial integrity of the Islamic homeland. In short, implementation of all laws relating to government devolves upon the *fuqaha*: the collection of *khums*, *zakat*, *sadaqa*, *jizya*, and *kharaj* and the expenditure of the money thus collected in accordance with the public interest; the implementation of the penal provisions of the law and the enactment of retribution (which must take place under the direct supervision of the ruler, failing which the next of kin of the murdered person has no authority to act); the guarding the frontiers; and the securing of public order.

Just as the Most Noble Messenger (peace and blessings be upon him) was entrusted with the implementation of divine ordinances and the establishment of the institutions of Islam, and just as God Almighty set him up over the Muslims as their leader and ruler, making obedience to him obligatory, so, too, the just *fuqaha* must be leaders and rulers, implementing divine ordinances and establishing the institutions of Islam.

Since Islamic government is a government of law, those acquainted with the law, or more precisely, with religion—i.e., the *fuqaha*—must supervise its functioning. It is they who supervise all executive and administrative affairs of the country, together with all planning. . . .

Law is actually the ruler; the security of all is guaranteed by the law, and law is their refuge. Muslims and the people in general are free within the limits laid down by the law; when they are acting in accordance with the provisions of the law, no one has the right to tell them, "Sit here," or "Go there." An Islamic government does not resemble states where the people are deprived of all security and everyone sits at home trembling for fear of a sudden raid or attack by the agents of the state. It was that way under Mu'awiya and similar rulers: the people had no security, and they were killed or banished, or imprisoned for lengthy periods, on the strength of an accusation or a mere suspicion, because the government was not Islamic. When an Islamic government is established, all will live with complete security under the protection of the law, and no ruler will have the right to take any step contrary to the provisions and laws of the immaculate *shari'a*.

The meaning of "trustee," then, is that the *fuqaha* execute as a trust all the affairs for which Islam has legislated—not that they simply offer legal judgments on given questions. Was that the function of the Imam? Did he merely expound the law? Was it the function of the prophets, from whom the *fuqaha* have inherited it as a trust? To offer judgment on a question of law or to expound the laws in general is, of course, one of the dimensions of *fiqh*. But Islam regards law as a tool, not as an end in itself. Law is a tool and an instrument for the establishment of justice in society, a means for man's intellectual and moral reform and his purification. Law exists to be implemented for the sake of establishing a just society that will morally and spiritually nourish refined human beings. The most significant duty of the prophets was the implementation of divine ordinances, and this necessarily involved supervision and rule.

There is a tradition of Imam Riza (upon whom be peace) in which he says approximately the following: "An upright, protecting, and trustworthy *imam* is necessary for the community in order to preserve it from decline," and then reasserts that the *fuqaha* are the trustees of the prophets. Combining the two halves of the tradition, we reach the conclusion that the *fuqaha* must be the leaders of the people in order to prevent Islam from falling into decline and its ordinances from falling into abeyance.

Indeed it is precisely because the just *fuqaha* have not had executive power in the lands inhabited by Muslims and their governance has not been established that Islam has declined and its ordinances have fallen into abeyance. The words of the Imam Riza have fulfilled themselves; experience has demonstrated their truth. . . .

"In Commemoration of the Martyrs of Tehran,"
11 October 1978

Now that forty days have passed since the death of our beloved martyrs in Tehran, after so many similar days of commemoration following massacres, and now that government by the bayonet has been officially established, we must anticipate still more such days. Now that the sinister specter of military government has added its dark shadow to the darkness of monarchy and inflicted further misery on our deprived people; now that the hands of the oppressive superpowers can be seen emerging from the sleeves of the Shah's butchers and slaughtering the dear Muslims—the superpowers that plunder our abundant resources despite the firm resolve of our people to prevent them; now that the "guardians of human rights" are peddling the wares of the "great civilization" over the heaped-up corpses of our young, now that, thanks to Carter, our people have attained the freedom and independence the Shah feels they deserve—now that all of this has happened, our country sits mourning without any protector. I am mourning here in the West, and you are mourning in the East.

As long as the criminal hands of the oil-hungry superpowers are at work in our country, the gates of happiness and freedom will remain closed to us.

My beloved ones, summon up all your strength and break open the chains of slavery! One after the other, remove the treacherous pawns of the Shah from the scene and cut off the greedy hands of those that manipulate them and their like in the Islamic countries. The way to happiness, freedom, and independence is barred by those pawns and those who manipulate them, so scatter their ranks and save the country!

According to the way Carter thinks, all the crimes, savagery, and repression the Shah practices represent efforts to establish democracy and find progressive solutions for social problems. He accuses the Iranian people of being opposed to the freedom the Shah wishes to give them—as if all the strikes and protest movements taking place all over Iran were an attempt to evade freedom! But he should realize that this kind of nonsense no longer has any effect and people have come to recognize the Shah for what he is.

Great people of Iran! The history of Iran, even world history, has never witnessed a movement like yours; it has never experienced a universal uprising like yours, noble people!

Today primary school children of seven or eight stand ready to sacrifice themselves and shed their blood for the sake of Islam and the nation; when has anything like that been seen? Our lionhearted women snatch up their infants and go to confront the machine guns and tanks of the regime; where in history has such valiant and heroic behavior by women been recorded? Today the thunderous cry of "Death to the Shah!" arises from the heart of the primary school child and the infirm old man alike, and it has blackened the days of this vile Pahlavi regime and so shattered the nerves of the Shah that he seeks to calm himself with the blood of our children and young people.

Beloved sisters and brothers! Be steadfast; do not weaken or slacken your efforts. Your path is the path of God and His elect. Your blood is being shed for the same cause as the blood of the prophets and the Imams and the righteous. You will join them, and you have no cause to grieve, therefore, but every reason for joy.

Make first your ranks, strengthen your resolve, preserve your unity of purpose, and join together with all Muslim elements, particularly those in the army. Convey my greetings to them, and tell them that those people their machine guns are killing are their brothers and sisters. Tell them not to disgrace themselves before God and man any longer in order to satisfy the passions of the Shah, but instead to accept the welcoming embrace of the people.

My dear ones! Avoid all disagreement, for disagreement is the work of the devil. Continue your sacred movement in unison for the sake of the ultimate goal, which is the overthrow of the corrupt Pahlavi regime and the liberation of the destiny and resources of our country from foreign control. Fear nothing in your pursuit of these Islamic goals, for no power can halt this great movement. You are in the right; the hand of God Almighty is with you, and it is His will that those who have been oppressed should assume leadership and become heirs to their own destiny and resources.

At the earliest opportunity, I will go to an Islamic country where I will be able to continue my activities, and God Almighty willing, I will spend the rest of my life in the path of God, which means serving you. Until now, none of the Muslim governments have issued me an invitation, but as soon as I am assured freedom of speech and expression in some Muslim country, I shall go there. For the time being, I shall remain here.

When one is in the service of Islam, the question of inconvenience—the inconvenience that may arise from being in some particular location—does not arise. What is important is duty and the voice of one's conscience. Whatever I may be able to do and whatever ultimately happens to me, I am embarrassed in front of you who are shedding your blood for the sake of freedom and Islam. What gladdens my heart in this painful place is the opportunity to serve you. I share the sorrow of those families throughout the country who, in the midst of their bereavement, are the pride of Iran, and my heart is pained by the memory of those primary school children who were recently killed by the tyrant Shah.

I declare the fortieth day after the massacre in Tehran to be a day of public mourning, and I too will be in mourning.

I ask of God Almighty that our movement may continue.

And peace be upon you, and the mercy and blessings of God.

"The First Day of God's Government," 1 April 1979

"We desired to grant Our favor to those that were oppressed in the land, and to make of them leaders and the inheritors" (Qur'an, 28:4).

I offer my sincere congratulations to the great people of Iran, who were despised and oppressed by arrogant kings throughout the history of the monarchy. God Almighty has granted us His favor and destroyed the regime of arrogance by His powerful hand, which has shown itself as the power of the oppressed. He has made our great people into leaders and exemplars for all the world's oppressed, and He has granted them their just heritage by the establishment of this Islamic Republic.

On this blessed day, the day the Islamic community assumes leadership, the day of the victory and triumph of our people, I declare the Islamic Republic of Iran. . . .

The country has been delivered from the clutches of domestic and foreign enemies, from the thieves and plunderers, and you, courageous people, are now the guardians of the Islamic Republic. It is you who must preserve this divine legacy with strength and determination and must not permit the remnants of the putrid regime of the Shah who now lie in wait, or the supporters of the international thieves and oil-bandits, to penetrate your serried ranks. You must now assume control of your own destiny and not give the opportunists any occasion to assert themselves. Relying on the divine power that is manifested in communal solidarity, take the next steps by sending virtuous, trustworthy representatives to the Constituent Assembly, so that they may revise the constitution of the Islamic Republic. Just as you voted with ardor and enthusiasm for the Islamic Republic, vote, too, for your representatives, so that the malevolent will have no excuse to object.

This day of Farvardin 12, the first day of God's government, is to be one of our foremost religious and national festivals; the people must celebrate this day and keep its remembrance alive, for it is the day on which the battlements of the twenty-five-hundred-year-old fortress of tyrannical government crumbled, a satanic power departed forever, and the government of the oppressed—which is the government of God—was established in its place.

Beloved people! Cherish and protect the rights you have attained through the blood of your young people and help to enact Islamic justice under the banner of Islam and the flag of the Qur'an. I stand ready to serve you and Islam with all the strength at my disposal during these last days of my life, and I expect the nation to devote itself similarly to guarding Islam and the Islamic Republic.

I ask the government that, fearing neither East nor West and cultivating an independent outlook and will, it purge all remnants of the tyrannical regime, which left deep traces upon all the affairs of our country. It should transform our educational and judicial systems, as well as all the ministries and government offices that are now run on

Western lines or in slavish imitation of Western models, and make them compatible to Islam, thus demonstrating to the world true social justice and true cultural, economic, and political independence.

I ask God Almighty that He grant dignity and independence to our country and the nation of Islam.

Peace be upon you, and also the blessings and mercy of God.

"The Religious Scholars Led the Revolt," 2 January 1980

It is apparent to everyone that the militant religious scholars, led by yourself, have played an important role in the Islamic Revolution. One of the factors enabling them to play this role has no doubt been the independence they have enjoyed vis-à-vis the state, an independence that was often complete. Now that, as a result of the Revolution, an Islamic government has come into being in Iran, will the religious scholars continue to function as a separate institution, or will some form of merger take place between them and the state? The latter possibility is suggested by the fact that certain religious scholars have already assumed executive functions.

You know that under the former regime, and also under the other monarchies that existed throughout Iranian history, not to mention the other forms of government in different parts of the world that contravened divine law and the principles of tauhid, the laws enforced were man-made laws, the product of the human mind. Whatever the specific form of government in each case, the laws enforced all had that common characteristic, and they were generally inspired by a desire to dominate the people. Of course, it occasionally happened that laws were put into effect for the sake of assuring order in society and the liberty of the people. But if we are looking for a government that is based on the principle of tauhid and follows divine law, it is to Islam that we must turn. If such government did exist before Islam, examples of it must be extremely rare.

The sole determining principle in a government based on tauhid is divine law, law that is the expression of divine will, not the product of the human mind. Now in the first age of Islam—an age nearer to us in time, of course, than that of the earlier prophets—such a government existed. It was at first weak and limited in scope, and then later it ruled over vast areas, but insofar as it was Islamic and did not pursue any aims other than those of Islam, its ruling principle was always divine law, or God Himself. The government was the government of God. The prophets and those who succeeded them did not introduce anything of their own devising; their sole aim was to implement divine law. In certain matters of detail, they naturally had recourse to measures of their own, but as far as fundamental matters were concerned—those aspects of government that have to exist in every country—they followed divine law. The Messenger of God (peace and blessings be upon him), who is of course our exemplar, never enacted a single judgment or executed a single law in opposition to God's decree; on the contrary, he executed God's law.

There is a great different between all the various man-made forms of government in the world, on the one hand—whatever their precise nature—and a divine government, on the other hand, which follows divine law. Governments that do not base themselves on divine law conceive of justice only in the natural realm; you will find them concerned only with the prevention of disorder and not with the moral refinement of the people. Whatever a person does in his own home is of no importance, so long as he causes no disorder in the street. In other words, people are free to do as they please at home. Divine governments, however, set themselves the task of making man into what he should be. In his unredeemed state, man is like an animal, even worse than the other animals. Left to his own devices, he will always be inferior to the animals, for he surpasses them in passion, evil, and rapacity. As originally created, man is superior to all other beings, but at the same time, his capacities for passion, anger, and other forms of evil are virtually boundless. For example, if a person acquires a house, he will begin to desire another house. If a person conquers a country, he will begin plotting to conquer another country. And if a person were to conquer the entire globe, he would begin planning the conquest of the moon or Mars. Men's passions and covetousness, then, are unlimited, and it was in order to limit men, to tame them, that the prophets were sent. If this animal that has broken its bridle is allowed to roam freely outside all recognizable bounds, if it is left to itself and no attempt is made to train it, it will desire everything for itself and be prepared to sacrifice everyone to its desires. The prophets came to tame this unbridled beast and to make it subject to certain restraints. After taming it, they showed it how to achieve the perfections that constitute its true happiness, and here it is not a question of this world and the natural realm only. In the prophets' view, the world is merely a means, a path by which to achieve a noble aim that man is himself unaware of but that is known to the prophets. They know what the final destiny of man will be if he continues in his unfettered state, and they also know how different it will be if man is tamed and follows the path leading to the noble rank of true humanity.

All the concerns that, taken together, form the objective of most governments are but a path or a means in the view of the prophets. For them, the world cannot be an objective or a point of orientation, but only a path of ascent leading to the rank of true humanity. If a person embarks on this path, he will attain true happiness. The happiness he may enjoy in this world will not be confined to it, for his ultimate goal is a world that lies beyond the present one. The prophets have seen that world, which is unknown to us because it is beyond the range of sensory perception.

So the prophets came, first, to tame the forces of anger, passion, and evil that are present in man, and then to guide him on the path of ascent to which those forces are in opposition. Unfortunately, there were many obstacles in their way and they rarely succeeded in attaining their goal. For men are inclined by their very natures to passion, anger, and evil, and even those who do wish to tame those forces within themselves face all kinds of opposition and impediment. But whatever salvation or blessing does exist in the world is the result of the exertions of the prophets. Within the limits that were set for them, and as far as the rays of their teaching extended, they were able to impose certain bounds on the evil forces present in man. Their task was extremely difficult, but whatever good does exist in the world proceeds from them. If we were to exclude the prophets from the world, it would collapse, and everyone would see what chaos would ensue. It was the prophets who were responsible for imposing some limits on man, and whatever good and blessedness exist in this world are their work. . . .

The people were ready for revolution: they were dissatisfied with their government and discontented with their lives, and—most importantly—God had brought about a spiritual transformation in them. The essence of this transformation, which still persists to some extent, is that people began to yearn for martyrdom, just as they had done in the earliest age of Islam. Look at the demonstrations that are still taking place; you will see people wearing shrouds and proclaiming their readiness for martyrdom. Mothers who have lost children come to me and ask me to pray that one or two more of their children may be martyred. Young people, both men and women, also ask me to pray that they may become martyrs. This, then, is a spiritual transformation being wrought in our people by God's will.

In addition, the whole nation was unanimous in its dissatisfaction. Muhammad Riza had done nothing to satisfy any segment of the population. He cared only for the upper echelons of the army and the security forces; he despised everyone else. He took no account of anyone: not of the civil service, nor the army (its lower ranks, that is), nor the bazaar, nor the mosque, nor the religious institution, nor the university. In fact, that was his greatest mistake: he regarded the people as nothing.

The people, then, were united in their dissatisfaction, and when the demand for an Islamic republic was raised, no one opposed it. The whole country in unison demanded the foundation of an Islamic republic and the abolition of the monarchy, and since the people were strengthened by divine support, they reached their goal despite the support and protection that were being extended to Muhammad Riza by various powers, great and small—particularly America and Britain (unfortunately, the governments of most Muslim countries adopted their attitude). . . .

Throughout the different stages of the revolution, the religious leaders played the primary role. Of course, others also took part—university professors, intellectuals, merchants, students—but it was the religious leaders who mobilized the whole people.

In every region there are three or four mosques, presided over by a religious scholar whom the people believe in. I have always advised the Iranian people not to overlook the impregnable fortress that the religious leaders provide for them, and I have particularly advised the intellectuals who might desire the independence of their country that the religious institution constitutes a great barrier to foreign domination, and its loss would leave them powerless.

If the religious scholars were eliminated from this movement, there would not have been a movement. The people do not listen to anyone else. They do not listen to the intellectuals. Political parties, unless they are Islamic, cannot gather more than a thousand or so members, and the people will not listen to them. However much the party leaders try to attract their attention, the people say to themselves, "They're talking nonsense."

It is this group alone, the religious leaders, who are capable of arousing the people and inspiring them to self-sacrifice. Your remark that they have played a great role is quite true, although of course individual religious leaders have different degrees of influence according to their status. But in proportion to the scope of his influence, each has his words heeded by those who comprise his audience. People understand that he seeks their well-being; if they follow him, they will attain true happiness, and even if they are killed, they will die martyrs.

So it was the religious leaders who mobilized the people all over Iran, and it was from the mosques that the people set out behind their preachers and leaders to participate in demonstrations.

I ask all the factions of the people—including those who regard themselves as nationalist—to protect the religious leaders. God is protecting them; the nationalists should also do so, and be careful not to lose them. You see some people today wanting to drag them into discussions in order to weaken them, but it is not in the worldly or the religious interest of these people to do so.

It is not my intention to proclaim the whole class of religious scholars free from blemish, or to say that anyone who wears a turban is a virtuous, upright, and pious person. I am not making any such claim, nor is anyone else. But those who oppose the religious scholars are not opposing the bad ones who may exist among them; they are opposing the good ones, those who have influence on the people. If their opposition were directed against evil elements among the religious scholars, their aim would be justified; such elements must be purged (I accept this, and the purge will take place at the appropriate time). But when our nation is in a state of upheaval in the aftermath of a revolution, when it is beginning successfully to confront the problems that always exist under such circumstances and that have been especially acute in our case, when it is facing the enmity of a super-power, indeed of all superpowers—it is not the time to endanger this great support of the nation, the element that is capable of mobilizing the people. It may be that we have a grievance against a particular religious leader, or objections to another, but this is not the time to pursue these matters. The problem must be solved gradually. . . .

I do not believe that Jesus held the views on this question of religion and politics that are now attributed to him. Could Jesus ever have taught people to accept oppression? All the prophets, including Jesus, were sent to root out injustice, but later, institutions arose that distorted the nature of religion. This happened also in the case of Islam; in every age, there were attempts to prevent its correct implementation.

So yes, the religious scholar will have a role in government. He does not want to be the ruler, but he does want to have a role. On this question of the presidency, there were proposals made to me, some of which even originated in the universities, that the President ought to be a religious leader, and I realized that that was because no one else would be trusted in the role. But I said, "No, the religious scholar does not wish to be President himself; he wishes instead to have a role in the presidency, a supervisory role. He will exercise this role on behalf of the people. If the government begins to misbehave, the religious scholar will stand in its way."

Now the constitution makes some provision for the principle of the governance of the faqih. In my opinion, it is deficient in this regard. The religious scholars have more prerogatives in Islam than are specified in the constitution, and the gentlemen in the Assembly of Experts stopped short of the ideal in their desire not to antagonize the intellectuals! In any event, only part of the principle of the governance of the faqih is present in the constitution, not all of it. Given the contingencies with which Islam has surrounded the operation of this principle, it cannot harm anyone. Particular attributes have been set down as necessary for the "holder of authority" (vali amr) and faqih, and they are attributes that prevent him from going astray. If he utters a single lie, or takes a single wrong step, he forfeits his claim to governance. The whole purpose of the clause in the constitution relating to the governance of the faqih is to prevent tyranny and despotism. Those who opposed the constitution said that it instituted a form of tyranny, but how can that be? Whatever we do, it is always possible that some despot will come along in the future and try to do whatever he wants, but the faqih who possesses the attributes mentioned in the constitution cannot, in the very nature of things, be a tyrant. On the contrary, he is just, not in the limited sense of social justice, but in the more rigorous and comprehensive sense that his quality of being just would be annulled if he were to utter a single lie, or cast a single glance at a woman past the degrees that are forbidden. Such a person will not act wrongly; on the contrary, he will seek to prevent others from acting wrongly. Justice, in this sense, has not been made an essential qualification for the president; it is possible that he might wish to do something wrong, in which case the faqih will prevent him. If the head of the army tries one day to go beyond his functions, the faqih has the legal right to dismiss him. The most valuable part of the entire constitution is that which relates to the governance of the faqih; those who oppose it are acting out of either ignorance or self-interest.

The religious scholars do not wish to become prime minister or president, and indeed it is not in their interest to do so. They do, however, have a role to play, a role that has always existed, even though they were pushed aside. Now God has given them the opportunity to fulfill this role as a result of the deeds wrought by our people: they rose up in revolt, and the religious scholars assumed their role. The role that they have is one of supervision, not of assuming executive positions without the proper expertise. It would make no sense, for example, for a religious leader to become the commander of a battalion if he is ignorant of military science. The expertise of the religious scholar lies in the area of Islamic law, that law which, if properly executed, secures us all our goals; and if he sees any mistake being made or any deviation from Islamic law occurring, he will move to prevent it.

This supervisory role is subject to particular conditions and principles to which we are bound. In addition, we are bound to follow the expressed wishes of the people. Once a religious leader has a role in government, he will not permit the president or the prime minister to practice oppression. Any power center that wishes to go beyond its bounds he will prevent from doing so. Any act tending toward dictatorship or the curbing of freedom he will also prevent. If the government wishes to conclude an agreement with a foreign power that brings about a relationship of dependence, the religious scholar will prevent it.

In summary, the religious leaders do not wish to be the government, but neither are they separate from the government. They do not wish to sit in the prime minister's residence and fulfill the duties of premiership, but at the same time, they will intervene to stop the prime minister if he takes a false step. The principle of the governance of the *faqih*, then, is a noble one, conducive to the welfare of the country. Once implemented, it will lead to the fulfillment of the hopes of the people.

"Lectures on Surat al-Fatiha," December 1979 to January 1980

Who can escape this temple of the self, this idol-temple that is situated within man himself? Man needs a helping hand from the world of the unseen to reach him and lead him out. It is precisely for this purpose, to lead man out of his idol-temple, that all the prophets have been sent and all the heavenly books revealed. They have enabled man to shatter the idol and begin worshiping God.

The prophets all came to make this world a divine world after it had been a satanic world, a world governed by Satan. It is Satan that is ruling us, too; we follow him, and our vain desires are a manifestation of him. As long as that great Satan that is our unredeemed soul exists within us, whatever we do will be done in egoism. We must destroy the government of Satan within us.

When we migrate to the teachings of the prophets and the *awliya*, turn our backs on egoism, we will have begun to emerge from the pit. Some will even succeed, while still in this world, in reaching a stage that is now beyond our imagination—that of nonbeing, of being effaced in God. We must desire to make this migration from egoism, and be prepared to struggle in order to migrate.

The Prophet said, "You have now returned from the lesser *jihad*; the greater *jihad* still remains as a duty for you." All forms of *jihad* that may be waged in the world depend on this greater *jihad*; if we succeed in the greater *jihad*, then all our other strivings will count as *jihad*, and if not, they will be satanic. Some who waged *jihad* may have been given simply a slavegirl as their just reward, whereas others who made the migration to God received God as their reward.

There are different categories of deeds. The deeds of the *awliya* are completely different from our deeds because of the source from which they spring. It is said of the Commander of the Faithful, for example, that a single blow struck by him during the Battle of the Ditch was better than all the deeds of worship performed by both men and jinn. Part of the explanation is, of course, that the blow he delivered that day to kill an enemy was struck during a confrontation between Islam and all the forces of kufr; if Islam had been defeated on that day, it would have been destroyed. The other part of the explanation, however, lies in his pure intention, sincerity, and absorption in God. Was this not the same Commander of the Faithful who once rose from the breast of an enemy he was about to kill, because the man spat in his face and he feared that his deed might be diminished by egoism? . . .

But we engage in worship for our own sakes. At most, if one of us is very good, he engages in worship for the sake of paradise. But take away paradise and see how many people will be left praying! One should aspire to the state of the Commander of the Faithful, who was "enamored of worship and embraced it." There is no question of paradise for him; he is unaware of it, having died, or been "overtaken by death." Since he no longer has any consciousness of the self, paradise and hell are equal in his view. His worship and praise are devoted exclusively to the Essence of God Almighty, for he has recognized God as deserving to be worshiped. This is the degree of a person who is "enamored of worship"; he worships God because He deserves to be worshiped.

This, then, is the first step: to quit your home of egoism, to take a step in the direction of God. We must awaken from our sleep, for it is only the animal dimension of our being that is now awake; the human dimension is sound asleep. . . .

Yes, we must wake up while there is still time, and embark on the straight path under the guidance of the prophets. The prophets, without a single exception, all had as their mission the reformation of man. Both justice and injustice arise from men's deeds, and the purpose of justice, therefore, is to transform the unjust into the just, the mushrik into the believer. So the person who, if left to his own devices, would have headed for the deepest pit of hellfire will listen and obey when he is shown the path he must take. . . .

Gradually, you must extricate yourself from the demands of your ego; naturally, this cannot be achieved all at once. All our worldly hopes and desires will be buried with us, and all this incessant attention to the self will work to our disadvantage. For all that can remain in the hereafter is what belongs to God: "What is with you will perish, and what is with God will remain" (16:96). Man has what is "with himself" and he also has what is "with God." What is "with himself" is all that comes from his preoccupation with himself, and it will inevitably perish. But whatever he has that relates to God, what is "with God," will remain by virtue of the divine name Eternal (Baqi).

So let us strive to extricate ourselves from the situation in which we find ourselves. Those who fight in jihad against the external enemy never fear superior numbers, for the Prophet said that he would never turn back even if all the Arabs united against him. His cause was the cause of God, and the cause of God can never be defeated, nor is there any turning back from it.

Those who engaged in jihad in the first age of Islam advanced and pushed forward without any regard for themselves or their personal desires, for they had earlier waged a jihad against their selves. Without the inner jihad, the outer jihad is impossible. Jihad is inconceivable unless a person turns his back on his own desires and the world. For what we mean here by "world" is the aggregate of man's aspirations that effectively constitute his world, not the external world of nature with the sun and the moon, which are manifestations of God. It is the world in this narrow, individual sense that prevents man from drawing near to the realm of sanctity and perfection.

May God grant us success in emerging from the pit and following the path of the prophets and the awliya, for it is they who have been "overtaken by death." And may peace be upon you.

Reference

Khomeini, Imam (Ruhollah), *Islam and the Revolution: Writings and Declarations*, translated and annotated by Hamid Algar (London: KPI, 1985).

AUTHORITARIAN
LEADERS

ABDEL NASSER

FULL NAME:

Gamal Abdel Nasser

BORN:

15 January 1918, Alexandria, Egypt

DIED:

28 September 1970, Cairo, Egypt

Army officer who overthrew regime of King Farouk. Prime Minister from 1954 to 56, then President of Egypt, 1956–70. Creator of the United Arab Republic, 1958–1961.

His writings include: *Egypt's Liberation: The Philosophy of the Revolution* (Washington, DC: Public Affairs Press, 1955). Biographies include: Robert St. John, *The Book: The Story of General Abdel Nasser* (New York: McGraw, 1960); and Mohammed Haykal, *The Cairo Documents: The Inside Story of Nasser and His Relationship with World Leaders, Rebels, and Statesmen* (Garden City, NY: Doubleday, 1973).

Speeches and Press Interviews

Speech on the occasion of the ninth anniversary of the revolution, 22 July 1961

Fellow Citizens: The tenth year of your revolution will begin in the early morning hours of tomorrow. At this hour nine years ago the revolution was still an unfulfilled plan, an aspiration in the heart, an effort at awaiting the first morning hours for realization with the rays of light to start a new era for the entire Arab nation, whose will derives from God's will.

The revolutionary vanguards ready on the night of 23 July 1952 were there in response to a popular appeal and a popular need. It is this which gives 23 July its greatest significance, its tremendous value in the history of our nation.

The success of the revolution was not due to preciseness of planning or the skill with which it was carried out.

The great success of the revolution was decided by the unanimous popular support that was extended to it from the first moment by the masses, who threw their strength behind the vanguard and brought about victory.

The revolution, in its reality, was a desperate bid by the masses who refused to be defeated by the forces of tyranny—the occupying imperialist and exploiting reactionary. It was not the vanguards that made the revolution. It was made by larger armies of a nation that wished to see its life based on a new foundation of complete liberty. . . .

No individual, Fellow Citizens, is immortal. Regardless of how valuable an individual might be to his nation, this individual can but be a page in the history of the nation. It is only the people as a whole who are immortal and eternal. It is the people who remain, who are renewed, and who are the makers of the whole history. . . .

Why did the revolution succeed?

The people and their consciousness were the strong shield of this revolution. It was the people who rose to defend the revolution and the political structure against armed aggression.

When we were exposed to armed aggression in 1956 the entire people rose to carry arms, and the Arab people in every Arab country rose against this armed aggression because they felt that the entire Arab nation had awakened. This tripartite aggression was the final attempt on the part of imperialism and reactionary elements to obstruct the new revival of the Arab nation. . . .

Speech at the Naval Academy, 27 July 1961

. . . We said this from the first day of the revolution and repeated our principles about imperialism, feudalism, and the monopolists. We spoke about the domination exercised by capital and the establishment of social equity. Have we forgotten all this? Have the people forgotten all these hopes? Have those who led the revolution forgotten all these words? Some time ago, someone was saying that the president had isolated himself, did not see the people and did not mix with anybody. I heard this. But when the president isolates himself, he does so with forethought, for a very simple reason. When, for example, I go to Alexandria, where shall I go to in Alexandria? If I am invited to dinner, I shall not be invited by foreman Mohamed or by Abdel Samie, the agricultural worker, or by a seasonal worker or by the fellah who has half a feddan planted with rice.

None of these will invite me. Those who will invite me to dinner are those persons who can afford a sumptuous dinner. Those who invite the president have a sumptuous dinner, a luxurious palace, or something of this sort. What shall I do with all this? If the president is therefore isolating, if those who carried out the revolution now isolate themselves, they do so in order that their way of thinking may remain unchanged. When one comes in contact with private opinion, one will be influenced by it. There is public opinion and private opinion, and private opinion is the opinion of the special clique or group one is with and this clique keeps pouring its opinion into one's ear until it penetrates his heart. . . .

Address at the opening of the preparatory committee of the National Congress for Popular Powers, 25 November 1961

. . . The experience of 23rd July—when I talk about this experience of the past ten years, I want us to look at the lessons that we learnt. On 23rd July it was not in our minds to govern—it was not in our minds, in any way whatsoever, to take over the government. We were expressing the people's hope in eradicating the corrupt kingdom and the rule of the palaces, the rule of the court, of foreign embassies, and the rule of the agents of imperialism. But it was not in our minds to govern. We thought that we would be able to effect the sixth principle, or the sixth aim of the revolution—the establishment of sound democratic life in the shortest possible time.

From the first day this task appeared to us to be easy, especially after the king had left and after we found ourselves free of the power or the authority of the palace.

During the first days of the revolution we asked the parties to get ready to assume power. We asked the Wafd Party to purge itself first from exploiters and then to get ready to assume power as a party that had previously represented the majority. However, we had one request, which was that when we achieve the sixth goal or when we put the sixth principle of the revolution's principles into force, i.e., the establishment of a sound democratic life, we should by no means neglect the other five goals—the goals that put to end imperialism and the agents of imperialism, feudalism, monopoly, domination of capital and the establishment of social justice, and a strong national army. We asked the parties or the Wafd Party in particular to put these goals into force. . . .

Many people say we have no theory, we would like you to give us a theory. What is the theory we are following? We answer, a socialist, democratic, cooperative society. But they persist in asking for a clearly defined theory.

I ask them, what is the object of a theory? I say that I was not asked on 23rd July to stage the revolution with a printed book including my theory. This is impossible. If we had stopped to write such a book before 23rd July, we would never have succeeded in carrying out two operations at the same time. Those who ask for a theory are greatly complicating matters. This is torture.

God Almighty gave an example in this respect, which we should follow in actual life.

In Islam, Gabriel could have come down with a printed and bound book, which he could have said was the theory, the Koran, the faith. Yet God did not act in this manner so that we may have an example to follow.

The first words in Islam were: I believe that there is no other God but Allah and that Mohammed is his Prophet. Islam began with these two sentences; it did not begin with all the contents of the Koran. Following that, Islam began to give us a lesson and an example, first among which were alcoholic drinks. It pointed out that it is partly sinful and partly beneficial but its disadvantages exceed its advantages, which means that drink is permitted.

Next the Koran said: "You shall not approach prayer while you are inebriated." This means drinks are prohibited all day long until evening prayers after which they become permissible. Then it stated that drinking and gambling, etc., should be avoided because they are of the work of the devil. This was a definite and final prohibition; but why did not the last verse come at the beginning of the Koran? It permitted drinks at first stating that they were partly beneficial and partly harmful but their harm exceeds their use. From this it showed us a way and a guide by which to work. It gave the people a chance to proceed gradually from one stage to the next until the final stage was reached and with it came the actual prohibition. The people were convinced of the need of prohibition for twenty-three years, until the Koran appeared and was completed. Why did God do this? This was done to give us a chance, a proof, and a means that would guide us in our lives.

Things have gone this way in all religions. No prophet had received his message all at once, always one step followed another. When we start to work, we must follow in this line. We must follow this way of thinking when we work. If I stayed with you on the 23rd of July, the words, I say today, I would not have known how to say then because I had not yet gone through the ten-years' experience in which I have lived. If you had asked me to give a lecture about tactics, I could have given you such a lecture or in any other military subject; if you had asked me to talk about the Revolution, about the processes of which we talk today, of course it would have been a very difficult subject for me to talk about.

But we have the six principles in which, when interpreted, we find everything: eradication of colonialism and its stooges, eradication of feudalism, eradication of monopoly and domination of capital over government, the establishment of social justice, the establishment of a strong national army, and the establishment of a democratic life.

Everything is included in these six principles. We find that these six principles when interpreted in detail give us the theory of the revolution.

Our circumstances were that the revolutionary application, our revolutionary application, may be prior to the theory. Then what is the theory? The theory is the evidence of the action.

In my opinion, they do not represent the people but something else. In our battle against imperialism, the people fought both imperialism and its stooges. We appealed for the elimination of imperialist agents and stooges from among the Egyptian traitors.

This was the first principle of the Revolution. We defined this principle directly and without any misunderstanding. We made it clear that imperialism was supported by the imperialistic stooges and that we could not destroy imperialism without destroying its stooges.

We must be frank without any equivocation. The people constitute all the groups supporting the social revolution. Placards bearing socialist mottos do not necessarily support the social revolution. Those who do not support the socialist revolution are the enemies of the people. . . .

Reference

Nasser, Gamal Abdel, *Speeches and Press Interviews*, January–December, 1961 (Cairo: Information Department, 1961).

NIKITA KHRUSHCHEV

FULL NAME:

Nikita Sergeyevich Khrushchev

BORN:

17 April 1894, Kalinovka, Ukraine, U.S.S.R.

DIED:

11 September 1971, Moscow, U.S.S.R.

Member of the Bolshevik Party in 1918. First Secretary of the Ukrainian Party organization in 1938 and member of the Politburo in 1940. Anti-Stalin speech at the Twentieth Party Congress in 1956. First Secretary of the Communist Party of the Soviet Union, 1952–1964. Premier of the U.S.S.R. from 1958 to 1964, when removed.

There is some controversy about Khrushchev's memoirs, but it is generally accepted that *Khrushchev Remembers*, edited by Edward Crankshaw and Strobe Talbott (Boston: Little Brown, 1970), is authentic. Also *Khrushchev Speaks: Selected Speeches, Articles, and Press Conferences, 1949–1961*, edited by Thomas Whitney (Ann Arbor: University of Michigan, 1963). Biographies include: Edward Crankshaw, *Khrushchev: A Biography* (London: Collins, 1966); Myron Rush, *The Rise of Khrushchev* (Washington, DC: Public Affairs Press, 1958); and Roy and Zhores Medvedev, *Khrushchev: The Years in Power* (New York: W. W. Norton, 1976).

Khrushchev Speaks

"Stalinist Friendship of Peoples—Guarantee of our Motherland's Invincibility," 21 December 1949*

All peoples of the Soviet Union and progressive mankind throughout the world are observing a precious date—the seventieth birthday of our inspired leader and teacher, Josef Vissarionovich Stalin. Millions of persons turn to Comrade Stalin with the most profound feelings of love and devotion because he, together with Lenin, formed the great party of the Bolsheviks and our socialist state, because he enriched Marxist-Leninist theory and raised it to a new, higher level. [Comrade Stalin, the brilliant leader and teacher of our party, defended and developed the Leninist theory of the victory of socialism in one country. Armed with this theory, the Bolshevik party, under the leadership of Comrade Stalin, rallied the peoples of our country and led them to the triumph of socialism. The victory of socialism found its expression in the new constitution, which has justly been called by the peoples of the U.S.S.R., the Stalinist Constitution.]

The despised enemies of our people have more than once attempted to shatter the unity of the Bolshevist Party, to ruin Soviet rule. A great service of Comrade Stalin is that he, in mortal combat with the enemies of the people—Mensheviks, Socialist Revolutionaries, Trotskyites, Zinovievites, Bukharinites, bourgeois nationalists—upheld the purity of Lenin's teaching, the unity and iron solidarity of our party's ranks. [Led by the great Stalin, the party of Bolsheviks guided with confidence the peoples of our country along the Leninist-Stalinist path to communism.]

Soviet citizens link all their achievements in the struggle for Communism, in rebuilding a multinational socialist state, with the name of the immortal Lenin, with the name of the great continuer of Lenin's cause—Comrade Stalin. Comrade Stalin's name is the banner of all victories of the Soviet people, the banner of struggle for the workers of the entire world against capitalist slavery and national oppression, for peace and socialism.

Prepared for and executed under the leadership of Lenin and Stalin, the great October Socialist Revolution shattered and destroyed forever the chains of social slavery and national oppression. Relying on Lenin's and Stalin's teaching, our party has in fact effected a proletarian solution of the national question, has established equal rights for all peoples and nations of our country and has created the great

*This article was published over the signature "N. Khrushchev" in Pravda, Dec. 21, 1949, page 9.

friendship of peoples that is a source of our motherland's strength and might. Herein lies Comrade Stalin's tremendous and invaluable service. He is the true friend and comrade-in-arms of the great Lenin.

From the very first days after the victory of the great October Socialist Revolution, Comrade Stalin, as the outstanding leader of the national policy of the Party and the Soviet state, did much to rally all nationalities of former Tsarist Russia in the formation of national Soviet republics and regions and in the creation of friendship among peoples. . . .

[. . . Lenin and Stalin stood by the cradle of every Soviet republic, defended it against threatening dangers, helped in a fatherly way its growth and strengthening. If today all the republics of the Soviet Union stand before the world in the flowering of their material and spiritual forces, for these they are obliged to the brilliant teaching of Lenin-Stalin, to the wise leadership of Comrade Stalin. That is why all the peoples of our country with unusual warmth and a feeling of filial love call the great Stalin their dear father, our great leader, and their brilliant teacher.]

After the victory of the great October Socialist Revolution a national revival of all the formerly oppressed nations of our country began. New socialist nations arose and developed on the ruins of the old order. [On the basis of the historical experiment of completing the first multinational socialist state in the world, Comrade Stalin developed and enriched Marxist-Leninist thought on the national question.] . . .

Like a careful gardener, Comrade Stalin cultivates and trains this personnel in a spirit of ardent Soviet patriotism. He has taught and is teaching them the Bolshevist mode of work and sharp implacability toward the slightest manifestation of alien bourgeois ideology, toward the ideology of bourgeois nationalism, rootless cosmopolitanism, and servility before decadent bourgeois culture. . . .

The freedom-loving peoples of the world and all progressive mankind brand with shame these betrayers and traitors. They rally still more closely around the great, invincible banner of Lenin and Stalin, for the decisive struggle against the enemies of the Soviet Union, the enemies of proletarian internationalism. [On the day of the seventieth birthday of Comrade Stalin, all the Soviet peoples give to their dear teacher and leader an oath—incessantly to strengthen the Lenin-Stalin friendship of the peoples as the indestructible basis for happiness and prosperity of our country, as the powerful guarantee of its national independence and statehood, the guarantee of the further prosperity of the Soviet Union and of every Soviet Republic entering into its composition.]

Today the peoples of the great Soviet Union and all advanced progressive mankind greet our own Comrade Stalin, inspirer of the indissoluble friendship of peoples wholeheartedly. [Glory to our dear father, our wise teacher, to the brilliant leader of the party of the Soviet people and of the workers of the entire world, Comrade Stalin!]

Speech on the Stalin Cult, delivered 25 February 1956 at a closed session of the Twentieth Congress of the Soviet Communist Party

Comrades! In the party Central Committee report to the Twentieth Congress, in a number of speeches by delegates to the Congress, and earlier at plenary sessions of the party Central Committee, quite a lot has been said about the cult of the individual leader and its harmful consequences.

After Stalin's death the party Central Committee began to implement a policy of explaining concisely and consistently that it is impermissible and foreign to the spirit of Marxism-Leninism to elevate one person, to transform him into a superman possessing supernatural characteristics akin to those of a god. Such a man supposedly knows everything, sees everything, thinks for everyone, can do anything, is infallible in his behavior.

Such a belief about a man—specifically about Stalin—was cultivated among us for many years.

The objective of the present report is not a thorough evaluation of Stalin's life and work. Concerning Stalin's merits, an entirely sufficient number of books, pamphlets, and studies had already been written in his lifetime. Stalin's role in the preparation and execution of the socialist revolution, in the civil war, and in the fight for the construction of socialism in our country is universally known. Everyone knows this well. At present we are concerned with a question that has immense importance for the Party now and in the future—[we are concerned] with how the Stalin cult gradually grew, the cult that became at a certain specific stage the source of a whole series of exceedingly serious and grave perversions of party principles, of party democracy, of revolutionary legality.

Because not all as yet realize fully the practical consequences resulting from the cult of the individual leader, the great harm caused by the violation of the principle of collective direction of the Party, and because immense and limitless power was gathered in the hands of one person, the party Central Committee considers it absolutely necessary to make the material pertaining to this matter available to the Twentieth Congress of the Communist Party of the Soviet Union.

Allow me first of all to remind you how severely the founders of

Marxism-Leninism denounced every manifestation of the cult of the individual leader. In a letter to the German political worker Wilhelm Bloss, Marx stated: "Because of my antipathy to any cult of the individual, I never made public during the existence of the International the numerous addresses from various countries that recognized my merits, and that annoyed me. I did not even reply to them, except sometimes to rebuke their authors. Engels and I first joined the secret society of Communists on the condition that everything making for superstitious worship of authority would be deleted from its statutes. [Ferdinand] Lassalle subsequently did quite the opposite."

Some time later Engels wrote: "Both Marx and I have always been against any public manifestation with regard to individuals, with the exception of cases when it had an important purpose; and we most strongly opposed such manifestations as during our lifetime concerned us personally."

The great modesty of the genius of the revolution, Vladimir Ilyich Lenin, is known. Lenin had always stressed the role of the people as the creator of history, the directing and organizing role of the Party as a living and creative organism, and also the role of the Central Committee.

Marxism does not negate the role of the leaders of the working class in directing the revolutionary liberation movement.

While ascribing great importance to the role of the leaders and organizers of the masses, Lenin at the same time mercilessly stigmatized every manifestation of the cult of the individual leader, inexorably combated "hero-and-the-crowd" views—views alien to Marxism—and countered all efforts to oppose a "hero" to the masses and to the people.

Lenin taught that the party's strength depends on its indissoluble unity with the masses, on the fact that the people—the workers, peasants, and intelligentsia—follow the Party. "Only he will win and retain power," said Lenin, "who believes in the people, who submerges himself in the fountain of the people's living creativeness." . . .

In addition to V. I. Lenin's great accomplishments for the victory of the working class and working peasants, for the victory of our party, and for the application of the ideas of scientific communism to life, his keen mind expressed itself also in that he detected in Stalin in time those negative characteristics that resulted later in grave consequences. Fearing the future destiny of the Party and of the Soviet country, V. I. Lenin gave a quite correct characterization of Stalin, pointing out that it was necessary to consider the question of transferring Stalin from the position of secretary general because Stalin was excessively rude, did not have a proper attitude toward his comrades, was capricious, and abused his power.

In December 1922, in a letter to the party Congress Vladimir Ilyich wrote: "Having become secretary general, Comrade Stalin has acquired immeasurable power in his hands, and I am not sure that he will always know how to use this power with sufficient caution."

This letter, a political document of tremendous importance, known in party history as Lenin's "testament," has been distributed among the delegates to the Twentieth Party Congress. You have read it, and will undoubtedly read it again more than once. You might reflect on Lenin's plain words, in which expression is given to Vladimir Ilyich's anxiety concerning the Party, the people, the state, and the future direction of party policy.

Vladimir Ilyich said: "Stalin is too rude, and this failing, which is quite tolerable in our midst and in relations among us Communists, becomes intolerable in the office of secretary general. Therefore, I propose to the comrades that they think of a way of removing Stalin from this post and appointing to it another person who in all other respects differs from Comrade Stalin in one advantage alone, namely, that he be more tolerant, more loyal, more courteous, and more considerate to comrades, less capricious, etc."

This document of Lenin's was made known to the delegates to the Thirteenth Party Congress, who discussed the question of transferring Stalin from the position of secretary general. The delegates declared themselves in favor of retaining Stalin in this post, hoping that he would heed Vladimir Ilyich's critical remarks and would be able to overcome the defects which caused Lenin serious anxiety.

Comrades! The party Congress should become acquainted with two new documents, which confirm Stalin's character as already outlined by Vladimir Ilyich Lenin in his "testament." These documents are a letter from Nadezhda Konstantinovna Krupskaya [Lenin's wife] to [Lev Borisovich] Kamenev, who was at that time head of the Politburo, and a personal letter from Vladimir Ilyich Lenin to Stalin.

I will now read these documents:

"Lev Borisovich! Because of a short letter that I had written in words dictated to me by Vladimir Ilyich by permission of the doctors, Stalin allowed himself yesterday an unusually rude outburst directed at me. This is not my first day in the Party. During all these thirty years I have never heard from any Comrade one word of rudeness. The cause of the Party and of Ilyich is not less dear to me than to Stalin. At present I need maximum self-control. I know better than any doctor what one can and what one cannot discuss with Ilyich, because I know what disturbs him and what does not; in any case, I know better than Stalin. I am turning to you and to Grigori [Zinoviev], as much closer comrades of V. I., and I beg you to protect me from rude interference with my private life and from vile invective and threats. I have no doubt as to what will be the unanimous decision of the Central Commission, with which Stalin sees fit to threaten me; however, I have neither the strength nor the time to waste on this foolish quarrel. And I am a living person and my nerves are strained to the utmost.—N. KRUPSKAYA."

Nadezhda Konstantinovna wrote this letter on 23 December 1922. Two and a half months later, in March 1923, Vladimir Ilyich Lenin sent Stalin the following letter:

"To Comrade Stalin.

"Copies to: Kamenev and Zinoviev.

"Dear Comrade Stalin! You permitted yourself a rude summons of my wife to the telephone and a rude reprimand of her. Despite the fact that she told you that she agreed to forget what was said, nevertheless Zinoviev and Kamenev heard about it from her. I have no intention to forget so easily what is being done against me, and I need not stress here that I consider as directed against me what is being done against my wife. I ask you, therefore, to weigh carefully whether you are agreeable to retracting your words and apologizing or whether you prefer the severance of relations between us." Sincerely, LENIN— 5 March 1923."

Comrades! I shall not comment on these documents. They speak eloquently for themselves. Since Stalin could behave in this manner during Lenin's life, could thus behave toward Nadezhda Konstantinovna Krupskaya, whom the Party knows well and values highly as a loyal friend of Lenin and as an active fighter for the cause of the Party since its creation, we can easily imagine how Stalin treated other people. These negative characteristics of his developed steadily and during the last years acquired an absolutely insufferable character.

As later events proved, Lenin's anxiety was justified: In the first period after Lenin's death Stalin still paid attention to his [Lenin's] advice, but later he began to disregard the serious admonitions of Vladimir Ilyich.

When we analyze Stalin's practice in directing the Party and the country, when we pause to consider everything Stalin perpetrated, we must be convinced that Lenin's fears were justified. Stalin's negative characteristics, which in Lenin's time were only incipient, turned during the last years into grave abuse of power by Stalin, which caused untold harm to our party.

We have to consider this matter seriously and analyze it correctly in order that we may preclude any possibility of a repetition, in any form whatever, of what took place during the life of Stalin, who absolutely did not tolerate collegiality in leadership and in work and who practiced brutal violence not only toward everything that opposed him, but also toward what seemed, to his capricious and despotic character, contrary to his concepts.

Stalin acted not through persuasion, explanation, and patient cooperation with people, but by imposing his concepts and demanding absolute submission to his opinion. Whoever opposed this concept or tried to prove his viewpoint and the correctness of his position was doomed to removal from the leading collective and to subsequent moral and physical annihilation. This was especially true during the period following the Seventeenth Party Congress, when many prominent Party leaders and rank-and-file party workers, honest and dedicated to the cause of communism, fell victim to Stalin's despotism.

We must affirm that the Party fought a serious fight against the Trotskyites, rightists, and bourgeois nationalists, and that it disarmed ideologically all the enemies of Leninism. This ideological fight was carried on successfully, and as a result the Party was strengthened and tempered. Here Stalin played a positive role.

The Party led a great political ideological struggle against those in its own ranks who proposed anti-Leninist theses, who represented a political line hostile to the Party and to the cause of socialism. This was a stubborn and a difficult fight but a necessary one, because the political line of both the Trotskyite-Zinovievite bloc and of the Bukharinites led actually toward the restoration of capitalism and capitulation to the world bourgeoisie. Let us consider for a moment what would have happened if in 1928–1929 the political line of right deviation had prevailed among us, or orientation toward "cotton-dress industrialization," or toward the kulak, etc. We would not now have a powerful heavy industry, we would not have the collective farms, we would find ourselves disarmed and weak in a capitalist encirclement.

It was for this reason that the Party led an inexorable ideological fight and explained to all party members and to the non-party masses the harm and the danger of the anti-Leninist proposals of the Trotskyite opposition and the rightist opportunists. And this great work of explaining the party line bore fruit; both the Trotskyites and the rightist opportunists were politically isolated; the overwhelming party majority supported the Leninist line and the Party was able to awaken and organize the working masses to apply the Leninist party line and to build socialism.

Worth noting is the fact that even during the progress of the furious ideological fight against the Trotskyites, the Zinovievites, the Bukharinites, and others, extreme repressive measures were not used against them. The fight was on ideological grounds. But some years later, when socialism in our country had been fundamentally established, when the exploiting classes had been generally liquidated, when the Soviet social structure had radically changed, when the social base for political movements and groups hostile to the Party had shrunk sharply, when the ideological opponents of the Party had long since been defeated politically, then the repression directed against them began.

It was precisely during this period (1935–1937–1938) that the practice of mass repression through the state apparatus was born, first against the enemies of Leninism—Trotskyites, Zinovievites, Bukharinites, long since politically defeated by the Party—and subsequently also against many honest Communists, against those party cadres that had borne the heavy burden of the civil war and the first and most difficult years of industrialization and collectivization, that had fought actively against the Trotskyites and the rightists for the Leninist party line.

Stalin originated the concept "enemy of the people." This term automatically rendered it unnecessary that the ideological errors of a man or men engaged in a controversy be proved; this term made possible the use of the most cruel repression, violating all norms of revolutionary legality, against anyone who in any way disagreed with Stalin, against those who were only suspected of hostile intent, against those who had bad reputations. This concept, "enemy of the people," actually eliminated the possibility of any kind of ideological fight or the making of one's views known on this or that issue, even issues of a practical nature. In the main, and in actuality, the only proof of guilt used, contrary to all norms of current law, was the "confession" of the accused himself; and, as subsequent investigation has proved, "confessions" were obtained through physical pressures against the accused.

This led to glaring violations of revolutionary legality, and to the fact that many entirely innocent persons, who in the past had defended the party line, became victims.

We must assert that, in regard to those persons who in their time had opposed the party line, there were often no sufficiently serious reasons for their physical annihilation. The formula "enemy of the people" was specifically introduced for the purpose of physically annihilating such individuals. . . .

An entirely different relationship with people characterized Stalin. Lenin's traits—patient work with people; stubborn and painstaking education of them; the ability to induce people to follow him without using compulsion, but rather through the ideological influence on them of the whole collective—were entirely foreign to Stalin. He [Stalin] discarded the Leninist method of persuading and educating; he abandoned the method of ideological struggle for that of administrative violence, mass repressions, and terror. He acted on an increasingly larger scale and more stubbornly through punitive organs, at the same time often violating all existing standards of morality and of Soviet law.

Arbitrary behavior by one person encouraged and permitted arbitrariness in others. Mass arrests and deportations of many thousands of people, execution without trial and without normal investigation created conditions of insecurity, fear, and even desperation.

This, of course, did not contribute toward unity of the party ranks and of all strata of the working people, but, on the contrary, brought about annihilation and the expulsion from the Party of workers who were loyal but inconvenient to Stalin.

Our party fought for the implementation of Lenin's plans for the construction of socialism. This was an ideological fight. Had Leninist principles been observed during the course of this fight, had the Party's devotion to principles been skillfully combined with a keen and solicitous concern for people, had they not been repelled and wasted, but rather drawn to our side, we certainly would not have had such a brutal violation of revolutionary legality and many thousands of people would not have fallen victim to the method of terror. Extraordinary methods would then have been resorted to only against those people who had in fact committed criminal acts against the Soviet system. . . .

Lenin used severe methods only in the most necessary cases, when the exploiting classes were still in existence and were vigorously opposing the revolution, when the struggle for survival was decidedly assuming the sharpest forms, even including a civil war.

Stalin, on the other hand, used extreme methods and mass repressions at a time when the revolution was already victorious, when the Soviet state was strengthened, when the exploiting classes were already liquidated and socialist relations were rooted solidly in all phases of national economy, when our party was politically consolidated and had strengthened itself both numerically and ideologically. It is clear that here Stalin showed in a whole series of cases his intolerance, his brutality, and his abuse of power. Instead of proving his political correctness and mobilizing the masses, he often chose the path of repression and physical annihilation, not only against actual enemies, but also against individuals who had not committed any crimes against the Party and the Soviet government. Here we see no wisdom but only a demonstration of the brutal force that had once so alarmed V. I. Lenin.

Lately, especially after the unmasking of the Beria gang, the Central Committee has looked into a series of cases fabricated by this gang. This disclosed a very ugly picture of brutal willfulness connected with the incorrect behavior of Stalin. As facts prove, Stalin, using his unlimited power, allowed himself many abuses. He acted in the name of the

Central Committee, not asking for the opinion of the Committee members or even of the members of the Central Committee's Politburo; often he did not inform them about his personal decisions concerning very important party and government matters.

In considering the question of the cult of the individual leader, we must first of all show everyone what harm this caused to the interests of our party.

Vladimir Ilyich Lenin had always stressed the Party's role and importance in directing the socialist government of workers and peasants; he saw in this the chief precondition for successfully building socialism in our country. Pointing to the great responsibility of the Bolshevist Party, as the ruling party in the Soviet state, Lenin called for the most meticulous observance of all norms of party life; he called for the realization of the principles of collegiality in the direction of the Party and the state.

Collegiality of leadership flows from the very nature of our party, a party built on the principles of democratic centralism. "This means," said Lenin, "that all party business is accomplished by all the party members—directly or through representatives—who, without any exceptions, are subject to the same rules; in addition, all administrative members, all directing collegiums, all holders of party positions are elected, are accountable for their activities, and are subject to recall." . . .

It is very characteristic that Lenin addressed to the party Congress, as the highest party body, his last articles, letters, and remarks. During the period between Congresses, the party Central Committee, acting as the most authoritative directing collective, meticulously observed the principles of the Party and carried out its policy.

So it was during Lenin's lifetime.

Were our party's sacred Leninist principles observed after the death of Vladimir Ilyich?

During the first few years after Lenin's death party Congresses and Central Committee plenary sessions took place more or less regularly, but later, when Stalin began increasingly to abuse his power, these principles were brutally violated. This was especially evident during the last fifteen years of his life. Was it a normal situation when thirteen years elapsed between the Eighteenth and Nineteenth Party Congresses, years during which our party and our country experienced so many important events? These events demanded categorically that the Party should have adopted decisions pertaining to the country's defense during the patriotic war [World War II] and to peacetime construction after the war. Even after the end of the war, a Congress was not convened for more than seven years.

Central Committee plenary sessions were hardly ever called. Suffice it to mention that during all the years of the patriotic war not a single Central Committee plenary session took place. It is true that there was an attempt to call a Central Committee plenary session in October 1941, when Central Committee members from the whole country were called to Moscow. They waited two days for the opening of the plenary session, but in vain. Stalin did not even want to meet and to talk to the Central Committee members. This fact shows how demoralized Stalin was in the first months of the war and how haughtily and disdainfully he treated the Central Committee members.

In practice Stalin ignored the norms of party life and trampled on the Leninist principle of collective party leadership. . . .

The majority of the Central Committee members and candidates elected at the Seventeenth Congress and arrested in 1937–1938 were expelled from the Party illegally through gross violation of the party statutes, since the question of their expulsion was never studied at a Central Committee plenary session.

Now when the cases of some of these so-called "spies" and "saboteurs" were examined it was found that all their cases were fabricated. Confessions of guilt of many arrested and charged with enemy activity were gained with the help of cruel and inhuman tortures.

At the same time Stalin, as we have been informed by members of the Politburo of that time, did not show them the statements of many accused political activists who retracted their confessions before the military tribunal and asked for an objective examination of their cases. There were many such declarations, and Stalin doubtless knew of them. . . .

Facts prove that many abuses were committed on Stalin's orders without reckoning with any norms of party and Soviet legality. Stalin was a very distrustful man, sickly suspicious; we knew this from our work with him. He could look at a man and say: "Why are your eyes so shifty today?" or "Why are you turning so much today and avoiding looking me directly in the eyes?" The sickly suspicion created in him a general distrust even toward eminent party workers whom he had known for years. Everywhere and in everything he saw "enemies," "double-dealers," and "spies."

Possessing unlimited power, he indulged in great willfulness and strangled a person morally and physically. A situation was created in which one could not express one's own will.

When Stalin said that one or another should be arrested, it was necessary to accept on faith that he was an "enemy of the people." Meanwhile, Beria's gang, which ran the organs of state security, outdid itself in proving the guilt of the arrested and the truth of materials that it had falsified. And what proofs were offered? The confessions of the arrested, and the investigative judges accepted these "confessions." And how is it possible that a person confesses to crimes that he has not committed? Only in one way—because of application of physical methods of pressuring him, tortures, bringing him to a state of unconsciousness, depriving him of his judgment, taking away his human dignity. In this manner were "confessions" acquired. . . .

Comrades, the cult of the individual acquired such monstrous proportions chiefly because Stalin himself, using all conceivable methods, supported the glorification of his own person. This is confirmed by numerous facts. One of the most characteristic examples of Stalin's self-glorification and of his lack of even elementary modesty is the edition of his *Short Biography*, which was published in 1948.

This book is an expression of the most dissolute flattery, an example of making a man into a godhead, of transforming him into an infallible sage, "the greatest leader," "sublime strategist of all times and nations." Finally, no other words could be found with which to exalt Stalin to the heavens.

We need not give here examples of the loathsome adulation filling this book. All we need to add is that they all were approved and edited by Stalin personally and some of them were added in his own handwriting to the draft text of the book.

What did Stalin consider essential to write into this book? Did he want to cool the ardor of his flatterers who were composing his *Short Biography*? No! He marked the very places where he thought that the praise of his services was insufficient.

Here are some examples characterizing Stalin's activity, added in Stalin's own hand:

"In this fight against the skeptics and capitulators, the Trotskyites, Zinovievites, Bukharinites, and Kamenevites, there was definitely welded together, after Lenin's death, that leading core of the Party . . . that upheld the great banner of Lenin, rallied the Party behind Lenin's behests, and brought the Soviet people onto the broad road of industrializing the country and collectivizing the rural economy. The leader of this core and the guiding force of the Party and the state was Comrade Stalin."

Thus writes Stalin himself! Then he adds:

"Although he performed his task of leader of the Party and the people with consummate skill and enjoyed the unreserved support of the entire Soviet people, Stalin never allowed his work to be marred by the slightest hint of vanity, conceit, or self-adulation."

Where and when could a leader so praise himself? Is this worthy of a leader of the Marxist-Leninist type? No. It was precisely against this that Marx and Engels took such a strong position. This was always sharply condemned by Vladimir Ilyich Lenin, too. . . .

And when Stalin himself asserts that he himself wrote the *History of the Communist Party of the Soviet Union (Short Course)*, this calls at the least for amazement. Can a Marxist-Leninist write about himself thus, praising his own person to the heavens?

Or let us take the matter of the Stalin Prizes. Not even the Tsars created prizes that they named after themselves.

Stalin recognized as the best a text of the national anthem of the Soviet Union that contains not a word about the Communist Party; it contains, however, the following unprecedented praise of Stalin: "Stalin brought us up in loyalty to the people/He inspired us to great labors and feats."

In these lines of the anthem the whole educational, directing, and inspirational activity of the great Leninist Party is ascribed to Stalin. This is, of course, a clear deviation from Marxism-Leninism, a clear debasing and belittling of the role of the Party. We should add for your information that the Presidium of the Central Committee has already adopted a decision concerning the composition of a new text of the anthem that will reflect the role of the people and the role of the Party. . . .

Comrades! The cult of the individual leader caused the employment of faulty principles in party work and in economic activity; it brought about gross violation of inner-party and Soviet democracy, sterile administration by fiat, deviations of all sorts, covering up of shortcomings and varnishing of reality. Our country gave birth to many flatterers and specialists in false optimism and deceit.

We should also not forget that due to numerous arrests of party, Soviet, and economic leaders, many workers began to work uncertainly, showed overcautiousness, feared everything that was new, feared their own shadows, and began to show less initiative in their work. . . .

In the recent years when we managed to free ourselves of the harmful practice of the cult of the individual leader and took several appropriate steps in the sphere of domestic and foreign policies, everyone saw how activity grew before their very eyes, how favorably all this influenced the development of the economy and of culture.

Some comrades may ask us: Where were the members of the Politburo of the Central Committee? Why did they not assert themselves against the cult of the individual leader in time? Why is this being done only now?

First of all we have to consider the fact that the members of the Politburo viewed these matters in a different way at different times. Initially, many of them backed Stalin actively because Stalin was one of the strongest Marxists and his logic, his strength, and his will greatly influenced the cadres and party work.

It is known that Stalin, after Lenin's death, especially during the first years, fought actively for Leninism against the foes of Leninist theory and against those who deviated. Basing itself on Leninist theory, the Party, headed by its Central Committee, started on a great scale the work of socialist industrialization of the country, agricultural collectivization, and the cultural revolution.

At that time Stalin gained great popularity, sympathy, and support. The Party had to fight those who attempted to lead the country away from the correct Leninist path; it had to fight Trotskyites, Zinovievites and rightists, and the bourgeois nationalists. This fight was indispensable. Later, however, Stalin, abusing his power more and more, began to fight eminent party and government leaders and to use terroristic methods against honest Soviet people. As we have already shown, Stalin thus treated such eminent party and government leaders as Kossior, Rudzutak, Eikhe, Postyshev, and many others.

Attempts to oppose groundless suspicions and charges resulted in the opponent falling victim of the repression. This characterized the fall of Comrade Postyshev.

In one of his speeches Stalin expressed his dissatisfaction with Postyshev and asked him, "What are you actually?"

Postyshev answered clearly, "I am a Bolshevik, Comrade Stalin, a Bolshevik."

This assertion was at first considered to show a lack of respect for Stalin; later it was considered a harmful act, and consequently resulted in Postyshev's annihilation and in his being branded without reason as an "enemy of the people."

In the situation that then prevailed I talked with Nikolai Alexandrovich Bulganin. Once when we two were traveling in a car, he said: "It has happened sometimes that a man goes to Stalin by invitation, as a friend. And when he sits with Stalin, he does not know where he will be sent next, home or to jail."

It is clear that such conditions put every member of the Politburo in a very difficult situation. And when we also consider the fact that in the last years Central Committee plenary sessions were not convened and that the sessions of the Politburo occurred only occasionally, from time to time, then we shall understand how difficult it was for any member of the Politburo to take a stand against one or another unjust or improper procedure, against serious errors and shortcomings in the practice of leadership. . . .

Comrades! In order not to repeat errors of the past, the Central Committee has declared itself resolutely against the cult of the individual leader. We consider that Stalin was excessively extolled. However, in the past Stalin undoubtedly performed great services to the Party, to the working class, and to the international workers' movement.

This question is complicated by the fact that all that we have just discussed was done during Stalin's life, under his leadership, and with his concurrence; here Stalin was convinced that it was necessary for the defense of the interests of the working classes against the plotting of the enemies and against the attack of the imperialist camp. He saw this from the position of the interests of the working class, the interests of the working people, the interests of the victory of socialism and communism. We cannot say that these were the deeds of a giddy despot. He considered that this should be done in the interests of the Party, of the working masses, in the name of defense of the revolution's gains. In this lies the whole tragedy!

Comrades! Lenin often stressed that modesty is an absolutely integral part of a real Bolshevik. Lenin himself was the living personification of the greatest modesty. We cannot say that we have been following this Leninist example in all respects. Suffice it to point out that we have called many cities, factories and industrial enterprises, collective and state farms, Soviet institutions, and cultural institutions after the private names—as if they were the private property, if I may express it so—of various government or party leaders who were still active and in good health. Many of us participated in the act of assigning our names to various cities, districts, factories, and collective farms. We must correct this.

But this should be done calmly and slowly. The Central Committee will discuss this matter and consider it carefully to prevent errors and excesses. I can remember how the Ukraine learned about Kossior's arrest. The Kiev radio used to start its programs thus: "This is the Radio Station [named for] Kossior." When one day the programs began without naming Kossior, everyone was quite certain that something had happened to Kossior, that he probably had been arrested.

Thus, if today we begin to remove the signs everywhere and to change names, people will think that the comrades in whose honor the given enterprises, collective farms, or cities are named also met some bad fate and that they have also been arrested.

How is the prestige and importance of this or that leader judged? By the number of cities, industrial enterprises, factories, collective and state farms that bear his name. Is it not time we ended this "private property" and "nationalized" the factories, the industrial enterprises, the collective and state farms? This will benefit our cause. After all, the cult of the individual leader is manifested also in this way.

We should consider the question of the cult of the individual leader quite seriously. We cannot let this matter get out of the Party, especially not to the press. It is for this reason that we are considering it here at a closed Congress session. We should know the limits; we should not give ammunition to the enemy; we should not wash our dirty linen before their eyes. I think that the delegates to the Congress will understand and assess all these proposals properly.

Comrades! We must resolutely abolish the cult of the individual leader once and for all; we must draw the proper conclusions concerning both ideological-theoretical and practical work.

It is necessary for this purpose:

First, in a Bolshevist manner to condemn and to eradicate the cult of the individual leader as alien to Marxism-Leninism and not consonant with the principles of party leadership and the norms of party life, and to fight inexorably all attempts at bringing back this practice in one form or another.

To return to and actually practice in all our ideological work the very important Marxist-Leninist theses about the people as the maker of history and the creator of all mankind's material and spiritual benefits, about the decisive role of the Marxist party in the revolutionary struggle to change society, about the victory of communism.

In this connection we shall be obliged to do much to examine critically from the Marxist-Leninist viewpoint and to correct the widespread, erroneous views connected with the cult of the individual leader in the spheres of history, philosophy, economics, and other sciences, as well as in literature and the fine arts. It is especially necessary that in the immediate future we compile a serious textbook of the history of our party, edited in accordance with scientific Marxist objectivism, a textbook of the history of Soviet society, a book pertaining to the events of the civil war and the great patriotic war.

Secondly, to continue systematically and consistently the work done by the Party Central Committee during the past years, work characterized by scrupulous observance—in all party organizations, from bottom to top—of the Leninist principles of party leadership; characterized above all by the main principle, collective leadership; characterized by observance of the norms of party life described in the statutes of our Party; and, finally, characterized by wide practice of criticism and self-criticism.

Thirdly, to restore completely the Leninist principles of Soviet, socialist democracy expressed in the constitution of the Soviet Union; to fight willfulness of individuals abusing their power. The evil caused by acts violating revolutionary socialist legality that accumulated over a long period as a result of the negative influence of the cult of the individual leader must be completely corrected.

Comrades! The Twentieth Congress of the Communist Party of the Soviet Union has manifested with new strength the unshakable unity of our party, its cohesiveness around the Central Committee, its resolute will to accomplish the great task of building communism. And the fact that we present in all their ramifications the basic problems of overcoming the cult of the individual leader, a cult alien to Marxism-Leninism, as well as the problem of liquidating its burdensome consequences, is evidence of the great moral and political strength of our Party.

We are absolutely certain that our Party, armed with the historic resolutions of the Twentieth Congress, will lead the Soviet people along the Leninist path to new successes, to new victories.

Long live the victorious banner of our Pary—Leninism!

Reference

Khrushchev, Nikita, *Khrushchev Speaks: Selected Speeches, Articles, and Press Conferences, 1949–1961*, edited by Thomas Whitney (Ann Arbor: University of Michigan Press, 1963).

MIKHAIL GORBACHEV

FULL NAME:

Mikhail Sergeyevich Gorbachev

BORN:

21 March 1931, Privol'mae, Russia, U.S.S.R.

Party official careerist. General Secretary of the Communist Party of the Soviet Union, 1985–1991. Chairman of the Supreme Soviet of the U.S.S.R., 1988–March 1990. President of the U.S.S.R., 1990–1991.

Publications include: *A Time for Peace* (New York: Richard and Steirman, 1985); *Toward A Better World* (New York: Richardson and Steirman, 1987); *Perestroika: New Thinking for Our Country and the World* (New York: Harper and Row, 1987); and *Speeches and Writings* (New York: Pergamon, 1987). Biographies include: Martin Lawrence, *Breaking with History: The Gorbachev Revolution* (Toronto: Doubleday, 1989); Zhores Medvedev, *Gorbachev* (Oxford, UK: Blackwell, 1986); and Stephen White, *Gorbachev and After* (New York: Cambridge University Press, 1992).

October and Perestroika

Report of the CPSU Central Committee on the occasion of the seventieth anniversary of the October Revolution, 2 November 1987

It is essential to assess the past with a sense of historical responsibility and on the basis of the historical truth . . . We need truthful assessments . . . especially now with the restructuring in full swing. We need them not to settle political scores or, as they say, to let off steam, but to pay due credit to all the heroic things in the past, and to draw lessons from mistakes and miscalculations.

And so, about the 1920s and the 1930s after Lenin. Although the Party and society had Lenin's conception of building socialism and Lenin's works of the post-revolution period to go by, the search for the way was not at all simple; it was marked by keen ideological struggle and political discussions. In their center were the basic problems of society's development, and above all the question of whether socialism could be built in our country. . . .

To understand the situation of those years it must be borne in mind that the administrative command system, which had begun to take shape in the process of industrialization and which had received a fresh impetus during collectivization, had told on the whole sociopolitical life of the country. Once established in the economy, it had spread to its superstructure, restricting the development of the democratic potential of socialism and holding back the progress of socialist democracy.

Quite obviously, it was the absence of a proper level of democratization in Soviet society that made possible the personality cult, the violations of legality, the wanton repressive measures of the thirties. Putting things bluntly, those were real crimes stemming from an abuse of power. Many thousands of people inside and outside the Party were subjected to wholesale repression. Such, comrades, is the bitter truth. Serious damage was done to the cause of socialism and to the authority of the Party. And we must state this bluntly. This is necessary to assert Lenin's ideal of socialism once and for all.

There is now much discussion about the role of Stalin in our history. His was an extremely contradictory personality. To remain faithful to historical truth we must see both Stalin's incontestable contribution to the struggle for socialism, to the defense of its gains, and the gross political errors, and the abuses committed by him and by those around him, for which our people paid a heavy price and which had grave consequences for the life of our society. It is sometimes said that

Stalin did not know about instances of lawlessness. Documents at our disposal show that this is not so. The guilt of Stalin and his immediate entourage before the Party and the people for the wholesale repressive measures and acts of lawlessness is enormous and unforgivable. This is a lesson for all generations.

Contrary to the assertions of our ideological opponents, the personality cult was certainly not inevitable. It was alien to the nature of socialism, represented a departure from its fundamental principles, and therefore, has no justification. At its Twentieth and Twenty-second Congresses the Party severely condemned the Stalin cult itself and its consequences. We now know that the political accusations and repressive measures against a number of party leaders and statesmen, against many Communists and non-party people, against economic executives and military men, against scientists and cultural personalities were a result of deliberate falsification.

The Politburo of the Central Committee has set up a commission for comprehensively examining new and already known facts and documents pertaining to these matters. Appropriate decisions will be taken on the basis of the commission's findings.

In drawing up a general balance sheet of the period of the twenties and thirties after Lenin, we can say that we have covered a difficult road, replete with contradictions and complexities, but a truly heroic one. Neither gross errors, nor departures from the principles of socialism could divert our people, our country from the road it embarked upon by the choice it made in 1917. The momentum of the October Revolution was too great! The ideas of socialism that had gripped the masses were too strong! The people felt themselves involved in a great effort and began enjoying the fruits of their work. Their patriotism acquired a new, socialist meaning.

It may be said with confidence: the years of the great patriotic war are one of the most glorious and heroic pages in the history of the Party, pages inscribed by the courage and valor, by the supreme dedication and self-sacrifice of millions of Communists. The war showed that the Soviet people, the Party, socialism, and the October Revolution are inseparable and that nothing on earth can shatter this unity.

Socialism did not just stand fast and did not simply achieve victory. It emerged from this most terrible and destructive of wars stronger morally and politically, having enhanced its authority and influence through the world.

It was the heroism of everyday work in those difficult postwar years that was the source of our achievements, of economic, scientific, and technical progress, of the harnessing of atomic energy, of the launching of the first spaceships, and of the growth of the people's economic and cultural standards.

But during this very same time—a time of new exploits by the people in the name of socialism—a contradiction between what our society had become and the old methods of leadership was making itself felt ever more appreciably. Abuses of power and violations of socialist legality continued. The "Leningrad case" and the "doctors' case" were fabricated. In short, there was a deficit of genuine respect for the people. People were devotedly working, studying, seeking new knowledge, accepting difficulties and shortages, but sensing that alarm and hope were building up in society. And all this gripped the public's consciousness soon after Stalin's death.

In the middle of the fifties, especially after the Twentieth Congress of the Communist Party, a wind of change swept the country. The people's spirits rose, they took heart, became bolder and more confident. It required no small courage of the Party and its leadership headed by Nikita Khrushchev to criticize the personality cult and its consequences, and to reestablish socialist legality. The old stereotypes in domestic and foreign policy began to crumble. Attempts were made to break down the command-bureaucratic methods of administration established in the thirties and the forties, to make socialism more dynamic, to emphasize humanitarian ideals and values, and to revive the creative spirit of Leninism in theory and practice.

The desire to change the priorities of economic development, to bring into play incentives related to a personal interest in work results keynoted the decisions of the September 1953 and July 1955 plenary meetings of the party Central Committee. More attention began to be devoted to the development of agriculture, housing, the light industry, the sphere of consumption, and to everything related to satisfying human needs.

In short, there were changes for the better—in Soviet society and in international relations. However, no small number of subjectivist errors were committed, and they handicapped socialism's advance to a new stage, moreover doing much to discredit progressive initiatives. The fact is that fundamentally new problems of domestic and foreign policies and of party development were often being solved by voluntaristic methods, with the aid of the old political and economic mechanism. But the failures of the reforms undertaken in that period were mainly due to the fact that they were not backed up by a broad development of democratization processes.

At the October 1964 plenary meeting of the party Central Committee there was a change of the leadership of the Party and the country, and decisions were taken to overcome voluntaristic tendencies and distortions in domestic and foreign policies. The Party sought to achieve a certain stabilization in policy, and to give it realistic features and thoroughness.

The March and September 1965 plenary meetings of the party Central Committee formulated new approaches to economic management. An economic reform and big programs for developing new areas and promoting the productive forces were worked out and began to be put into effect. In the first few years this changed the situation in the country for the better. The economic and scientific potential was increasing, the defense capacity was being strengthened, and the standard of living was rising. Many foreign policy moves enhanced the international prestige of our state. Strategic parity with the U.S.A. was achieved.

The country had at its disposal extensive resources for further accelerating its development. But to utilize these resources and put them to work, cardinal new changes were needed to society and, of course, the corresponding political will. There was a shortage of both. And even much of what had been decided remained on paper, was left suspended in midair. The pace of our development was substantially retarded.

At the April 1985 plenary meeting of its Central Committee and at its Twenty-seventh Congress the Party frankly identified the causes of the situation that had arisen, laid bare the mechanism retarding our development, and gave it a fundamental assessment.

It was stated that in the latter years of the life and activities of Leonid Brezhnev the search for ways of further advancement had been largely hampered by an addiction to habitual formulas and schemes that did not reflect the new realities. The gap between word and deed had widened. Negative processes in the economy were gathering momentum and had, in effect, created a pre-crisis situation. Many aberrations had arisen in the social, spiritual, and moral spheres, and they were distorting and deforming the principles of socialist justice, undermining the people's faith in it, and giving rise to social alienation and immorality in various forms. The growing discrepancy between the lofty principles of socialism and the everyday realities of life was becoming intolerable.

Perestroika implies not only eliminating the stagnation and conservatism of the preceding period and correcting the mistakes committed, but also overcoming historically limited, outdated features of social organization and work methods. It implies imparting to socialism the most contemporary forms, corresponding to the conditions and needs of the scientific and technological revolution, and to the intellectual progress of Soviet society. This is a relatively lengthy process of the revolutionary renewal of society, a process that has its own logic and stages.

The purpose of perestroika is the full theoretical and practical reestablishment of Lenin's conception of socialism, in which indisputable priority belongs to the working man with his ideals and interests, to humanitarian values in the economy, in social and political relations, and in culture.

Our hope of achieving revolutionary purification and renewal requires tapping the enormous social potentialities of socialism by invigorating the individual, the human factor. As a result of perestroika socialism can and must make full use of its potentialities as a truly humanitarian system serving and elevating man. This is a society for people, for the flourishing of their creative work, well-being, health, physical and spiritual development, a society where man feels he is the full-fledged master and is indeed that.

Two key problems of the development of society determine the fate of perestroika. These are the democratization of all social life and a radical economic reform.

Today we can say that we are entering a new stage of perestroika.

The difficulty of the forthcoming period also lies in the fact that the transformations will come to affect the interests of ever greater masses of people, social groups and strata, and of all cadres. We are confident that widespread support of perestroika by the people and a profound understanding of the need for the changes, for the vigorous and unflagging pursuit of perestroika despite the difficulties arising in its course will continue to shape the situation in our country.

But it would be a mistake to take no notice of a certain increase in the resistance of the conservative forces that see perestroika simply as a threat to their selfish interests and objectives. This resistance can be felt not only at management level but also in work collectives.

We should learn to spot, expose, and neutralize the maneuvers of the opponents of perestroika: those who act to impede our advance and trip us up, who gloat over our difficulties and setbacks, who try to drag us back into the past. Nor should we succumb to the pressure of the overly zealous and impatient: those who refuse to accept the objective logic of perestroika, who voice their disappointment with what they regard as a slow rate of change, who claim that this change does not yield the necessary results fast enough. It should be clear that one cannot leap over essential stages and try to accomplish everything at one go. . . .

The grandeur and novelty of our time is determined by the people's increasingly obvious and open presence in the foreground of history. Their present positions are such that they must be heeded immediately rather than in the long run. The new truth thereby brought into sharp focus is that the constant need to make a choice is becoming increasingly characteristic of historical advancement on the threshold of the twenty-first century. And the right choice depends on the extent to which the interests and aspirations of millions, of hundreds of millions of people are heeded.

Hence the politicians' responsibility. For policy can only be effective if the novelty of the time is taken into account: today the human factor figures on the political plane not as a remote and more or less spontaneous side effect of the life, activity, and intentions of the masses. It directly invades world affairs. Unless this is realized, in other words, unless a new thinking, one based on current realities and the people's will, is adopted, politics turn into an unpredictable improvisation posing a risk both to one's own country and to other nations. Such politics have no lasting support.

The socialist system, the quests and experience it has tested in practice are of importance to the whole of mankind. It has offered to the world its own answers to the main questions of human existence, and confirmed its humanitarian and collectivist values centered on the working man.

The socialist world appears before us in all its national and social variety. This is good and useful. We have become convinced that unity does not mean identity and uniformity. We have also become convinced that there is no model of socialism to be emulated by everyone, nor can there be any.

We can see today that humanity is not really doomed to always live in the way it did before October 1917. Socialism has evolved into a powerful growing and developing reality. It is the October Revolution and socialism that show humankind the road to the future and identify the new values of truly human relations:

Collectivism instead of egoism.

Freedom and equality instead of exploitation and oppression.

Toward a Better World

Political report of the CPSU Central Committee to the Twenty-seventh Congress of the Communist Party of the Soviet Union, 25 February 1986

Comrades,

The magnitude and novelty of what we have to do make exceptionally high demands on the character of the political, ideological, and organizational work conducted by the CPSU, which today has more than nineteen million members welded together by unity of purpose, will, and discipline.

The Party's strength is that it has a feel for the time, that it feels the pulse of life, and always works among the people. Whenever the country faces new problems the Party finds ways of resolving them, restructures and remolds leadership methods, demonstrating its ability to measure up to its historic responsibility for the country's destiny, for the cause of socialism and communism.

Life constantly verifies our potentialities. Last year was special in this respect. As never before there was a need for unity in the party ranks and unity in the Central Committee. We saw clearly that it was no longer possible to evade pressing issues of society's development, to remain reconciled to irresponsibility, laxity, and inertness. Under these conditions the Politburo, the CC Secretariat, and the Central Committee itself decided that the cardinal issues dictated by the times had to be resolved. An important landmark on this road was the April plenary meeting of the Central Committee. We told the people frankly about the difficulties and omissions in our work and about the plans for the immediate future and the long term. Today, at this Congress, we can state with confidence that the course set by the April plenary meeting received the active support of the Communists, of millions of working people.

The present stage, which is one of society's qualitative transformation, requires the Party and each of its organizations to make new efforts, to be principled in assessing their own work, and to show efficiency and dedication. The draft new edition of the party program and the draft amendments in the party rules presented to the Congress proceed from the premise that the task of mobilizing all the factors of acceleration can only be carried out by a party that has the interests of the people at heart, a party having a scientifically substantiated perspective, asserting by its labor the confidence that the set targets would be attained.

The Party can resolve new problems successfully if it is itself in uninterrupted development, free of the "infallibility" complex, critically assesses the results that have been attained, and clearly sees what has to be done. The new requirements being made of cadres, of the entire style, methods, and character of work are dictated by the magnitude and complexity of the problems and the need to draw lessons from the past without compromise or reservations.

At present, Comrades, we have a focus on the practical organization of our work and the placing and education of cadres, of the body of party activists, and to take a fresh look at our entire work from the Party's point of view—at all levels, in all echelons. In this context, I should like to remind you of Lenin's words: "When the situation has changed and different problems have to be solved, we cannot look back and attempt to solve them by yesterday's methods. Don't try—you won't succeed!"

The purpose of restructuring party work is that each party organization—from republican to primary—should vigorously implement the course set by the April plenary meeting and live in an atmosphere of quest, of renewal of the forms and methods of its activity. This can only be done through the efforts of all the Communists, the utmost promotion of democracy within the Party itself, the application of the principle of collective leadership at all levels, the promotion of criticism and self-criticism, control, and a responsible attitude to the work at hand. It is only then that the spirit of novelty is generated, that inertness and stagnation become intolerable.

We feel just indignation about all sorts of shortcomings and those responsible for them—people who neglect their duties and are indifferent to society's interests: hack worker and idler, grabber and writer of anonymous letters, petty bureaucrat and bribe-taker. But they live and work in a concrete collective, town, or village, in a given organization and not some place away from us. Then who but the collective and the Communists should openly declare that in our working society each person is obliged to work conscientiously and abide strictly by the norms of socialist human association, which are the same for everybody? What and who prevents this?

This is where the task of enhancing the role of the party organization rises to its full stature. It does not become us, the Communists, to put the blame on somebody else. If a party organization lives a full-blooded life founded on relations of principle, if Communists are engaged in concrete matters and not in a chitchat on general subjects, success is assured. It is not enough to see shortcomings and defects, to stigmatize them. It is necessary to do everything so that they should not exist. *There is no such thing as Communists' vanguard role in general: it is expressed in practical deeds.*

Party life that is healthy, businesslike, multiform in its concrete manifestations and concerns, characterized by openness and publicity of plans and decisions, by the humaneness and modesty of Communists—that is what we need today. We, the Communists, are looked upon as a model in everything—in work and behavior. We have to live and work in such a way that the working person could say: "Yes, this is a real Communist." And the brighter and cleaner life is within the Party, the sooner we shall cope with the complex problems that are typical of the present time of change.

Guided by the decisions of the April and subsequent plenary meetings of the Central Committee and working boldly and perseveringly, many party organizations have achieved good results. In defining the ways for advancement, the CPSU Central Committee relies chiefly on that experience, striving to make it common property. For example, the decisions on accelerating scientific and technological progress are based to a large extent on the innovatory approach to these matters in the Leningrad party organization, and its experience underlies the drafting of the programs for the intensification and integration of science and production, and socio-economic planning. Party organizations in the Ukraine should be commended for creating scientific and technological complexes and engineering centers and for their productive work in effectively utilizing recycled resources. The measures to form a unified agro-industrial complex in the country underwent a preliminary trial in Georgia and Estonia.

Many examples could be given of a modern approach to work. A feel for the new, and active restructuring in accordance with the changing conditions are a characteristic of the Byelorussian, Latvian, Sverdlovsk, Chelyabinsk, Krasnodar, Omsk, Ulyanovsk, and other Party organizations. Evidence of this is also provided by many election meetings, conferences, and republican congresses. They were notable for their businesslike formulation of issues, the commitment of Communists to seeking untapped resources and ways of speeding up our progress, and exactingness in assessing the work of elective bodies.

But not everybody can see the need for restructuring, and not everywhere. There still are many organizations, as is also confirmed by the election campaign, in which one does not feel the proper frame of mind for a serious, self-critical analysis, for drawing practical conclusions. This is the effect of adherence to the old, the absence of a feel for the time, a propensity for excessive organization, the habit of speaking vaguely, and the fear of revealing the real state of affairs.

We shall not be able to move a single step forward if we do not learn to work in a new way, do not put an end to inertness and conservatism in any of their forms, if we lose the courage to assess the situation realistically and see it as it actually is. To make irresponsibility recede into the past, we have to make a rule of calling things by their names, of judging everything openly. It is about time to stop exercises in misplaced tact where there should be exactingness and honesty, a party conscience. Nobody has the right to forget Lenin's stern warning: "False rhetoric and false boastfulness spell moral ruin and lead unfailingly to political extinction."

The consistent implementation of the *principle of collectivism* is a key condition for a healthy life in every party organization. But in some organizations the role of plenary meetings and of the bureaus as collegiate bodies was downgraded, and the joint drafting of decisions was replaced by instructions issued by one individual, and this often led to gross errors. Such sidetracking from the norms of party life was tolerated in the Central Committee of the Communist Party of Kirghizia. A principled assessment was given at the Congress of the Republic's Communist Party of the activities not only of the former first secretary but also of those who connived at unscrupulousness and servility.

It is only strict compliance with and the utmost strengthening of the principle of collective leadership that can be a barrier to subjectivist excesses and create the conditions for the adoption of considered and substantiated decisions. A leader who understands this clearly has the right to count on long and productive work.

More urgently than before there is now the *need to promote criticism and self-criticism and step up the efforts to combat window dressing.* From the recent past we know that where criticism and self-criticism are smothered, where talk about successes is substituted for a party analysis of the actual situation, all party activity is deformed and a situation of complacency, permissiveness, and impunity arises that leads to the most serious consequences. In the localities and even in the center there appeared quite a few officials who are oversensitive to critical remarks leveled at them and who go so far as to harass people who come up with criticism.

The labor achievements of the people of Moscow are widely known. But one can say confidently that these accomplishments would have been much greater had the city party organization not lost since some time ago the spirit of self-criticism and a healthy dissatisfaction with what had been achieved, had complacency not surfaced. As was noted at a city party conference, the leadership of the city committee had evaded decisions on complex problems while parading its successes. This is what generated complacency and was an impediment to making a principled evaluation of serious shortcomings.

Perhaps in their most glaring form negative processes stemming from an absence of criticism and self-criticism manifested themselves in Uzbekistan. Having lost touch with life the republic's former top leadership made it a rule to speak only of successes, paper over shortcomings, and respond irritably to any criticism. In the republican party organization discipline slackened, and persons for whom the sole principle was lack of principles, their own well-being, and careerist considerations were in favor. Toadyism and unbridled laudation of those "senior in rank" became widespread. All this could not but affect the state of affairs. The situation in the economy and in the social sphere deteriorated markedly, machinations, embezzlement, and bribery thrived, and socialist legality was grossly transgressed.

It required intervention by the CPSU Central Committee to normalize the situation. The republic was given all-sided assistance. Many sectors of party, governmental, and economic work were reinforced with cadres. These measures won the approval and active support of the Communists and the working people of Uzbekistan.

There is something else that causes concern. The shortcomings in the republic did not appear overnight, they piled up over the years, growing from small to big. Officials from all-Union bodies, including the Central Committee, went to Uzbekistan on many occasions and they must have noticed what was happening. Working people of the

Republic wrote indignant letters to the central bodies about the malpractices. But these signals were not duly investigated.

The reason for this is that at some stage some republics, territories, regions, and cities were placed out of bounds to criticism. As a result, in the localities there began to appear districts, collective farms, state farms, industrial facilities, and so on that enjoyed a kind of immunity. From this we have to draw the firm conclusion that *in the Party there neither are nor should be organizations outside the pale of control and closed to criticism, there neither are nor should be leaders fenced off from party responsibility.*

This applies equally to ministries, departments, and any enterprises and organizations. The CPSU Central Committee considers that the role of party committees of ministries and departments must be enhanced significantly, that their role in restructuring the work of the management apparatus and of industries as a whole must be raised. An examination of the reports of the party committees of some ministries in the Central Committee shows that they are still using their right of control very timidly and warily, that they are not catalysts of the new, of the struggle against departmentalism, paperwork, and red tape.

The Party provides political leadership and defines the general prospect for development. It formulates the main tasks in socio-economic and intellectual life, selects and places cadres, and exercises general control. As regards the ways and means of resolving specific economic and socio-cultural problems, wide freedom of choice is given to each management body and work collective, and managerial personnel.

In improving the forms and methods of leadership, the Party is emphatically against confusing the functions of party committees with those of governmental and public bodies. This is not a simple question. In life it is sometimes hard to see the boundary beyond which party control and the organization of the fulfillment of practical tasks become petty tutelage or even substitution for governmental and economic bodies. Needless to say, each situation requires a specific approach, and here much is determined by the political culture and maturity of leaders. The Party will endeavor to organize work so that everyone on his job will act professionally and energetically, unafraid to shoulder responsibility. Such is the principled Leninist decision on this question and we should abide strictly by it at all levels of party activity. . . .

Perestroika: New Thinking for Our Country and the World

. . . I want to make the reader understand that the energy for revolutionary change has been accumulating amid our people and in the

Party for some time. And the ideas of perestroika have been prompted not just by pragmatic interests and considerations but also by our troubled conscience, by the indomitable commitment to ideals that we inherited from the revolution and as a result of a theoretical quest that gave us a better knowledge of society and reinforced our determination to go ahead.

The life-giving impetus of our great revolution was too powerful for the Party and people to reconcile themselves to phenomena that were threatening to squander its gains. The works of Lenin and his ideals of socialism remained for us an inexhaustible source of dialectical creative thought, theoretical wealth, and political sagacity. His very image is an undying example of lofty moral strength, all-around spiritual culture, and selfless devotion to the cause of the people and to socialism. Lenin lives on in the minds and hearts of millions of people. Breaking down all the barriers erected by scholastics and dogmatists, an interest in Lenin's legacy and a thirst to know him more extensively in the original grew as negative phenomena in society accumulated.

Turning to Lenin has greatly stimulated the Party and society in their search to find explanations and answers to the questions that have arisen. Lenin's works in the last years of his life have drawn particular attention. I shall adduce my own experience to corroborate this point. In my report of 22 April 1983, at a gala session dedicated to the 113th anniversary of Lenin's birth, I referred to Lenin's tenets on the need for taking into account the requirements of objective economic laws, on planning and cost accounting, and intelligent use of commodity-money relations and material and moral incentives. The audience enthusiastically supported this reference to Lenin's ideas. I felt, once again, that my reflections coincided with the sentiments of my fellow party members and the many people who were seriously concerned about our problems and sincerely wanted to rectify matters. Indeed, many of my fellow party members felt an urgent need for the renewal of society, for changes. However, I should say that I also sensed that not everybody liked the report, but felt that it was not as optimistic as the time required.

Today we have a better understanding of Lenin's last works, which were in essence his political bequest, and we more clearly understand why these works appeared. Gravely ill, Lenin was deeply concerned for the future of socialism. He perceived the lurking dangers for the new system. We, too, must understand this concern. He saw that socialism was encountering enormous problems and that it had to contend with a great deal of what the bourgeois revolution had failed to accomplish. Hence the utilization of methods that did not seem to be intrinsic to socialism itself or, at least, diverged in some respects from generally accepted classical notions of socialist development.

The Leninist period is indeed very important. It is instructive in that it proved the strength of Marxist-Leninist dialectics, the conclusions of which are based on an analysis of the actual historical situation. Many of us realized even long before the April plenary meeting that everything pertaining to the economy, culture, democracy, foreign policy—all spheres—had to be reappraised. The important thing was to translate it into the practical language of everyday life. . . .

The concept of restructuring with all the problems involved had been evolving gradually. Way back before the April plenary meeting a group of party and state leaders had begun a comprehensive analysis of the state of the economy. Their analysis then became the basis for the documents of perestroika. Using the recommendations of scientists and experts, our entire potential, all the best that social thought had created, we elaborated the basic ideas and drafted a policy that we subsequently began to implement.

Thus, an arsenal of constructive ideas had been accumulated. Therefore, at the April 1985 plenary meeting we managed to propose a more or less well-considered, systematized program and to outline a concrete strategy for the country's further development and a plan of action. It was clear that cosmetic repairs and patching would not do; a major overhaul was required. Nor was it possible to wait, for much time had been lost as it was.

The first question to arise was one of improving the economic situation, stopping and reversing the unfavorable trends in that sphere.

The most immediate priority, which we naturally first looked to, was to put the economy into some kind of order, to tighten up discipline, to raise the level of organization and responsibility, and to catch up in areas where we were behind. A great deal of hard work was done and, for that matter, is continuing. As expected, it has produced its first results. The rates of economic growth have stopped declining and are even showing some signs of improvement. . . .

References

Gorbachev, Mikhail, *Perestroika: New Thinking for Our Country and the World* (New York: Harper and Row, 1987).

Gorbachev, Mikhail, *Toward a Better World* (New York: Richardson and Steirman, 1987).

Gorbachev, Mikhail, "October and Perestroika" from *Report by General Secretary of the CPSA Central Committee*, Moscow, November 2, 1987.

JOMO KENYATTA

FULL NAME:

Jomo Kenyatta (Kamau Ngengi)

BORN:

c. 1894, at Ichaweri, southwest of Mount Kenya
in what is now Kenya

DIED:

22 August 1978, Mombasa, Kenya

Early nationalist leader who went to London in 1929, studied anthropology at the London School of Economics, and returned to Kenya in 1946 as the leader of the Kenya African Union. In prison for suspicion of being a Mau Mau leader from 1953 to 1961. Provisional Prime Minister on release. First Prime Minister of Independent Kenya, 1963–1964; President from 1964 until his death in 1978.

His major works include: *Facing Mount Kenya: The Tribal Life of the Gikuyu* (New York: Vintage Books, 1965); *Harambee!* (Nairobi, Oxford University Press, 1965); and *Suffering Without Bitterness* (Nairobi: East African Publishing House, 1968). Biographies include: Guy Arnold, *Kenyatta and the Politics of Kenya* (London: Dent, 1974); and Jeremy Murray-Brown, *Kenyatta* (London: Allen and Unwin, 1972).

Suffering Without Bitterness

Excerpts

It has been my intention for some time to make known, as a broad and factual coverage, the backgaround of events that preceded my arrest and imprisonment, and subsequent patterns that led to my release and assumption of leadership in the government and public life of Kenya. . . .

Politics is an arena with formidable pitfalls for the man of ideals. Yet without the driving-force of some idealism, the politician is a sterile man. I have spent my entire adult life in the service of my people. Like many others I have at times regarded and used politics as the weapon underlying both the language and the medium of public undertaking, in pursuit of such objectives here as meaningful independence, enduring stability, national unity, economic progress, and social justice. Once or twice, in all this long period, the pendulum of political fortune has swung me toward some uncomfortable situations. There were evenings of bitterness. But I could never find solace in despair.

Kenya is a living entity. On our intensive farms and ranches and plantations, as well as in the wilderness of bush and plain, life is surarounded and influenced by natural phenomena. Although the Republic of Kenya, with its refineries and factories, its power projects and research institutions, its services as a hub of communications and a center of business, is rapidly and desirably emerging as a modern state, yet still our real problems arise more from natural causes and effects than they do from the machines.

In a life of close association with the soil of Kenya, I have found joy and humility in the seasonal rhythms both of plant and of animal life, and in the crafts of careful husbandry. But I have seen draught and flood, hail and tempest. I have seen locusts come, and crops destroyed by virus or fungus, and livestock stricken by rinderpest or tick-borne disease. One must learn to suffer and endure, to replant or rebuild, to move on again. And as with farming, so in politics, the practitioner must never lose faith. . . .

I have always believed that the best way to achieve worthwhile human ambitions is through hard work. To me, "Uhuru na Kazi" is a living reality. My day is taken up with all the tasks that can beset a head of government who is also head of state, although my diaries bear witness to duties as well as a party president and a constituency member of Parliament, as a host, and even as a farmer! My home in Gatundu is open to and entered by many groups and delegations, since the work I undertake in every role would be of small account if I failed to maintain contact with the people.

This outline is not plaintively put in; still less in search of admiration. I believe in the fullest utilization of each fleeting day. Of all the deadly sins, that of sloth seems to me the most contemptible, a flaunting of the very purpose of Creation. There is so much, always, for the wit and resourcefulness of man—driven by the will—to conquer or contrive. . . .

My work and my beliefs have always had their roots in service to the people, fortified at all important times by their mandate and by mutual bonds of faith. This, it may be felt, is an almost obligatory submission for any statesman to advance. But I have had the good fortune, throughout my long life, for this always to be meaningful. Today, I go onto the farms or into the homes of the people, not as royalty bestowing condescension, but unaffectedly, understanding and sharing the tempo and tribulations of their lives. I have never grown away from the people, and at massive public rallies we meet on common garound as fellow men. They know me best as I have always been: as one of them.

No man has ever devised any wiser criterion, for the national direction of public affairs, than government of the people, by the people, and for the people. Distorted as this simple cause may be, in sundry blocs or regions, by ambition or autocracy, by fear disguised as freedom, it has always been the core of my political purpose. And there is more to this than just morality. The latent achievement and potential contribution of the people of Africa require foundations in basic freedoms of expression, in the sense both of participation and of influence, on the road to social justice.

When approaching such challenges in Kenya as national unity and effective nation-building, I have always told my people what I believed to be the simple truth, never employing tricks to win some cheap applause or to gloss over setbacks or reality. I have left the people in no doubt about my views and intentions, or about the national policies of the Kenya Republic. It has been my task to point the way, to encourage and measure advancement, to some extent perhaps to inspire our national progress. . . .

Speech delivered on Kenyatta Day, 20 October 1964

On this day that bears my name, I want to speak to you all without formality, in your homes or in community centers or wherever you might be. And I want to speak to all, today, not just as a prime minister, but as a man. For although—by your wish—I am the leader of my country, the recollection of this day in all your hearts and minds means more than just a tribute to a title. It reaches back in time. And it reminds me very vividly of all the phases and milestones of more than forty years of work and service, dedicated to the freedom and the dignity of Africa, and to pan-African ideals.

This is the first celebration of Kenyatta Day since, here in Kenya, our struggle for Uhuru was ended, and we became an independent sovereign state. I am proud to think back on the part that I played in this struggle. Much was direct contribution. But it gladdened me to know, through a long period of anxieties and sufferings, that my conception of duty—to this country and its people—inspired and upheld others, when I could not be there.

Our struggle was a just one. All the noble charters and declarations of history, and all the constitutions that enshrine human rights, have sprung from one paramount truth: that men in their spirit and in their striving, under the law, have the right to be free. The world in these past years has moved rapidly forward, from the colonial age. Peoples in many countries have been freed, and not just from political bondage. Their talents and their ambitions and their cultures have all been released. Their productive energies have altered the old pattern of economic privilege. Their philosophies have made impact on the thinking of mankind, bringing fresh hope to the cause of world peace.

All this is what we sought for ourselves. And on this day, I share your joy that we in Kenya have the rights and the responsibilities of free men. To me, this is a monument to years of service.

What I want to say to you now is what these years have taught me. Triumph in a struggle of this kind cannot be achieved without a long history of setbacks and sufferings, of failure and humiliation. But all this is worthwhile, and all can be forgotten, when its outcome is the foundation on which a future can be built. It is the future, my friends, that is living, and the past that is dead. In all that I have seen, in many countries and at many periods of my life, never has there seemed any purpose in arguments about the past, or any nobility in motives of revenge.

There have been murmurs here in Kenya about the part played by one set of people, or another set of people, in the struggle for Uhuru. There has been talk of the contribution made, or refused, by this group or that. There has been—at times—vindictive comment, and a finger of scorn has been pointed at some selected race, or group, or tribe. All this is unworthy of our future here.

I want this celebration of Kenyatta Day to mean more to you all than just some particular Tuesday in the calendar. Let this be the day on which all of us commit ourselves to erase from our minds all the hatreds and the difficulties of those years that now belong to history. Let us agree that we shall never refer to the past. Let us instead unite, in all our utterances and activities, in concern for the reconstruction of our country and the vitality of Kenya's future. . . .

I would be satisfied now, with my life, simply through knowing that I had made some contribution to a free and better life for Kenya's people. I would be satisfied even if I were not prime minister, with many grave tasks and responsibilities still lying ahead.

The fruits of life, my friends, are there, for as long as one has the strength to seek them. I say to you now that service to one's fellow man can never be confined by a price or a reward. Its true satisfaction comes in the nature of dedication. In my long life, this has been dedication to my country and its people, to the cause of freedom and pan-African ideals, to progress through unity and the bounty of our land.

Not all of you can be leaders. But all of you have your families, your farms or businesses, your daily tasks. By applying all that you are and all that you do to the cause of national unity and the progress of our country, then this dedication that I have known and enjoyed will be something we all can share.

Harambee!

Uhuru Independence Day Speech, December 12, 1963

. . . An African government wants faithfulness. It wants the laws to be obeyed. This is what government is for, and what it should be. I do not want to burden you. But I do want those who will help me in building our nation, and making it a worthwhile place to live in, to be faithful. Those present who are prepared to help me in this vital task should raise their hands. . . . I thank you all.

I thank you as well for electing me to lead you into a new phase in the progress of our country. In the past, we used to blame the Europeans for everything that went wrong. When things went wrong, we used to say Europeans are bad, they are sucking our blood. When we lacked education, we said the Europeans were only educating their children, and the Asians were only educating their children, so when will ours be educated?

Now the government is ours. Maybe you will now be blaming Kenyatta, saying: Kenyatta, we elected you, but where is this or that? But you must know that Kenyatta alone cannot give you everything. All things we must do together. You and I must work together to develop our country, to get education for our children, to have doctors, to build roads, to improve or provide all day-to-day essentials. This should be our work, in the spirit that I am going to ask you to echo, to shout aloud, to shatter the foundations of the past with the strength of our new purpose . . . HARAMBEE! . . . HARAMBEE!

There have been reports of people trying to sow the seeds of dissension. Instead of releasing their energies to reconstruct Kenya, these people go about trying to create confusion. To such people I would say: Since the beginning of the world, how many people have come and gone? All people come and go. So please do not spoil the world, because you will not live forever. Try to live in peace, and leave the world a better place than you found it. . . .

There are people who call themselves leaders, and who say they have no confidence in this government. I must know whether or not you have confidence in your government, and whether you have given these people any mandate to oppose the government. . . .

Anyone who wants to weaken this government will be dealt with ruthlessly by the government. We recognize the Opposition, but we cannot allow anyone to belittle this government. This is not the government of Nairobi, or Nakuru, or Kisumu, but the government of Kenya, and the sooner the Opposition recognizes this the better. . . .

There are those who keep going aaround saying "this government has not given us jobs." Some of you are in fact being misled by troublemakers, whose only interest is to see you in difficulties. My government is a government of action, and will not hesitate to deal with these few troublemakers in the country. . . . We have gained a good reputation in the world, and throughout Asia and Africa; but there are still a few people here who want to spoil our good name abroad. . . .

I must warn these people . . . (those who took bribes from foreigners in order to cause confusion in the country) . . . that the government is fully aware of their activities, and a full-scale investigation is going on. I will deal with them very firmly when they are known. . . .

References

Kenyatta, Jomo, *Suffering Without Bitterness* (Nairobi: East African Publishing House, 1968).

Kenyatta, Jomo, *Harambee! The Prime Minister of Kenya's Speeches, 1963–1964* (Nairobi: Oxford University Press, 1964).

JULIUS K. NYERERE

FULL NAME:

Julius Kambarage Nyerere

BORN:

1 March 1922, Butiama, Tanganyika
(now Tanzania)

Teacher who was elected member of the Legislative Council, Chief Minister, and Prime Minister of Tanganyika, 1961–1962. First President of the United Republic of Tanzania, 1964–1985. Chairman of the ruling party TANU, renamed Chama Cha Mapinduzi, from 1954 on.

Author of *Ujamaa: Essays on Socialism* (Dar es Salaam: Oxford University Press, 1968); *Freedom and Unity: Uhuru na Umoja, A Selection from Writings and Speeches 1952–1965* (Dar es Salaam: Oxford University Press, 1966); *Freedom and Socialism: Uhuru na Ujamaa, A Selection from Writings and Speeches, 1965–1967* (Dar es Salaam: Oxford University Press, 1968); and *Freedom and Development: Uhuru na Maendeleo, A Selection from Writings and Speeches, 1968–1973* (Dar es Salaam: Oxford University Press, 1973). Biographies include: William Dugan and John Civille, *Tanzania and Nyerere* (Maryknoll, NY: Orbis Books, 1976); and William Edgett Smith, *We Must Run While They Walk: A Portrait of Africa's Julius Nyerere* (New York: Random House, 1972).

Freedom and Unity

Inaugural address, 10 December 1962

The first thing I want to do is to say thank you. You, the people of Tanganyika, have laid upon me a heavy burden of responsibility. This burden I have accepted with a sense of humility and of gratitude. And by the Grace of Almighty God, and with your help, I shall endeavor faithfully to carry out my duties. . . . For the past ten months our government has carried on under the leadership of the Honorable Rashidi Kawawa. He, together with his colleagues, has set before us a splendid example of unhesitating acceptance of responsibility, and of the use of that responsibility in the service of our country—a service untainted by any of the envious bickerings and squabbles of the position-seeker. I am sure the nation as a whole would wish me to extend to Mr. Kawawa and his colleagues the gratitude we all feel for the service they have rendered us during these past months. And I know that all of you in this assembly, and in the whole country, will wish them well and will continue to help them carry out their new duties just as you have helped them in the past. . . .

Yesterday I took an oath. I swore that as president of the Republic of Tanganyika I would do my duty and carry out my work without fear or favor, affection or ill will toward anyone. That was no hollow formula, to be spoken and forgotten. It was a most solemn promise, made before Almighty God, that with His help I shall prove myself worthy of the responsibility that you—the people of Tanganyika— have entrusted to me; that I shall strive to fulfill the task laid upon me, without permitting myself to be influenced by any personal likes or dislikes, nor by consideration of my own comfort or convenience. I say "I" swore. But in actual fact it is true to say that "WE" swore; for I took that oath on your behalf. Every citizen of Tanganyika, whether he be the president, a politician, a civil servant, a farmer, a teacher, or the lowest-paid worker in the land, every single one of us has an equal duty to give of his best. Every one of us has an equal duty to do the work entrusted to him—whatever that work may be—as if he too had taken a solemn oath to devote himself, without thought for his own advantage, to building our new Republic of Tanganyika.

Speech commemorating the opening of the Police College, 1 August 1961

In less than a week I have participated in three very happy and very significant events. On the 28th of last month, only six days ago, I opened TANU's new building that I mentioned is being rented to the government for the purpose of the Dar es Salaam University College, which is expected to receive its first students before the end of the year. On the following day I opened Kivukoni College, another educational institution to serve the New Tanganyika we are trying to build. Today I find myself very happily opening this Police College. These events are indicative, but no more than indicative, of government's relentless efforts to educate our people for the responsibilities they must shoulder in an independent Tanganyika. Government is determined to continue this work in spite of difficulties. . . .

On the great tasks that face our country none is more important than the provision of leaders in every sphere of the national life. It is said that leaders are born and not made, but this phrase is a deceptive half-truth; there is no man living whose qualities of leadership cannot be improved and developed by training.

Leadership has many aspects but, most of all, it is the qualities of the mind that establish a man among his fellows. The ability to think logically, the capacity to express himself clearly and concisely, that mastery of his job that enables him to understand fully the implications of his decisions, all these are the hallmarks of the competent leader. . . .

To be a good leader it helps to be a good administrator and it is with this in mind that the syllabus of the college has been designed. You will be taught to appreciate a problem in a logical fashion, to think objectively, and to express yourselves clearly and concisely. You will be taught to accept the responsibilities of command, including the grave responsibility you bear toward your subordinates. Far too much is made of the word "welfare." The well-being of your men is not an isolated issue to be conveniently tagged with an overworked word. The contentment of your men is a fundamental matter upon which all discipline and efficiency rests. It is inextricably bound up with good administration and, therefore, good leadership.

Letter to government ministers and officials, 13 July 1963, based on speech delivered 7 July 1963 at a mass rally

My dear Colleagues,

On Saba Saba Day I was obliged to speak publicly against something that I have been complaining about for some time; that is, the growing tendency within the government to confuse dignity with what I consider to be sheer pomposity. This is a tendency that must be checked at once if it is not to destroy the very thing it is, presumably, intended to emphasize—the dignity of the Republic and the respect due to the government of the Republic.

By this letter I am asking every person in a responsible position both in TANU and government to help in stamping out this disease.

I will give a few examples to illustrate the sort of thing I mean by pomposity. I could give many more. You all know them.

When we became independent, we started by singing the national anthem every time the prime minister arrived anywhere, even at supposedly informal dinner parties. This, already, was rather unnecessary; but, as a little overenthusiasm was fairly understandable just at first, I had hoped that in time we should learn to reserve the anthem for the really ceremonial functions at which its playing is appropriate. It seems I was too hopeful; for now we sing it whenever a minister, a parliamentary secretary, a regional commissioner, or an area commissioner arrives at a gathering of any kind anywhere in Tanganyika!

Nothing could be more disrespectful to our national anthem than to treat it as a popular song-hit, or a "signature-tune" to be "plugged" the moment any member of the government appears on the scene. Yet this is exactly what we are doing. We sing the national anthem on the most unsuitable and unlikely occasions; and, if some unfortunate passerby does not happen to notice us, we take very serious offense and start shouting about "insults to the Republic"! This is not only ridiculous, but very undignified. It is we who must learn to treat our national anthem with more respect. Indeed, if it is true that overfamiliarity breeds contempt, then we are ourselves guilty of exposing the anthem to the risk of ridicule.

It is exceedingly unlikely that anybody, whether he is a Tanganyika citizen or a foreigner, would deliberately ignore the playing of the national anthem. After all, it is customary in every country in the world for visiting foreigners, as well as the local public, to show their respect by standing to attention while the anthem is being played. But it is not customary in other countries to play or sing their national anthem without any warning, just because some official of the government happens to have dropped in unexpectedly at a small gathering, or landed at an airstrip on a visit to his mother-in-law! Supposing we were on holiday in another country, and we happened to overhear a small group of young people burst into song as they greeted some— to us—unknown figure; we should be very startled to find ourselves suddenly accused of insulting behavior because we had failed to recognize the tune as their national anthem!

It is the same with police escorts. We managed to get about quite well without them when we were not in the government; but I am told we cannot now do without them altogether. I admit, therefore, that there may be certain ceremonial occasions when it is necessary for the president, or the vice president, to have a police escort. For example, when receiving a state visit or when there is to be a state opening of

Parliament we have to make sure the roads are clear so that the president arrives punctually at his destination. In a case like that the preliminary clearing of the road from the State House to Karimjee Hall is necessary, and the public can easily appreciate why it is so. But, as with the playing of the national anthem, the intrinsic importance of the occasion must itself be sufficient to warrant the use of a police escort. It is meaningless, in fact it is insulting to the public, if we try and use an escort, or play the national anthem, as a means of embroidering the most ordinary occasion with a sham pomp that it does not merit!

The office of president, in this or any other sovereign republic, carries with it the duties and the responsibilities of the head of state. It does not, or it most certainly should not, oblige its holder to become also the greatest public nuisance in the capital city! Yet, as a result of this growing insistence on pomposity and ostentation, the president of Tanganyika is fast becoming the worst public nuisance the city of Dar es Salaam has ever had to put up with! Whenever he decides to go out, whether to a dinner, a dance, or even to visit some friends, the normal flow of traffic has now to be interfered with. If he has not had time to warn the police well in advance, then other road-users on the route to his destination will suddenly find themselves being cleared out of the way (like so much unsightly rubbish) to leave the road clear for the president's car. And, acting under orders to get it clear immediately, the unfortunate police outriders have no time for courteous explanations; so that the mere "ordinary" motorist has to be waved off the road with a rude abruptness, and sublime disregard for his own convenience, which can do little to enhance his respect for the cause of it all! If, on the other hand, the police have had sufficient warning to enable them to do their work efficiently, then all traffic within a quarter of a mile of the route may be brought to a standstill for anything from half an hour to an hour before the president leaves the State House.

If I were not myself the president, I should by now have taken to ringing up the State House before ever attempting to fix any appointment with a friend; for it is rapidly becoming impossible for anybody in Dar es Salaam to guess how long it will take him to drive from point A to point B without first finding out whether the president also intends to go out on that particular day!

And it is not only the public who suffer, but the police themselves. It is difficult, to say the least, for them to live up to the repeated injunctions of TANU and the government to "treat the public with consideration and courtesy," and at the same time to carry out sudden orders to clear bewildered motorists from the public thoroughfares in a matter of minutes! Once we even had a serious accident as a direct result of this insistence on the very maximum of pomp. I was going to Morogoro. Two police cars had been provided as escort, but at the last moment it was decided that this was not impressive enough, so a motorcycle outrider was ordered to go ahead of the police cars. As he was hurrying to obey this order something happened, and his motorcycle overturned. He was severely injured, and lost four of his teeth—all in the cause of enhancing the presidential pomp.

Then, too, there is the question of the State House garounds. It is much more difficult to enter the State House garounds now than it was under colonial rule. There have been several occasions when I have wanted passersby to be allowed into the garounds to enjoy a ngoma that was going on there. But it has proved impossible for me or anybody else to get the gate opened. Presumably this could only be authorized by means of a cabinet directive! I, myself, cannot leave the State House garounds without the guard at the gate being called out to announce to the whole city—by a fanfare of trumpets—that the president is going out!

Hitherto, whenever I have questioned the value of all this very undemocratic pomposity, I have been assured that "the people like it." But this is highly doubtful. Do the people really like being refused permission to join in the ngomas which they can see going on on the other side of the State House barriers? Do they really love being shouted at to get off the road because the president, or a minister, or a regional commissioner, is taking an afternoon drive? Do they really feel a surge of pride and patriotism every time they are expected to stop what they are doing and stand to attention just because some newly appointed official, whom they may not even have seen before, is being "serenaded" by his friends with the national anthem?

We should stop deceiving ourselves. This sort of pomposity has nothing to do with the people, for it is the very reverse of democratic. We must stop it. We must begin to treat pomposity with the scorn it deserves. Dignity does not need pomposity to uphold it; and pomposity in all its forms is a wrong. Even if it were proved that the people really did enjoy it—which I very much doubt—it would still be a wrong; and as such it would still be our duty to put a stop to it, and to tell the people that what they had learned to enjoy was wrong.

Freedom and Socialism

Speech on Mafia Island, February 1966

. . . I was the first to use the word "ujamaa" in order to explain the kind of life we wish to live in our country. The word ujamaa denotes the kind of life lived by a man and his family—father, mother, children, and near relatives. Our Africa was a poor country before it was invaded and ruled by foreigners. There were no rich people in Africa. There was no person or group of persons who had exclusive claim to the ownership of the land. Land was the property of all the people, and those who used it did not do so because it was their property. They used it because they needed it, and it was their responsibility to use it carefully and hand it over in good condition for use by future generations. Life was easy. It was possible for a man to live with his wife, his children, and other close relatives. Wealth belonged to the family as a whole; and every member of a family had the right to the use of family property. No one used wealth for the purpose of dominating others. This is how we want to live as a nation. We want the whole nation to live as one family.

This is the basis of socialism. Yet we say we want socialism and want to build a socialist state. What do we mean by this? We mean two things. First, that we do not already have what we are looking for. Secondly, we believe that the thing we want is good. If you know that something is bad, you will not waste time trying to get it: it will not benefit you. This means that if we want socialism and aim at developing our country on the basis of socialist principles, it is because we believe that socialism is good.

Let me first explain that many countries are not socialist. Many countries in the world want to be socialist, and different people give different names to this concept of socialism. I have said I chose the word "ujamaa" to explain socialism. I shall now try to explain why I chose the word ujamaa.

Normally a country is divided into two sections. Some people are called "masters" and others are called "servants." We accept this division of people into classes of "masters" and "slaves." Sometimes we are even content to live with these divisions and to accept them as they are. I will tell you an example that one old man told me. During the German administration a group of people were told to do a certain job. They did not do it. Then they were called to a meeting where their German master told them to divide themselves between "masters" and "slaves." Some of the slaves joined the masters' group, hoping that they would escape punishment if the slaves were going to be punished. After the division, the German master allowed the slaves to go home, but immediately ordered the masters to be caned because they were lazy, and also because they were inducing the slaves to be lazy, too. Those slaves who had joined the group of masters regretted their decision.

. . . Yet it is true that even in countries where such divisions between masters (who cannot be bought like sheep) and servants (who are bought like sheep) are absent, the people are divided into classes. This division exists even though there are no slaves in a country. In such a case the masters have the habit of being served by other people. The wives of masters do not work; they do not cook, or wash clothes, or make their beds. These things are done for them by other people. The masters have cars, but they do not drive them; they are driven. Masters can eat without working despite the fact that a man normally works in order to eat, except if he is ill, crippled, a child, or mad. What these masters are capable of doing is to give instructions to their servants. Sometimes, however, they employ other people to instruct servants on their behalf. The master does not have to do any work; other people will work for him and report to him month after month. They will report to him about the total harvest from one of his farms, and also about the total income obtained through the sale of his crops. These masters live comfortable lives, despite the fact that they do not work.

But this does not mean that all masters are equal; some are more equal than others. There are two groups of masters—the big masters and the little masters. Then there is the group of workers and servants who are often oppressed by the masters. Our aim is to abolish this division of people between masters and servants, and to make every person a master—not a master who oppresses others, but one who serves himself. A person who serves himself is a true master. He has no worries, he has confidence in himself and is confident of his own actions. He dislikes being pushed aaround and being told what to do. Why should a person who is his own master be pushed into doing work that will not benefit him?

Let me go back to what I said earlier in order to explain what I mean. I said that I did not make speeches at any of the places I had visited on my current tour of this island. Instead, I told the people I met to ask me questions, or to tell me the problems that face them in their everyday lives. It was difficult to get people to ask me questions. They told me they had no problems and that all was well. They were afraid to speak, probably thinking they would be punished. Why should they be punished? In the past years and centuries, we were greatly intimidated and harassed by the colonialists. If you stood before a colonial leader to speak or to ask him a question, you would be harassed by his juniors, who would ask you why you spoke or asked questions. This practice instilled fear in the minds of many citizens. The people did not respect their seniors; they simply feared them. This practice has not ended yet, and it explains why people did not want to tell me their problems when I asked them to. They refused to speak not because they had no problems, but because they were afraid to speak.

This is a bad habit. This is your country. We tell you every day that this is your country and that you have the freedom of speech. If you do not accept your responsibility for this country, I shall claim ownership of it! Any country must be looked after by people. If you do not like to accept the responsibility for looking after this country, I shall get a few clever people, and together we will declare this country to be our property. If we are asked why we are taking it, we shall say you do not want it. But this habit of evading responsibility has been inherited. We have been led to accept the division of men into masters and slaves. Sometimes you hear people talk about themselves as being simply ordinary men. They think their leaders know everything. When you talk to them and explain an issue to them, they will simply say, "What can we say? You leaders know everything."

This is a bad habit. You have been brought up badly. We have been treated as slaves and we have accepted that status. This is bad. What is the meaning of leadership? When you are selected to lead your fellow men, it does not mean that you know everything better than they do. It does not even mean that you are more intelligent than they are—especially the elders. Sometimes my own mother calls me and gives me some advice. She tells me not to do this or that. She advises me even in matters of government. Why must she not advise me? She is a parent and parents are not afraid of their children. She advises me even though she has no formal school education. Why? Does it mean that a person who does not have formal education is a fool? What does education mean? An uneducated man has a brain—given to him by God. Does a man become a goat because he is uneducated? No! Such a person understands the nature of his children; he will know when one of them goes astray. It may be true that I am educated; but how can this mean that I am more intelligent than my mother?

At the moment our aim is to remove fear from the minds of our people. The fear that our people have can be removed from their minds. It was instilled in us by the Portuguese, the Germans, the Arabs, and the British. We have been told that we are not capable of doing this or that, and we have accepted this verdict. We are not even sure where to live. We fear to make decisions. This is why some people tell me to decide things for them on the garounds that we know better. This is not true. You must not fear your leaders. Our aim is to hand over responsibility to the people to make their own decisions. Our leaders are not leaders by birth; they are elected by the people. For why should a person be a leader by birth? Our leaders must be chosen by us. There is no need to have hereditary leaders.

This area commissioner is your son. He is not a district commissioner. If he behaves like a district commissioner we shall terminate his services. He is not supposed to act like a district commissioner. He will be making a mistake if he acted as if he were a district commissioner. We did not want to replace a white DC by a black DC. The area commissioner is the servant of the people. He is here to listen to the problems of the people, and to report to us about those problems or the progress being made to remove the problems. I shall keep on urging Tanzanians not to fear their leaders. . . .

Campaign address broadcast on the radio
10 September 1965

On the 21, 23, and 26 September—that is before the end of this month—the people of Tanzania will have their first opportunity to elect the president of the United Republic. Until now I have been president of our nation because at the time of the Union between Tanganyika and Zanzibar it was agreed that the person who had been elected president of Tanganyika in 1962 should be the head of the Union. Now the people of the mainland and the people of the islands, acting as one, will decide whether they wish me to continue to be president of our country.

At the same time as this election is held, the people on the mainland will also have the opportunity to choose their member of Parliament from among the two people who have been presented to them by TANU.

I want to talk about both these elections tonight, but before I do so I want to stress their importance for all of us. Free elections in an independent country give meaning to independence, because it is through them that we govern ourselves, and decide what sort of country ours will become. When we elect the president and the Parliament of the United Republic we are deciding what will be the laws of our country, how much tax we will pay in order to get public and social services, and who will talk on our behalf with foreign countries, as well as very many other things.

This is what we were claiming for ourselves when we campaigned for independence. We said that we had a right to run our own country in accordance with our own desires, and that no man had the right to govern another. We won that right for ourselves; elections are an occasion on which we exercise it. They are the means through which we choose, and later call to account, the people who have the responsibility of making laws, and leading us. There is no other way in which we can freely govern ourselves because—as we know very well—life in any community brings duties as well as rights. We cannot all do just as we like all of the time. Real freedom therefore means that a man has the right to join with his fellows, on terms of equality and absolute freedom, in deciding what are the citizen's duties and rights, and what proportion of our time and our wealth shall be devoted to common activities for the benefit of our future, and so on.

In very small societies, like the village, this self-government can be effected through community discussions, where every adult joins in, and the group talk until they have reached agreement. Then everyone knows that he has participated in his own government, and knows the decision and how it was arrived at.

Clearly this method is not possible when very large communities are involved, and some other method has to be found whereby each individual can have the same freedom to express his views, and after which a decision can be reached. In a democratic country like Tanzania there are many ways through which this is done. One of the most important for us is through membership of TANU or the Afro-Shirazi Party, and participation in the free discussion at Party meetings. But there are many other ways; it can be done through joining in the discussions of the Village Development Committees, through active membership of NUTA, the cooperative societies and the UWT, through writing to the members of Parliament, and to the newspapers.

By any and all of these methods every citizen of our country can make sure that his ideas are heard and understood. But in addition to all of these methods of exerting democratic rights, there is the basic right of a citizen to choose his representative in Parliament, and to choose his president. This is done periodically; our next opportunity will be through the elections which are to be held later this month. . . .

Those who do not wish me to be president of Tanzania for the next five years have simply to put a tick in the space on the ballot paper underneath where it says "Hapana"—that is, underneath the shaded space. If the majority of the people who voted do this, then the two parties will meet again and select another name to put before you for your consideration; another presidential election will be held, and as soon as you have chosen another person he will take over from me.

I am explaining this point not because I want the people to reject the TANU/Afro-Shirazi recommendation that I should be the president again. I hope that a very large majority of people will agree with the Party on its selection, because it is a very important matter—perhaps the most important single choice our two parties make. Therefore, if the parties have not chosen according to your wishes then they are out of touch with the people as a whole, and this would be very bad. But it is important that everyone should understand that the president of this country is the people's president, chosen by them, and responsible to them for his actions. Therefore the people have, and must have, absolute freedom to vote for or against the man who is put forward by the two parties. The voting is secret so that a voter's choice may be quite free and not influenced by fear or anything except his own judgment.

But every citizen should use his vote. Any person holding this responsible position of president in Tanzania is carrying on his work on behalf of the people, and he can only do it well if the people fully and wholeheartedly support him, and if they show that they do. If, therefore, you as a voter feel that I should continue as president, I hope you will go to the polls and vote for me by putting your tick on the presidential ballot paper under the word "ndiyo"—that is, underneath the black spot. The more people who do this the more help I receive in doing my work properly, and the more obvious it is to people from other countries that I really do speak for Tanzania, and in accordance with the wishes of the people of Tanzania. But if you do not think I am the right person, then it is your duty to vote "Hapana," and to ask the parties to make another recommendation. What you must not do is assume that it does not matter. Your vote does matter very much indeed.

I am saying all these things, which most of you know already, because it is my duty as your president to uphold the constitution of this country. The constitution gives to the people an absolutely free choice in their voting according to law. If your votes go against me I shall accept your decision. If you endorse the Party choice—as I hope you will—I will then accept the heavy responsibilities of president from you again.

If you elect me, I will then once again do my best to serve my country, and to lead the people of Tanzania in the long and hard fight against poverty, ignorance, and disease. I will strive to work with you, the people, in maintaining the complete independence of our country from outside control. And I will uphold the laws and the constitution of this country, and the sovereignty of the people. At the same time I shall continue to work for the unity and liberation of Africa, and for the closer cooperation between Tanzania and her neighboring states.

More than this I do not think it is necessary for me to say about my own candidacy. You have had many opportunities to hear me speak, and on many different subjects. You know my views and my attitudes. I think we know each other. I ask you to consider carefully whether you think I have done well as your president, and whether you think I shall do well in the future. And if you can then do so with a clear conscience I ask you to vote "ndiyo" on polling day. . . .

The Arusha Declaration, speech given on 29 January 1967

TANU believes that everybody who loves his nation has a duty to serve it by cooperating with his fellows in building the country for the benefit of all the people of Tanzania. In order to maintain our independence and our people's freedom we ought to be self-reliant in every possible way and avoid depending upon other countries for assistance. If every individual is self-reliant the ten-house cell will be self-reliant; if all the cells are self-reliant the whole ward will be self-reliant; and if the wards are self-reliant the district will be self-reliant. If the districts are self-reliant, then the region is self-reliant, and if the regions are self-reliant, then the whole nation is self-reliant, and this is our aim.

Good Leadership

TANU recognizes the urgency and importance of good leadership. But we have not yet produced systematic training for our leaders; it is necessary that TANU Headquarters should now prepare a program of training for all leaders—from the national level to the ten-house-cell level—so that every one of them understands our political and economic policies. Leaders must set a good example to the rest of the people in their lives and in all their activities.

TANU Membership

Since the Party was founded we have put great emphasis on getting as many members as possible. This was the right policy during the independence struggle. But now the national executive feels that the time has come when we should put more emphasis on the beliefs of our Party and its policies of socialism.

That part of the TANU Constitution that relates to the admission of a member should be adhered to, and if it is discovered that a man does not appear to accept the faith, the objects, and the rules and regulations of the Party, then he should not be accepted as a member. In particular, it should not be forgotten that TANU is a Party of peasants and workers.

The Arusha Resolution

Therefore, the National Executive Committee, meeting in the Community Center at Arusha from 26.1.67 to 29.1.67, resolves:

(a) *The Leadership*

1. Every TANU and government leader must be either a peasant or a worker, and should in no way be associated with the practices of capitalism or feudalism.
2. No TANU or government leader should hold shares in any company.
3. No TANU or government leader should hold directorships in any privately owned enterprise.
4. No TANU or government leader should receive two or more salaries.
5. No TANU or government leader should own houses that he rents to others.

6. For the purposes of this Resolution the term "leader" should comprise the following:
members of the TANU National Executive Committee; ministers; members of Parliament; senior officials of organizations affiliated to TANU; senior officials of para-statal organizations; all those appointed or elected under any clause of the TANU Constitution; councillors; and civil servants in the high and middle cadres. (In this context "leader" means a man, or a man and his wife; a woman, or a woman and her husband.)

(b) *The Government and Other Institutions*

1. Congratulates the government for the steps it has taken so far in the implementation of the policy of socialism.
2. Calls upon the government to take further steps in the implementation of our policy of socialism as described in Part Two of this document without waiting for a presidential commission on socialism.
3. Calls upon the government to put emphasis, when preparing its development plans, on the ability of this country to implement the plans rather than depending on foreign loans and grants as has been done in the current Five-Year Development Plan. The National Executive Committee also resolves that the plan should be amended so as to make it fit in with the policy of self-reliance.
4. Calls upon the government to take action designed to ensure that the incomes of workers in the private sector are not very different from the incomes of workers in the public sector.
5. Calls upon the government to put great emphasis on actions that will raise the standard of living of the peasants, and the rural community.
6. Calls upon NUTA, the cooperatives, TAPA, UWT, TYL, and other government institutions to take steps to implement the policy of socialism and self-reliance.

(c) *Membership*

Members should get thorough teaching on Party ideology so that they may understand it, and they should always be reminded of the importance of living up to its principles.

Speech "After the Arusha Declaration" 17 October 1967
Responsibilities of Leadership

In this field, as in so many others, what is called for is good, honest leadership from people who are really committed to the welfare of the citizens of Tanzania. And the kind of honest leadership that is required is not necessarily the noisiest. If a leader can encourage the people and help them to understand problems and policies by his constructive oratory, that is a very good thing. But it is not entertainment that our people want and expect from their leaders; nor do they want a lot of false promises about a Utopia that someone will bring to them; nor do they want to listen to their leader abusing some person or some group that he has set up as a scapegoat for the problems the people are experiencing.

The leaders of Tanzania—and that includes everyone present at this conference, as well as many other people—have to show, in both actions and words, that they recognize one central fact. Leaders cannot do anything for the people. We can only provide the necessary information, guidance, and organization for the people to build their own country for themselves. Leaders of Tanzania should not be making promises; we cannot fulfill them for others. We should not be complaining; complaints help no one. We should know the facts of Tanzania's situation, understand them, and give guidance to the people in the light of them.

This is essential. Leaders have to know the reality of our present position, and then show the people how, by our own efforts, we can change our present poverty into something better. It is no use pretending that certain facts are not facts; it is no use talking about "alleged" low prices of sisal, etc., when the low world price of sisal is a fact, and has been for many years, and a fact that has very important implications for the plans we should be making. Bad things do not disappear because we pretend they are not there, or because we accuse other people of causing them. We cannot run this country by complaining, and we have been entrusted with the responsibility of running this country. Complaining that we are poor, or that world prices are low, is as useless as complaining that the rains do not fall. We have to assess our present situation—which includes many things beyond our control—and work out plans to change the situation and to counteract the effect of the things we cannot alter. Then we have to execute our plans by hard and intelligent work. There is no other way. There is no shortcut.

Our people are poor. That is a fact. It is also a fact that every human being finds it easier to see the greater wealth or the greater privilege of other people than he does to see his own advantages. It is not part of a Tanzanian leader's duty simply to encourage the people in envy, or to turn that envy into hostility or hatred against others. But he does have to make it clear to the people that he is not himself among a group that is unfairly privileged. It is for this reason that the leadership qualifications have been laid down in the Arusha Declaration.

For at the very least it must be clear to our people that no leader will become wealthy by abusing his position or by exploiting others. They must know that any wealth he gains will be from wise use of the payment the people make to him in return for his service. But even this is not enough. Leaders must show the way to the development of our country and our people. If ten hunters have trapped a rabbit they are foolish idiots, wasting their energies, if they stop their hunting in order to fight over the distribution of the meat on that rabbit. They would do better to concentrate their energies on working out a better system of hunting so that they can increase the amount of meat available to them all. . . .

Freedom and Development

Speech "Implementation of Rural Socialism," 1 January 1968

In all this discussion we must realize the central fact; that an ujamaa village must be governed by the members themselves, equally. I have already stated this, but I make no apology for saying it again; it is the essence of rural socialism. Members must jointly make their own decisions on everything that is of exclusive concern to the village— where to plant, what to plant, how to share the work, how to share the returns, what to invest in the future development, and so on. Obviously the communities, and their members, must obey the laws of the land; they cannot be exempt from taxation or other national responsibilities. But the decisions about the way they run their farm and their village—the amount of private farming and ownership they allow, etc.—must be made by them, and not by others.

There will, in fact, probably be no shortage of people who come to a new embryonic village and tell the members what to do. Indeed, I hope the Agricultural Field Workers and other skilled and trained people will be offering their advice freely, and doing all they can to encourage ujamaa villages to adopt modern methods from the start. But the decisions must be made by the members, not by anyone else— even area commissioners or visiting presidents.

Yet we must be clear what we are saying here; for we have a real dilemma. It may easily happen that a visiting political or government leader knows that the people are making a mistake that could prove fatal to their ambition, either in organization, in their selection of their leader, or in their methods. The temptation to intervene must surely be very great indeed under these circumstances; part of the visitor's job is to help these communities. Obviously he should explain his point, illustrate his argument by pointing to experience elsewhere, and discuss the whole question with the members. But suppose the members still insist on their own decision? It is at that point that we have to go back to the essence of these villages; people must be allowed to make their own decisions, and therefore their own mistakes. Only if we accept this are we really accepting the philosophy of socialism and rural development. If we prevent people making their own mistakes we are preventing the establishment of ujamaa villages; we can advise and warn, but if we try to run them we are destroying them. We may have to pay a price in failures and disappointments as a result, but it cannot be avoided. And in any case obstinate local people can sometimes prove all previous experience, and all skilled advice, to be wrong! The fact that a man is employed by government, or elected in TANU—or even educated at University College—does not make him infallible!

In one sense all that I have been saying so far is a call for leadership. We need people to lead others into an understanding of the concept of ujamaa villages, to lead the members in the villages, to promote good methods of husbandry and practical methods of organization; we need people to rally the members when they get discouraged, show them the way out of their difficulties, and so on. Progress in socialist rural development does in fact depend almost entirely on leadership at all levels; it needs leadership to get the groups started, and it needs leadership to maintain them and have them grow.

Let me emphasize that this leadership I am now talking about does not imply control, any more than it implies bullying or intimidating people. A good leader will explain, teach, and inspire. In an ujamaa village he will do more; he will lead by doing. He is in the front of the people, showing them what can be done, guiding them, and encouraging them. But he is with them. You do not lead people by being so far in front or so theoretical in your teaching that the people cannot see what you are doing or saying. You do not lead people by yapping at their heels like a dog herding cattle. You can lead the people only by being one of them, by just being more active as well as more thoughtful, and more willing to teach as well as more willing to learn—from them and others.

The members of an ujamaa village must control their own affairs—I say it again! But the role of a leader is crucial and good leadership will make all the difference to the socialist success and the material success of such a community.

Let me give one example of the kind of leadership that is needed. Suppose a group of families have decided to start a cooperative farm and village, and are discussing where to build their houses. The problem is whether to build on a hill or down in the valley; and the argument is about the ease of getting water versus the danger of flooding. A good leader who is a member of this group may argue that it is better to build on the hill and face the drudgery of carrying the water until they can afford a pump and pipes; but let us suppose that despite all his efforts the general opinion is to build near the water's edge. What should he do? The answer is clear: he must play a very full part in the work of building the village in the valley. Having done that he must also think out plans for action if his fears are proved well-founded. He might persuade the members to build some of their stores on the hill so as to have a reserve in case of trouble; he might persuade them to keep a reserve of poles and thatching material on the hill that can then be used wherever and whenever it is necessary; and he will certainly work out in his own mind a plan for rescue and shelter on higher garound so that he at least knows what must be done in case of emergency.

But this kind of leadership is only one of many different kinds that will be needed. There is the same problem of management—although on a different scale—for an ujamaa farm as for a capitalist farm which employs many people. Work has still to be organized, the crops harvested and sold, etc. This will require some delegation, by the members, of their power over themselves—for you cannot have a members' meeting every day in order to decide whether to weed the beans or the tobacco! The selection of the right person as the "farm manager" or as the "farm treasurer" can be of vital importance; how then can the members be helped to choose the best man from among their number? And if they do make a mistake, how can they be sure of effecting a change, without having so much daily "democracy" in the running of the farm that no work gets done because of the time spent in talking?

These are practical questions. The little experience we have so far in Tanzania shows the importance of the village leaders. It is clear they must be strong men, yet humble; they must be capable of ensuring that everyone does a fair share of the work—including themselves—and at the same time they must be willing to accept group decisions on basic issues. For example, they must be able to convince the members that everyone will have to work for eight hours a day in order to get through all the jobs; able to accept a group decision that this will be done from 6:00 A.M. until 2:00 P.M.; and then able to allocate different members to different jobs in rotation—and see that they are done.

This brings me to the final problem that I intend to refer to today— the problem of incentives. For it is all very well so say that members will "live together and work together for the common good"; it is all very well to say a leader's job is to see that everyone does his fair share.

But we are not all angels, and it is not unknown for everyone to do a fair share on a communal project just because everyone does as much as the laziest member, and no more! What kind of organization, or what kind of rules about distribution of returns, should be recommended to groups setting up together, so as to ensure that between them they produce the maximum? For if there is no difference in return, is it not likely that the good and fast worker may get tired of putting his best efforts forward while another member merely does the bare minimum that keeps him in the scheme? In an ideal world he might shrug his shoulders and carry on; in the world as it is he might decide to do less himself, too!

Is it enough, therefore, to rely upon every member understanding the benefit to himself of everyone putting forward his maximum effort? Is it enough to rely upon social sanctions as a discipline against those who slack, with explusion as the only and final weapon against them? Or would such groups be advised to work out some system of division according to the amount of work done, or the number of hours spent on the communal projects? If you do this, are you breaking the socialist principle of equality—for it will lead to some differences in income between the members? And if you do not do it, are you allowing the poor workers, or the lazy ones, to exploit the others? But again, if you do advocate payment by work done, what about those people who work to the best of their ability, but who are sick, or weak, or just not very capable?

Mr. Chairman, there are many other problems I could raise—some of which may be raised by other speakers. . . .

. . . For the policy outlined in "Socialism and Rural Development" is not the work of a month or a year; it is the work for ten or twenty years ahead. What we have to do now is start; and the more people who understand the objectives, and who are willing to join in, the greater—and the quicker—will be our success.

Speech "Freedom and Development," 16 October 1968

. . . If the purpose of development is the greater freedom and well-being of the people, it cannot result from force. For the proverb tells the truth in this matter: you can drive a donkey to water, but you cannot make it drink. By orders, or even by slavery, you can build pyramids and magnificent roads, you can achieve expanded acreages of cultivation, and increases in the quantity of goods produced in your factories. All these things, and many more, can be achieved through the use of force; but none of them result in the development of people. Force, and deceitful promises can, in fact, only achieve short-term material goals. They cannot bring strength to a nation or a community, and they cannot provide a basis for the freedom of the people, or security for any individual or group of persons.

There is only one way in which you can cause people to undertake their own development. That is by education and leadership. Through these means—and no other—people can be helped to understand both their own needs and the things that they can do to satisfy these needs. This is the kind of leadership that TANU and government officials should be giving the people; this is the way in which we can bring development to Tanzania. But, although we must give this leadership, the decisions must come from the people themselves, and they themselves must carry out the programs they have decided upon.

There are thus two factors that are essential in the development of people. The first is leadership through education, and the second is democracy in decision-making. For leadership does not mean shouting at people; it does not mean abusing individuals or groups of people you disagree with; even less does it mean ordering people to do this or that. Leadership means talking and discussing with the people, explaining and persuading. It means making constructive suggestions, and working with the people to show by actions what it is that you are urging them to do. It means being one of the people, and recognizing your equality with them.

In particular, at this stage in our history we should not be trying to blame particular groups or individuals for things that are not to our liking, or not to the liking of the people. The exploiters, who are now apparently so beloved by our leaders that they spend all their time talking about them, are a negligible factor in our development now. Those few who remain can most effectively be dealt with by constructive development work on the part of the people and their leaders; it is certainly absurd that we leaders should spend all our time abusing exploiters—especially as some of us do not understand the work that is being done by some of the individuals we abuse. Instead we should be providing creative and positive leadership. We should have taken the trouble to understand the development policies our Party is trying to pursue, and we should be explaining these policies to the people. When we have convinced the people that TANU's policies are good and sound, then we should be working with them to create a society in which exploiters will find no opportunities for their evil doing.

But giving leadership does not mean usurping the role of the people. The people must make the decisions about their own future through democratic procedures. Leadership cannot replace democracy; it must be part of democracy. If the decision relates to national affairs, then the people make it through the National Executive Committee, and Parliament, and through the National Conference of TANU. If it is a decision about district affairs, the people make it through the district committee and district council. If it is a question of purely local interest—for example, whether to undertake a particular self-help scheme—then the people directly concerned must make the decision following a free debate. There is no other way in which real development can take place. For just as real freedom for the people requires development, so real development of the people requires freedom. . . .

References

Nyerere, Julius K., *Freedom and Unity: Uhuru na Umoja, A Selection from Writings and Speeches 1952–1965* (Dar es Salaam: Oxford University Press, 1966).

Nyerere, Julius K., *Freedom and Socialism: Uhuru na Ujamaa, A Selection from Writings and Speeches, 1965–1967* (Dar es Salaam: Oxford University Press, 1968).

Nyerere, Julius K., *Freedom and Development: Uhuru na Maendeleo, A Selection from Writings and Speeches, 1968–1973* (Dar es Salaam: Oxford University Press 1973).

FELIX HOUPHOUËT-BOIGNY

> **BORN:**
>
> *18 October 1905, Yamousoukro, Ivory Coast*
>
> **DIED:**
>
> *7 December 1993, Ivory Coast*

Physician who became founder and President of the ruling party, Parti Démocratique de la Côte d'Ivoire. Member of the French National Assembly, 1946. President of the Territorial Assembly, 1957–1959; Prime Minister, 1959–1960. First President of Côte d'Ivoire from 1960 until his death in 1993.

Houphouët-Boigny was not a writer. A collection of his thoughts, *Houphouët Speaks,* was published in 1985 through Offset-Aubin, Poitiers, France.

Houphouët Speaks

"Houphouëtism"

. . . I, personally, have never spoken of "Houphouëtism." I have done what I could to serve my country, by bringing together our sixty tribes—by involving them in a harmonious process of development, and giving equal opportunities to our farmers. They earn the same wages for their work, whether they are in the north or the west. Whether it is for crops of coffee, cocoa, cotton, hevea, palm seed, it is the same price. The state undertakes to provide transport. We also give equal opportunities to our children, irrespective of their social background. From primary level to university, education is free for the best. We practice solidarity between us.

One example: in order to ease the distress of our unemployed people, civil servants, Ivorians in the private sector, and in their turn, foreign workers, have consented, despite their reduced revenue, to a deduction of one-hundredth of their income for their brothers who have been hit by unemployment, and for their young brothers waiting to find work on coming out of university.

Effective solidarity is not an empty term with us. Tolerance is absolute. We do not have political tribunals. We have never spilled the blood of others. We assume our responsibilities at the head of this country.

May God forbid that a single drop of human blood be spilt by me, or because of me, in the Ivory Coast or anywhere in the world! God grant that all the differences that might arise between myself and others, between my country and other countries, be always solved peacefully, through dialogue, and to the exclusion of all recourse to violence.

Some say, "that is Houphouëtism." And yet, you know, I never wrote a thing. I say that with a certain amount of humor, but it's true. The two historical characters who never wrote a word, or a letter, are the most widely read in the world: Mohammed and Jesus. I am a humble man. I am not of that class. But, I too have disciples. Let the disciples speak, and write about "Houphouëtism." Don't ask me to define it. . . .

Reference

Houphouët-Boigny, Felix, *Houphouët Speaks* (Poitiers, France: 1985).

DEMOCRATIC

LEADERS

MAHATMA GANDHI

FULL NAME:

Mohandas Karamchand Gandhi

BORN:

2 October 1869, Porbandar, India

DIED:

30 January 1948, Delhi, India

Lawyer in South Africa, 1893–1914, where he was imprisoned. In 1919 Leader of the Indian Nationalist Movement against British rule. Head of the Indian National Congress. A leading theorist of ideas on nonviolence and a great moral force in India and beyond its borders. Leading nationalist who was imprisoned by the British during much of World War II. Negotiator for an independent India. Victim of assassination in January 1948.

Gandhi was prolific. His works include: *All Men Are Brothers* (Lausanne: UNESCO, 1958); *Gandhi's Autobiography* (Ahmed-abad: Navajivan Publishing House, 1986); and *Communal Unity* (Ahmedabad: Navajivan Publishing House, 1949). Biographies are many, among them: Erik Erickson, *Gandhi's Truth* (New York: W. W. Norton, 1966); and Louis Fischer, *The Life of Mahatma Gandhi* (New York: Harper, 1950).

All Men Are Brothers

There are limits to the capacity of an individual, and the moment he flatters himself that he can undertake all tasks, God is there to humble his pride. For myself, I am gifted with enough humility to look even to babes and sucklings for help.

A drop in the ocean partakes of the greatness of its parent although it is unconscious of it. But it is dried up as soon as it enters upon an existence independent of the ocean. We do not exaggerate when we say that life is a mere bubble.

I am an irrepressible optimist, because I believe in myself. That sounds very arrogant, doesn't it? But I say it from the depths of my humility. I believe in the supreme power of God. I believe in Truth and, therefore, I have no doubt in the future of this country or the future of humanity.

Mine is not a religion of the prison-house. It has room for the least among God's creation. But it is proof against insolence, pride of race, religion, or color.

I do not share the belief that there can or will be on earth one religion. I am striving, therefore, to find a common factor and to induce mutual tolerance.

I hold that a life of perfect continence in thought, speech, and action is necessary for reaching spiritual perfection. And a nation that does not possess such men is poorer for the want.

A sinner is equal to a saint in the eye of God. Both will have equal justice, and both an equal opportunity either to go forward or to go backward. Both are His children, His creation. A saint who considers himself superior to a sinner forfeits his sainthood and becomes worse than the sinner, who, unlike the proud saint, knows not what he is doing.

We often confuse spiritual knowledge with spiritual attainment. Spirituality is not a matter of knowing scriptures and engaging in philosophical discussions. It is a matter of heart culture, of unmeasurable strength. Fearlessness is the first requisite of spirituality. Cowards can never be moral.

Man should earnestly desire the well-being of all God's creation and pray that he might have the strength to do so. In desiring the well-being of all lies his own welfare; he who desires only his own or his community's welfare is selfish and it can never be well with him. . . . It is essential for man to discriminate between what he may consider to be good and what is really good for him.

I believe in the absolute oneness of God and, therefore, of humanity. What though we have many bodies? We have but one soul. The rays of the sun are many through refraction. But they have the same source. I cannot, therefore, detach myself from the wickedest soul nor may I be denied identity with the most virtuous.

If I were a dictator, religion and state would separate. I swear by my religion. I will die for it. But it is my personal affair. The state has nothing to do with it. The state would look after secular welfare, health, communications, foreign relations, currency, and so on, but not your or my religion. That is everybody's personal concern.

I am surrounded by exaggeration and untruth. In spite of my best efforts to find it, I do not know where Truth lies. But it seems to me that I have come nearer to God and Truth. It has cost me old friendships but I am not sorry for it. To me it is a sign of my having come nearer to God that I can write and speak to everybody plainly and fearlessly about the delicate issue in the teeth of the fiercest opposition, practice in full the eleven vows that I have professed, without the slightest feeling of perturbation or unrest. Sixty years of striving have at last enabled me to realize the ideal of truth and purity that I have ever set before myself.

All that we know is that one should do one's duty and leave the results in the hands of God. Man is supposed to be master of his own destiny, but it is only partly true. He can make his own destiny only in so far as he is allowed by the Great Power which overrides all our intentions, all our plans and carries out His own plans. I call that Power not by the name of Allah, Khuda, or God, but Truth. The whole truth is embodied only within the heart of that Great Power—Truth.

I know of no greater sin than to oppress the innocent in the name of God.

When I think of my littleness and my limitations on the one hand and of the expectations raised about me on the other, I become dazed for the moment, but I come to myself as soon as I realize that these expectations are a tribute not to me, a curious mixture of Jekyll and Hyde, but to the incarnation, however imperfect but comparatively great in me, of the two priceless qualities of truth and nonviolence.

There is nothing on earth that I would not give up for the sake of the country excepting of course two things and two only, namely, truth and nonviolence. I would not sacrifice these two for all the world. For to me Truth is God and there is no way to find Truth except the way of nonviolence. I do not seek to serve India at the sacrifice of Truth or God. For I know that a man who forsakes Truth can forsake his country, and his nearest and dearest ones.

* * *

Means and end are convertible terms in my philosophy of life.

They say "means are after all means." I would say "means are after all everything." As the means so the end. There is no wall of separation between means and end. Indeed the Creator has given us control (and that too very limited) over means, none over the end. Realization of the goal is in exact proportion to that of the means. This is a proposition that admits of no exception. . . .

I do not believe in short-violent-cuts to success. . . . However much I may sympathize with and admire worthy motives, I am an uncompromising opponent of violent methods even to serve the noblest of causes. There is, therefore, really no meeting-ground between the school of violence and myself. But my creed of nonviolence not only does not preclude me but compels me even to associate with anarchists and all those who believe in violence. But that association is always with the sole object of weaning them from what appears to me their error. For experience convinces me that permanent good can never be the outcome of untruth and violence. Even if my belief is a fond delusion, it will be admitted that it is a fascinating delusion.

Your belief that there is no connection between the means and the end is a great mistake. Through that mistake even men who have been considered religious have committed grievous crimes. Your reasoning is the same as saying that we can get a rose through planting a noxious weed. If I want to cross the ocean, I can do so only by means of a vessel; if I were to use a cart for that purpose, both the cart and I would soon find the bottom. "As is the God, so is the votary" is a maxim worth considering. Its meaning has been distorted and men have gone astray. The means may be likened to a seed, the end to a tree; and there is just the same inviolable connection between the means and the end as there is between the seed and the tree. I am not likely to obtain the result flowing from the worship of God by laying myself prostrate before Satan. If, therefore, anyone were to say: "I want to worship God; it does not matter that I do so by means of Satan," it would be set down as ignorant folly. We reap exactly as we sow.

Socialism is a beautiful word and so far as I am aware, in socialism all the members of society are equal—none low, none high. In the individual body, the head is not high because it is the top of the body, nor are the soles of the feet low because they touch the earth. Even as members of the individual body are equal, so are the members of society. This is socialism.

In it the prince and the peasant, the wealthy and the poor, the employer and the employee are all on the same level. In terms of religion, there is no duality in socialism. It is all unity. Looking at society all the world over, there is nothing but duality or plurality. Unity is conspicuous by its absence. . . . In the unity of my conception there is perfect unity in the plurality of designs. . . .

The spiritual weapon of self-purification, intangible as it seems, is the most potent means of revolutionizing one's environment and loosening external shackles. It works subtly and invisibly; it is an intense process though it might often seem a weary and long-drawn process, it is the straightest way to liberation, the surest and quickest and no effort can be too great for it. What it requires is faith—an unshakable mountainlike faith that flinches from nothing.

I am more concerned in preventing the brutalization of human nature than in the prevention of the sufferings of my own people. I know that people who voluntarily undergo a course of suffering raise themselves and the whole of humanity; but I also know that people who become brutalized in their desperate efforts to get victory over their opponents or to exploit weaker nations or weaker men, not only drag down themselves but mankind also. And it cannot be a matter of pleasure to me or anyone else to see human nature dragged to the mire. If we are all sons of the same God and partake of the same divine essence, we must partake of the sin of every person whether he belongs to us or to another race. You can understand how repugnant it must be to invoke the beast in any human being, how much more so in Englishmen, among whom I count numerous friends.

The method of passive resistance is the clearest and safest, because, if the cause is not true, it is the resisters, and they alone, who suffer.

* * *

Nonviolence is the greatest force at the disposal of mankind. It is mightier than the mightiest weapon of destruction devised by the ingenuity of man. Destruction is not the law of the humans. Man lives freely by his readiness to die, if need be, at the hands of his brother, never by killing him. Every murder or other injury, no matter for what cause, committed or inflicted on another is a crime against humanity.

The first condition of nonviolence is justice all around in every department of life. Perhaps, it is too much to expect of human nature. I do not, however, think so. No one should dogmatize about the capacity of human nature for degradation or exaltation.

Just as one must learn the art of killing in the training for violence, so one must learn the art of dying in the training for nonviolence. Violence does not mean emancipation from fear, but discovering the means of combating the cause of fear. Nonviolence, on the other hand, has no cause for fear. The votary of nonviolence has to cultivate the capacity for sacrifice of the highest type in order to be free from fear. He recks not if he should lose his land, his wealth, his life. He who has not overcome all fear cannot practice *ahimsā* to perfection. The votary of *ahimsā* has only one fear, that is of God. He who seeks refuge in God ought to have a glimpse of the *Atma* that transcends the body; and the moment one has a glimpse of the imperishable *Atma* one sheds the love of the perishable body. Training in nonviolence is thus diametrically opposed to training in violence. . . .

I would say to my critics to enter with me into the sufferings, not only of the people of India but of those, whether engaged in the war or not, of the whole world. I cannot look at this butchery going on in the world with indifference. I have an unchangeable faith that it is beneath the dignity of man to resort to mutual slaughter. I have no doubt that there is a way out.

Perfect nonviolence is impossible so long as we exist physically, for we would want some space at least to occupy. Perfect nonviolence whilst you are inhabiting the body is only a theory like Euclid's point or straight line, but we have to endeavor every moment of our lives. . . .

Having flung aside the sword, there is nothing except the cup of love that I can offer to those who oppose me. It is by offering that cup that I expect to draw them close to me. I cannot think of permanent enmity between man and man, and believing as I do in the theory of rebirth, I live in the hope that if not in this birth, in some other birth, I shall be able to hug all humanity in friendly embrace.

Love is the strongest force the world possesses and yet it is the humblest imaginable.

The hardest heart and the grossest ignorance must disappear before the rising sun of suffering without anger and without malice.

Nonviolence is "not a resignation from all real fighting against wickedness." On the contrary, the nonviolence of my conception is a more active and real fight against wickedness than retaliation, whose very nature is to increase wickedness. I contemplate a mental and therefore a moral opposition to immoralities. I seek entirely to blunt the edge of the tyrant's sword, not by putting up against it a sharper-edged weapon, but by disappointing his expectation that I would be offering physical resistance. The resistance of the soul that I should offer would elude him. It would at first dazzle him and at last compel recognition from him, which recognition would not humiliate but would uplift him. It may be urged that this is an ideal state. And so it is. . . .

I am but a weak aspirant, ever failing, ever trying. My failures make me more vigilant than before and intensify my faith. I can see with the eye of faith that the observance of the twin doctrine of truth and nonviolence has possibilities of which we have but very inadequate conception.

I am an irrepressible optimist. My optimism rests on my belief in the infinite possibilities of the individual to develop nonviolence. The more you develop it in your own being, the more infectious it becomes till it overwhelms your surroundings and by and by might oversweep the world. . . .

It has become the fashion these days to say that society cannot be organized or run on nonviolent lines. I join issue on that point. In a family, when a father slaps his delinquent child, the latter does not think of retaliating. He obeys his father not because of the deterrent effect of the slap but because of the offended love that he senses behind it. That, in my opinion, is an epitome of the way in which society is or should be governed. What is true of the family must be true of society, which is but a larger family.

I do not want to live at the cost of the life even of a snake. I should let him bite me to death rather than kill him. But it is likely that if God puts me to that cruel test and permits a snake to assault me, I may not have the courage to die, but that the beast in me may assert itself and I may seek to kill the snake in defending this perishable body. I admit that my belief has not become so incarnate in me as to warrant my stating emphatically that I have shed all fear of snakes so as to befriend them as I would like to be able to.

I am not opposed to the progress of science as such. On the contrary, the scientific spirit of the West commands my admiration and if that admiration is qualified, it is because the scientist of the West takes no note of God's lower creation. I abhor vivisection with my whole soul. I detest the unpardonable slaughter of innocent life in the name of science and humanity so-called, and all the scientific discoveries stained with innocent blood I count as of no consequence. If the circulation of blood theory could not have been discovered without vivisection, the human kind could well have done without it. And I see the day clearly dawning when the honest scientist of the West will put limitations upon the present methods of pursuing knowledge. . . .

Jesus Christ, Daniel, and Socrates represented the purest form of passive resistance or soul-force. All these teachers counted their bodies as nothing in comparison to their soul. Tolstoy was the best and brightest (modern) exponent of the doctrine. He not only expounded it, but lived according to it. In India, the doctrine was understood and commonly practiced long before it came into vogue in Europe. It is easy to see that soul-force is infinitely superior to body-force. If people in order to secure redress of wrongs resort to soul-force, much of the present suffering will be avoided.

Buddha fearlessly carried the war into the enemy's camp and brought down on its knees an arrogant priesthood. Christ drove out the money changers from the temple of Jerusalem and drew down curses from Heaven upon the hypocrites and the Pharisees. Both were for intensely direct action. But even as Buddha and Christ chastised, they showed unmistakable gentleness and love behind every act of theirs. They would not raise a finger against their enemies, but would gladly surrender themselves rather than the truth for which they lived. Buddha would have died resisting the priesthood, if the majesty of his love had not proved to be equal to the task of bending the priesthood. Christ died on the cross with a crown of thorns on his head defying the might of a whole empire. And if I raise resistances of a nonviolent character, I simply and humbly follow in the footsteps of the great teachers. . . .

To me political power is not an end but one of the means of enabling people to better their condition in every department of life. Political power means capacity to regulate national life through national representatives. If national life becomes so perfect as to become self-regulated, no representation becomes necessary. There is then a state of enlightened anarchy. In such a state everyone is his own ruler. He rules himself in such a manner that he is never a hindrance to his neighbor. In the ideal state, therefore, there is no political power because there is no state. But the ideal is never fully realized in life. Hence the classical statement of Thoreau that that government is best which governs the least.

I believe that true democracy can only be an outcome of nonviolence. The structure of a world federation can be raised only on a foundation of nonviolence, and violence will have to be totally given up in world affairs.

My idea of society is that while we are born equal, meaning that we have a right to equal opportunity, all have not the same capacity. It is, in the nature of things, impossible. For instance, all cannot have the same height, or color, or degree of intelligence, etc.; therefore in the nature of things, some will have ability to earn more and others less. People with talents will have more, and they will utilize their talents for this purpose. If they utilize kindly, they will be performing the work of the state. Such people exist as trustees, on no other terms. I would allow a man of intellect to earn more, I would not cramp his talent. But the bulk of his greater earnings must be used for the good of the state, just as the income of all earning sons of the father go to the common family fund. They would have their earnings only as trustees. It may be that I would fail miserably in this. But that is what I am sailing for. . . .

Mere withdrawal of the English is not independence. It means the consciousness in the average villager that he is the maker of his own destiny, he is his own legislator through his chosen representative.

We have long been accustomed to think that power comes only through legislative assemblies. I have regarded this belief as a grave error brought about by inertia or hypnotism. A superficial study of the British history has made us think that all power percolates to the people from parliaments. The truth is that power resides in the people and it is entrusted for the time being to those whom they may choose as their representatives. The parliaments have no power or even existence independently of the people. It has been my effort for the last twenty-one years to convince the people of this simple truth. Civil disobedience is the storehouse of power. Imagine a whole people unwilling to conform to the laws of the legislature and prepared to suffer the consequences of noncompliance! They will bring the whole legislative and the executive machinery to a standstill. The police and the military are of use to coerce minorities however powerful they may be. But no police or military coercion can bend the resolute will of a people, out for suffering to the uttermost.

And parliamentary procedure is good only when its members are willing to conform to the will of the majority. In other words, it is fairly effective only among compatibles.

What we want, I hope, is a government not based on coercion even of a minority but on its conversion. If it is a change from white military rule to a brown, we hardly need make any fuss. At any rate the masses then do not count. They will be subject to the same spoliation as now, if not even worse. . . .

I am not interested in freeing India merely from the English yoke. I am bent upon freeing India from any yoke whatsoever. I have no desire to exchange "king log for king stork." Hence for me the movement of swarāj is a movement of self-purification.

Our tyranny, if we impose our will on others, will be infinitely worse than that of the handful of Englishmen who form the bureaucracy. Theirs is a terrorism imposed by a minority struggling to exist in the midst of opposition. Ours will be a terrorism imposed by a majority and therefore worse and really more godless than the first. We must therefore eliminate compulsion in any shape from our struggle. If we are only a handful holding freely the doctrine of noncooperation, we may have to die in the attempt to convert others to our view, but we shall have truly defended and represented our cause. If however we enlist under our banner men by force, we shall be denying our cause and God, and if we seem to succeed for the moment, we shall have succeeded in establishing a worse terror.

A born democrat is a born disciplinarian. Democracy comes naturally to him who is habituated normally to yield willing obedience to all laws, human or divine. I claim to be a democrat both by instinct and training. Let those who are ambitious to serve democracy qualify themselves by satisfying first this acid test of democracy. Moreover, a democrat must be utterly selfless. He must think and dream not in terms of self or party but only of democracy. Only then does he acquire the right of civil disobedience. I do not want anybody to give up his convictions or to suppress himself. I do not believe that a healthy and honest difference of opinion will injure our cause. But opportunism, camouflage, or patched-up compromises certainly will. If you must dissent, you should take care that your opinions voice your innermost convictions and are not intended merely as a convenient party cry.

I value individual freedom but you must not forget that man is essentially a social being. He has risen to his present status by learning to adjust his individualism to the requirements of social progress. Unrestricted individualism is the law of the beast of the jungle. We have learnt to strike the mean between individual freedom and social restraint. Willing submission to social restraint for the sake of the well-being of the whole society enriches both the individual and the society of which one is a member.

The golden rule of conduct, therefore, is mutual toleration, seeing that we will never all think alike and we shall see Truth in fragments and from different angles of vision. Conscience is not the same thing for all. Whilst, therefore, it is a good guide for individual conduct, imposition of that conduct upon all will be an insufferable interference with everybody's freedom of conscience.

Differences of opinion should never mean hostility. If they did, my wife and I should be sworn enemies of one another. I do not know two persons in the world who had no difference of opinion, and as I am a follower of the Gita, I have always attempted to regard those who differ from me with the same affection as I have for my nearest and dearest.

I shall continue to confess blunders each time the people commit them. The only tyrant I accept in this world is the "still small voice" within me. And even though I have to face the prospect of a minority of one, I humbly believe I have the courage to be in such a hopeless minority.

I can truthfully say that I am slow to see the blemishes of fellow beings, being myself full of them, and therefore being in need of their charity. I have learnt not to judge anyone harshly and to make allowances for defects that I may detect.

I have often been charged with having an unyielding nature. I have been told that I would not bow to the decisions of the majority. I have been accused of being autocratic. . . . I have never been able to subscribe to the charge of obstinacy or autocracy. On the contrary, I pride myself on my yielding nature in nonvital matters. I detest autocracy. Valuing my freedom and independence I equally cherish them for others. I have no desire to carry a single soul with me, if I cannot appeal to his or her reason. My unconventionality I carry to the point of rejecting the divinity of the oldest *shāstras* if they cannot convince my reason. But I have found by experience that, if I wish to live in society and still retain my independence, I must limit the points of utter independence to matters of first-rate importance. In all others which do not involve a departure from one's personal religion or moral code, one must yield to the majority.

I do not believe in the doctrine of the greatest good of the greatest number. It means in its nakedness that in order to achieve the supposed good of 51 percent the interest of 49 percent may be, or rather, should be sacrificed. It is a heartless doctrine and has done harm to humanity. The only real, dignified, human doctrine is the greatest good of all, and this can only be achieved by uttermost self-sacrifice.

Those who claim to lead the masses must resolutely refuse to be led by them, if we want to avoid mob law and desire ordered progress for the country. I believe that mere protestation of one's opinion and surrender to the mass opinion is not only not enough, but in matters of vital importance, leaders must *act* contrary to the mass of opinion if it does not commend itself to their reason.

A leader is useless when he acts against the prompting of his own conscience, surrounded as he must be by people holding all kinds of views. He will drift like an anchorless ship, if he has not the inner voice to hold him firm and guide him.

While admitting that man actually lives by habit, I hold that it is better for him to live by the exercise of will. I also believe that men are capable of developing their will to an extent that will reduce the exploitation to a minimum. I look upon an increase of the power of the state with the greatest fear because, although while apparently doing good by minimizing exploitation, it does the greatest harm to mankind by destroying individuality, which lies at the root of all progress. We know of so many cases where men have adopted trusteeship, but none where the state has really lived for the poor.

The state represents violence in a concentrated and organized form. The individual has a soul, but as the state is a soulless machine, it can never be weaned from the violence to which it owes its very existence.

It is my firm conviction that if the state suppressed capitalism by violence, it will be caught in the coil of violence itself and fail to develop nonviolence at any time.

Self-government means continuous effort to be independent of government control whether it is foreign government or whether it is national. *Swaraj* government will be a sorry affair if people look up to it for the regulation of every detail of life.

We must be content to die, if we cannot live as free men and women.

The rule of majority has a narrow application, i.e., one should yield to the majority in matters of detail. But it is slavery to be amenable to the majority, no matter what its decisions are. Democracy is not a state in which people act like sheep. Under democracy individual liberty of opinion and action is jealously guarded.

In matters of conscience the law of majority has no place.

It is my certain conviction that no man loses his freedom except through his own weakness.

It is not so much British guns that are responsible for our subjection as our voluntary cooperation.

Even the most despotic government cannot stand except for the consent of the governed, which consent is often forcibly procured by the despot. Immediately the subject ceases to fear the despotic force, his power is gone. . . .

Reference

Gandhi, Mahatma, *All Men Are Brothers* (Lausanne: UNESCO, 1958).

JAWAHARLAL NEHRU

BORN:

14 November 1889, Allahabad, India

DIED:

27 May 1964, New Delhi, India

General Secretary of the Congress Party in 1923. President of the Congress Party in 1929. Gandhi's political heir. In prison in 1940 and 1942–1945. First Prime Minister of independent India, 1947–1964.

His writings include: *Jawaharlal Nehru: An Autobiography* (London: Jonathan Cape, 1941). Biographies include: Michael Brecher, *Nehru* (Boston: Beacon Press, 1962) and Sarvepalli Gopal, *Jawaharlal Nehru: A Biography* (London: Jonathan Cape, 1975); *Nehru: The First Sixty Years* (New York: The John Day Company, 1965); *Jawaharlal Nehru: Reminiscences* (New Delhi: Sterling Publishers, 1989).

Nehru: The First Sixty Years

1947 correspondence referring to Gandhi

This little man has been and is a colossus before whom others, big in their own way and in their own space and time, are small of stature. In this world of hatred and uttermost violence and the atom bomb, this man of peace and goodwill stands out, a contrast and a challenge. In an acquisitive society madly searching for new gadgets and new luxuries, he takes to his loincloth and his mud hut. In man's race for wealth and authority and power, he seems to be a nonstarter, looking the other way; and yet that authority looks out of his gentle but hard eyes, that power seems to fill his slight and emaciated frame, and flows out to others. Wherein does his strength lie, wherein this power and authority? . . .

Often we do not understand him; we argue with him and get angry sometimes. But the anger passes, leaving us rather ashamed of our lack of balance and restraint. Only that pervasive influence remains and he seems to become the vehicle and embodiment of some greater force of which even he is perhaps only dimly conscious. Is that the spirit of India, the accumulated experience of the millennia that lie behind our race, the memory of a thousand tortured lives?

Conditions all over India to some extent are very unsatisfactory. There is a certain disruptive tendency at work which affects our work in every direction. The whole Congress organization is suffering from it and we, who are in the government, have no time at all to give to any work except the immediate problems that confront us. . . . I want you to realize that there is in some ways a progressive deterioration in the situation and I feel very unhappy about it. . . .

When our own approach is not quite clear and there are different viewpoints and pulls, then it becomes even more difficult to deal with the problem.

I know that we must learn to rely upon ourselves and not run to you for help on every occasion. But we have got into this bad habit and we do often feel that if you had been easier of access our difficulties would have been less.

Speech commemorating the immersion of Gandhi's ashes in the Ganges, 12 February 1948

The last journey has ended. The final pilgrimage has been made. For over fifty years Mahatma Gandhi wandered all over our great country, from the Himalayas and the North Western Frontier and the Brahmaputra in the North East to Kanya Kumari (Cape Comorin) in the far South. He visited every part and corner of this country, not as a mere tourist or visitor for the sake of amusement, but in order to understand and serve the Indian people. Perhaps no other Indian in history has traveled so much in India or got to know the common people so well and served them so abundantly. And now his journey in this world is over, though we have still to continue for a while. Many people are moved to grief, and this is proper and natural. But why should we grieve? Do we grieve for him or for something else? In his life as in his death there has been a radiance that will illumine our country for ages to come. Why then should we grieve for him? Let us grieve rather for ourselves, for our own weaknesses, for the ill will in our hearts, for our dissensions and for our conflicts. Remember that it was to remove all these that Mahatmaji gave his life. Remember that during the past few months it was on this that he concentrated his vast energy and service. If we honor him, do we honor his name only or do we honor what he stood for, his advice and teachings, and more especially what he died for?

Let us, standing here on the banks of the Ganga, search our own hearts and ask ourselves the question: how far have we followed the path shown to us by Gandhiji and how far have we tried to live in peace and cooperation with others? If even now we follow the right path, it will be well with us and well with our country.

Our country gave birth to a mighty soul and he shone like a beacon not only for India but for the whole world. And yet he was done to death by one of our own brothers and compatriots. How did this happen? You might think that it was an act of madness, but that does not explain this tragedy. It could only occur because the seed for it was sown in the poison of hatred and enmity that spread throughout the country and affected so many of our people. Out of that seed grew this poisonous plant. It is the duty of all of us to fight this poison of hatred and ill will. If we have learned anything from Gandhiji, we must bear no ill will or enmity toward any person. The individual is not our enemy. It is the poison within him that we fight and that we must put an end to. We are weak and feeble, but Gandhiji's strength passed to us also to some extent. In his reflected glory we also gained in stature. The splendor and the strength were his and the path he showed was also his. We stumbled often enough and fell down in our attempts to follow that path and serve our people as he wanted us to serve them.

Our pillar of strength is no more. But why do we say that? His image is enshrined in the hearts of the million men and women who are present here today, and hundreds of millions of our countrymen, who are not present here, will also never forget him. Future generations of our people, who have not seen him or heard him, will also have that image in their hearts because that image is now a part of India's inheritance and history. Thirty or forty years ago began in India what is called the Gandhi Age. It has come to an end today. And yet I am wrong, for it has not ended. Perhaps it has really begun now, although somewhat differently. Thus far we have been leaning on him for advice and support, from now onwards we have to stand on our own feet and to rely on ourselves. May his memory inspire us and his teachings light our path. Remember his ever recurring message: "Root out fear from your hearts, and malice, put an end to violence and internecine conflict, keep your country free."

He brought us to freedom and the world marveled at the way he did it. But at the very moment of gaining our freedom we forgot the lesson of the Master. A wave of frenzy and fanaticism overtook our people and we disgraced the fair name of India. Many of our youth were misled and took to wrong paths. Are we to drive them away and crush them? They are our own people and we have to win them over and mold them and train them to right thought and action.

The communal poison, which has brought disaster upon us, will put an end to our freedom also if we are not vigilant and if we do not take action in time. It was to awaken us to this impending danger that Gandhiji undertook his last fast two or three weeks ago. His self-crucifixion roused the nation's conscience and we pledged before him to behave better. It was only then that he broke his fast.

Gandhiji used to observe silence for one day in every week. Now that voice is silenced forever and there is unending silence. And yet that voice resounds in our ears and in our hearts, and it will resound in the minds and hearts of our people and even beyond the borders of India, in the long ages to come. For that voice is the voice of truth, and though truth may occasionally be suppressed it can never be put down. Violence for him was the opposite of truth and therefore he preached to us against violence not only of the hand but of the mind and heart. If we do not give up this internecine violence and have the utmost forbearance and friendliness for others, we are doomed as a nation. The path of violence is perilous and freedom seldom exists for long where there is violence. Our talk of Swarajya and the people's freedom is meaningless, if we have internal violence and conflict. . . .

Democracy demands discipline, tolerance, and mutual regard. Freedom demands respect for the freedom of others. In a democracy changes are made by mutual discussion and persuasion and not by violent means. If a government has no popular support, another government that commands that popular support takes its place. It is only small groups who know that they cannot get sufficient popular support that resort to methods of violence, imagining in their folly that they can gain their ends in this way. This is not only utterly wrong but it is also utterly foolish. For the reaction to the violence of the minority, which seeks to coerce the majority, is to provoke the majority into violence against them.

This great tragedy has happened because many persons, including some in high places, have poisoned the atmosphere of this country of ours. It is the duty of the government as well as the people to root out this poison. We have had our lesson at a terrible cost. Is there anyone amongst us now who will not pledge himself after Gandhiji's death to fulfill his mission—a mission for which the greatest man of our country, the greatest man in the world, has laid down his life?

You and I and all of us will go back from these sands of our noble river, the Ganga. We shall feel sad and lonely. We shall never see Gandhiji again. We used to run to him for advice and guidance whenever we were confronted with any great problem or when we felt ill at ease or in doubt. There is none to advise us now or to share our burdens. It is not I alone or a few of us who looked up to him for help. Thousands and hundreds of thousands of our countrymen considered him their intimate friend and counselor. All of us felt that we were his children. Rightly he was called the Father of our Nation and in millions of homes today there is mourning as on the passing away of a beloved father. . . .

What kind of triumph did Gandhiji wish for us? Not the triumph for which most people and countries strive through violence, fraud, treachery, and evil means. That kind of victory is not stable. For the foundations of a lasting victory can only be laid on the rock of truth. Gandhiji gave us a new method of struggle and political warfare and a new kind of diplomacy. He demonstrated the efficacy of truth and goodwill and nonviolence in politics. He taught us to respect and cooperate with every Indian as a man and as a fellow citizen, irrespective of his political belief or religious creed. We all belong to Mother India and have to live and die here. We are all equal partners in the freedom that we have won. Every one of our three or four hundred million people must have an equal right to the opportunities and blessings that free India has to offer. It was not a few privileged persons that Gandhiji strove and died for. We have to strive for the same ideal and in the same way. Then only shall we be worthy to say, "Mahatma Gandhi ki Jai." . . .

An Autobiography

. . . It was true that I had achieved, almost accidentally as it were, an unusual degree of popularity with the masses; I was appreciated by the intelligentsia; and to young men and women I was a bit of a hero, and a halo of romance seemed to surround me in their eyes. Songs had been written about me, and the most impossible and ridiculous legends had grown up. Even my opponents had often put in a good word for me and patronizingly admitted that I was not lacking in competence or in good faith.

Only a saint, perhaps, or an inhuman monster could survive all this, unscathed and unaffected, and I can place myself in neither of these categories. It went to my head, intoxicated me a little, and gave me confidence and strength. I became (I imagine so, for it is a difficult task to look at oneself from outside) just a little bit autocratic in my ways, just a shade dictatorial. And yet I do not think that my conceit increased markedly. I had a fair measure of my abilities, I thought, and I was by no means humble about them. But I knew well enough that there was nothing at all remarkable about them, and I was very conscious of my failings. A habit of introspection probably helped me to retain my balance and view many happenings connected with myself in a detached manner. Experience of public life showed me that popularity was often the handmaiden of undesirable persons; it was certainly not an invariable sign of virtue or intelligence. Was I popular then because of my failings or my accomplishments? Why indeed was I popular?

Not because of intellectual attainments, for they were not extraordinary, and, in any event, they do not make for popularity. Not because of so-called sacrifices, for it is patent that hundreds and thousands in our own day in India have suffered infinitely more, even to the point of the last sacrifice. My reputation as a hero is entirely a bogus one, and I do not feel at all heroic, and generally the heroic attitude or the dramatic pose in life strikes me as silly. As for romance, I should say that I am the least romantic of individuals. It is true that I have some physical and mental courage, but the background of that is probably pride: personal, group, and national, and a reluctance to be coerced into anything.

I had no satisfactory answer to my question. Then I proceeded along a different line of inquiry. I found that one of the most persistent legends about my father and myself was to the effect that we used to send our linen weekly from India to a Paris laundry. We have repeatedly contradicted this, but the legend persists. Anything more fantastic and absurd it is difficult for me to imagine, and if anyone is foolish enough to indulge in this wasteful snobbery, I should have thought he would get a special mention for being a prize fool.

Another equally persistent legend, often repeated in spite of denial, is that I was at school with the Prince of Wales. The story goes on to say that when the Prince came to India in 1921 he asked for me; I was then in jail. As a matter of fact, I was not only not at school with him, but I have never had the advantage of meeting him or speaking to him.

I do not mean to imply that my reputation or popularity, such as they are, depend on these or similar legends. They may have a more secure foundation, but there is no doubt that the superstructure has a thick covering of snobbery, as is evidenced by these stories. At any rate, there is the idea of mixing in high society and living a life of luxury and then renouncing it all, and renunciation has always appealed to the Indian mind. As a basis for a reputation this does not at all appeal to me. I prefer the active virtues to the passive ones, and renunciation and sacrifice for their own sakes have little appeal for me. I do value them from another point of view—that of mental and spiritual training—just as a simple and regular life is necessary for the athlete to keep in good physical condition. And the capacity for endurance and perseverance in spite of hard knocks is essential for those who wish to dabble in great undertakings. But I have no liking or attraction for the ascetic view of life, the negation of life, the terrified abstention from its joys and sensations. I have not consciously renounced anything that I really valued; but then values change.

The question that my friend had asked me still remained unanswered: did I not feel proud of this hero worship of the crowd? I disliked it and wanted to run away from it, and yet I had got used to it, and when it was wholly absent, I rather missed it. Neither way brought satisfaction, but, on the whole, the crowd had filled some inner need of mine. The notion that I could influence them and move them to action gave me a sense of authority over their minds and hearts; and this satisfied, to some extent, my will to power. On their part, they exercised a subtle tyranny over me, for their confidence and affection moved inner depths within me and evoked emotional responses. Individualist as I was, sometimes the barriers of individuality seemed to melt away, and I felt that it would be better to be accursed with these unhappy people than to be saved alone. But the barriers were too solid to disappear, and I peeped over them with wondering eyes at this phenomenon that I failed to understand.

Conceit, like fat on the human body, grows imperceptibly, layer upon layer, and the person whom it affects is unconscious of the daily accretion. Fortunately the hard knocks of a mad world tone it down or even squash it completely, and there has been no lack of these hard knocks for us in India during recent years. The school of life has been a difficult one for us, and suffering is a hard taskmaster.

I have been fortunate in another respect also—the possession of family members and friends and comrades, who have helped me to retain a proper perspective and not to lose my mental equilibrium. Public functions, addresses by municipalities and local boards and other public bodies, processions and the like, used to be a great strain on my nerves and my sense of humor and reality. The most extravagant and pompous language would be used, and everybody would look so solemn and pious that I felt an almost uncontrollable desire to laugh, or to stick out my tongue, or stand on my head, just for the pleasure of shocking and watching the reactions on the faces at that august assembly! Fortunately for my reputation and for the sober respectability of public life in India, I have suppressed this mad desire and usually behaved with due propriety. But not always. Sometimes there has been an exhibition on my part in a crowded meeting, or more often in processions, which I find extraordinarily trying. I have suddenly left a procession, arranged in our honor, and disappeared in the crowd, leaving my wife or some other person to carry on, perched up in a car or carriage, with that procession.

This continuous effort to suppress one's feelings and behave in public is a bit of a strain, and the usual result is that one puts on a glum and solid look on public occasions. Perhaps because of this I was once described in an article in a Hindu magazine as resembling a Hindu widow! I must say that, much as I admire Hindu widows of the old type, this gave me a shock. The author evidently meant to praise me for some qualities he thought I possessed—a spirit of gentle resignation and renunciation and a smileless devotion to work. I had hoped that I possessed—and, indeed, I wish that Hindu widows would possess—more active and aggressive qualities and the capacity for humor and laughter. Gandhiji once told an interviewer that if he had not had the gift of humor he might have committed suicide, or something to this effect. I would not presume to go so far, but life certainly would have been almost intolerable for me but for the humor and light touches that some people gave to it.

My very popularity and the brave addresses that came my way, full (as is, indeed, the custom of all such addresses in India) of choice and flowery language and extravagant conceits, became subjects of raillery in the circle of my family and intimate friends. The high-sounding and pompous words and titles that were often used for all those prominent in the national movement, were picked out by my wife and sisters and others and bandied about irreverently. I was addressed as Bharat Bhushan—"Jewel of India" Tyagamurti—"O Embodiment of Sacrifice," and this lighthearted treatment soothed me, and the tension of those solemn public gatherings, where I had to remain on my best behavior, gradually relaxed. Even my little daughter joined in the game. Only my mother insisted on taking me seriously, and she never wholly approved of any sarcasm or raillery at the expense of her darling boy. Father was amused; he had a way of quietly expressing his deep understanding and sympathy.

But all these shouting crowds, and dull and wearying public functions, and interminable arguments, and the dust and tumble of politics touched me on the surface only, though sometimes the touch was sharp and pointed. My real conflict lay within me, a conflict of ideas, desires, and loyalties, of subconscious depths struggling with outer circumstances, of an inner hunger unsatisfied. I became a battleground, where various forces struggled for mastery. I sought an escape from this; I tried to find harmony and equilibrium, and in this attempt I rushed into action. That gave me some peace; outer conflict relieved the strain of the inner struggle.

Why am I writing all this sitting here in prison? The quest is still the same, in prison or outside, and I write down my past feelings and experiences in the hope that this may bring me some peace and psychic satisfaction. . . .

References

Nehru, Jawaharlal, *Nehru: The First Sixty Years* (New York: The John Day Company, 1965).

Nehru, Jawaharlal, *An Autobiography* (London: Jonathan Cape, 1941).

INDIRA GANDHI

FULL NAME:

Indira Nehru Gandhi

BORN:

19 November 1917, Allahabad, India

DIED:

31 October 1984, New Delhi, India

Only child of Jawaharlal Nehru. President of the Congress Party in 1959 and Minister of Information in 1964. Leader of the Congress Party and Prime Minister in 1966 and served three consecutive terms as Prime Minister of India from 1966 to 1977 and a fourth term from 1980 to 1984. Assassination victim in 1984.

Most of Indira Gandhi's work are selected speeches for different years, published by the Ministry of Information, Publications Division, New Delhi, 1966–1972. Biographies include: Krishha Bhatia, *Indira: A Biography of Prime Minister Gandhi* (New York: Praeger, 1974); and Dom F. Moraes, *Indira Gandhi* (Boston: Little Brown, 1980).

Selected Speeches

"The Message of Mahatma," 1968

Each person's understanding of Gandhiji is a measure of his own change and growth. Whilst Gandhiji was alive, many of my age group found it difficult to understand him. Some of us were impatient with what we considered to be his fads, and we found some of his formulations obscure. We took his Mahatma-hood for granted, but quarreled with him for bringing mysticism into politics.

This applied not only to my generation. In his *Autobiography*, my father describes the difficulty which he and others of his generation felt in integrating Gandhian ideas into their own thought structure. But little by little, the experience of the ebb and flow of our national movement enabled my father to arrive at a fuller understanding of Gandhiji and to weave the essential elements of Gandhiji's thinking into his own. He called him a "magician" and devotedly attempted to translate Gandhian thought into contemporary terms, to make it more comprehensible and to extend its influence to young people and intellectuals.

Gandhiji himself did not demand unquestioning obedience. He did not want acceptance of his ends and means without a full examination. He encouraged discussion. How many times have I not argued with him, even when a mere girl? He regarded no honest opinion as trivial and always found time for those who dissented from him—a quality rare in teachers in our country or in prophets anywhere. He was an untypical prophet also in that he did not lay claim to revelation. He held forth neither blandishment of reward nor fear of punishment. Nor was he weighed down by the burden of his mission. He was a saint who quipped and had use for laughter.

The centenary year of Gandhiji's birth also marks the fiftieth anniversary of the Jallianwala Bagh tragedy. Those who confuse rigidity or harshness with strength would do well to ponder over the effect of this so-called strong-handed action on the future of the British Empire. Seldom has a single event so moved an entire nation, shocking it into a reappraisal of values and aims. It made a powerful impact on men like Motilal Nehru and the poet Rabindranath Tagore. Tagore gave up his knighthood and wrote passionately and understandingly on the problems of colonialism. My grandfather was drawn, along with the entire family, into Gandhiji's circle. Our lives changed. The mood of the entire country changed. It was the year which brought Gandhiji to the helm of our political movement. Looking back on this half century, we are better able to realize the full impact of his personality and of his teaching, though a total assessment is still beyond us. We are too near to him and are still in a state of transition. Not for decades will we be able to wholly measure the extent of his work for India and for all mankind. Even so, one cannot but marvel at the turn Gandhiji gave to our history in that one year. It was as though with his two thin hands he lifted up a whole people. What changes he brought about in the personal lives of such a vast number of people, eminent and humble alike! To be the prime mover of politics is not a greater achievement than to influence so profoundly the inner lives of people. Gandhiji differs from his forerunners on the national scene in that he rejected the politics of the elite and found the key to mass action. He was a leader closely in tune with the mass mind, interpreting it and at the same time molding it. He was the crest of the wave but they, the people, were the wave itself.

Gandhiji freed us from fear. The political liberation of the country was not the culmination but a mere by-product of his liberation of the spirit. Even more far-reaching was the alteration he brought about in the social climate of India. Gandhiji set us free also from the walls and fetters of our social tradition. It was his axiomatic assumption of the equality of women and men, of the supposedly lowborn and highborn, the urban and the rural, that inducted the masses into the Gandhian movement. In the long history of India, every reformer has fought against the hierarchy of caste and the debasement of women but no one succeeded in breaking down discrimination to the extent that Gandhiji did. The women of India owe him a special debt of gratitude. And so do all other groups who suffered from age-old handicaps.

Mahatma Gandhi once wrote, "Let no one say that he is a follower of Gandhi. It is enough that I should be my own follower. I know what an inadequate follower I am of myself, for I cannot live up to the convictions I stand for."

The Gandhians would have us believe that Gandhiji evolved a universal philosophy, analyzing everything, reconciling everything and prescribing for every contingency. How unfair this would be to a man who never assumed omniscience and never stopped his experiments with truth and understanding. He was an integrated being but he did not deal in absolutes. Few men were greater idealists than he, but few more practical. He propounded fundamental truths, but in every plan of action that he drew up, he proceeded on the basis of "One step is enough for me." . . .

To me, Gandhiji is not a collection of dry thoughts and dicta but a living man who reminds one of the highest level to which a human being can evolve. Containing the best from the past, he lived in the present, yet for the future. Hence the timelessness of his highest thoughts.

Much that he said and wrote was for the solution of immediate problems; some was for the inner guidance of individuals. His intellect did not feed on derived information. He fashioned his ideas as tools in the course of his experiments in the laboratory of his own life.

Speaking of Gandhiji's work in South Africa, Gopal Krishna Gokhale said that he made heroes out of clay. Sometimes I wonder whether we have not become clay again. The exaltation which a truly great teacher produces in his time cannot last very long. But the teaching and thought of such people have a reach farther than their own time and country. We who were born in Gandhiji's own time and country have a special obligation to cherish his image. More than his words, his life was his message.

It is not despite but through his time and place that man achieves true universality. Gandhiji identified himself totally with the common people of India. For this he even changed his mode of dress. Yet he was receptive to the best thought from other parts of the world. The impact on him of his days in England and South Africa as a student and practitioner of law was evident in his insistence on sanitation and in his habit of examining all that he heard by strictly applying the evidence test. But he assimilated everything he adopted and evolved Indian solutions to Indian problems.

I hesitate to speak of the other great teaching left us by Gandhiji, namely, nonviolence. I hesitate not because I find any justification for violence. Mankind has accumulated such a fearful store of weapons of destruction that I sometimes wonder whether we have any right to hope. Wars still erupt here and there, but even more distressing and alarming is the growth in all parts of the world of hatred in thought and violence in action, and the reckless recourse to the agitational approach. Gandhiji said, "In the midst of darkness, light persists." We must have faith. The ultimate justification of Gandhiji is that he showed how armed strength could be matched without arms. If this could happen once, can it not happen again?

Life means struggle, and the higher you aim, the more you wish to achieve, the greater is the work and sacrifice demanded of you. Men of all religions have evoked the eternal truths. It is the great good fortune of India that she has given birth to great sons who have again and again revitalized her ancient thought to make it a part of the lives of the people. In our own lives, we were guided through perilous times by Mahatma Gandhi and Jawaharlal Nehru, who merged themselves in the general good. Each complemented the other. Each taught that every decision should be put to the acid test of its relevance to the welfare of the multitude. More than any ism, this guiding principle will save us from error. As Jawaharlal Nehru said, "The greatest prayer that we can offer is to take a pledge to dedicate ourselves to the truth, and to the cause for which this great countryman of ours lived and for which he has died."

* * *

"In the history of India, there have been occasions when a cloud, no bigger than a man's hand, has soon covered the whole sky," so wrote Mahatma Gandhi in 1921. He himself poured life-giving water on a land thirsting for freedom.

In just four weeks in 1919, he changed the outlook of his subcontinent. He transformed the cowed and the weak into a nation that fearlessly asserted its right to be free. He gave his people a new weapon, which ultimately delivered them from colonial rule. This weapon was *satyagraha*, civil disobedience or nonviolent noncooperation. Literally, the word means "insistence on truth." It was a weapon that did not need physical strength. But to be effective it did need the greatest self-discipline.

After Mahatma Gandhi conducted his first *satyagraha* campaigns in the country, it took India thirty long years to wrest freedom. During this time we learnt the full meaning of freedom. He taught us that a people who permitted injustice and inequality in their own society did not deserve freedom and could not preserve it. Thus equality of opportunity, irrespective of birth, sex, or religion, became the objectives of our struggle for freedom.

These ideals have come down to us through the ages, from the Buddha, Ashoka, and Akbar, to name only three of the many wise and great men who have molded our history. Mahatma Gandhi reinterpreted these old truths and applied them to our daily lives, and so made them comprehensible to the humblest of us. He forged them as instruments for a mass struggle for a peaceful political and social revolution. His stress was on reconciliation, whether amongst classes or amongst nations.

Mahatma Gandhi interpreted the yearnings of the inarticulate masses and spoke the words that they themselves were struggling to express. Wearing the loincloth, which was then all that the vast majority of our peasants could afford, he identified himself with the downtrodden and the poor. To those whom Indian society had regarded as untouchables, he gave the name "men of God," and to the last days of his life he worked ceaselessly for their uplift and emancipation. During the communal riots, this frail and aged man walked amongst the people and, through sheer faith and force of spirit, achieved miracles of reconciliation, which peacekeeping armies could not have wrought. He met his martyrdom because he refused to compromise with hatred and intolerance.

Mahatma Gandhi relied on spiritual strength. He believed in limiting one's wants and in working with one's hands. He modeled his life according to the ancient Hindu book, the Bhagavad Gita or "the Lord's Song," but he drew inspiration also from Christianity and Islam. Indeed he thought that no man could follow his own religion truly unless he equally honored other religions. Long before him, in the third century B.C., the Emperor Ashoka had written, "In reverencing the faith of others, you will exalt your own faith and will get your own faith honored by others."

Mahatma Gandhi called his life-story "My Experiments with Truth." His truth was neither exclusive nor dogmatic. As he once wrote, "There are many ways to truth, and each of us sees truth in fragment." Thus, tolerance is essential to truth; violence is incompatible with it. Nor can peace come from violence. To him, ends and means are equally important. He believed that no worthy objective could be achieved through an unworthy instrument.

Mahatma Gandhi will be remembered as a prophet and a revolutionary. He stood for resistance—nonviolent resistance—to tyranny and social injustice. He asked us to apply a test, which I quote, "Whenever you are in doubt, or when the self becomes too much with you, recall the case of the poorest and weakest man who you may have seen, and ask yourself if the step you contemplate is going to be any use to him. Will he gain anything by it? Will it restore him control over his own life and destiny? Will it lead to *swaraj*, that is self-government, for the hungry and spiritually starving millions? Then, you will find your doubts and self melting away." This test is valid for our times, indeed for all times. It is valid for India and for the world.

As long as there is oppression and degradation of the human spirit, people will seek guidance from him to assert their dignity. The weapon of nonviolent resistance which he has given mankind, is today used in other lands and other climes. The world rightly regards Gandhi as the greatest Indian since the Buddha. Like the Buddha, he will continue to inspire mankind in its progress to a higher level of civilization. In India, it is our endeavor to build a future that is worthy of him.

Speech on the occasion of the first Nehru Memorial Lecture,
New Delhi, 14 November 1961

My father, as you all know, was the staunchest of nationalists with a deep and abiding love for India, for her traditions, and for her culture.

But he projected, in international assemblies and wherever he went, a new and dynamic image of India. To the downtrodden and underprivileged and the oppressed all over the world, he became the very personification of freedom, not merely freedom as the opposite of enslavement but freedom in its wider sense, that is, a liberation of the spirit. He realized fully that political freedom would always be endangered if it were not accompanied by economic regeneration of self-reliance. A perceptive historian, he was deeply conscious of weaknesses in our society and strove relentlessly to cut asunder the old rusty chains of superstition and narrowness of mind which isolated us from the growth of science and technology. He knew the spirit could be liberated and free only when there was rational thinking and rational living. He felt that India could be vibrant and alive only if it could liberate its spirit. But he thought also, as indeed did Gandhiji, that no one can attain to it unless certain basic needs of the body are also met. This is why he laid so much stress on the utilization of science and technology for improving the conditions of living of our people, for widening their horizon in every way.

Speech at a function arranged by the Uruguayan Ministry of Culture and UNESCO, Montevideo, 28 September 1968

All true cultures are integrative. Our great men have interpreted the ancient thought of our sages and have made it comprehensible to the common man. We in India do have a philosophical outlook on life. But it is only half the truth. We could not have built up a magnificent civilization if we had not had a well-organized material base. But it is true that Indian culture has had a capacity to assimilate ideas and make them its own. We have learned to create unity out of diversity.

It has been our good fortune that in time of need India has produced many great men. One such was Jawaharlal Nehru. He loved the Indian people and worked for India. Once he wrote, "If any people choose to think of me then I should like them to say: this was a man who with all his mind and heart loved India and the Indian people and they in turn were indulgent to him and gave him all their love most abundantly and extravagantly."

Yet, he was universal in spirit, and his mind and heart encompassed the whole world. One prime minister of Britain called Jawaharlal Nehru the first citizen of the modern world and another, Sir Winston Churchill, described him as a man who had conquered hatred and fear. Amongst his personal friends, he counted some of the great minds of his time—in science and arts and literature no less than in politics. Yet he was completely at home with the simplest peasant. I am glad to see the honor and affection in which he is held here.

Reference

Gandhi, Indira, *Selected Speeches* 1966–1969 (New Delhi: Ministry of Information, 1971).

CHARLES DE GAULLE

BORN:

22 November 1890, Lille, France

DIED:

9 November 1970, Colombery-les-Deux-Eglises

Soldier, statesman, and writer. He led the resistance to Nazi Germany from abroad. Prior to the German occupation of France, de Gaulle entered the government as Undersecretary of State for Defense and War. He left for England and in 1943 moved to Algiers, where he became President of the French Committee for National Liberation. He headed two provisional governments after the war, resigning in January 1946 and returning to his home. He was invested as Prime Minister in June 1958 and on December 21 was elected President. He was reelected in 1965. He resigned on April 28, 1968.

De Gaulle was a prolific writer. His works include: *France and Her Army*, translated by F. L. Dash (London: Hutchinson & Co., 1945); *The Complete War Memoirs of Charles de Gaulle*, Three Volumes (New York: Simon and Schuster, 1960–64); *The Edge of the Sword*, translated by Gerard Hopkins (New York: Criterion Books, 1960). Biographies include Jean Lacoutre, *De Gaulle* (London: Hutchinson, 1970); Brian Crozier, *De Gaulle* (New York: Scribner's, 1973); Raymond Aron, *An Explanation of de Gaulle* (New York: Harper & Row, 1966).

The Edge of the Sword*

"Of Politics and the Soldier"

They will go two by two/Till the world's end, step by step and side by side.
                                                        —MUSSET

I

In the theater of peacetime, it is the statesman who plays the chief rôle. Whether the masses greet him with applause or boos, it is for him first of all that they have eyes and ears. Then suddenly war calls another actor from the wings, pushes him to the middle of the stage, and trains the limelight on him: the military chief appears. A drama is about to begin which will be played by statesman and soldier in concert. No matter how great the crowd of extras, how noisy the audience, it is on these two performers that attention will be centered. So closely interwoven is their dialogue that nothing said by either has any relevance, point, or effect except with reference to the other. If one of them misses his cue, then disaster overwhelms them both. However widely in fact the work of the civil government differs from that of the High Command, no one would seriously question the interdependence of the two authorities. What policy can hope to succeed if the country's arms are brought low? Of what use is strategical planning if the means of carrying it out are not forthcoming? Without the legions the skill of the Roman Senate would have gone for nothing. What could Richelieu, Mazarin, and Louvois have achieved if they had not had the royal army at their backs? Had Dumouriez been defeated at Valmy, the Revolution would have been strangled at birth. The names of Bismarck and Moltke are inseparably connected with German unity. The statesmen and the great soldiers of the recent war will, in spite of everything, be inextricably mingled in our memories of the final triumph.

It is the task of political leaders to dominate opinion: that of the monarch, of the council, of the people, since it is from these that they draw their authority. They have no value, and can do nothing, except in the name of the sovereign power. But their abilities matter less than their skill in pleasing, and promises are more effective than arguments. The statesman, therefore, must concentrate all his efforts on captivating men's minds. He must know when to dissemble, when to be frank. He must pose as the servant of the public in order to become its master. He must outbid his rivals in self-confidence, and only after a thousand intrigues and solemn undertakings will he find himself

* First published in 1930

entrusted with full power. Even when he has it in his grasp, he can never be completely open in his dealings, for he must still be concerned to please, to know how to convince prince or parliament, how to gratify popular passions and soothe the anxieties of vested interests. His authority, no matter how unquestioned, is precarious. Public opinion, that inconstant mistress, follows his lead with a capricious step, ready to stop dead should he race too far ahead, to take giant strides when he thinks it advisable to move with caution. Ungrateful, it rates at a low price the efforts he has made, and, even at the moment of success, is only too ready to listen to his opponents. But, if he makes a mistake, the pack is at his heels; if he shows signs of weakness it hurls itself upon him. What does the statesman's empire amount to? A court cabal, an intrigue in the Council, a shift of opinion in the Assembly can snatch it from him in a moment. Toppled from his pedestal he finds nothing but injustice awaiting him. Great or small, historic figure or colorless politician, he comes and goes between power and powerlessness, between prestige and public ingratitude. The whole of his life and the sum total of his work are marked by instability, restlessness, and storm, and so are very different from those of the soldier. The soldier's profession is that of arms, but the power they give him has to be strictly organized. From the moment that he embarks upon it he becomes a slave of a body of regulations, and so remains all through his active life. The army is generous but jealous. It guides his steps, supports him in his moments of weakness, develops such gifts as he may have. But it also keeps a tight hold on him, overriding his doubts and holding his enthusiasm in check. As a man he suffers much from its demands, for he must renounce his personal liberty, his chances of making money, and, sometimes, sacrifice his life, and what greater offering could there be? But at this high cost it opens the door for him to the empire of armed might. That is why, though he often grumbles at his slavery, he clings to it; nay, more, he loves it, and glories in the price he has to pay. "It is my honor!" he says.

In the company of his fellows he rises to a position of power, but by degrees, for the hierarchy of which he is a member is strict and uncompromising. For the soldier there is always yet some higher rank to attain, some recognition to be gained. On the other hand, such authority as he may wield is absolute. Supported by discipline and strengthened by tradition, it makes use of everything in the way of credit and prestige which the military order gives to him who holds command. Under the iron rod and the shield of the "regulations" he marches with a firm step along a road that, grueling though it may be, points straight ahead.

The statesman and the soldier bring, therefore, to a common task very different characters, methods, and anxieties. The former reaches his goal by roundabout ways, the latter by direct approach. The one is long-sighted though his vision may be clouded, sees realities as complex, and sets himself to master them by trickery and calculation. The other sees with clear eyes what there is to be seen straight in front of his nose and thinks it simple and capable of being controlled by resolution. In dealing with immediate problems, the statesman's first concern is what people will say of him; the soldier looks for counsel to principles.

This unlikeness is the cause of a certain amount of mutual misunderstanding. The soldier often regards the man of politics as unreliable, inconstant, and greedy for the limelight. Bred on imperatives, the military temperament is astonished by the number of pretenses in which the statesman has to indulge. The terrible simplicities of war are in strong contrast to the devious methods demanded by the art of government. The impassioned twists and turns, the dominant concern with the effect to be produced, the appearance of weighing others in terms not of their merit but of their influence—all inevitable characteristics in the civilian whose authority rests upon the popular will—cannot but worry the professional soldier, broken in as he is to a life of hard duties, self-effacement, and respect shown for services rendered. . . .

II

When faced with the challenge of events, the man of character has recourse to himself. His instinctive response is to leave his mark on action, to take responsibility for it, to make it *his own business*. Far from seeking shelter behind his professional superiors, taking refuge in textbooks, or making the regulations bear the responsibility for any decision he may make, he sets his shoulders, takes a firm stand, and looks the problem straight in the face. It is not that he wishes to turn a blind eye to orders, or to sweep aside advice, but only that he is passionately anxious to exert his own will, to make up his own mind. It is not that he is unaware of the risks involved, or careless of consequences, but that he takes their measure honestly, and frankly accepts them. Better still, he embraces action with the pride of a master; for if he takes a hand in it, it will become his, and he is ready to enjoy success on condition that it is really *his own*, and that he derives no profit from it. He is equally prepared to bear the weight of failure, though not without a bitter sense of satisfaction. In short, a fighter who finds within himself all the zest and support he needs, a gambler more intent on success than profits, a man who pays his debts with his own money lends nobility to action. Without him there is but the dreary task of the slave; thanks to him, it becomes the divine sport of the hero.

This does not mean that he carries out his purpose unaided. Others share in it who are not without the merit of self-sacrifice and obedience, and give of their best when carrying out his orders. Some there are who even contribute to his planning—technicians or advisers. But it is character that supplies the essential element, the creative touch, the divine spark; in other words, the basic fact of initiative. Just as talent gives to a work of art a special stamp of understanding and expression, character imparts its own dynamic quality to the elements of action, and gives it personality which, when all is said, makes it live and move, just as the talent of the artist breathes life into matter.

The power to vivify an undertaking implies an energy sufficient to shoulder the burden of its consequences. The man of character finds an especial attractiveness in difficulty, since it is only by coming to grips with difficulty that he can realize his potentialities. Whether or not he proves himself the stronger is a matter between it and him. He is a jealous lover and will share with no one the prizes or the pains that may be his as a result of trying to overcome obstacles. Whatever the cost to himself, he looks for no higher reward than the harsh pleasure of knowing himself to be the man responsible.

This passion for self-reliance is obviously accompanied by some roughness in method. The man of character incorporates in his own person the severity inherent in his effort. This is felt by his subordinates, and at times they groan under it. In any event, a leader of this quality is inevitably aloof, for there can be no authority without prestige, nor prestige unless he keeps his distance. Those under his command mutter in whispers about his arrogance and the demands he makes. But once action starts, criticism disappears. The man of character then draws to himself the hopes and the wills of everyone as the magnet draws iron. When the crisis comes, it is him they follow, it is he who carries the burden on his own shoulders, even though they collapse under it. On the other hand, the knowledge that the lesser men have confidence in him exalts the man of character. The confidence of those under him gives him a sense of obligation. It strengthens his determination but also increase his benevolence, for he is a born protector. If success attends upon his efforts he distributes its advantages with a generous hand. If he meets with failure, he will not let the blame fall on anybody but himself. The security he offers is repaid by the esteem of his men.

In his relationship with his superiors he is generally at a disadvantage. He is too sure of himself, too conscious of his strength to let his conduct be influenced by a mere wish to please. The fact that he finds his powers of decision within himself, and not imposed upon him by an order, often disinclines him to adopt an attitude of passive obedience. All he asks is that he shall be given a task to do, and then be left alone to do it. He wants to be the captain of his own ship, and this many senior officers find intolerable since, temperamentally incapable of taking a wide view, they concentrate on details and draw their mental sustenance from formalities. And so it comes about that the authorities dread any officer who has the gift of making decisions and cares nothing for routine and soothing words. "Arrogant and undisciplined" is what the mediocrities say of him, treating the thoroughbred with a tender mouth as they would a donkey that refuses to move, not realizing that asperity is, more often than not, the reverse side of a strong character, that you can only lean on something that offers resistance, and that resolute and inconvenient men are to be preferred to easygoing natures without initiative.

But when the position becomes serious, when the nation is in urgent need of leaders with initiative who can be relied upon, and are willing to take risks, then matters are seen in a very different light, and credit goes to whom credit is due. A sort of a ground swell brings the man of character to the surface. His advice is listened to, his abilities are praised, and his true worth becomes apparent. To him is entrusted, as a matter of course, the difficult task, the direction of the main effort, the decisive mission. Everything he suggests is given serious consideration; all his demands are met. He, for his part, does not take advantage of this change in his fortunes, but shows a generous temperament and responds wholeheartedly when he is called upon. Scarcely, even, does he taste the sweet savor of revenge, for his every faculty is brought to bear upon the action he must take.

This rallying to character when danger threatens is the outward manifestation of an instinctive urge, for all men at heart realize the supreme value of self-reliance, and know that without it there can be no action of value. In the last resort, we must, to quote Cicero, "judge all conduct in the light of the best examples available," for nothing great has ever been achieved without that passion and that confidence which is to be found only in the man of character. Alexander would never have conquered Asia, Galileo would never have demonstrated the movement of the earth, Columbus would never have discovered America, nor Richelieu have restored the authority of the crown, had they not believed in themselves and taken full control of the task in hand. Boileau would never have established the laws of classic taste, Napoleon would never have founded an empire, Lesseps would never have pierced the isthmus of Suez, Bismarck would never have achieved German unity, nor Clemenceau have saved his country, had they hearkened to the counsels of shortsighted prudence or the promptings of fainthearted modesty. We can go further and say that those who have done great deeds have often had to take the risk of ignoring the merely routine aspects of discipline. Examples are plentiful: Pélissier at Sebastopol stuffing the Emperor's threatening dispatches into his pocket unopened and reading them only after the action was over; Lanrezac saving his army after Charleroi by breaking off the battle, contrary to orders; Lyautey keeping the whole of Morocco in 1914, in the teeth of instructions issued at a higher level. After the Battle of Jutland and the English failure to take the opportunity offered them of destroying the German fleet, Admiral Fisher, then First Sea Lord, exclaimed in a fury after reading Jellicoe's dispatch: "He has all Nelson's qualities but one: he doesn't know how to disobey!"

It goes without saying that the successes achieved by great men have always depended on their possessing many different faculties. Character alone, if unsupported by other qualities, results only in rashness and obstinacy. On the other hand, purely intellectual gifts, even of the highest order, are not sufficient. History is filled with examples of men who, though they were gifted beyond the ordinary, saw their labors brought to nothing because they were lacking in character. Whether serving, or betraying, their masters in the most expert fashion, they were entirely uncreative. Notable they may have been, but famous never. . . .

"Of Prestige"

To carry glory in one's inmost self . . .
—VILLIERS DE L'ISLE-ADAM

I

These are hard days for authority. Current custom attacks it and legislation tends to weaken it. In the home and in the factory, in the State and in the street, it arouses impatience and criticism rather than confidence and obedience. Jostled from below whenever it shows its head, it has come to doubt itself, to feel its way, to assert itself at the wrong moment; when it is unsure, with reticence, excuses, and extreme caution; when it is overconfident, harshly, roughly, and with a niggling formalism.

This decay of public authority has followed hard on the heels of a decline in the moral standards, both in society and in politics, from what they were in an older Europe. For many centuries, whether from conviction or self-interest, men have sought a basis for power, and, for an élite, a justification which led to the creation of hierarchies. But cracks have appeared in the fabric of these old conventions, and it is now in a sorry state. Our contemporaries, by reason of their shifting beliefs, their anemic traditions, and exhausted loyalties, have lost the sense of deference and no longer wish to observe the rules of conduct that were once firmly established.

"*Nos dieux sont décrépits et la misère en tombe.*"

A crisis of this kind, no matter how general it may appear to be, cannot last indefinitely. Men, in their hearts, can no more do without being controlled than they can live without food, drink, and sleep. As political animals they feel the need for organization, that is to say for an established order and for leaders. Authority may totter on its shaken foundations, but sooner or later the natural equilibrium that lies at the base of all things will provide it with new ones, better, or less good, but, in any case, firm enough to establish discipline in a new form. These new foundations are, even now, emerging into the light of day. They are apparent in the recognition given to the value of individuals, and to the ascendancy of a few men. What the masses once granted to birth or office, they now give to those who can assert themselves. What legitimate prince was ever so blindly obeyed as is now the dictator who owes his rise to nothing but his own audacity? What established authority ever so left its mark upon events as does the proficiency of an engineer in the modern world? What conquerors were ever so wildly acclaimed as are our athletes who owe success only to their own endeavors?

This transformation of authority cannot but have its effect upon military discipline. In the army, as elsewhere, they say: "Respect is disappearing." But in fact it has only changed its object. To be obeyed, the man in command must today rely less on his rank than on his own value. We can no longer confuse power and its attributes.

This does not, of course, mean that none of the things in which discipline used to be steeped can be dispensed with. Men do not change so quickly or so completely, nor does human nature move by leaps and bounds. Authority exercised over other people still depends to a large extent upon the aura that surrounds rank and seniority. At the same time, the ascendancy exercised by the personality of the master, and his consequent ability to ensure obedience, have always existed. But in these unsettled times, and in a society where traditions and institutions have been violently disturbed, the conventions of obedience are growing weaker, and the mainspring of command is now to be found in the personal prestige of the leader.

II

Prestige is largely a matter of feeling, suggestion, and impression, and it depends primarily on the possession of an elementary gift, a natural aptitude that defies analysis. The fact of the matter is that certain men have, one might almost say from birth, the quality of exuding authority, as though it were a liquid, though it is impossible to say precisely of what it consists. Even those who come under its influence frequently feel surprised by their own reactions to it. This phenomenon has something in common with the emotion of love which cannot be explained without the presence of what we call "charm," for want of a better word. Still stranger is the fact that the authority exerted by certain individuals has often nothing to do with their intrinsic gifts or abilities. It is no rare thing to find men of outstanding intellect who are without it, whereas others far less highly endowed possess it in a very high degree.

But though there is something in what we call a "natural gift of authority" which cannot be acquired, but comes from the innermost being of some individuals, and varies in each, there are also a number of constant and necessary elements on which it is possible to lay one's finger, and these can be acquired or developed. The true leader, like the great artist, is a man with an inborn propensity that can be strengthened and exploited by the exercise of his craft.

First and foremost, there can be no prestige without mystery, for familiarity breeds contempt. All religions have their holy of holies, and no man is a hero to his valet. In the designs, the demeanor and the mental operations of a leader there must be always a "something" which others cannot altogether fathom, which puzzles them, stirs them, and rivets their attention. In saying this I do not mean that he must shut himself away in an ivory tower, remote from, and inaccessible to, his subordinates. On the contrary, if one is to influence men's minds, one must observe them carefully and make it clear that each has been marked out from among his fellows, but only on condition that this goes with a determination to give nothing away, to hold in reserve some piece of secret knowledge which may at any moment intervene, and the more effectively from being in the nature of a surprise. The latent faith of the masses will do the rest. Once the leader has been judged capable of adding the weight of his personality to the known factors of any situation, the ensuing hope and confidence will add immensely to the faith reposed in him.

This attitude of reserve demands, as a rule, a corresponding economy of words and gestures. No doubt these things are of the surface only, but they play a large part in determining the reaction of the crowd. There would even seem to be some relationship between a man's inner force and his outward seeming. No experienced soldier has ever underrated the importance of appearances. Whereas ordinary officers must be content with behaving correctly in front of their men, the great leaders have always carefully stage-managed their effects. They have made of this a very special art, as Flaubert very well knew when, in *Salammbô*, he described the stimulus imparted to the vacillating troops by the calculated arrival of Hamilcar upon the scene. Every page of the *Commentaries* provides us with evidence of the studied manner in which Caesar moved and held himself in public. We know how much thought Napoleon gave to showing himself in such a manner as to impress his audience.

Sobriety of speech supplies a useful contrast to theatricality of manner. Nothing more enhances authority than silence. It is the crowning virtue of the strong, the refuge of the weak, the modesty of the proud, the pride of the humble, the prudence of the wise, and the sense of fools. The man who is moved by desire or fear is naturally led to seek relief in words. If he yields to the temptation it is because by *externalizing* his passion or his terror he can come to terms with them. To speak is to dilute one's thoughts, to give vent to one's ardor, in short, to dissipate one's strength, whereas, what action demands is concentration. Silence is a necessary preliminary to the ordering of one's thoughts. One calls troops to attention before explaining what is expected of them. Since everything that comes from the leader is in the highest degree contagious, he can be sure, in that way, of establishing an atmosphere of calmness and alertness, provided he does not say a word more than is necessary. Men instinctively distrust an officer who is prodigal of speech. *Imperatoria brevitas* said the Romans. Regulations have always laid it down that orders should be concise and to the point, and we, today, have only too good reason to know how easily authority is undermined when it is swamped under floods of paper or drowned in torrents of oratory. . . .

But this systematic habit of reserve adopted by the leader produces little or no effect unless it is felt to conceal strength of mind and determination. It is no rare thing to come on men whose impassivity has earned them a brief reputation for sphinxlike wisdom, though they are very soon seen to be no better than nitwits. It is precisely from the contrast between inner power and outward control that ascendancy is gained, just as style in a gambler consists in his ability to show greater coolness than usual when he has raised his stake, and an actor's most notable effects depend upon his skill in producing the appearance of emotion when he is keeping strong control of himself. Barrès had only to look at the statues of Alexander, with their evidence of com-

bined passion and serenity, of the august and the terrible, to understand how he came to possess that authority which enabled him, for
thirteen years of the most exacting trials and tribulations, to maintain
order among a host of jealous underlings and unruly troops, and to
impose Hellenism on a corrupt and savage world.

What, above all else, we look for in a leader is the power to dominate events, to leave his mark on them, and to assume responsibility
for the consequences of his actions. The setting up of one man over
his fellows can be justified only if he can bring to the common task
the drive and certainty that comes of character. But why, for that matter, should a man be granted, free gratis and for nothing, the privilege
of domination, the right to issue orders, the pride of seeing them
obeyed, the thousand and one tokens of respect, unquestioning obedience, and loyalty that surround the seat of power? To him goes the
greater part of the honor and glory. But that is fair enough, for he
makes the best repayment that he can by shouldering the risks. Obedience would be intolerable if he who demands it did not use it to produce effective results, and how can he do so if he does not possess the
qualities of daring, decision, and initiative?

The masses are the less deceived in this matter since, deprived of a
master, they soon suffer from the results of their own turbulence. Not
even the best trained and most experienced sailors could get their ship
out of harbor if there were not someone to direct the operation. No
four men, even though each was as strong as Hercules, could lift and
carry a stretcher without there being somebody to see that they move
in step. A disorganized crowd faced by the need to act is fearful, and
the apprehension of each man's neighbor adds to his own. "Fear is the
mainspring of assemblies." Ardant du Picq has shown how easy it is
for troops to be carried away by it. That is why the energy of a leader
is so necessary to stiffen those under his command, just as the presence of life buoys reassures the passengers on board a ship. It is
enough for them to know that they are available; that, should danger
come, they can cling to them with confidence. . . .

It is essential that the plan on which the leader has concentrated all
his faculties shall bear the mark of grandeur. It must, indeed, respond
to the cravings felt by men who, imperfect themselves, seek perfection
in the end they are called upon to serve. Conscious of their own limitations and restricted by nature, they give free rein to unlimited hopes,
and each measuring his own littleness, accepts the need for collective
action on condition that it contribute to an end which is, in itself,
great. No leader will ever succeed in asserting himself unless he can
touch that spring. All whose rôle it is to command and direct the
crowd are fully aware of this fact. It is the basis of eloquence. There is

not an orator but will dress up the poorest argument in the garments of greatness. It is the king post of big business: every company prospectus commends itself to the public by talking of progress. It is the springboard of political parties, each one of which unceasingly declares that universal happiness is the end and purpose of its program. Consequently, whatever orders the leader may give, they must be swathed in the robes of nobility. He must aim high, show that he has vision, act on the grand scale, and so establish his authority over the generality of men who splash in shallow water. He must personify contempt for contingencies, and leave it to his subordinates to be bogged down in detail. He must put from him all that smacks of niggling and leave it to the humdrum individuals to be circumspect and wary. The question of virtue does not arise. The perfection preached in the Gospels never yet built up an empire. Every man of action has a strong dose of egotism, pride, hardness, and cunning. But all those things will be forgiven him, indeed, they will be regarded as high qualities, if he can make of them the means to achieve great ends. Thus, by satisfying the secret desires of men's hearts, by providing compensation for the cramped conditions of their lives, he will capture their imagination, and, even should he fall by the way, will retain, in their eyes, the prestige of those heights to which he did his best to lead them. But he who never rises above the commonplace and is content with little, will never be of much account. At most he will be remembered as a good servant, but never as a master who can draw to himself the faith and the dreams of mankind.

It is, indeed, an observable fact that all leaders of men, whether as political figures, prophets, or soldiers, all those who can get the best out of others, have always identified themselves with high ideals, and this has given added scope and strength to their influence. Followed in their lifetime because they stand for greatness of mind rather than self-interest, they are later remembered less for the usefulness of what they have achieved than for the sweep of their endeavors. Though sometimes reason may condemn them, feeling clothes them in an aura of glory. In the concourse of great men Napoleon will always rank higher than Parmentier. So true is this that history gives a sort of somber magnificence to certain men whose claim to fame rests merely on the fact that they were the instigators of revolts and brutalities, because their crimes were committed in the name of some high-sounding cause.

Aloofness, character, and the personification of greatness, these qualities it is that surround with prestige those who are prepared to carry a burden that is too heavy for lesser mortals. The price they have to pay for leadership is unceasing self-discipline, the constant taking of risks, and a perpetual inner struggle. The degree of suffering involved varies according to the temperament of the individual; but it is bound to be no less tormenting than the hair shirt of the penitent. This helps to explain those cases of withdrawal that, otherwise, are so hard to understand. It constantly happens that men with an unbroken record of success and public applause suddenly lay the burden down. For, in addition to everything else, the leader who keeps himself, perforce, in isolation from his fellows, turns his back upon those simpler pleasures that are the gift of unconstraint, familiar intercourse, and, even, of friendship. He must accept the loneliness that, according to Faguet, is the "wretchedness of superior beings." Contentment and tranquility and the simple joys that go by the name of happiness are denied to those who fill positions of great power. The choice must be made, and it is a hard one: whence that vague sense of melancholy that hangs about the skirts of majesty, in things no less than in people. One day somebody said to Napoleon, as they were looking at an old and noble monument: "How sad it is!" "Yes," came the reply, "as sad as greatness."

III

Not only is the spirit of the age sapping the foundations of individual authority; it is delivering a determined attack on the time-honored prestige of public authorities. The intrinsic features of the organs of government may not have shown much change, but it is an undoubted fact that criticism and irreverence are pressing harder on them than before, and dealing shrewder blows. . . .

Reference

de Gaulle, Charles, *The Edge of the Sword* (New York: Greenwood Press, Criterion Books, 1960).

SIR WINSTON CHURCHILL

FULL NAME:

Sir Winston Leonard Spencer Churchill

BORN:

30 November 1874 at Blenheim Palace,
Great Britain

DIED:

25 January 1965, London, Great Britain

Home Secretary, 1910–1911; First Lord of Admiralty, 1911–1915; Secretary for War and Air, 1919–1921; Chancellor of the Exchequer, 1924–1929; again First Lord of the Admiralty, 1939. Prime Minister of Great Britain, May 1940 to July 1945; 1951–1955.

A prolific author, his works include: *The Second World War*, Six Volumes (Boston: Houghton Mifflin, 1948–1953); and *Complete Speeches*, 1897–1965, edited by Robert Rhodes James (New York: Chelsea House, 1974). Awarded Nobel Prize in literature, 1953.

He was himself the biographer of Lord Randolph Churchill and of Marlborough, Four Volumes (London: 1933–1938). Among the many biographies of Churchill are: Joseph P. Lash, *Roosevelt and Churchill*, 1934–1941 (Franklin Center, PA: 1976), and Henry Pelling, *Winston Churchill* (London: Macmillan, 1974). A multivolume biography of Churchill was written by his son, Randolph Churchill, and Martin Gilbert; also A.J.P. Taylor, *Churchill Revised* (New York: Dial Press, 1969).

The Second World War:
Triumph and Tragedy

"Message to the Nation from the Prime Minister,"
26 July 1945

The decision of the British people has been recorded in the votes counted today. I have therefore laid down the charge that was placed upon me in darker times. I regret that I have not been permitted to finish the work against Japan. For this however all plans and preparations have been made, and the results may come much quicker than we have hitherto been entitled to expect. Immense responsibilities abroad and at home fall upon the new government, and we must all hope that they will be successful in bearing them.

It only remains for me to express to the British people, for whom I have acted in these perilous years, my profound gratitude for the unflinching, unswerving support that they have given me during my task, and for the many expressions of kindness that they have shown toward their servant.

Great Destiny

Speech delivered to the House of Commons,
3 September 1939

. . . We must expect many disappointments, and many unpleasant surprises, but we may be sure that the task that we have freely accepted is one not beyond the compass and the strength of the British Empire and the French Republic. The prime minister said it was a sad day, and that is indeed true, but at the present time there is another note that may be present, and that is a feeling of thankfulness that, if these great trials were to come upon our island, there is a generation of Britons here now ready to prove itself not unworthy of the days of yore and not unworthy of those great men, the fathers of our land, who laid the foundations of our laws and shaped the greatness of our country.

This is not a question of fighting for Danzig or fighting for Poland. We are fighting to save the whole world from the pestilence of Nazi tyranny and in defense of all that is most sacred to man. This is no war of domination or imperial aggrandizement or material gain; no war to shut any country out of its sunlight and means of progress. It is a war, viewed in its inherent quality, to establish, on impregnable rocks, the rights of the individual, and it is a war to establish and revive the stature of man. Perhaps it might seem a paradox that a war undertaken in the name of liberty and right should require, as a necessary part of its processes, the surrender for the time being of so many of the dearly valued liberties and rights. In these last few days the House of Commons has been voting dozens of bills that hand over to the executive our most dearly valued traditional liberties. We are sure that these liberties will be in hands that will not abuse them, that will use them for no class or party interests, that will cherish and guard them, and we look forward to the day, surely and confidently we look forward to the day, when our liberties and rights will be restored for us, and when we shall be able to share them with the peoples to whom such blessings are unknown.

Address broadcast 1 October 1939

. . . Here I am in the same post as I was twenty-five years ago. Rough times lie ahead; but how different is the scene from that of October 1914! Then the French front, with its British army fighting in the line, seemed to be about to break under the terrible impact of German Imperialism. Then Russia had been laid low at Tannenberg; then the whole might of the Austro-Hungarian Empire was in battle against us; then the brave, warlike Turks were about to join our enemies. Then we had to be ready night and day to fight a decisive sea battle with a formidable German fleet almost, in many respects, the equal of our own. We faced those adverse conditions then; we have nothing worse to face tonight.

In those days of 1914 also, Italy was neutral; but we did not know the reason for her neutrality. It was only later on that we learned that by a secret clause in the original Treaty of the Triple Alliance, Italy had expressly reserved to herself the right to stand aside from any war that brought her into conflict with Great Britain. Much has happened since then. Misunderstandings and disputes have arisen, but all the more do we appreciate in England the reason why this great and friendly nation of Italy, with whom we have never been at war, has not seen fit to enter the struggle.

I do not underrate what lies before us, but I must say this: I cannot doubt we have the strength to carry a good cause forward, and to break down the barriers that stand between the wage-earning masses of every land and that free and more abundant daily life, which science is ready to afford. That is my conviction, and I look back upon the history of the past to find many sources of encouragement. Of all the wars that men have fought in their hard pilgrimage, none was more noble than the great Civil War in America nearly eighty years ago. Both sides fought with high conviction, and the war was long and hard. All the heroism of the South could not redeem their cause from the stain of slavery, just as all the courage and skill that the Germans always show in war will not free them from the reproach of Nazism, with its intolerance and its brutality. We may take good heart from what happened in America in those famous days of the nineteenth century. We may be sure that the world will roll forward into broader destinies. We may remember the words of old John Bright after the American Civil War was over, when he said to an audience of English working folk: "At last after the smoke of the battlefield had cleared away, the horrid shape which had cast its shadow over the whole continent had vanished and was gone forever."

Address given at the Free Trade Hall, Manchester, 27 January 1940

We have been five months at war against the world's greatest military power and the world's greatest air power. When the war began in September most of us expected that very soon our cities would be torn and charred by explosion and fire, and few would have dared to plan for the end of January a splendid gathering such as I see before me here this afternoon. I know of nothing more remarkable in our long history than the willingness to encounter the unknown, and to face and endure whatever might be coming to us, which was shown in September by the whole mass of the people of this island in the discharge of what they felt sure was their duty. There never was a war that seemed so likely to carry its terrors at once into every home, and there never was a war into which the whole people entered with the same united conviction that, God helping, they could do no other.

This was no war planned and entered upon by a government, or a class, or a party. On the contrary, the government labored for peace to the very end; and during those last days the only fear in Britain was lest, weighted down by their awful responsibilities, they should fail to rise up to the height of the occasion. They did not fail, and the prime minister led us forward in one great body into a struggle against aggression and oppression, against wrongdoing, faithlessness, and cruelty, from which there can be no turning back. We cannot tell what the course of that struggle will be, into what regions it will carry us, how long it will last, or who will fall by the way. But we are sure that in the end right will win, that freedom will not be trampled down, that a truer progress will open, and a broader justice will reign. And we are determined to play our part worthily, faithfully, and to the end.

Come then: let us to the task, to the battle, to the toil—each to our part, each to our station. Fill the armies, rule the air, pour out the munitions, strangle the U-boats, sweep the mines, plow the land, build the ships, guard the streets, succor the wounded, uplift the downcast, and honor the brave. Let us go forward together in all parts of the Empire, in all parts of the island. There is not a week, nor a day, nor an hour to lose.

Speech to the House of Commons, 13 May 1940

On Friday evening last I received His Majesty's commission to form a new administration. It was the evident wish and will of Parliament and the nation that this should be conceived on the broadest possible basis and that it should include all parties, both those who supported the late government and also the parties of the Opposition. I have completed the most important part of this task. A war cabinet has been formed of five members, representing, with the Opposition Liberals, the unity of the nation. The three party leaders have agreed to serve, either in the war cabinet or in high executive office. The three fighting services have been filled. It was necessary that this should be done in one single day, on account of the extreme urgency and rigor of events. A number of other key positions were filled yesterday, and I am submitting a further list to His Majesty tonight. I hope to complete the appointment of the principal ministers during tomorrow. The appointment of the other ministers usually takes a little longer, but I trust that, when Parliament meets again, this part of my task will be completed, and that the administration will be complete in all respects. . . .

To form an administration of this scale and complexity is a serious undertaking in itself, but it must be remembered that we are in the preliminary stage of one of the greatest battles in history, that we are in action at many points in Norway and in Holland, that we have to be prepared in the Mediterranean, that the air battle is continuous and that many preparations have to be made here at home. In this crisis I hope I may be pardoned if I do not address the House at any length today. I hope that any of my friends and colleagues, or former colleagues, who are affected by the political reconstruction, will make all allowance for any lack of ceremony with which it has been necessary to act. I would say to the House, as I said to those who have joined this government: "I have nothing to offer but blood, toil, tears, and sweat."

We have before us an ordeal of the most grievous kind. We have before us many, many long months of struggle and of suffering. You ask, what is our policy? I will say: it is to wage war, by sea, land, and air, with all our might and with all the strength that God can give us: to wage war against a monstrous tyranny, never surpassed in the dark, lamentable catalogue of human crime. That is our policy. You ask, what is our aim? I can answer in one word: Victory—victory at all costs, victory in spite of all terror, victory, however long and hard the road may be; for without victory, there is no survival. Let that be realized; no survival for the British Empire; no survival for all that the British Empire has stood for, no survival for the urge and impulse of the ages, that mankind will move forward toward its goal. But I take up my task with buoyancy and hope. I feel sure that our cause will not be suffered to fail among men. At this time I feel entitled to claim the aid of all, and I say, "Come, then, let us go forward together with our united strength."

Address broadcast 19 May 1940

. . . Our task is not only to win the battle—but to win the war. After this battle in France abates its force, there will come the battle for our island—for all that Britain is, and all that Britain means. That will be the struggle. In that supreme emergency we shall not hesitate to take every step, even the most drastic, to call forth from our people the last ounce and the last inch of effort of which they are capable. The interests of property, the hours of labor, are nothing compared with the struggle for life and honor, for right and freedom, to which we have vowed ourselves.

I have received from the chiefs of the French Republic, and in particular from its indomitable prime minister, M. Reynaud, the most sacred pledges that whatever happens they will fight to the end, be it bitter or be it glorious. Nay, if we fight to the end, it can only be glorious.

Having received His Majesty's commission, I have formed an administration of men and women of every party and of almost every point of view. We have differed and quarreled in the past; but now one bond unites us all—to wage war until victory is won, and never to surrender ourselves to servitude and shame, whatever the cost and the agony may be. This is one of the most awe-striking periods in the long history of France and Britain. It is also beyond doubt the most sublime. Side by side, unaided except by their kith and kin in the great dominions and by the wide empires that rest beneath their shield—side by side, the British and French peoples have advanced to rescue not only Europe but mankind from the foulest and most soul-destroying tyranny that has ever darkened and stained the pages of history. Behind them—behind us—behind the armies and fleets of Britain and France—gather a group of shattered States and bludgeoned races: the Czechs, the Poles, the Norwegians, the Danes, the Dutch, the Belgians—upon all of whom the long night of barbarism will descend, unbroken even by a star of hope, unless we conquer, as conquer we must; as conquer we shall.

Today is Trinity Sunday. Centuries ago words were written to be a call and a spur to the faithful servants of Truth and Justice: "Arm yourselves, and be ye men of valor, and be in readiness for the conflict; for it is better for us to perish in battle than to look upon the outrage of our nation and our altar. As the Will of God is in Heaven, even so let it be."

"Message to the People," broadcast 17 June 1940

The news from France is very bad and I grieve for the gallant French people who have fallen into this terrible misfortune. Nothing will alter our feelings toward them or our faith that the genius of France will rise again. What has happened in France makes no difference to our actions and purpose. We have become the sole champions now in arms to defend the world cause. We shall do our best to be worthy of this high honor. We shall defend our island home and with the British Empire we shall fight on unconquerable until the curse of Hitler is lifted from the brows of mankind. We are sure that in the end all will come right.

Speech to the House of Commons, 18 June 1940

. . . Much will depend upon this; every man and every woman will have the chance to show the finest qualities of their race, and render the highest service to their cause. For all of us, at this time, whatever our sphere, our station, our occupation, or our duties, it will be a help to remember the famous lines:

> He nothing common did or mean,
> Upon that memorable scene.

I have thought it right upon this occasion to give the House and the country some indication of the solid, practical grounds upon which we base our inflexible resolve to continue the war. There are a good many people who say, "Never mind. Win or lose, sink or swim, better die than submit to tyranny—and such a tyranny." And I do not dissociate myself from them. But I can assure them that our professional advisers of the three services unitedly advise that we should carry on the war, and that there are good and reasonable hopes of final victory. We have fully informed and consulted all the self-governing dominions, these great communities far beyond the oceans who have been built up on our laws and on our civilization, and who are absolutely free to choose their course, but are absolutely devoted to the ancient motherland, and who feel themselves inspired by the same emotions that lead me to stake our all upon duty and honor. We have fully consulted them, and I have received from their prime ministers, Mr. Mackenzie King of Canada, Mr. Menzies of Australia, Mr. Fraser of New Zealand, and General Smuts of South Africa—that wonderful man, with his immense, profound mind, and his eye watching from a distance the whole panorama of European affairs—I have received from all these eminent men, who all have governments behind them elected on wide franchises, who are all there because they represent the will of their people, messages couched in the most moving terms in which they endorse our decision to fight on, and declare themselves ready to share our fortunes and to persevere to the end. That is what we are going to do. . . .

What General Weygand called the Battle of France is over. I expect that the battle of Britain is about to begin. Upon this battle depends the survival of Christian civilization. Upon it depends our own British life, and the long continuity of our institutions and our Empire. The whole fury and might of the enemy must very soon be turned on us. Hitler knows that he will have to break us in this island or lose the war. If we can stand up to him, all Europe may be free and the life of the world may move forward into broad, sunlit uplands. But if we fail, then the whole world, including the United States, including all that we have known and cared for, will sink into the abyss of a new Dark Age made more sinister, and perhaps more protracted, by the lights of perverted science. Let us therefore brace ourselves to our duties, and so bear ourselves that, if the British Empire and its Commonwealth last for a thousand years, men will still say, "This was their finest hour."

Speech to the boys of Harrow, 18 December 1940

It is a great pleasure and a refreshing treat to me and those of my parliamentary ministerial colleagues who have come to Harrow with me this afternoon to join the school in singing Harrow songs. When I was here as a boy I was thrilled by them, and they have often come back to me in afterlife. I feel that they are one of the greatest treasures of the school, passing as they do from one generation to another and pointing with bright hopes toward the future.

We have sung of "the wonderful giants of old" but can anyone doubt that this generation is as good and as noble as any the nation has ever produced, and that its men and women can stand against all tests? Can anyone doubt that this generation is in every way capable of carrying on the traditions of the nation and handing down its love of justice and liberty and its message undiminished and unimpaired?

I like the song "Boy," although when I was at the school I did not advance to that position of authority that entitles one to make that call. The songs and their spirit form a bond between Harrovians all over the world, and they have played a great part in the influence that has been exercised in national affairs by men who have had their education here.

Hitler, in one of his recent discourses, declared that the fight was between those who have been through the Adolf Hitler Schools and those who have been at Eton. Hitler has forgotten Harrow, and he has also overlooked the vast majority of the youth of this country who have never had the advantage of attending such schools, but who have by their skill and prowess won the admiration of the whole world.

When this war is won, as it surely will be, it must be one of our aims to work to establish a state of society where the advantages and privileges, which hitherto have been enjoyed only by the few, shall be far more widely shared by the many, and by the youth of the nation as a whole.

It is a great time in which you are called upon to begin your life. You have already had the honor of being under the fire of the enemy, and no doubt you acquitted yourself with befitting composure and decorum. You are here at this most important period of your lives, at a moment when our country stands forth almost alone as the champion of right and freedom all over the world. You, the young men, will be the heirs of the victory that we shall surely achieve, and perhaps some of you in this Speech Room will derive from these songs and Harrow associations the impulse to render that victory fruitful and lasting.

Address broadcast 9 February 1941

I have been so very careful, since I have been prime minister, not to encourage false hopes or prophesy smooth and easy things, and yet the tale that I have to tell today is one that must justly and rightly give us cause for deep thankfulness, and also, I think, for strong comfort and even rejoicing. But now I must dwell upon the more serious, darker, and more dangerous aspects of the vast scene of the war. We must all of us have been asking ourselves: what has that wicked man whose crime-stained regime and system are at bay and in the toils— what has he been preparing during these winter months? What new devilry is he planning? What new small country will he overrun or strike down? What fresh form of assault will he make upon our island home and fortress; which—let there be no mistake about it—is all that stands between him and the dominion of the world?

But after all, the fate of this war is going to be settled by what happens on the oceans, in the air, and—above all—in this island. It seems now to be certain that the government and people of the United States intend to supply us with all that is necessary for victory. In the last war the United States sent two million men across the Atlantic. But this is not a war of vast armies, firing immense masses of shells at one another. We do not need the gallant armies that are forming throughout the American Union. We do not need them this year, nor next year; nor any year that I can foresee. But we do need most urgently an immense and continuous supply of war materials and technical apparatus of all kinds. We need them here and we need to bring them here. We shall need a great mass of shipping in 1942, far more than we can build ourselves, if we are to maintain and augment our war effort in the West and in the East.

These facts are, of course, all well known to the enemy, and we must therefore expect that Herr Hitler will do his utmost to prey upon our shipping and to reduce the volume of American supplies entering these islands. Having conquered France and Norway, his clutching fingers reach out on both sides of us into the ocean. I have never underrated this danger, and you know I have never concealed it from you. Therefore, I hope you will believe me when I say that I have complete confidence in the Royal Navy, aided by the Air Force of the Coastal Command, and that in one way or another I am sure they will be able to meet every changing phase of this truly mortal struggle, and that sustained by the courage of our merchant seamen, and of the dockers and workmen of all our ports, we shall outwit, outmaneuver, outfight, and outlast the worst that the enemy's malice and ingenuity can contrive.

In order to win the war Hitler must destroy Great Britain. He may carry havoc into the Balkan States; he may tear great provinces out of Russia; he may march to the Caspian; he may march to the gates of India. All this will avail him nothing. It may spread his curse more widely throughout Europe and Asia, but it will not avert his doom. With every month that passes the many proud and once happy countries he is now holding down by brute force and vile intrigue are learning to hate the Prussian yoke and the Nazi name as nothing has ever been hated so fiercely and so widely among men before. And all the time, masters of the sea and air, the British Empire—nay, in a certain sense, the whole English-speaking world—will be on his track, bearing with them the swords of justice.

The other day, President Roosevelt gave his opponent in the late presidential election a letter of introduction to me, and in it he wrote out a verse, in his own handwriting, from Longfellow, which he said, "applies to you people as it does to us." Here is the verse:

> . . . Sail on, O Ship of State!
> Sail on, O Union, strong and great!
> Humanity with all its fears,
> With all the hopes of future years,
> Is hanging breathless on thy fate!

What is the answer that I shall give, in your name, to this great man, the thrice-chosen head of a nation of 130 millions? Here is the answer which I will give to President Roosevelt: Put your confidence in us. Give us your faith and your blessing, and, under Providence, all will be well.

We shall not fail or falter; we shall not weaken or tire. Neither the sudden shock of battle, nor the long-drawn trials of vigilance and exertion will wear us down. Give us the tools, and we will finish the job.

World broadcast, 10 May 1942

The tremendous period through which we have passed has certainly been full of anxieties and exertions; it has been marked by many misfortunes and disappointments. This time two years ago the Germans were beating down Holland and Belgium by unprovoked brutal, merciless invasion, and very soon there came upon us the total defeat of France and the fatal surrender at Bordeaux. Mussolini, the Italian miscalculator, thought he saw his chance of a cheap and easy triumph, and rich plunder for no fighting. He struck at the back of a dying France, and at what he believed was a doomed Britain. We were left alone—our quarter of a million Dunkirk troops saved, only disarmed; ourselves, as yet unarmed—to face the might of victorious Germany, to face also the carefully saved-up strength of an Italy, which then still ranked as a first-class power.

Here at home in this island, invasion was near; the Mediterranean was closed to us; the long route round the Cape, where General Smuts stands on guard, alone was open; our small, ill-equipped forces in Egypt and the Sudan seemed to await destruction. All the world, even our best friends, thought that our end had come. Accordingly, we prepared ourselves to conquer or to perish. We were united in that solemn, majestic hour; we were all equally resolved at least to go down fighting. We cast calculation to the winds; no wavering voice was heard; we hurled defiance at our foes; we faced our duty, and, by the mercy of God, we were preserved.

It fell to me in those days to express the sentiments and resolves of the British nation in that supreme crisis of its life. That was to me an honor far beyond any dreams or ambitions I had ever nursed, and it is one that cannot be taken away. For a whole year after the fall of France we stood alone, keeping the flag of freedom flying, and the hopes of the world alive. We conquered the Italian Empire, we destroyed or captured almost all Mussolini's African army; we liberated Abyssinia; we have so far successfully protected Palestine, Syria, Persia, and Iraq from German designs. We have suffered grievous reverses in going to the aid of the heroic Greeks; we bore unflinching many a heavy blow abroad, and still more in our cities here at home; and all this time, cheered and helped by President Roosevelt and the United States, we stood alone, neither faltering nor flagging.

Where are we now? Can anyone doubt that if we are worthy of it, as we shall be, we have in our hands our own future? As in the last war, so in this, we are moving through many reverses and defeats to complete and final victory. We have only to endure and to persevere, to conquer. Now we are no longer unarmed; we are well armed. Now we are not alone; we have mighty allies, bound irrevocably by solemn faith and common interests to stand with us in the ranks of the United Nations. There can only be one end. When it will come, or how it will come, I cannot tell. But, when we survey the overwhelming resources that are at our disposal, once they are fully marshaled and developed—as they can be, as they will be—we may stride forward into the unknown with growing confidence. . . .

Speech in Usher Hall, Edinburgh, 12 October 1942

. . . When peaceful nations like the British and the Americans, very careless in peacetime about their defenses, carefree, unsuspecting nations, peoples who have never known defeat—improvident nations, I will say, feckless nations, nations who despise the military art and thought war so wicked that it could never happen again—when nations like these are set upon by highly organized, heavily armed conspirators, planning and calculating in secret for years on end, exalting war as the highest form of human effort, glorifying slaughter and aggression, prepared and trained to the last point science and discipline can carry them, is it not natural that the peaceful, unprepared, improvident peoples should suffer terribly and that the wicked, scheming aggressors should have their reign of savage exaltation?

Ah! But that is not the end of the story. It is only the first chapter. If the great, peaceful democracies could survive the first few years of the aggressors' attack, another chapter had to be written. It is to that chapter we shall come in due time.

It will ever be the glory of this island and its Empire that we stood alone for one whole year of mortal peril, and gained the time for the good cause to arm, to organize and slowly bring the conjoined, united, irresistible forces of outraged civilization to bear upon the criminals. That is our greatest glory.

Surveying both sides of the account—the good and the bad, with equal composure and coolness—we must see that we have reached a stern and somber moment in the war, one that calls in a high degree for firmness of spirit and constancy of soul.

The excitement and the emotion of those great days when we stood alone and unaided against what seemed overwhelming odds and, single-handed, saved the future of the world, are not present now. We are surrounded by a concourse of governments and nations, all of us bound together in solemn unbreakable alliance, bound together by ties not only of honor but of self-preservation. We are able to plan our slow but sure march onward. Deadly dangers still beset us. Weariness, complacency, or discord, squabbles over petty matters, would mar our prospects.

We must all drive ourselves to the utmost limit of our strength. We must preserve and refine our sense of proportion. We must strive to combine the virtues of wisdom and of daring. We must move forward together, united and inexorable.

Thus, with God's blessing, the hopes that are now justified, that we are now entitled to feel, will not fail or wither. The light is broadening on the track, and the light is brighter too. Among the qualities for which Scotland is renowned, steadfastness holds perhaps the highest place.

Be steadfast, then, that is the message that I bring to you, that is my invocation to the Scottish people, here in this ancient capital city, one of whose burgesses I now have the honor to be. Let me use the words of your famous minstrel [Sir Harry Lauder]—he is here today—words that have given comfort and renewed strength to many a burdened heart:

> Keep right on to the end of the road,
> Keep right on to the end.

References

Churchill, Sir Winston S., *The Second World War: Triumph and Tragedy* (Boston: Houghton Mifflin, 1953).

Churchill, Sir Winston, *Great Destiny*, edited by F. W. Heath (New York: G.P. Putnam's Sons, 1965).

GOLDA MEIR

FULL NAME:

Golda Meir (Goldie Mabovitch)

BORN:

3 May 1898, Kiev, Ukraine

DIED:

8 December 1978, Israel

Family migrated to Wisconsin in 1906, where she later taught school. In 1921, to Palestine, where she served as Minister of Labor from 1949 to 1956 and as Minister of Foreign Affairs from 1956 to 1966. Secretary General of the Labor Party from 1966 to 1969. Prime Minister of Israel, 1969–1974.

Her major work is: My Life (New York: G.P. Putnam's Sons, 1975). Biographies include: Eliyahu Agres, *Golda Meir: Portrait of a Prime Minister* (New York: Sabra Books, 1969); and Marie Syrkin, *Golda Meir, Woman with a Cause* (New York: G.P. Putnam's Sons, 1963).

My Life

. . . So I moved again, this time to the large, not especially attractive prime minister's residence in Jerusalem—in which Ben-Gurion, Sharett, and Eshkol had lived before me—and began to accustom myself to the permanent presence of police and bodyguards, to a workday of at least sixteen hours and to the minimum of privacy. Obviously some days were easier, shorter and less tense than others, and I have no intention of pretending that I spent the five years that I was prime minister of Israel in a state of martyrdom or that I never enjoyed myself at all. But my term of office began with one war and ended with another, and I can't help thinking how symbolic it was that the very first instruction I gave to anyone in my capacity as prime minister was to tell my military secretary, Yisrael Lior, that I was to be informed as soon as the reports from any military action came in—even if it was in the middle of the night.

"I want to know the moment that the boys get back," I told him, "and I want to know how they are." I didn't use the word "casualties" but Lior understood and was horrified by the request.

"You don't really want me to phone you at three A.M.?" he said. "After all, there is nothing you can do about it if there are any casualties. I promise to call you first thing in the morning."

But I knew that I wouldn't be able to bear the idea of sleeping soundly through the night not even knowing if soldiers had been killed or wounded, and I forced poor Lior to obey me. When the news was bad, of course, I couldn't fall asleep again, and I spent more nights than I care to remember padding around that big, empty house, waiting for morning and for more detailed information. Sometimes the bodyguards outside the house would see that the kitchen light was on at 4 A.M., and one of them would look in to make sure that I was all right. I'd make us both a cup of tea, and we'd talk about what was happening at the Canal or in the north until I felt that I could go back to bed again. . . .

The other (though minor) bane of my life during all the time that I was prime minister—and one that it took me months to accustom myself to, even partially—was the freedom with which various ministers confided in the press, to put it very politely. The constant leaks from cabinet meetings infuriated me, and although I had my own suspicions all along as to the source of the sensational revelations by so-called diplomatic correspondents that greeted me so often in the morning papers, I could never prove them—which meant that I couldn't do much about them. But my staff very quickly got used to seeing me turn up at the office on the day after a cabinet meeting looking as black as thunder because over breakfast I had read something garbled in the paper that shouldn't have been there at all, garbled or otherwise. But these, need I say, were not my major anxieties. The real problems, as they had been for so long, were survival and peace, in that order. . . .

Of all the members of the cabinet, Dayan was, of course, the most controversial and probably the most complicated. He is, and always has been, a man who elicits very strong responses from the public. Naturally, he has his faults, and like his virtues, they are not small ones. One of the things of which I am most proud, to be quite frank, is that for more than five years I kept together a cabinet that included not only Dayan, but also a number of men who greatly disliked and resented him. But from the start I had a good idea of the problems I was likely to face in this respect. I had known Dayan for years, and I knew that he had opposed my becoming prime minister when Eshkol died. The only way in which I could operate, therefore, was to take whatever stands I would have to take on the essence of each and every issue and to prove to the cabinet—and to Dayan himself—that I was not in the habit of evaluating propositions according to who fathered them.

To his credit, I must say that when I did not support Dayan in something, he always took it very well, although he doesn't work easily with people and is used to getting his own way. In the end we became good friends, and there was not a single occasion when I could complain of any disloyalty on his part. Not once. Even on military matters, he would always come—with the chief of staff—to talk to me first. Sometimes I said to him, "I won't vote in favor of this, but you are free to take your proposal to the cabinet." But if I didn't go along with one of his ideas, he never took it any further. Considering Dayan's reputation for not being able to function as part of a team—and mine for not being able to compromise easily—I think that on the whole we did very well.

It is also not true that he is a hard man. I saw him come back shattered from those agonizing funerals following the war, when children were pushed at him by mothers who shrieked, "You killed their father," and mourners shook their fists at him and called him a murderer. I know how I felt—and I know how Dayan felt. In the first days of the Yom Kippur War, he was very pessimistic and wanted to prepare the nation for the worst. He called a meeting of newspaper editors to describe to them the situation as he saw it—which was certainly not easy for him.

I kept him from resigning during the war, but I think perhaps he should have done so immediately after the Agranat Commission of Inquiry published its first preliminary report on 2 April 1974. That report cleared Dayan (and myself) of any "direct responsibility" for Israel's unpreparedness on Yom Kippur, but it dealt so harshly with the chief of staff and the head of military intelligence that Dado resigned at once. I have always suspected that Dayan might have retained his "charismatic" image—or at least some of it—had he then, publicly, stuck by his comrades-in-arms. He read that preliminary (and only partial) report in my office and, for the third time, asked me whether he should resign. "This time," I said, "it must be the decision of the party." But he was following a logic of his own, and I didn't feel that on such a weighty matter I should give him advice. Now I am sorry that I didn't, though he may not have taken it in any case.

As for me, the commission said that on Yom Kippur morning "she decided wisely, with common sense and speedily, in favor of the full mobilization of the reserves, as recommended by the chief of staff despite weighty political considerations, thereby performing a most important service for the defense of the state."

To many outsiders the situation in Israel appeared brighter in the winter of 1973–74 than it did to the Israelis themselves. One of my visitors around that time was the late Richard Crossman, who had been so involved in the birth of the state and couldn't understand the current gloom and despondency. "You people have gone crazy," he said to me. "What's happening to all of you?"

"Tell me," I asked him, "what would have been the reaction in England if something similar had happened to the British?" He was so astonished at my question that he almost dropped his coffee cup.

"Do you think things like that haven't happened to us?" he said. "That Churchill never made a mistake during the war? That we had no Dunkirk and a great many other setbacks as well? We just didn't take things in such an intense way."

But we are different, I suppose, and the word "trauma" that was on everyone's lips all that winter most accurately describes the national sense of loss and injury that Crossman thought was so excessive. . . .

On 31 December we held our elections. The ballots showed that the country was not keen on changing horses in midstream, and although we lost some votes—as did the National Religious Party—the Ma'arach still came out as the leading bloc. But the opposition to the Ma'arach had become more forceful because the entire right wing had now combined into a bloc of its own. A coalition would have to be formed again, and it would clearly be a backbreaking job to form it, since the religious bloc, which was a traditional coalition partner of ours, was itself deeply divided on the question of who should lead it and what its policy should be at this tremendously difficult time.

I was beginning to feel the physical and psychological effects of the draining past few months. I was dead tired and not at all sure that, in this kind of situation, I could ever succeed in forming a government—or even whether I should go on trying to do so. Not only were there problems from without, but there were also difficultes within the party. At the beginning of March I felt I couldn't go on, and I told the party that I had had enough. But I was bombarded by delegations imploring me to change my mind. It was still quite likely that war would break out again since there was still no disengagement of forces with Syria and the Syrians were continually violating the cease-fire. And again I was told that the Ma'arach would disintegrate unless I stayed on.

Sometimes it seemed to me that everything that had happened since the afternoon of 6 October had happened on one endless day—and I wanted that day to end. I was deeply distressed by the breaking down of solidarity within the inner circle of the party. People who had been ministers in my government, colleagues with whom I had worked closely throughout my years in office and who had been full partners in the formation of government policy now appeared unwilling to stand up to the barrage of unjust criticism, even slander, that was being hurled against Dayan, Galili, and myself on the grounds that the three of us—without consulting others—had presumed to make crucial decisions that had allegedly led to the war. I also resented the irresponsible talk of my so-called kitchen cabinet that had supposedly replaced the government to some extent by acting as a decision-making body. This accusation was utterly without foundation. It was only natural on my part to seek the advice of people whose judgment I valued. At no time and in no way, however, did these informal consultations ever take the place of government decisions.

Nonetheless, throughout March I went on with the struggle to form a government, though, increasingly, it began to look like an impossible task, particularly in the face of growing demands for a "wall-to-wall" coalition, something to which both I and most of the party were more opposed than ever. This was certainly not the time for political experimentation, and I had no more faith than I ever had in the ability of the opposition to apply good judgment, common sense, or flexibility to Israel's attempts to arrive, at last, at some sort of understanding with our neighbors. I didn't want the cabinet to be burdened by an element that would refuse to negotiate—if and when the time came—because of its totally negative attitude toward any territorial compromise, especially as far as the West Bank was concerned. I knew that—for historical reasons—there was a difference in the attitude of the population regarding territorial compromise on the Sinai, for instance, and on the West Bank—though I myself felt that most Israelis would be prepared for a reasonable compromise on the West Bank, too. However, I also thought it necessary to include in the government's policy statement a clause to the effect that although the cabinet was authorized to negotiate and decide on territorial compromise with Jordan, before any actual treaty was signed, the issue would be taken to the people in the form of new elections. . . .

The more I talked with my colleagues about the ongoing conflict in the party and the more I analyzed it for myself, the more I began to feel that I couldn't go on any longer. I had reached a point where I felt that without the support of the entire party (the majority was with me all the time) I couldn't function as its head anymore. And the moment came when I said to myself, "This is it. I am going to resign, and other people will have to see what they can do about forming a coalition. There is a limit to what I can take, and I have now reached that limit."

During all those weeks of interminable talk, argument and bitterness, I had been getting the most moving letters of encouragement and support from people all over Israel whom I had never met but who seemed to understand what I was going through. Some of these were wounded soldiers, still in the hospital; others were parents of boys who had fallen. "Be well. Be strong. Everything will be all right," they wrote to me. I truly didn't want to fail them, but on 10 April I told the party leadership that I had had enough.

"Five years are sufficient," I said. "It is beyond my strength to continue carrying this burden. I don't belong to any circle or faction within the party. I have only a circle of one to consult—myself. And this time my decision is final, irrevocable. I beg of you not to try to persuade me to change my mind for any reason at all. It will not help." Of course, attempts were made all the same to talk me out of my decision, but they were to no avail. I was about to conclude fifty years of public service, and I knew with absolute certainty that I was doing the right thing. I had wanted to do it much earlier, but now nothing was going to stop me, and nothing did. My political career was over. . . .

Like my generation, this generation of sabras will strive, struggle, make mistakes, and achieve. Like us, they are totally committed to the development and security of the state of Israel and to the dream of a just society here. Like us, they know that for the Jewish people to remain a people, it is essential that there be a Jewish state where Jews can live as Jews, not on sufferance and not as a minority. I am certain that they will bring at least as much credit to the Jewish people everywhere as we tried to bring. And at this point I would like to add something about being Jewish. It is not only a matter, I believe, of religious observance and practice. To me, being Jewish means and has always meant being proud to be part of a people that has maintained its distinct identity for more than 2,000 years, with all the pain and torment that have been inflicted upon it. Those who have been unable to endure and who have tried to opt out of their Jewishness have done so, I believe, at the expense of their own basic identity. They have pitifully impoverished themselves.

I don't know what forms the practice of Judaism will assume in the future or how Jews, in Israel and elsewhere, will express their Jewishness 1,000 years hence. But I do know that Israel is not just some small beleaguered country in which 3,000,000 people are trying hard to survive; Israel is a Jewish state that has come into existence as the result of the longing, the faith, and the determination of an ancient people. We in Israel are only one part of the Jewish nation, and not even its largest part; but because Israel exists Jewish history has been changed forever, and it is my deepest conviction that there are few Israelis today who do not understand and fully accept the responsibility that history has placed on their shoulders as Jews.

As for me, my life has been greatly blessed. Not only have I lived to see the State of Israel born, but I have also seen it take in and successfully absorb masses of Jews from all parts of the world. When I came to this country in 1921, its Jewish population amounted to 80,000, and the entry of each Jew depended on permission granted by the mandatory government. We are now a population of over 3,000,000, of whom more than 1,000,000 are Jews who have arrived since the establishment of the state under Israel's Law of Return, a law that guarantees the right of every Jew to settle here. I am also grateful that I live in a country whose people have learned how to go on living in a sea of hatred without hating those who want to destroy them and without abandoning their own vision of peace. To have learned this is a great art, the prescription for which is not written down anywhere. It is part of our way of life in Israel.

Finally, I wish to say that from the time I came to Palestine as a young woman, we have been forced to choose between what is more dangerous and what is less dangerous for us. At times we have all been tempted to give in to various pressures and to accept proposals that might guarantee us a little quiet for a few months, or maybe even for a few years, but that could only lead us eventually into even greater peril. We have always been faced by the question "Which is the greater danger?" And we are still in that situation or perhaps in an even graver one. The world is harsh, selfish, and materialistic. It is insensitive to the sufferings of small nations. Even the most enlightened of governments, democracies that are led by decent leaders who represent fine, decent people, are not much inclined today to concern themselves with problems of justice in international relations. At a time when great nations are capable of knuckling under to blackmail and decisions are being made on the basis of big-power politics, we cannot always be expected to take their advice, and therefore, we must have the capacity and the courage to go on seeing things as they really are and to act on our own most fundamental instincts for self-preservation. So to those who ask, "What of the future?" I still have only one answer: I believe that we will have peace with our neighbors, but I am sure that no one will make peace with a weak Israel. If Israel is not strong, there will be no peace.

My vision of our future? A Jewish state in which masses of Jews from all over the world will continue to settle and to build; an Israel bound in a collaborative effort with its neighbors on behalf of all the people of this region; an Israel that remains a flourishing democracy and a society resting firmly on social justice and equality.

And now I have only one desire left: never to lose the feeling that it is I who am indebted for what has been given to me from the time that I first learned about Zionism in a small room in tsarist Russia all the way through to my half century here, where I have seen my five grandchildren grow up as free Jews in a country that is their own. Let no one anywhere have any doubts about this: Our children and our children's children will never settle for anything less.

Reference

Meir, Golda, My Life (New York: G.P. Putnam's Sons, 1975).

F. W. DE KLERK

FULL NAME:

Frederik Willem de Klerk

BORN:

18 March 1936, Johannesburg, South Africa

Son of a politician, he practiced law, became a member of Parliament in 1972, and joined the cabinet in 1978. He served as Education Minister from 1984 to 1989 and succeeded P. W. Botha in 1989 as President. He dismantled the apartheid system and paved the way for the drafting of a new constitution. He contested and lost the presidential elections of 1994 but became Vice President.

The New York Times International

Speech conceding defeat in the 2 May 1994 election

Mr. Mandela will soon assume the highest office of the land with all the awesome responsibility that it bears. He will have to exercise this great responsibility in a balanced manner that will assure South Africans from all our communities that he has all their interests at heart.

I am confident that this will be his intention.

Mr. Mandela has walked a long road and now stands at the top of the hill. A traveler would sit down and admire the view. But a man of destiny knows that beyond this hill lies another and another. The journey is never complete. As he contemplates the next hill I hold out my hand in friendship and in cooperation.

As far as my own position is concerned, I should like to make clear that I believe that my political task is just beginning. Everything that we have done so far—the four years of difficult and often frustrating negotiations, the problems and the crises—have been simply a preparation for the work that lies ahead.

The greatest challenge that we will face in the government of national unity will be to defend and nurture our new constitution. Our greatest task will be to ensure our young and vulnerable democracy will take root and flourish.

Principles for Economy

We must also ensure that we adopt the right approaches in the economic and social spheres. We need a strong and a vibrant economy based on the tried and tested principles of free enterprise. Only then can we ensure that we will generate the wealth that we need to address the pressing social needs of large sections of our population. We must ensure that social services are affordable, caring, and effective.

I will be in a good position in the government of national unity to promote these objectives. I will not be there at the whim of any person or any party, but in my own right as the representative of many millions of South Africans.

Just as we could not rule South Africa effectively without the support of the A.N.C. and its supporters, no government will be able to rule South Africa effectively without the support of the people and the institutions that I represent.

I enthusiastically pledge that support in the spirit of national reconciliation.

Reference

"The South African Vote: Words of Peace, Deeds of Death," *The New York Times International*, 3 May 1994.

NELSON MANDELA

FULL NAME:

Nelson Rolihahla Mandela

BORN:

18 July 1918, Transkei Region, South Africa

Member of a royal family and a lawyer. He became a leader of the African National Congress; was arrested in 1963 and sentenced to life imprisonment in 1964. In 1990, the de Klerk government released him. He contested and won the presidential elections of 1994, becoming the first Black African president of South Africa.

Books include: *The Struggle Is My Life* (London: IDAF Publications, 1990); *No Easy Walk to Freedom* (London: Heinemann Educational, 1973).

Books about Mandela include: Ronald Harwood, *Mandela* (New York: New American Library, 1987); Sheridan Johns and R. Hunt Davis, editors, *Mandela, Tambo and the African National Congress: A Documentary Survey* (New York: Oxford University Press, 1991).

The New York Times International

Victory speech after the 2 May 1994 election

This is indeed a joyous night. Although not yet final, we have received the provisional results of the election. My friends, I can tell you that we are delighted by the overwhelming support for the African National Congress.

Within the last few hours I have received telephone calls from State President de Klerk, General Constandt Viljoen [leader of the right-wing Freedom Front], Dr. Zach de Beer [of the Democratic Party] and Mr. Johnson Mlambo, the first deputy president of the P.A.C. [Pan Africanist Congress], who pledged their full cooperation and offered their sincere congratulations.

I thank them all for their support and look forward to working together for our beloved country. I would also like to congratulate President de Klerk for the strong showing the National Party has displayed in this election. I also want to congratulate him for the many days, weeks and months and the four years that we have worked together, quarreled, addressed sensitive problems and at the end of our heated exchanges were able to shake hands and to drink coffee.

To all those in the African National Congress and the democratic movement who worked so hard these last few days and through these many decades, I thank you and honor you. To the people of South Africa and the world who are watching: This is indeed a joyous night for the human spirit. This is your victory, too. You helped end apartheid, you stood with us through the transition.

I watched, along with you all, as the tens of thousands of our people stood patiently in long queues for many hours, some sleeping on the open ground overnight to cast this momentous vote.

South Africa's heroes are legend across the generations. But it is you, the people, who are our true heroes.

This is one of the most important moments in the life of our country. I stand before you filled with deep pride and joy—pride in the ordinary, humble people of this country. You have shown such a calm, patient determination to reclaim this country as your own. And joy that we can loudly proclaim from the rooftops—free at last!

I am your servant. I don't come to you as a leader, as one above others. We are a great team.

Leaders come and go, but the organization and the collective leadership that has looked after the fortunes and reversals of this organization will always be there. And the ideas I express are not ideas invented in my own mind.

They stem from our fundamental policy document, the Freedom Charter, from the decisions, resolutions of the national conference and from the decisions of the national executive committee. That is the nature of our organization. It is not the individuals that matter, it is the collective leadership which has led this organization so skillfully.

I stand before you humbled by your courage, with a heart full of love for all of you. I regard it as the highest honor to lead the A.N.C. at this moment in our history, and that we have been chosen to lead our country into the new century.

I pledge to use all my strength and ability to live up to your expectations of me as well as the A.N.C.

I am personally indebted and pay tribute to some of South Africa's greatest leaders, including John Dube, Josiah Gumede, G. M. Naicker, Dr. Abduraman, Chief Luthuli, Lilian Ngoyi, Bram Fisher, Helen Joseph, Yusuf Dadoo, Moses Kotane, Chris Hani, and Oliver Tambo. They should have been here to celebrate with us, for this is their achievement, too.

Let's get South Africa working. For we must together and without delay begin to build a better life for all South Africans. This means creating jobs, building houses, providing education, and bringing peace and security for all. This is going to be the acid test of the government of national unity.

We have emerged as the majority party on the basis of the program that is contained in the reconstruction and development program. There we have outlined the steps that we are going to take in order to ensure a better life for all South Africans.

Almost all the organizations that are going to take part in the government of national unity have undertaken during the course of the campaign to contribute to the better life of our people. That is going to be the cornerstone, the foundation on which the government of national unity is going to be based.

And I appeal to all the leaders who are going to serve in this government to honor that program and to go there determined to contribute toward its immediate implementation. If there are attempts on the part of anybody to undermine that program, there will be serious tension in the government of national unity.

We are here to honor our promises. If we fail to implement this program, that will be a betrayal of the trust that the people of South Africa have vested in us. It is a program that was developed by the masses of the people themselves in people's forums. It has been accepted by state corporations, by government departments, by business, academics, by religious leaders, youth movements, women's organizations. And nobody will be entitled to participate in that government of national unity to oppose that plan.

But I must add we are not going to make the government of national unity an empty shell. We want every political organization that participates in that government to feel that they are part and parcel of a government machine that is happy to accommodate their views within the context of the reconstruction and development program.

We do not want to reduce them into mere rubber stamps to rubber-stamp the decisions of any organization except to say that that program has to be carried out without reservation.

The calm and tolerant atmosphere that prevailed during the election depicts the type of South Africa we can build. It set the tone for the future. We might have our differences, but we are one people with a common destiny in our rich variety of culture, race, and tradition.

People have voted for the party of their choice and we respect that. This is democracy.

I hold out a hand of friendship to the leaders of all parties and their members, and ask all of them to join us in working together to tackle the problems we face as a nation. An A.N.C. government will serve all the people of South Africa, not just A.N.C. members.

We are looking forward to working together in a government of national unity.

Now is the time for celebration, for South Africans to join together to celebrate the birth of democracy. Let our celebrations be in keeping with the mood set in the elections, peaceful, respectful and disciplined, showing we are a people ready to assume the responsibilities of government.

Reference

"The South African Vote: Words of Peace, Deeds of Death," The New York Times International, 3 May 1994.

PRESIDENTS

OF THE

UNITED STATES

THEODORE ROOSEVELT

BORN:

27 October 1858, New York, New York

DIED:

6 January 1919, Oyster Bay, New York

Twenty-sixth President of the United States. Soldier, Assistant Secretary of the Navy, and Governor of New York from 1898 to 1900. Vice President under William McKinley, 1900. President when McKinley was assassinated on 13 September 1901. Elected President in 1904 and stepped down in 1909. Unsuccessful bids for Republican nomination against William Howard Taft and then as Progressive candidate in 1912.

Roosevelt wrote prolifically on hunting, citizenship, and history. His works include: *The Free Citizen* (New York: Macmillan, 1956); and *The Works of Theodore Roosevelt*, Twenty Volumes (New York: Scribner's Sons, 1926). His letters are collected in Elting E. Morrison et al., editors, *The Letters of Theodore Roosevelt*, Eight Volumes (Cambridge, MA: 1951–1954). Biographies include: William H. Harbaugh, *The Life and Times of Theodore Roosevelt* (New York: Oxford University Press, 1975); and Howard K. Beale, *Theodore Roosevelt and the Rise of America to World Power* (Baltimore, MD: Johns Hopkins Press, 1956).

An Autobiography

. . . The most important factor in getting the right spirit in my administration, next to the insistence upon courage, honesty, and a genuine democracy of desire to serve the plain people, was my insistence upon the theory that the executive power was limited only by specific restrictions and prohibitions appearing in the Constitution or imposed by the Congress under its constitutional powers. My view was that every executive officer, and above all every executive officer in high position, was a steward of the people bound actively and affirmatively to do all he could for the people, and not to content himself with the negative merit of keeping his talents undamaged in a napkin. I declined to adopt the view that what was imperatively necessary for the nation could not be done by the president unless he could find some specific authorization to do it. My belief was that it was not only his right but his duty to do anything that the needs of the nation demanded unless such action was forbidden by the Constitution or by the laws. Under this interpretation of executive power I did and caused to be done many things not previously done by the president and the heads of the departments. I did not usurp power, but I did greatly broaden the use of executive power. In other words, I acted for the public welfare, I acted for the common well-being of all our people, whenever and in whatever manner was necessary, unless prevented by direct constitutional or legislative prohibition. I did not care a rap for the mere form and show of power; I cared immensely for the use that could be made of the substance. The Senate at one time objected to my communicating with them in printing, preferring the expensive, foolish, and laborious practice of writing out the messages by hand. It was not possible to return to the outworn archaism of handwriting; but we endeavored to have the printing made as pretty as possible. Whether I communicated with the Congress in writing or by word of mouth, and whether the writing was by a machine, or a pen, were equally, and absolutely, unimportant matters. The importance lay in what I said and in the heed paid to what I said. So as to my meeting and consulting senators, congressmen, politicians, financiers, and labor men. I consulted all who wished to see me; and if I wished to see anyone, I sent for him; and where the consultation took place was a matter of supreme unimportance. I consulted every man with the sincere hope that I could profit by and follow his advice. . . .

In internal affairs I cannot say that I entered the presidency with any deliberately planned and far-reaching scheme of social betterment. I had, however, certain strong convictions; and I was on the lookout for every opportunity of realizing those convictions. I was bent upon making the government the most efficient possible instrument in helping the people of the United States to better themselves in every way, politically, socially, and industrially. I believed with all my heart in real and thoroughgoing democracy, and I wished to make this democracy industrial as well as political, although I had only partially formulated the methods I believed we should follow. I believed in the people's rights, and therefore in national rights and states' rights just exactly to the degree in which they severally secured popular rights. I believed in invoking the national power with absolute freedom for every national need; and I believed that the Constitution should be treated as the greatest document ever devised by the wit of man to aid a people in exercising every power necessary for its own betterment, and not as a straitjacket cunningly fashioned to strangle growth. As for the particular methods of realizing these various beliefs, I was content to wait and see what method might be necessary in each given case as it arose; and I was certain that the cases would arise fast enough. . . .

To play the demagogue for purposes of self-interest is a cardinal sin against the people in a democracy, exactly as to play the courtier for such purposes is a cardinal sin against the people under other forms of government. A man who stays long in our American political life, if he has in his soul the generous desire to do effective service for great causes, inevitably grows to regard himself merely as one of many instruments, all of which it may be necessary to use, one at one time, one at another, in achieving the triumph of those causes; and whenever the usefulness of any one has been exhausted, it is to be thrown aside. If such a man is wise, he will gladly do the thing that is next, when the time and the need come together, without asking what the future holds for him. Let the half-god play his part well and manfully, and then be content to draw aside when the god appears. Nor should he feel vain regrets that to another it is given to render greater services and reap a greater reward. Let it be enough for him that he too has served, and that by doing well he has prepared the way for the other man who can do better. . . .

American Ideals

"The Manly Virtues", The Forum, *July 1894*

. . . A man must not only be disinterested, but he must be efficient. If he goes into politics he must go into practical politics, in order to make his influence felt. Practical politics must not be construed to mean dirty politics. On the contrary, in the long run the politics of fraud and treachery and foulness are unpractical politics, and the most practical of all politicians is the politician who is clean and decent and upright. But a man who goes into the actual battles of the political world must prepare himself much as he would for the struggle in any other branch of our life. He must be prepared to meet men of far lower ideals than his own, and to face things, not as he would wish them, but as they are. He must not lose his own high ideal, and yet he must face the fact that the majority of the men with whom he must work have lower ideals. He must stand firmly for what he believes, and yet he must realize that political action, to be effective, must be the joint action of many men, and that he must sacrifice somewhat of his own opinions to those of his associates if he ever hopes to see his desires take practical shape.

The prime thing that every man who takes an interest in politics should remember is that he must act, and not merely criticize the actions of others. It is not the man who sits by his fireside reading his evening paper, and saying how bad our politics and politicians are, who will ever do anything to save us; it is the man who goes out into the rough hurly-burly of the caucus, the primary, and the political meeting, and there faces his fellows on equal terms. The real service is rendered, not by the critic who stands aloof from the contest, but by the man who enters into it and bears his part as a man should, undeterred by the blood and the sweat. It is a pleasant but a dangerous thing to associate merely with cultivated, refined men of high ideals and sincere purpose to do right, and to think that one has done one's duty by discussing politics with such associates. It is a good thing to meet men of this stamp; indeed it is a necessary thing, for we thereby brighten our ideals, and keep in touch with the people who are unselfish in their purposes; but if we associate with such men exclusively we can accomplish nothing. The actual battle must be fought out on other and less pleasant fields. The actual advance must be made in the field of practical politics among the men who represent or guide or control the mass of the voters, the men who are sometimes rough and coarse, who sometimes have lower ideals than they should, but who are capable, masterful, and efficient. It is only by mingling on equal terms with such men, by showing them that one is able to give and to receive heavy punishment without flinching, and that one can master the details of political management as well as they can, that it is possible for a man to establish a standing that will be useful to him in fighting for a great reform. Every man who wishes well to his country is in honor bound to take an active part in political life. If he does his duty and takes that active part he will be sure occasionally to commit mistakes and to be guilty of shortcomings. For these mistakes and shortcomings he will receive the unmeasured denunciation of the critics who commit neither because they never do anything but criticize. Nevertheless he will have the satisfaction of knowing that the salvation of the country ultimately lies, not in the hands of his critics, but in the hands of those who, however imperfectly, actually do the work of the nation. I would not for one moment be understood as objecting to criticism or failing to appreciate its importance. We need fearless criticism of our public men and public parties; we need unsparing condemnation of all persons and all principles that count for evil in our public life: but it behooves every man to remember that the work of the critic, important though it is, is of altogether secondary importance, and that, in the end, progress is accomplished by the man who does the things, and not by the man who talks about how they ought or ought not to be done.

Therefore the man who wishes to do good in his community must go into active political life. . . . Of course, in a government like ours, a man can accomplish anything only by acting in combination with others, and equally, of course, a number of people can act together only by each sacrificing certain of his beliefs or prejudices. That man is indeed unfortunate who cannot in any given district find some people with whom he can conscientiously act. He may find that he can do best by acting within a party organization; he may find that he can do best by acting, at least for certain purposes, or at certain times, outside of party organizations, in an independent body of some kind; but with some association he must act if he wishes to exert any real influence.

One thing to be always remembered is that neither independence on the one hand nor party fealty on the other can ever be accepted as an excuse for failure to do active work in politics. The party man who offers his allegiance to party as an excuse for blindly following his party, right or wrong, and who fails to try to make that party in any way better, commits a crime against the country; and a crime quite as serious is committed by the independent who makes his independence an excuse for easy self-indulgence, and who thinks that when he says he belongs to neither party he is excused from the duty of taking part in the practical work of party organizations. The party man is bound to do his share in party management. He is bound to attend the caucuses and the primaries, to see that only good men are put up, and to exert his influence as strenuously against the foes of good government within his party, as, through his party machinery, he does against those who are without the party. In the same way the independent, if he cannot take part in the regular organizations, is bound to do just as much active constructive work (not merely the work of criticism) outside; he is bound to try to get up an organization of his own and to try to make that organization felt in some effective manner. Whatever course the man who wishes to do his duty by his country takes in reference to parties or to independence of parties, he is bound to try to put himself in touch with men who think as he does, and to help make their joint influence felt in behalf of the powers that go for decency and good government. He must try to accomplish things; he must not vote in the air unless it is really necessary. Occasionally a man must cast a "conscience vote," when there is no possibility of carrying to victory his principles or his nominees; at times, indeed, this may be his highest duty; but ordinarily this is not the case. As a general rule a man ought to work and vote for something that there is at least a fair chance of putting into effect.

Yet another thing to be remembered by the man who wishes to make his influence felt for good in our politics is that he must act purely as an American. If he is not deeply imbued with the American spirit he cannot succeed. Any organization that tries to work along the line of caste or creed, that fails to treat all American citizens on their merits as men, will fail, and will deserve to fail. . . . On the one side, there is nothing to be made of a political organization that draws an exclusive social line, and on the other it must be remembered that it is just as un-American to vote against a man because he is rich as to vote against him because he is poor. The one man has just as much right as the other to claim to be treated purely on his merits as a man. In short, to do good work in politics, the men who organize must organize wholly without regard to whether their associates were born here or abroad, whether they are Protestants or Catholics, Jews or Gentiles, whether they are bankers or butchers, professors or day laborers. All that can rightly be asked of one's political associates is that they shall be honest men, good Americans, and substantially in accord as regards their political ideas.

Another thing that must not be forgotten by the man desirous of doing good political work is the need of the rougher, manlier virtues, and above all the virtue of personal courage, physical as well as moral. If we wish to do good work for our country we must be unselfish, disinterested, sincerely desirous of the well-being of the common-wealth, and capable of devoted adherence to a lofty ideal; but in addition we must be vigorous in mind and body, able to hold our own in rough conflict with our fellows, able to suffer punishment without flinching, and, at need, to repay it in kind with full interest. A peaceful and commercial civilization is always in danger of suffering the loss of the virile fighting qualities without which no nation, however cultured, however refined, however thrifty and prosperous, can ever amount to anything. Every citizen should be taught, both in public and in private life, that while he must avoid brawling and quarreling, it is his duty to stand up for his rights. He must realize that the only man who is more contemptible than the blusterer and bully is the coward. No man is worth much to the commonwealth if he is not capable of feeling righteous wrath and just indignation, if he is not stirred to hot anger by misdoing, and is not impelled to see justice meted out to the wrongdoers. No man is worth much anywhere if he does not possess both moral and physical courage. A politician who really serves his country well, and deserves his country's gratitude, must usually possess some of the hardy virtues which we admire in the soldier who serves his country well in the field.

An ardent young reformer is very apt to try to begin by reforming too much. He needs always to keep in mind that he has got to serve as a sergeant before he assumes the duties of commander in chief. It is right for him from the beginning to take a great interest in national, state, and municipal affairs, and to try to make himself felt in them if the occasion arises; but the best work must be done by the citizen working in his own ward or district. Let him associate himself with men who think as he does, and who, like him, are sincerely devoted to the public good. Then let them try to make themselves felt in the choice of alderman, of councilman, of assemblyman. The politicians will be prompt to recognize their power, and the people will recognize it too, after a while. Let them organize and work, undaunted by any temporary defeat. If they fail at first, and if they fail again, let them merely make up their minds to redouble their efforts, and perhaps alter their methods; but let them keep on working.

It is sheer unmanliness and cowardice to shrink from the contest because at first there is failure, or because the work is difficult or repulsive. No man who is worth his salt has any right to abandon the effort to better our politics merely because he does not find it pleasant, merely because it entails associations that to him happen to be disagreeable. . . .

"The Higher Life of American Cities," The Outlook, December 21, 1895

Whether a man is a party man or an independent, he must, if a good citizen, make honesty the first requisite in a public officer, and must refuse to support any man who is not honest. Moreover, his virtue must not be of the milk-and-water kind, if he is going to do good work politically. If he does not possess the virile virtues, courage, hardiness, resolution; if he is not willing to give good blows and receive them, he cannot expect to accomplish anything of permanent good. In the third place, he must possess common sense. If he allows the friends of bad government to monopolize the intelligence of the community, he is going to get beaten most certainly. . . .

As to the first point, the need of honest officials, everyone admits it theoretically; the trouble is we have got to insist upon the admission being practical. As a corollary to it we must insist upon all of the minor officials whose duties are merely ministerial being appointed purely for their merits, and being retained exactly as long as they do their duty well. Until we take it as a matter of course that a policeman, or a laborer on the public works, or a clerk in the Dock Department, is appointed purely because of capacity, and is retained without regard to his politics just as long as he does his duty faithfully, we cannot expect to get proper service from the departments. . . .

The question at issue was really of infinitely more importance than whether beer shall or shall not be sold on Sundays—it was the question upon the final answer to which depends the continuance of the Republic. If public officers are to execute the laws at their caprice, or at the caprice of a section of their constituents, then we may not only expect to see corruption flourish in our great cities, to see the growth of a blackmailed and lawbreaking body of liquor-sellers, and the growth of venality among public officials and of indifference to law among citizens, but we may expect to see in other communities the white-capper and the lyncher flourish, and crimes of every kind go unpunished unless punished by the exercise of the right of private vengeance. The one all-important foundation of our system of orderly liberty is obedience to law. . . .

"The Presidency," 1900

The president of the United States occupies a position of peculiar importance. In the whole world there is probably no other ruler, certainly no other ruler under free institutions, whose power compares with his. Of course a despotic king has even more, but no constitutional monarch has as much.

In the republics of France and Switzerland the president is not a very important officer, at least, compared with the president of the United States. In England the sovereign has much less control in shaping the policy of the nation, the prime minister occupying a position more nearly analogous to that of our president. The prime minister, however, can at any time be thrown out of office by an adverse vote, while the president can only be removed before his term is out for some extraordinary crime or misdemeanor against the nation.

Of course, in the case of each there is the enormous personal factor of the incumbent himself to be considered, entirely apart from the power of the office itself. The power wielded by Andrew Jackson was out of all proportion to that wielded by Buchanan, although in theory each was alike. So a strong president may exert infinitely more influence than a weak prime minister, or vice versa. But this is merely another way of stating that in any office the personal equation is always of vital consequence.

It is customary to speak of the framers of our Constitution as having separated the judicial, the legislative, and the executive functions of the government. The separation, however, is not in all respects sharply defined. The president has certainly most important legislative functions, and the upper branch of the national legislature shares with the president one of the most important of his executive functions; that is, the president can either sign or veto the bills passed by Congress, while, on the other hand, the Senate confirms or rejects his nominations. Of course the president cannot initiate legislation, although he can recommend it. But unless two-thirds of Congress in both branches are hostile to him, he can stop any measure from becoming a law. This power is varyingly used by different presidents, but it always exists, and must always be reckoned with by Congress.

While Congress is in session, if the president neither signs nor vetoes the bill that is passed, the bill becomes a law without his signature. The effect is precisely the same as if he had signed it. Presidents who disapproved of details in a bill, but felt that on the whole it was advisable it should become a law, have at times used this method to emphasize the fact that they were not satisfied with the measure that they were yet unwilling to veto. A notable instance was afforded in President Cleveland's second term, when he thus treated the Wilson-Gorman tariff bill.

The immense federal service, including all the postal employees, all the customs employees, all the Indian agents, marshals, district attorneys, navy-yard employees, and so forth, is under the president. It would of course be a physical impossibility for him to appoint all the individuals in the service. His direct power lies over the heads of the departments, bureaus, and more important offices. But he does not appoint these by himself. His is only the nominating power. It rests with the Senate to confirm or reject the nominations.

The senators are the constitutional advisers of the president, for it must be remembered that his cabinet is not in the least like the cabinet of which the prime minister is head in the English Parliament. Under our government the secretaries who form the cabinet are in the strict-est sense the president's own ministerial appointees; the men, chosen out of all the nation, to whom he thinks he can best depute the most important and laborious of his executive duties. Of course they all ad-vise him on matters of general policy when he so desires it, and in practice each cabinet officer has a very free hand in managing his own department, and must have it if he is to do good work. But all this ad-vice and consultation is at the will of the president. With the Senate, on the other hand, the advice and consultation are obligatory under the Constitution.

The president and Congress are mutually necessary to one another in matters of legislation, and the president and Senate are mutually necessary in matters of appointment. Every now and then men who understand our Constitution but imperfectly raise an outcry against the president for consulting the senators in matters of appointment, and even talk about the senators "usurping" his functions. These men labor under a misapprehension. The Senate has no right to dictate to the president who shall be appointed, but they have an entire right to say who shall not be appointed, for under the Constitution this has been made their duty.

In practice, under our party system, it has come to be recognized that each senator has a special right to be consulted about the appoint-ments in his own state, if he is of the president's political party. Often the opponents of the senator in his state do not agree with him in the matter of appointments, and sometimes the president, in the exercise of his judgment, finds it right and desirable to disregard the senator. But the president and the senators must work together, if they desire to secure the best results.

But although many men must share with the president the respon-sibility for different individual actions, and although Congress must of course also very largely condition his usefulness, yet the fact remains that in his hands is infinitely more power than in the hands of any other man in our country during the time that he holds the office; that there is upon him always a heavy burden of responsibility; and that in certain crises this burden may become so great as to bear down any but the strongest and bravest man.

It is easy enough to give a bad administration; but to give a good administration demands the most anxious thought, the most wearing endeavor, no less than very unusual powers of mind. The chances for error are limitless, and in minor matters, where from the nature of the case it is absolutely inevitable that the president should rely upon the judgment of others, it is certain that under the best presidents some errors will be committed. The severest critics of a president's policy are apt to be, not those who know most about what is to be done and of the limitations under which it must be done, but those who know least.

In the aggregate, quite as much wrong is committed by improper denunciation of public servants who do well as by failure to attack those who do ill. There is every reason why the president, whoever he may be and to whatever party he may belong, should be held to a sharp accountability alike for what he does and for what he leaves undone. But we injure ourselves and the nation if we fail to treat with proper respect the man, whether he is politically opposed to us or not, who in the highest office in our land is striving to do his duty according to the strength that is in him.

We have had presidents who have acted very weakly or unwisely in particular crises. We have had presidents the sum of whose work has not been to the advantage of the Republic. But we have never had one concerning whose personal integrity there was so much as a shadow of a suspicion, or who has not been animated by an earnest desire to do the best possible work that he could for the people at large. Of course infirmity of purpose or wrongheadedness may mar this integrity and sincerity of intention; but the integrity and the good intentions have always existed. We have never had in the presidential chair any man who did not sincerely desire to benefit the people and whose own personal ambitions are not entirely honorable, although as much cannot be said of certain aspirants for the place, such as Aaron Burr.

Corruption, in the gross sense in which the word is used in ordinary conversation, has been absolutely unknown among our presidents, and it has been exceedingly rare in our presidents' cabinets. Inefficiency, whether due to lack of willpower, sheer deficiency in wisdom, or improper yielding either to the pressure of politicians or to the other kinds of pressure that must often be found even in a free democracy, has been far less uncommon. Of deliberate moral obliquity there has been but very little indeed.

In the easiest, quietest, most peaceful times the president is sure to have great tasks before him. The simple question of revenue and expenditure is as important to the nation as it is to the average household, and the president is the man to whom the nation looks and whom it holds accountable in the matter both of expenditure and of revenue. It is an entirely mistaken belief that the expenditure of money is simply due to a taste for recklessness and extravagance on the part of the people's representatives.

The representatives in the long run are sure to try to do what the people effectively want. The trouble is that although each group has, and all the groups taken together still more strongly have, an interest in keeping the expenditures down, each group has also a direct interest in keeping some particular expenditure up. This expenditure is usually entirely proper and desirable, save only that the aggregate of all such expenditures may be so great as to make it impossible for the nation to go into them.

It is a good deal the same thing in the nation as it is in a state. The demand may be for a consumptive hospital, or for pensions to veterans, or for a public building, or for an armory, or for cleaning out a harbor, or for starting irrigation. In each case the demand may be in itself entirely proper, and those interested in it, from whatever motives, may be both sincere and strenuous in their advocacy. But the president has to do on a large scale what every governor of a state has to do on a small scale, that is, balance the demands on the Treasury with the capacities of the Treasury.

Whichever way he decides, some people are sure to think that he has tipped the scale the wrong way, and from their point of view they may conscientiously think it; whereas from his point of view he may know with equal conscientiousness that he has done his best to strike an average that would on the one hand not be niggardly toward worthy objects, and on the other would not lay too heavy a burden of taxation upon the people.

Inasmuch as these particular questions have to be met every year in connection with every session of Congress and with the work of every department, it may readily be seen that even the president's everyday responsibilities are of no light order. So it is with his appointments. Entirely apart from the fact that there is a great pressure for place, it is also the fact that in all the higher and more important appointments there are usually conflicting interests that must somehow be reconciled to the best of the President's capacity.

Here again it must be remembered that the matter is not always by any means one of merely what we call politics. Where there is a really serious conflict in reference to an appointment, while it may be merely a factional fight, it is more apt to be because two groups of the president's supporters differ radically and honestly on some question of policy; so that whatever the president's decision may be, he cannot help arousing dissatisfaction.

One thing to be remembered is that appointments and policies that are normally routine and unimportant may suddenly become of absolutely vital consequence. For instance, the War Department was utterly neglected for over thirty years after the Civil War. This neglect was due less to the successive presidents than to Congress, and in Congress it was due to the fact that the people themselves did not take an interest in the army. Neither the regular officer nor the regular soldier takes any part in politics as a rule, so that the demagogue and the bread-and-butter politician have no fear of his vote; and to both of them, and also to the cheap sensational newspaper, the army offers a favorite subject for attack. So it often happens that some amiable people really get a little afraid of the army, and have some idea that it may be used some time or other against our liberties.

The army never has been and, I am sure, it never will be or can be a menace to anybody save America's foes, or aught but a source of pride to every good and farsighted American. But it is only in time of actual danger that such facts are brought home vividly to the minds of our people, and so the army is apt to receive far less than its proper share of attention. But when an emergency like that caused by the Spanish War arises, then the secretary of war becomes the most important officer in the cabinet, and the army steps into the place of foremost interest in all the country.

It is only once in a generation that such a crisis as the Spanish War or the Mexican War or the War of 1812 has to be confronted, but in almost every administration lesser crises do arise. They may be in connection with foreign affairs, as was the case with the Chilean trouble under President Harrison's administration, the Venezuelan matter in President Cleveland's second term, or the Boxer uprising in China last year. Much more often they relate to domestic affairs, as in the case of a disastrous panic, which produces terrible social and industrial convulsions. Whatever the problem may be, the president has got to meet it and to work out some kind of a solution. In midwinter or midsummer, with Congress sitting or absent, the president has always to be ready to devote every waking hour to some anxious, worrying, harassing matter, most difficult to decide, and yet which it is imperative immediately to decide.

An immense addition to the president's burden is caused by the entirely well-meaning people who ask him to do what he cannot possibly do. For the first few weeks after the inauguration a new president may receive on an average fifteen hundred letters a day. His mail is so enormous that often he cannot read one letter in a hundred, and rarely can he read one letter in ten. Even his private secretary can read only a small fraction of the mail. Often there are letters that the president would really be glad to see, but that are swamped in the great mass of demands for office, demands for pensions, notes of warning or advice, demands for charity, and requests of every conceivable character, not to speak of the letters from "cranks," which are always numerous in the president's mail.

One president, who was very anxious to help people whenever he could, made the statement that the requests for pecuniary aid received in a single fortnight would, if complied with, have eaten up considerably more than his entire year's salary. The requests themselves are frequently such as the president would like to comply with if there was any way of making a discrimination; but there is none.

One rather sad feature of the life of a president is the difficulty of making friends, because almost inevitably after a while the friend thinks there is some office he would like, applies for it, and when the president is obliged to refuse, feels that he has been injured. Those who were closest to Abraham Lincoln have said that this was one of the things that concerned him most in connection with his administration. It is hardly necessary to allude to the well-known fact that no president can gratify a hundredth part of the requests and demands made upon him for office, often by men who have rendered him real services and who are fit to fill the position they seek, but not so fit as somebody else. Of course the man does not realize that his successful rival was appointed because he really was more fit, and he goes away sour and embittered because of what he feels to be the President's ingratitude.

Perhaps the two most striking things in the presidency are the immense power of the president, in the first place; and in the second place, the fact that as soon as he has ceased being president he goes right back into the body of the people and becomes just like any other American citizen. While he is in office he is one of the half-dozen persons throughout the whole world who have most power to affect the destinies of the world.

He can set fleets and armies in motion; he can do more than any save one or two absolute sovereigns to affect the domestic welfare and happiness of scores of millions of people. Then when he goes out of office he takes up his regular round of duties like any other citizen, or if he is of advanced age retires from active life to rest, like any other man who has worked hard to earn his rest.

One president, John Quincy Adams, after leaving the presidency, again entered public life as a congressman, and achieved conspicuous successes in the Lower House. This, however, is a unique case. Many presidents have followed the examples of Jefferson and Jackson, and retired, as these two men retired to Monticello and the Hermitage. Others have gone into more or less active work, as practicing lawyers or as lecturers on law, or in business, or in some form of philanthropy.

During the president's actual incumbency of his office the tendency is perhaps to exaggerate not only his virtues but his faults. When he goes out he is simply one of the ordinary citizens, and perhaps for a time the importance of the role he has played is not recognized. True perspective is rarely gained until years have gone by.

Altogether, there are few harder tasks than that of filling well and ably the office of president of the United States. The labor is immense, the ceaseless worry and harassing anxiety are beyond description. But if the man at the close of his term is able to feel that he has done his duty well, that he has solved after the best fashion of which they were capable the great problems with which he was confronted, and has kept clean and in good running order the governmental machinery of the mighty Republic, he has the satisfaction of feeling that he has performed one of the great world-tasks, and that the mere performance is in itself the greatest of all possible rewards.

References

Roosevelt, Theodore, *An Autobiography* (New York: Macmillan Company, 1913).

Roosevelt, Theodore, *American Ideals, The Strenuous Life, Realizable Ideals* (New York: Charles Scribner's Sons, 1926).

WOODROW WILSON

FULL NAME:
Thomas Woodrow Wilson

BORN:
28 December 1856, Staunton, Virginia

DIED:
3 February 1924, Washington, D.C.

Twenty-eighth President of the United States. President of Princeton University, 1902–1910. Governor of New Jersey, 1911–1913. President in 1912 and reelected in 1916, serving two terms.

Wilson himself was a student of the presidency and published *Constitutional Government in the United States* in 1908 (New York: Columbia University, 1964). *The Papers of Woodrow Wilson*, edited by Arthur S. Link et al., is the comprehensive documentary collection (Princeton, NJ: Princeton University Press, 1966–1993). Among the biographies are: Arthur S. Link, *Wilson*, Five Volumes (Princeton, NJ: Princeton University Press, 1947–1965); and Ray Standard Baker, *Woodrow Wilson: Life and Letters*, Eight Volumes (Garden City, NY: Doubleday, 1927–1939).

The Papers of Woodrow Wilson

*Remarks at Democratic State Committee luncheon in
Trenton, New Jersey, on 13 January 1913*

I feel a natural embarrassment on this particular occasion, because in view of what is likely to happen immediately after 3 o'clock, I am again placed in the position of a blushing candidate. I think that one can predict what the choice is going to be at 3 o'clock. Nevertheless, I feel that it would be unbecoming in me to make a speech in any other tone than that of a man who believes that he is speaking for the men with whom he is associated. Some men have been slow to observe, but the majority of us have seen, that the people of the United States have made a definite choice. I happen to be one of the instruments through whom that choice is expressed, but I am for the time, and that choice is for the long future. The people of the United States have turned their faces in a definite direction, and any party, any man, who does not go with them in that direction, they will reject—and they ought to reject.

Therefore, in looking forward to the responsibilities that I am about to assume, I feel first, last, and all the time that I am acting in a representative capacity. I am bidden to interpret as well as I can the purposes of the people of the United States and to act, so far as my choice determines the action, only through the instrumentality of persons who also represent that choice. I have no liberty in the matter. I have given bonds. My sacred honor is involved, and nothing more could be involved. Therefore, I shall not be acting as a partisan when I pick out progressives, and only progressives. I shall be acting as a representative of the people of this great country. And, therefore, it is a matter of supreme pleasure to me to find in every direction, as I turn about from one group of men to another, that men's minds and men's consciences, and men's purposes, are yielding to that great impulse that now moves the whole people of the United States.

I do not foresee any serious divisions of counsel in the Democratic party as a national body. On the contrary, I find every evidence of solidarity. I see every evidence that men who have not hitherto yielded their judgment to the movement of the age are now about to yield their judgment. I will not say their will. They do not seem to be acting under compulsion; they are beginning to yield their judgment to the common judgment of the nation. Because I find in discussing questions of business—contrary to the impression that prevails in some editorial rooms—that in speaking to men of business, I am speaking to men whose vision is swinging around to the path that the nation has marked out for itself.

This nation is full of honorable men who have been engaged in large business in a way in which they thought they were permitted to do so, both by their consciences and the laws. But they have had their eyes so close to their ledgers, they have had their energies so absolutely absorbed in the undertakings with which they were individually identified, that they have not, until the nation spoke loud, raised their eyes from their books and papers and seen how the things they are doing stood related to the fortunes of mankind.

Now, they are beginning to see those relationships, and as they see those relationships they are beginning to feel the refreshment of men who look away from a particular task and extend their eyes to the fortunes of men lying outside their usual ken and beyond their touch— the great bodies of men who would along with them hope and struggle and achieve. I believe that I am not mistaken in seeing this new purpose come into the hearts of men who have not permitted themselves hitherto to see what they now look upon. For the nation cannot move successfully by anything except concert of purpose and of judgment. You cannot whip a nation into line. You cannot drive your leaders before you. You have got to have a spirit that thrills the whole body, and I believe that that spirit is now beginning to thrill the whole body. Men are finding that they will be bigger men and bigger businessmen as they will spend some of their brains on something that has nothing to do with themselves, and that the more you extend the use of your energy, the more energy you have got to spend even upon your own affairs; that enrichment comes from the enlargement, and that with the enrichment comes the increase of power.

Men, in the last analysis, even in the narrower field of business, have a grip upon their fellow men in the proportion as they enjoy the confidence and admiration of their fellow men. A man can accomplish a great deal more in business, as I need hardly tell you, by the belief that people have in him than by the fear that he inspires. And some men have made the profound mistake, so far as their individual success is concerned, of trying to succeed by fear and not by persuasion, not by confidence, but by creating the consciousness that they can spoil the careers of the men who do not work. They cannot get far that way. They may spoil a good many careers, but for every career they spoil this is the result:

Did you ever read that story of Poe's, that dreadful story of the man who was put in an iron room in a prison? The room had seven windows, and after he had slept through the first night he became conscious that something had changed in the room, and there were only six windows. He believed that he must have counted wrong the day before, for the proportions of the room seemed the same. On the second morning there were only five windows, and the room was closing about him. Men who shut themselves up in selfishness ought to read that story and realize that their life is closing about them, and that the end is inexorable. The only way to increase the number of windows and let in the air and see the horizon is the way of fairness and equity and love of your fellow men, and not the way of selfishness and of power.

This is not a new thing for America to see. She saw it at the first, but she forgot it for a little while. That is all. She diverted her energies. She thought that to be rich was to be great, and forgot that her only distinction is the way in which she uses her riches and her power; that she is great only as she differs from other nations, not as she resembles other nations. And she differed from other nations in setting up this standard of hope that was the standard of liberty, and so long as she can induce men to follow it as a standard of hope, so long will she lead the nations. We were just dreaming. We were astray in a dream. And now we have waked up and are recovering the road that we had gone aside from, and have set out again in the beginning of another century—for we choose a century as our dramatic unit in American history—rediscovering the standards of hope and liberty for mankind. And the Democratic Party is privileged to lead in that quest. And New Jersey is privileged to stand at the front in the hosts of the Democratic Party in that splendid enterprise. These are the things that make a man grateful who loves his state and who believes in the men who are associated with him. These are the things that make fighting worthwhile.

I suppose some people have the idea that I love to fight just for the fun of it. I had a friend of mine tell me that I reminded him of a Highlander's dog who was looking very dejected one day, and his owner was asked what was the matter with him. He said: "He can no jus' get enuch o' fichtin'." He was not able to find any dog that would give him the satisfaction. Now, that is not in the least my temperament. I am really a very tame, amenable person; but I do love to feel in my blood the splendid satisfaction of fighting for something, something that is bigger than myself, and trying for the time at least to think I am as big as the thing I am fighting for. That is a solid satisfaction. And when I can for the time being represent the Democratic Party and find that the nation as a whole is thawing out toward the Democratic Party and more and more coming to believe that the Democratic Party can do the thing that the country has been waiting for, then I enjoy the immense satisfaction of being part of a thing that is so much bigger than I am that I can dream, at any rate, that I am taking my own measure by the thing that I belong to.

Now, that is the kind of thought that I believe we are permitted to indulge in today, this common sense of being part of a new age and having our eyes forward and not backward, swearing allegiance to one another, that we are not going to allow ourselves or anything we are connected with to be caught in the old entanglements anymore. That is what I have sworn to. And the enterprise is easy, because, as I told some gentlemen in another place the other night, we have asked for and obtained a change of venue. The jury is not now the selected jury that was always summoned and always consisted of the same persons; but it is a jury consisting of all the people of the United States; and that jury will stand by you to the last ditch. And with that jury back of you, you may smile at all the gentlemen who meet in corners and in private rooms and arrange to beat you. The thing cannot be arranged. The game cannot be set up. Because all the walls are taken down now, and you are out in the open now. If you want to set up your game, come here in the center of the ring and let us see you set it up. That is the only way in which you can set it up. And if it is the right kind of a setting up, you will not mind setting it up here in our presence, and in the presence, by representation, of the rest of the people of the United States.

And so, gentlemen, our satisfaction today is handsome because it is unselfish. There is nothing handsome about boasting. There is nothing handsome about crowing over anybody else. That is a pretty mean business. But there is something very satisfactory in saying this: "Now we have left all those things behind; we have set forward in this journey that is ahead of us. We have found the old road, and we are going to follow it; and anybody is welcome to come along with us that wants to." And we are not going to remember whether he tried to find other roads or not, provided he comes along. But we are not going to take his word for it; we are going to look around and see if he is keeping step. Because he has got to get there when we get there, and he has got to get there by the same road we get there on or else he is not of our company. But he is welcome to come along if he will come along. And there is only one way to come along in this journey. There are inns and stages by the way, and there is good entertainment, I dare say, ahead, but the roll will have to be called occasionally, and we will have to see who is present or accounted for. It will not be military discipline, but we will all have to arrive at the same time.

I feel myself no bitterness about anything that has happened. There are some gentlemen who, I fear, think that I have entertained bitter feelings toward them, whom I would love to see and grasp hands with at the end of the journey.

Letter to Mary Allen Hulbert, 16 March 1913

. . . The days pass without variety. The work is hard and incessant. But it grows gradually familiar. The old kink in me is still there. Everything is persistently *impersonal*. I am administering a great office—no doubt the greatest in the world—but I do not seem to be identified with it: it is not me, and I am not it. I am only a commissioner, in charge of its apparatus, living in its offices, and taking upon myself its functions[.] This impersonality of my life is a very odd thing, and perhaps robs it of intensity, as it certainly does of pride and self-consciousness (and, maybe, of enjoyment) but it at least prevents me from becoming a fool, and thinking myself It! Everything has gone well, so far, and very generous opinions are expressed of the start the new administration has made.

We are all well. We think often, very, very often, of you, and all unite in messages of deep affection.

Your devoted friend, Woodrow Wilson
Love to Allen.

Letter to Mary Allen Hulbert, 21 September 1913

. . . I am perfectly well and strong, in spite of the strain that I had feared might be too much for me. Partly, perhaps, because so far all has gone singularly well in public matters. Do not believe anything you read in the newspapers. If you read the papers I see, they are utterly untrustworthy. They represent the obstacles as existing that they wish to have exist, whether they are actual or not. Read the editorial page and you will know what you will find in the news columns. For unless they are grossly careless the two always support one another. Their lying is shameless and colossal! Editorially the papers that are friendly (and some that are not) represent me, in the most foolish way, as master of the situation here, bending Congress to my indomitable individual will. That is, of course, silly. Congress is made up of thinking men who want the party to succeed as much as I do, and who wish to serve the country effectively and intelligently. They have found out that I am honest and that I have no personal purpose of my own to serve (except that "If it be a sin to covet honor, then am I the most offending soul alive!") and accept my guidance because they see that I am attempting only to mediate their own thoughts and purposes. I do not know how to wield a big stick, but I do know how to put my mind at the service of others for the accomplishment of a common purpose. They are using me; I am not driving them. But I need not tell you all this. The joy of a real friend is that one need not explain anything: it is known and comprehended already. You will know just how I accomplish anything that I do accomplish. And what a pleasure it is, what a deep human pleasure, to work with strong men, who do their own thinking and know how to put things in shape! Why a man should wish to be the whole show, and surround himself with weak men, I cannot imagine! How dull it would be! How tiresome to watch a plot that was only the result of your own action and every part of which you could predict before it was put on the boards! That is not power. Power consists in one's capacity to link his will with the purpose of others, to lead by reason and a gift for cooperation. It is a multiple of combined brains. But you know that, too. The fact is that you are a very wise lady, because you instinctively comprehend your fellow beings, both singly and in the mass. That explains the hold you have upon individuals and the power you have in society whenever you have the chance or the wish to exercise it. To comprehend people is to rule them. At any rate that is the root and source of the whole thing. See the thing from the point of view of those with whom you are dealing and your influence is established, and is welcome. But how are you? That's what I am really thinking about. I spoke of the rest only because your own gifts suggested it. I am waiting more anxiously than you know to learn how my dearest friend is.

Your devoted friend, Woodrow Wilson

Remarks to the National Press Club, 20 March 1914

My Lord, and fellow members: I feel a little bit as if it were Monday morning or Thursday afternoon, and questioning was to come from your end and then carefully guarded answers from mine. I can say without the least affectation that I really did not know that I was to make a speech this afternoon, but a man can always speak freely when he knows he is not going to be reported. So that perhaps things will come out of me spontaneously that would not come out if I knew I were on public parade.

Just here, among ourselves, I am very glad to say how sincerely I congratulate you on moving into these truly delightful quarters and how I congratulate you upon our elevation, so that we can look down even upon the Treasury and feel a condescension toward our fellow men who are on the outside.

I was just thinking, as Mr. Lord was speaking, of my sense of confusion of identity, sometimes, when I read articles about myself. I have never read an article about myself in which I recognized myself, and I have come to have the impression that I must be some kind of a fraud, because I think a great many of these articles are written in absolute good faith. I tremble to think of the variety and falseness in the impressions I make—and it is being borne in on me that it may change my very disposition—that I am a cold and removed person who has a thinking machine inside that he adjusts to the circumstances, that he does not allow to be moved by any winds of affection or emotion of any kind, but turns it like a cold searchlight on anything that is presented to his attention and makes it work. I am not aware of having any detachable apparatus inside of me. On the contrary, if I were to interpret myself, I would say that my constant embarrassment is to restrain the emotions that are inside of me. You may not believe it, but I sometimes feel like a fire from a far from extinct volcano, and if the lava does not seem to spill over it is because you are not high enough to see into the basin and see the caldron boil. Because, truly, gentlemen, in the position that I now occupy there is a sort of, I do not know how else to express it than to say, passionate sense of being connected with my fellow men in a peculiar relationship of responsibility. Not merely the responsibility of office, but God knows there are enough things in this world that need to be corrected. I have mixed, first and last, with all sorts and conditions of men—there are mighty few kinds of men that have to be described to me, and there are mighty few kinds of experiences that have to be described to me— and when I think of the number of men who are looking to me as the representative of a party with hope, with the hope for all varieties of salvation from the things they are struggling in the midst of it, it makes me tremble. It makes me tremble, not only with a sense of my own inadequacy and weakness, but as if I were shaken by the very things that are shaking them; and if I seem circumspect, it is because I am so diligently trying not to make any colossal blunders. If you just calculated the number of blunders a fellow can make in twenty-four hours if he is not careful and if he does not listen more than he talks, you would see something of the feeling that I have.

I was amused the other day at a remark that Senator Newlands made. I had read him the trust message that I was to deliver to Congress some ten days before I delivered it, and I never stop doctoring things of that kind until the day I have to deliver them. When he heard it read to Congress, he said, "I think it was better than it was when you read it to me." I said, "Senator, there is one thing that I do not think you understand. I not only use all the brains I have but all I can borrow, and I have borrowed a lot since I read it to you first." That, I dare say, is what gives the impression of circumspectness, and of the "velvet slipper." I am listening; I am diligently trying to collect all the brains that are borrowable in order that I may not make more blunders than it is inevitable that a man should make who has great limitations of knowledge and capacity. And the emotion of the thing is so great that I suppose I must be some kind of a mask to conceal it. I really feel sometimes as if I were masquerading when I catch a picture of myself in some printed description. When you fellows stand around me on Monday mornings and Thursday afternoons and ask me questions, I know what is in the back of your heads, and I could tell you sometimes more than I do tell you, but I do not tell you any more than I am sure of. I try to keep a grip on myself. The other day, the last time we were together, the natural man got to the front of the stage, and I had to talk to you as an individual and not as the president of the United States. I wish to God there were more occasions when I could do that, because I have this feeling, gentlemen: In between things that I have to do as a public officer, I never think of myself as the president of the United States, because I never have had any sense of being identified with that office. I feel like a person appointed for a certain length of time to administer that office, and I feel just as much outside of it at this moment as I did before I was elected to it. I feel just as much outside of it as I still feel outside of the government of the United States. No man could imagine himself the government of the United States; but he could understand that some part of his fellow citizens had told him to go and run a certain part of it the best he knew how. That would not make him the government itself or the thing itself. It would just make him responsible for running it the best he knew how. The machine is so much greater than himself, the office is so much greater than himself; the office is so much greater than he can ever be, and the most he can do is to look grave enough and self-possessed enough to seem to fill it. I can hardly refrain every now and again from tipping the public the wink, as much as to say, "It is only 'me' that is inside this thing. I know perfectly well that I will have to get out presently. I know that then I will look just my own proper size, and that for the time being the proportions are somewhat refracted and misrepresented to the eye by the large thing I am inside of, from which I am tipping you this wink."

For example, take matters of this sort: I will not say whether it is wise or unwise, silly or grave, but certain precedents have been established that, in certain companies, the president must leave the room first, and people must give way to him. They must not sit down if he is standing up. It is a very uncomfortable thing to have to think of all the other people every time I get up and sit down, and all that sort of thing. So that when I get guests in my own house and the public is shut out, I adjourn being president and take leave to be a gentleman. If they draw back and insist upon my doing something first, I firmly decline. There are blessed intervals when I forget by one means or another that I am president of the United States. One means by which I forget is to get a rattling good detective story, get after some imaginary offender, and chase him all over—preferably any continent but this. Because the various parts of this continent are becoming painfully suggestive to me. The post offices, the senators, and things like that, which encumber the land have "sicklied them o'er with a pale cast of thought." There are certain states I can't think of without thinking how difficult it is for those senators to suggest the same thing at the same time. There are post offices to which I wouldn't think of mailing a letter, which I can't think of without trembling with the knowledge of all the heartburnings of the struggle there was in connection with getting somebody installed as postmaster. Why anybody should wish to be postmaster, and get the postmastership at the sacrifice of the esteem of all his fellow citizens, I cannot understand. They do not think of their fellow citizens until they get it, and then they generally forget the office and let the deputy run it. I had been witness to one occasion of that sort for so many years that when I became President I put the deputy in as postmaster, because I knew he needed a vacation, he has been running the office so long. If there were only a deputy president, who could keep a straight face and a clear conscience and let the president go off on what may be called a mere vacation, adjourning the dignities and the requirements of his office, it would be a very delightful thing.

Now, if I were free, I would come not infrequently up to these rooms. You know I never was in Washington but a very few times and for a very few hours until I came down to admit that I had got into trouble, and I never expect to see the inside of the public buildings in Washington until my term is over. The minute I turn up anywhere, I am personally conducted to beat the band. The curator, and the assistant curators, and every other blooming thing turn up, and they show me so much attention that I don't see the building. I would have to say, "Stand aside and let me see what you are showing me." For example, I took a shortcut through the Treasury Department the other day, going in this door just opposite here and cutting through, and there was a great scampering of custodians and whatnot up to the secretary of the treasury's office crying, "The President is in the building"—as if some menagerie animal or something that had to be attended were loose. The secretary of the treasury a few days after said, "I understand you visited the Treasury." "Not at all," I said, "I took a shortcut through it, and escaped as soon as I could." Everywhere I go I have that. Someday, after I am through with this office, I am going to come back to Washington and see it. In the meantime, I am in the same category as the

National Museum, the Monument, the Smithsonian Institution, or the Congressional Library, and all the Sunday schools and everything else that comes down here has to be shown the president. If I only knew an exhibition appearance to assume—apparently I can assume other appearances that do not show what is going on inside—I would like to have it pointed out, so that I could practice it before the looking glass and see if I could not look like the Monument. Being regarded as a national exhibit, it would be much simpler than being shaken hands with by the whole United States.

And yet even that is interesting to me, simply because I like human beings. It is a pretty poor crowd that does not interest you. I think they would have to be all members of that class that devotes itself to "expense regardless of pleasure" in order to be entirely uninteresting. I think the highly elaborate and ably dressed rich people that look so much alike—they try, they spend their time trying to look so much alike and they so relieve themselves of all responsibility of thought—that they are very monotonous indeed to look at; whereas, a crowd picked up off the street is just a jolly lot—a job lot of average human beings, pulsating with life, with all kinds of passions and desires. It would be a great pleasure if, unobserved and unattended to and knocked around as I have been accustomed to most of my life, I could resort to these delightful quarters and to any place in Washington that I chose. I have sometimes thought of going to some costumer's—some theatrical costumer's—and buying an assortment of beards, rouge, and coloring and all the known means of disguising myself, if it were not against the law. You see, I have a scruple as president against breaking the law, and disguising one's self is against the law, but if I could disguise myself and not get caught, hang the law; I would go out, be a free American citizen once more, and have a jolly time. I might then meet some of you gentlemen and actually tell you what I really thought.

Reference

Wilson, Woodrow, *The Papers of Woodrow Wilson*, edited by Arthur S. Link, et al., Volumes 27, 28, 29 (Princeton, NJ: Princeton University Press, 1966–1993).

FRANKLIN D. ROOSEVELT

FULL NAME:

Franklin Delano Roosevelt

BORN:

30 January 1882, New York

DIED:

12 April 1945, Warm Springs, Georgia

Thirty-second President of the United States. State Legislator and Assistant Secretary of the Navy. Governor of New York, 1924–1933. President from 1933 until his death in 1945.

Roosevelt's books include: Franklin Delano Roosevelt, Looking Forward (New York: Day, 1933); and One Man's Philosophy (Chicago, IL: Kallis, 1934). His biographies include: Robert Dallek, Franklin D. Roosevelt and American Foreign Policy, 1932–1945 (New York: Oxford University Press, 1979); Frank Freidel, Franklin D. Roosevelt, Four Volumes (Boston: Little Brown, 1952–1973); Volume I, Arthur M. Schlesinger, Jr., The Age of Roosevelt, Three Volumes (Boston: Houghton Mifflin, 1957–1960); and James McGregor Burns, Roosevelt: The Soldier of Freedom (New York: Harcourt Brace Jovanovich, 1970).

The Speeches of Franklin Delano Roosevelt

First inaugural address, Washington, D.C., 4 March 1933

I am certain that my fellow Americans expect that on my induction into the presidency I will address them with a candor and a decision that the present situation of our nation impels. This is preeminently the time to speak the truth, the whole truth, frankly and boldly. Nor need we shrink from honestly facing conditions in our country today. This great nation will endure as it has endured, will revive and will prosper. So, first of all, let me assert my firm belief that the only thing we have to fear is fear itself—nameless, unreasoning, unjustified terror that paralyzes needed efforts to convert retreat into advance. In every dark hour of our national life a leadership of frankness and vigor has met with that understanding and support of the people themselves, which is essential to victory. I am convinced that you will again give that support to leadership in these critical days.

In such a spirit on my part and on yours we face our common difficulties. They concern, thank God, only material things. Values have shrunken to fantastic levels; taxes have risen; our ability to pay has fallen; government of all kinds is faced by serious curtailment of income; the means of exchange are frozen in the currents of trade; the withered leaves of industrial enterprise lie on every side; farmers find no markets for their produce; the savings of many years in thousands of families are gone.

More important, a host of unemployed citizens face the grim problem of existence, and an equally great number toil with little return. Only a foolish optimist can deny the dark realities of the moment.

Yet our distress comes from no failure of substance. We are stricken by no plague of locusts. Compared with the perils that our forefathers conquered because they believed and were not afraid, we have still much to be thankful for. Nature still offers her bounty and human efforts have multiplied it. Plenty is at our doorstep, but a generous use of it languishes in the very sight of the supply. Primarily this is because rulers of the exchange of mankind's goods have failed through their own stubbornness and their own incompetence, have admitted their failure, and have abdicated. Practices of the unscrupulous money changers stand indicted in the court of public opinion, rejected by the hearts and minds of men.

True they have tried, but their efforts have been cast in the pattern of an outworn tradition. Faced by failure of credit they have proposed only the lending of more money. Stripped of the lure of profit by which to induce our people to follow their false leadership, they have resorted to exhortations, pleading tearfully for restored confidence. They know only the rules of a generation of self-seekers. They have no vision, and when there is no vision the people perish.

The money changers have fled from their high seats in the temple of our civilization. We may now restore the temple to the ancient truths. The measure of the restoration lies in the extent to which we apply social values more noble than mere monetary profit.

Happiness lies not in the mere possession of money; it lies in the joy of achievement, in the thrill of creative effort. The joy and moral stimulation of work no longer must be forgotten in the mad chase of evanescent profits. These dark days will be worth all they cost us if they teach us that our true destiny is not to be ministered unto but to minister to ourselves and to our fellow men.

Recognition of the falsity of material wealth as the standard of success goes hand in hand with the abandonment of the false belief that public office and high political position are to be valued only by the standards of pride of place and personal profit; and there must be an end to a conduct in banking and in business that too often has given to a sacred trust the likeness of callous and selfish wrongdoing. Small wonder that confidence languishes, for it thrives only on honesty, on honor, on the sacredness of obligations, on faithful protection, on unselfish performance; without them it cannot live.

Restoration calls, however, not for changes in ethics alone. This nation asks for action, and action now.

Our greatest primary task is to put people to work. This is no unsolvable problem if we face it wisely and courageously. It can be accomplished in part by direct recruiting by the government itself, treating the task as we would treat the emergency of a war, but at the same time, through this employment, accomplishing greatly needed projects to stimulate and reorganize the use of our natural resources.

Hand in hand with this we must frankly recognize the overbalance of population in our industrial centers and, by engaging on a national scale in a redistribution, endeavor to provide a better use of the land for those best fitted for the land. The task can be helped by definite efforts to raise the values of agricultural products and with this the power to purchase the output of our cities. It can be helped by preventing realistically the tragedy of the growing loss through foreclosure of our small homes and our farms. It can be helped by insistence that the federal, state, and local governments act forthwith on the demand that their cost be drastically reduced. It can be helped by the unifying of relief activities which today are often scattered, uneconomical, and unequal. It can be helped by national planning for and supervision of all forms of transportation and of communications and other utilities which have a definitely public character. There are many ways in which it can be helped, but it can never be helped merely by talking about it. We must act and act quickly.

Finally, in our progress toward a resumption of work we require two safeguards against a return of the evils of the old order: there must be a strict supervision of all banking and credits and investments, so that there will be an end to speculation with other people's money; and there must be provision for an adequate but sound currency.

These are the lines of attack. I shall presently urge upon a new Congress, in special session, detailed measures for their fulfillment, and I shall seek the immediate assistance of the several states.

Through this program of action we address ourselves to putting our own national house in order and making income balance outgo. Our international trade relations, though vastly important, are in point of time and necessity secondary to the establishment of a sound national economy. I favor as a practical policy the putting of first things first. I shall spare no effort to restore world trade by international economic readjustment, but the emergency at home cannot wait on that accomplishment.

The basic thought that guides these specific means of national recovery is not narrowly nationalistic. It is the insistence, as a first consideration, upon the interdependence of the various elements in and parts of the United States—a recognition of the old and permanently important manifestation of the American spirit of the pioneer. It is the way to recovery. It is the immediate way. It is the strongest assurance that the recovery will endure.

In the field of world policy I would dedicate this nation to the policy of the good neighbor—the neighbor who resolutely respects himself and, because he does so, respects the rights of others—the neighbor who respects his obligations and respects the sanctity of his agreements in and with a world of neighbors.

If I read the temper of our people correctly, we now realize as we have never realized before our interdependence on each other; that we cannot merely take but we must give as well; that if we are to go forward, we must move as a trained and loyal army willing to sacrifice for the good of a common discipline, because without such discipline no progress is made, no leadership becomes effective. We are, I know, ready and willing to submit our lives and property to such discipline, because it makes possible a leadership that aims at a larger good. This I propose to offer, pledging that the larger purposes will bind upon us all as a sacred obligation with a unity of duty hitherto evoked only in time of armed strife.

With this pledge taken, I assume unhesitatingly the leadership of this great army of our people dedicated to a disciplined attack upon our common problems.

Action in this image and to this end is feasible under the form of government that we have inherited from our ancestors. Our Constitution is so simple and practical that it is possible always to meet extraordinary needs by changes in emphasis and arrangement without loss of essential form. That is why our constitutional system has proved itself the most superbly enduring political mechanism the modern world has produced. It has met every stress of vast expansion of territory, of foreign wars, of bitter internal strife, of world relations.

It is to be hoped that the normal balance of executive and legislative authority may be wholly adequate to meet the unprecedented task before us. But it may be that an unprecedented demand and need for undelayed action may call for temporary departure from that normal balance of public procedure.

I am prepared under my constitutional duty to recommend the measures that a stricken nation in the midst of a stricken world may require. These measures, or such other measures as the Congress may build out of its experience and wisdom, I shall seek, within my constitutional authority, to bring to speedy adoption.

But in the event that the Congress shall fail to take one of these two courses, and in the event that the national emergency is still critical, I shall not evade the clear course of duty that will then confront me. I shall ask the Congress for the one remaining instrument to meet the crisis—broad executive power to wage a war against the emergency, as great as the power that would be given to me if we were in fact invaded by a foreign foe.

For the trust reposed in me I will return the courage and the devotion that befit the time. I can do no less.

We face the arduous days that lie before us in the warm courage of national unity; with the clear consciousness of seeking old and precious moral values; with the clean satisfaction that comes from the stern performance of duty by old and young alike. We aim at the assurance of a rounded and permanent national life.

We do not distrust the future of essential democracy. The people of the United States have not failed. In their need they have registered a mandate that they want direct, vigorous action. They have asked for discipline and direction under leadership. They have made me the present instrument of their wishes. In the spirit of the gift I take it.

In this dedication of a nation we humbly ask the blessing of God. May He protect each and every one of us. May He guide me in the days to come.

Second inaugural address, Washington, D.C.,
20 January 1937

When four years ago we met to inaugurate a president, the Republic, single-minded in anxiety, stood in spirit here. We dedicated ourselves to the fulfillment of a vision—to speed the time when there would be for all the people that security and peace essential to the pursuit of happiness. We of the Republic pledged ourselves to drive from the temple of our ancient faith those who had profaned it; to end by action, tireless and unafraid, the stagnation and despair of that day. We did those first things first.

Our covenant with ourselves did not stop there. Instinctively we recognized a deeper need—the need to find through government the instrument of our united purpose to solve for the individual the ever-rising problems of a complex civilization. Repeated attempts at their solution without the aid of government had left us baffled and bewildered. For, without that aid, we had been unable to create those moral controls over the services of science that are necessary to make science a useful servant instead of a ruthless master of mankind. To do this we knew that we must find practical controls over blind economic forces and blindly selfish men.

We of the Republic sensed the truth that democratic government has innate capacity to protect its people against disasters once considered inevitable, to solve problems once considered unsolvable. We would not admit that we could not find a way to master economic epidemics just as, after centuries of fatalistic suffering, we had found a way to master epidemics of disease. We refused to leave the problems of our common welfare to be solved by the winds of chance and the hurricanes of disaster.

In this we Americans were discovering no wholly new truth; we were writing a new chapter in our book of self-government.

This year marks the one-hundred-and-fiftieth anniversary of the Constitutional Convention that made us a nation. At that convention our forefathers found the way out of the chaos that followed the Revolutionary War; they created a strong government with powers of united action sufficient then and now to solve problems utterly beyond individual or local solution. A century and a half ago they established the federal government in order to promote the general welfare and secure the blessings of liberty to the American people.

Today we invoke those same powers of government to achieve the same objectives.

Four years of new experience have not belied our historic instinct. They hold out the clear hope that government within communities, government within the separate states, and government of the United States can do the things the times require, without yielding its democracy. Our tasks in the last four years did not force democracy to take a holiday.

Nearly all of us recognize that as intricacies of human relationships increase, so power to govern them also must increase—power to stop evil; power to do good. The essential democracy of our nation and the safety of our people depend not upon the absence of power, but upon lodging it with those whom the people can change or continue at stated intervals through an honest and free system of elections. The Constitution of 1787 did not make our democracy impotent.

In fact, in these last four years, we have made the exercise of all power more democratic; for we have begun to bring private autocratic powers into their proper subordination to the public's government. The legend that they were invincible—above and beyond the processes of a democracy—has been shattered. They have been challenged and beaten.

Our progress out of the depression is obvious. But that is not all that you and I mean by the new order of things. Our pledge was not merely to do a patchwork job with secondhand materials. By using the new materials of social justice we have undertaken to erect on the old foundations a more enduring structure for the better use of future generations.

In that purpose we have been helped by achievements of mind and spirit. Old truths have been relearned; untruths have been unlearned. We have always known that heedless self-interest was bad morals; we know now that it is bad economics. Out of the collapse of a prosperity whose builders boasted their practicality has come the conviction that in the long run economic morality pays. We are beginning to wipe out the line that divides the practical from the ideal; and in so doing we are fashioning an instrument of unimagined power for the establishment of a morally better world.

This new understanding undermines the old admiration of worldly success as such. We are beginning to abandon our tolerance of the abuse of power by those who betray for profit the elementary decencies of life.

In this process evil things formerly accepted will not be so easily condoned. Hardheadedness will not so easily excuse hard-heartedness. We are moving toward an era of good feeling. But we realize that there can be no era of good feeling save among men of goodwill.

For these reasons I am justified in believing that the greatest change we have witnessed has been the change in the moral climate of America.

Among men of goodwill, science and democracy together offer an ever-richer life and ever-larger satisfaction to the individual. With this change in our moral climate and our rediscovered ability to improve our economic order, we have set our feet upon the road of enduring progress.

Shall we pause now and turn our back upon the road that lies ahead? Shall we call this the promised land? Or, shall we continue on our way? For "each age is a dream that is dying, or one that is coming to birth."

Many voices are heard as we face a great decision. Comfort says, "Tarry awhile." Opportunism says, "This is a good spot." Timidity asks, "How difficult is the road ahead?"

True, we have come far from the days of stagnation and despair. Vitality has been preserved. Courage and confidence have been restored. Mental and moral horizons have been extended.

But our present gains were won under the pressure of more than ordinary circumstance. Advance became imperative under the goad of fear and suffering. The times were on the side of progress.

To hold to progress today, however, is more difficult. Dulled conscience, irresponsibility, and ruthless self-interest already reappear. Such symptoms of prosperity may become portents of disaster! Prosperity already tests the persistence of our progressive purpose.

Let us ask again: Have we reached the goal of our vision of that fourth day of March 1933? Have we found our happy valley?

I see a great nation, upon a great continent, blessed with a great wealth of natural resources. Its hundred-and-thirty-million people are at peace among themselves; they are making their country a good neighbor among the nations. I see a United States that can demonstrate that, under democratic methods of government, national wealth can be translated into a spreading volume of human comforts hitherto unknown, and the lowest standard of living can be raised far above the level of mere subsistence.

But here is the challenge to our democracy: In this nation I see tens of millions of its citizens—a substantial part of its whole population—who at this very moment are denied the greater part of what the very lowest standards of today call the necessities of life.

I see millions of families trying to live on incomes so meager that the pall of family disaster hangs over them day by day.

I see millions whose daily lives in city and on farm continue under conditions labeled indecent by a so-called polite society half a century ago.

I see millions denied education, recreation, and the opportunity to better their lot and the lot of their children.

I see millions lacking the means to buy the products of farm and factory and by their poverty denying work and productiveness to many other millions.

I see one-third of a nation ill-housed, ill-clad, ill-nourished.

It is not in despair that I paint you that picture. I paint it for you in hope—because the nation, seeing and understanding the injustice in it, proposes to paint it out. We are determined to make every American citizen the subject of his country's interest and concern; and we will never regard any faithful, law-abiding group within our borders as superfluous. The test of our progress is not whether we add more to the abundance of those who have much; it is whether we provide enough for those who have too little.

If I know aught of the spirit and purpose of our nation, we will not listen to Comfort, Opportunism, and Timidity. We will carry on.

Overwhelmingly, we of the Republic are men and women of good-will; men and women who have more than warm hearts of dedication; men and women who have cool heads and willing hands of practical purpose as well. They will insist that every agency of popular government use effective instruments to carry out their will.

Government is competent when all who compose it work as trustees for the whole people. It can make constant progress when it keeps abreast of all the facts. It can obtain justified support and legitimate criticism when the people receive true information of all that government does.

If I know aught of the will of our people, they will demand that these conditions of effective government shall be created and maintained. They will demand a nation uncorrupted by cancers of injustice and, therefore, strong among the nations in its example of the will to peace.

Today we reconsecrate our country to long-cherished ideals in a suddenly changed civilization. In every land there are always at work forces that drive men apart and forces that draw men together. In our personal ambitions we are individualists. But in our seeking for economic and political progress as a nation, we all go up, or else we all go down, as one people.

To maintain a democracy of effort requires a vast amount of patience in dealing with differing methods, a vast amount of humility. But out of the confusion of many voices rises an understanding of dominant public need. Then political leadership can voice common ideals, and aid in their realization.

In taking again the oath of office as President of the United States, I assume the solemn obligation of leading the American people forward along the road over which they have chosen to advance.

While this duty rests upon me I shall do my utmost to speak their purpose and to do their will, seeking Divine guidance to help us each and every one to give light to them that sit in darkness and to guide our feet into the way of peace.

Address at the Jackson Day dinner, Washington, D.C., 8 January 1938

When speaking before a party gathering in these modern days, I am happy to realize that the audience is not confined to active members of my own party, and that there is less of unthinking partisanship in this country today than at any time since the administration of George Washington.

In the last campaign, in 1936, a very charming lady wrote me a letter. She said: "I believe in you and in what you are trying to do for the nation. I do wish I could vote for you—but you see my parents were Republicans and I was brought up as a Republican and so I have to vote for your opponent."

My reply to her ran as follows: "My father and grandfather were Democrats and I was born and brought up as a Democrat, but in 1904, when I cast my first vote for a president, I voted for the Republican candidate, Theodore Roosevelt, because I thought he was a better Democrat than the Democratic candidate."

I have told that story many times, and if I had to do it over again I would not alter that vote.

Conditions and parties change, as we know, with every generation. Nevertheless, I cannot help but feel pride in the fact that the Democratic Party, as it exists today, is a national party representing the essential unity of our country. As we move forward under our present momentum, it is not only necessary but it is right that the Party should slough off any remains of sectionalism and class consciousness. Party progress cannot stop just because some public officials and private or local groups fail to move along with the times. Their places will be amply filled by the arriving generation. That is on the principle that "Nature abhors a vacuum."

In these recent years the average American seldom thinks of Jefferson and Jackson as Democrats or of Lincoln and Theodore Roosevelt as Republicans; he labels each one of them according to his attitude toward the fundamental problems that confronted him as a president, when he was active in the affairs of government.

These men stand out because of the constructive battles they waged, not merely battles against things temporarily evil but battles for things permanently good—battles for the basic morals of democracy, which rest on respect for the right of self-government and faith in majority rule.

They knew, with the wisdom of experience, that the majority often makes mistakes. But they believed passionately that rule by a small minority class unfailingly makes worse mistakes—for rule by class takes counsel from itself and fails to heed the problems and, therefore, the good of all kinds and conditions of men. In the long run the instincts of the common man, willing to live and let live, work out the best and safest balance for the common good. And that is what I mean by the battle to restore and maintain the moral integrity of democracy.

At heart some of the small minority on the other side seek and use power to make themselves masters instead of servants of mankind. At heart they oppose our American form of government.

That is the cause of the great struggle that we are engaged in to-day—a struggle for the maintenance of the integrity of the morals of democracy. And we are in the process of winning it.

Let me talk history. President Washington, feeling his way through the organizing years of the infant Republic, questioned whether government would not be most safely conducted by the minority of education and of wealth.

But Jefferson saw that this control, if long exercised by a minority, would be destructive of a sound, representative, democratic system. He preached the extension of the franchise of government more responsive to the public will.

Against Jefferson were almost all the newspapers and magazines of the day. And so, to disseminate his policies in every hamlet and town his associates resorted to printing simple leaflets and pamphlets.

We know that the handful of printers and editors who helped them were harried and arrested under the sedition law with the full approval of the great papers and magazines of that time. That, my friends, was the first effort, with the cooperation of the owners of the press, to curb the essential freedom of the press. It failed just as any similar effort would fail today.

Time went by. Men were not eternally vigilant and once more the control of national affairs was maneuvered into the hands of a group of citizens small in number. The government's face was turned toward the handful of citizens of the seaboard—that small group that owned the Bank of the United States and the great merchant and shipping companies. The government's back was turned on the tens of thousands of pioneers who were settling the mountain regions and spreading over into the new country that lay westward to the Mississippi.

Jackson took up the battle of these pioneers of the West and South, and the battle of the inarticulate poor of the great cities. For that, like Jefferson, he was called a rabble-rouser.

He had to fight the same evil Jefferson fought—the control of government by a small minority instead of by a popular opinion duly heeded by the Congress, the courts, and the president.

The Bank of the United States was the purse and sword of the opposition, and with it were aligned all those who, like the early Federalists in Jefferson's time, were at heart in favor of control by the few.

With it were aligned all the nationally known press of the day, with the exception of three newspapers. The Bank sought to array all the money in the country against him.

No one who reads the history of that period can allege that either Jefferson or Jackson attacked all of the bankers, all of the merchants, or all of those of wealth. Nor can anyone say that even a majority of these elements of the population were opposed to either one of them.

The fight was won—as all such fights are won in the long run—because Jackson was fighting on the side of the people, whose instincts did not fail him. He was fighting for the integrity of the morals of democracy.

Another generation went by. Lincoln emerged—and was scorned for his uncouthness, his simplicity, his homely stories, and his solicitude for the little man. He faced opposition far behind his battle lines from those who thought first and last of their own selfish aims—gold speculators in Wall Street who cheered defeats of their own armies because thereby the price of their gold would rise; army contractors who founded fortunes at the expense of the boys at the front—a minority unwilling to support their people and their government unless the government would leave them free to pursue their private gains.

Lincoln, too, fought for the morals of democracy—and had he lived the South would have been allowed to rehabilitate itself on the basis of those morals instead of being "reconstructed" by martial law and carpetbaggers.

There followed, as we remember, after 1865, and lasting for many years, an uninspired commercialized era in our national life, lighted briefly by the stubborn integrity of Grover Cleveland.

Then came Theodore Roosevelt and resurgence of the morals of democracy. He, too, preached majority rule to end the autocracy of the same old type of opposition. He pleaded for decency—strenuous decency—in public as well as in private life. He laughed at those who called him unprintable names, and challenged again the small minority that claimed vested rights to power.

You and I, in our day and generation, know how Wilson carried on his fight. If the cataclysm of the World War had not stopped his hand, neither you nor I would today be facing such a difficult task of reconstruction and reform.

On the eighth of every January we honor Andrew Jackson for his unending contribution to the vitality of our democracy. We look back on his amazing personality, we review his battles because the struggles he went through, the enemies he encountered, the defeats he suffered, and the victories he won are part and parcel of the struggles, the enmities, the defeats, and the victories of those who have lived in all the generations that have followed.

In our nation today we have still the continuing menace of a comparatively small number of people who honestly believe in their superior right to influence and direct government, and who are unable to see or unwilling to admit that the practices by which they maintain their privileges are harmful to the body politic.

After Jefferson's election in 1800, an election over their violent opposition, such people came to him and said: "Let us alone—do not destroy confidence." After Jackson had won his fight against the Bank of the United States, they said the same thing. They said it to Lincoln, they said it to Theodore Roosevelt, and they said it to Wilson. Strangely enough, although they had no confidence in a people's government, they demanded that a people's government have confidence in them.

In my message to the Congress on Monday last, I made it abundantly clear that this administration seeks to serve the needs, and to make effective the will, of the overwhelming majority of our citizens and seeks to curb only abuses of power and privilege by small minorities. Thus we in turn are striving to uphold the integrity of the morals of our democracy. . . .

From address at the Jackson Day dinner, Washington, D.C., 8 January 1940

Seriously, the more I have studied American history and the more clearly I have seen what the problems are, I do believe that the common denominator of our great men in public life has not been mere allegiance to one political party, but the disinterested devotion with which they have tried to serve the whole country, and the relative unimportance that they have ascribed to politics, compared with the paramount importance of government.

By their motives may ye know them!

The relative importance of politics and government is something not always easy to see when you are in the front-line trenches of political organization.

In a period of thirty years, during which I have been more or less in public life—in my home county, in Albany, in Washington, in Europe during the World War, in New York City, in national conventions, back in Albany, and finally again in Washington—I have come to the conclusion that the closer people are to what may be called the front lines of government, of all kinds—local and state and federal—the easier it is to see the immediate underbrush, the individual tree trunks of the moment, and to forget the nobility, the usefulness, and the wide extent of the forest itself.

It is because party people in county courthouses, or city halls, or state capitals, or the District of Columbia are, most of them, so close to the picture of party or factional warfare, that they are apt to acquire a false perspective of what the "motives" and the purposes of both parties and their leaders should be for the common good today.

They forget that politics, after all, is only an instrument through which to achieve government. They forget that back of the jockeying for party position, back of the party generals, hundreds of thousands of men and women—officers and privates, foremen and workmen—have to get a good job done, have to put in day after day of honest, sincere work in carrying out the multitudinous functions that the policymakers in modern democracy assign to administrators in modern democracy.

People tell me that I hold to party ties less tenaciously than most of my predecessors in the presidency, and that I have too many people in my administration who are not active party Democrats. I must admit the soft impeachment.

My answer is that I do believe in party organization, but only in proportion to its proper place in government. I believe party organization—the existence of at least two effectively opposing parties—is a sound and necessary part of our American system; and that, effectively organized nationally and by states and by localities, parties are good instruments for the purpose of presenting and explaining issues, of drumming up interest in elections, and, incidentally, of improving the breed of candidates for public office.

But the future lies with those wise political leaders who realize that the great public is interested more in government than in politics; that the independent vote in this country has been steadily on the increase, at least for the past generation; that vast numbers of people consider themselves normally adherents of one party and still feel perfectly free to vote for one or more candidates of another party, come election day, and on the other hand, sometimes uphold party principles even when precinct captains decide "to take a walk."

The growing independence of voters, after all, has been proven by the votes in every presidential election since my childhood—and the tendency, frankly, is on the increase. I am too modest, of course, to refer to certain recent elections. Party regulars who want to win must hold their allies and supporters among those independent voters. And do not let us forget it.

There are, of course, some citizens—I hope a decreasing number—with whom I find it difficult to talk rationally on this subject of strict party voting. I have in mind, for example, some of my close friends down Georgia-way, who are under the impression that they would be ostracized in society and in business if it were to appear publicly that they had ever voted for a Republican. I also have in mind some very close friends in northern villages and counties who tell me, quite frankly, that though they would give anything in the world to be able to vote for me, a Democrat, it would hurt their influence and their social position in their own hometown.

I have in mind the predicament of one of the ablest editors of a great paper who some time ago said to me, very frankly:

"I am really in complete sympathy with your program, Mr. President, but I cannot say so publicly because the readers and the advertisers of my paper are 90 percent Republicans and I simply cannot afford to change its unalterable policy of traditional opposition to anything and everything that comes from Democratic sources. Of course, Mr. President, you understand."

And might I add, that the president understood.

Millions of unnecessary words and explanations and solemn comments are uttered and written year in and year out about the great men of American history—written with ample quotations—to prove what Jefferson or Hamilton, Jackson or Clay, Lincoln or Douglas, Cleveland or Blaine, Theodore Roosevelt or Bryan, would have said or would have done about some specific modern problems of government if they were alive today. The purpose of all these comments is either to induce the party leaders of today blindly to follow the words of leaders of yesterday; or to justify public acts or policies of today by the utterances of the past, often tortured out of context. Yes, the devil can quote past statesmen as readily as he can quote the Scriptures, in order to prove his purpose.

But most people, who are not on the actual firing line of the moment, have come to attach major importance only to the motives behind the leaders of the past. To them it matters, on the whole, very little what party label American statesmen bore, or what mistakes they made in the smaller things, so long as they did the big job that their times demanded be done.

Alexander Hamilton is a hero to me in spite of his position that the nation would be safer if our leaders were chosen exclusively from persons of higher education and of substantial property ownership; he is a hero because he did the job that then had to be done—to bring stability out of the chaos of currency and banking difficulties.

Thomas Jefferson is a hero to me despite the fact that the theories of the French Revolutionists at times overexcited his practical judgment. He is a hero because, in his many-sided genius, he too did the big job that then had to be done—to establish the new Republic as a real democracy based on universal suffrage and the inalienable rights of man, instead of a restricted suffrage in the hands of a small oligarchy. Jefferson realized that if the people were free to get and discourse all the facts, their composite judgment would be better than the judgment of a self-perpetuating few. That is why I think of Jefferson as belonging to the rank and file of both major political parties today.

I do not know which party Lincoln would belong to if he were alive in 1940—and I am not even concerned to speculate on it; a new party had to be created before he could be elected president. I am more interested in the fact that he did the big job that then had to be done—to preserve the Union and make possible, at a later time, the united country that we all live in today. His sympathies and his motives of championship of humanity itself have made him for all centuries to come the legitimate property of all parties—of every man and woman and child in every part of our land.

I feel very much the same way about Andrew Jackson—not Jackson the Democrat, but Jackson the American, who did the big job of his day—to save the economic democracy of the Union for its westward expansion into a great nation, strengthened in the ideals and practice of popular government.

I have always thought it a magnificent illustration of the public's instinct for the quality of a leader, that the people triumphantly reelected Jackson in spite of the fact that in the meantime, in his fight for economic democracy, Biddle and the Bank had sought to create an economic depression in order to ruin the president himself.

Of all of these great American figures, I like to think—and I know I am right—that their purposes, their objectives, and especially their motives placed the good of the nation always ahead of the good of the party; and while, properly, they used the mechanics of party organization in a thousand ways, they dropped mere partisanship when they considered partisanship to be different from the national interest.

As some of you know, I saw a good deal of the governorship of New York long before I became governor, and I saw a good deal of the inside of the White House for many years before I occupied it. Many years ago it had become clear to me that, properly availed of, the governorship and the presidency, instead of being merely a party headquarters, could become the most important clearinghouse for exchange of information and ideas, of facts and ideals, affecting the general welfare.

In practice, as you know, I have tried to follow out that concept. In the White House today we have built up a great mosaic of the state of the union from thousands of bits of information—from one man or woman this thought; from another, data on some event, a scrap here perhaps and a scrap there; from every congressional district in the Union; from rich and poor; from enthusiast and complainant; from liberal and conservative; from Republican and Democrat.

I like to think that most American governors or presidents have seen the same opportunity in their office, and that their motives have been primarily motives of service rather than of party or personal aggrandizement.

Doubtless they have all been irked by the commentators and interpreters of the day who ascribed other motives to them. Doubtless after much experience in the public life of America, with its free speech and its free press, the irksomeness wore off. Doubtless, all of them wore hair shirts when they started; but if they matured in public life most of them discarded those shirts in their earlier days. In other words, they had to drop their hair shirt or else lose their political shirt.

And when you have learned not to worry at all about all of these things, there is really a lot of fun in this job.

For when you reach that point of understanding, there is a deep satisfaction in pursuing the truth through the medley of information that reaches the White House, the overstatement, the half-truth, the glittering generality, the viewing-with-alarm, and, equally, the pointing-with-pride. There is practical satisfaction in sifting a tiny particle of truth from the mass of irrelevancies in which it is hidden. And there is the philosopher's satisfaction of trying to fit that particle of truth into the general scheme of things that are good and things that are bad for the people as a whole. . . .

Selected Speeches, Messages, Press Conferences, and Letters

Washington's Birthday radio address, 23 February 1942,

My Fellow Americans:

Washington's Birthday is a most appropriate occasion for us to talk with each other about things as they are today and things as we know they shall be in the future.

For eight years, General Washington and his Continental Army were faced continually with formidable odds and recurring defeats. Supplies and equipment were lacking. In a sense, every winter was a Valley Forge. Throughout the thirteen states there existed fifth columnists—and selfish men, jealous men, fearful men, who proclaimed that Washington's cause was hopeless, and that he should ask for a negotiated peace.

Washington's conduct in those hard times has provided the model for all Americans ever since—a model of moral stamina. He held to his course, as it had been charted in the Declaration of Independence. He and the brave men who served with him knew that no man's life or fortune was secure, without freedom and free institutions.

The present great struggle has taught us increasingly that freedom of person and security of property anywhere in the world depend upon the security of the rights and obligations of liberty and justice everywhere in the world.

This war is a new kind of war. It is different from all other wars of the past, not only in its methods and weapons but also in its geography. It is warfare in terms of every continent, every island, every sea, every air lane in the world. . . .

This generation of Americans has come to realize, with a present and personal realization, that there is something larger and more important than the life of any individual or of any individual group—something for which a man will sacrifice, and gladly sacrifice, not only his pleasures, not only his goods, not only his associations with those he loves, but his life itself. In time of crisis when the future is in the balance, we come to understand, with full recognition and devotion, what this nation is, and what we owe to it. . . .

The task that we Americans now face will test us to the uttermost.

Never before have we been called upon for such a prodigious effort. Never before have we had so little time in which to do so much.

"These are the times that try men's souls."

Tom Paine wrote those words on a drumhead, by the light of a campfire. That was when Washington's little army of ragged, rugged men was retreating across New Jersey, having tasted naught but defeat.

And General Washington ordered that these great words written by Tom Paine be read to the men of every regiment in the Continental Army, and this was the assurance given to the first American armed forces:

> The summer soldier and the sunshine patriot will, in this crisis, shrink from the service of their country; but he that stands it now, deserves the love and thanks of man and woman. Tyranny, like hell, is not easily conquered; yet we have this consolation with us, that the harder the sacrifice, the more glorious the triumph.

So spoke Americans in the year 1776.
So speak Americans today!

References

Roosevelt, Franklin D., *Nothing to Fear: The Speeches of Franklin Delano Roosevelt*, edited by B. D. Zevin (Boston: Houghton Mifflin, 1946).

Roosevelt, Franklin D., *Selected Speeches, Messages, Press Conferences, and Letters*, edited by Basil Rauch (New York: Rinehart and Company, Inc., 1957).

HARRY S. TRUMAN

FULL NAME:

Harry S. Truman

BORN:

8 May 1884, Lamar, Missouri

DIED:

26 December 1972, Kansas City, Missouri

Thirty-third President of the United States. Judge and United States Senator. Vice President under Franklin D. Roosevelt, assuming presidency on Roosevelt's death in 1945 until 1952.

His own writings include: Memoirs:Years of Decision (Garden City, NY: Doubleday, 1955); and Years of Trial and Hope (Garden City, NY: Doubleday, 1956). Studies of Truman include: Robert J. Donovan, Conflict and Crisis: The Presidency of Harry S. Truman, 1945–1948 (New York: W.W. Norton, 1977); and Margaret Truman, Harry S. Truman (New York: Morrow and Company, 1973).

Memoirs: Years of Trial and Hope

I have often thought in reading the history of our country how much is lost to us because so few of our presidents have told their own stories. It would have been helpful for us to know more of what was in their minds and what impelled them to do what they did.

The presidency of the United States carries with it a responsibility so personal as to be without parallel.

Very few are ever authorized to speak for the president. No one can make decisions for him. No one can know all the processes and stages of his thinking in making important decisions. Even those closest to him, even members of his immediate family, never know all the reasons why he does certain things and why he comes to certain conclusions. To be president of the United States is to be lonely, very lonely at times of great decisions.

Unfortunately some of our presidents were prevented from telling all the facts of their administrations because they died in office. Some were physically spent on leaving the White House and could not have undertaken to write even if they had wanted to. Some were embittered by the experience and did not care about living it again in telling about it.

As for myself, I should like to record, before it is too late, as much of the story of my occupancy of the White House as I am able to tell. The events, as I saw them and as I put them down here, I hope may prove helpful in informing some people and in setting others straight on the facts. . . .

* * *

Within the first few months I discovered that being a president is like riding a tiger. A man has to keep on riding or be swallowed. The fantastically crowded nine months of 1945 taught me that a president either is constantly on top of events or, if he hesitates, events will soon be on top of him. I never felt that I could let up for a single moment.

No one who has not had the responsibility can really understand what it is like to be president, not even his closest aides or members of his immediate family. There is no end to the chain of responsibility that binds him, and he is never allowed to forget that he is president. What kept me going in 1945 was my belief that there is far more good than evil in men and that it is the business of government to make the good prevail.

By nature not given to making snap judgments or easy decisions, I required all available facts and information before coming to a decision. But once a decision was made, I did not worry about it afterward. I had trained myself to look back into history for precedents, because instinctively I sought perspective in the span of history for the decisions I had to make. That is why I read and reread history. Most of the problems a president has to face have their roots in the past. . . .

. . . I had never underestimated my difficulties with MacArthur, but after the Wake Island meeting I had hoped that he would respect the authority of the president. I tried to place myself in his position, however, and tried to figure out why he was challenging the traditional civilian supremacy in our government.

Certainly his arguments and his proposals had always received full consideration by me and by the Joint Chiefs of Staff. If anything, they—and I—had leaned over backward in our respect for the man's military reputation. But all his statements since November—ever since the Chinese entry into Korea—had the earmarks of a man who performs for the galleries. It was difficult to explain this latest development unless it is assumed that it was of importance to the general to prevent any appearance that the credit for ending the fighting should go elsewhere.

I reflected on the similarities in the situation that had faced Abraham Lincoln in his efforts to deal with General McClellan. Carl Sandburg tells a story about Lincoln's relationship with McClellan: The general occasionally made political statements on matters outside the military field, and someone asked Lincoln what he would reply to McClellan. Lincoln's answer, so the story goes, was this: "Nothing—but it made me think of the man whose horse kicked up and stuck his foot through the stirrup. He said to the horse: 'If you are going to get on, I will get off.'"

Lincoln had had great and continuous trouble with McClellan, though the policy differences in those days were the opposite of mine: Lincoln wanted McClellan to attack, and McClellan would not budge. The general had his own ideas on how the war, and even the country, should be run. The President would issue direct orders to McClellan, and the general would ignore them. Half the country knew that McClellan had political ambitions, which men in opposition to Lincoln sought to use. Lincoln was patient, for that was his nature, but at long last he was compelled to relieve the Union army's principal commander. And though I gave this difficulty with MacArthur much wearisome thought, I realized that I would have no other choice myself than to relieve the nation's top field commander.

If there is one basic element in our Constitution, it is civilian control of the military. Policies are to be made by the elected political officials, not by generals or admirals. Yet time and again General MacArthur had shown that he was unwilling to accept the policies of the administration. By his repeated public statements he was not only confusing our allies as to the true course of our policies but, in fact, was also setting his policy against the president's.

I have always had, and I have to this day, the greatest respect for General MacArthur, the soldier. Nothing I could do, I knew, could change his stature as one of the outstanding military figures of our time—and I had no desire to diminish his stature. I had hoped, and I had tried to convince him, that the policy he was asked to follow was right. He had disagreed. He had been openly critical. Now, at last, his actions had frustrated a political course decided upon, in conjunction with its allies, by the government he was sworn to serve. If I allowed him to defy the civil authorities in this manner, I myself would be violating my oath to uphold and defend the Constitution.

I have always believed that civilian control of the military is one of the strongest foundations of our system of free government. Many of our people are descended from men and women who fled their native countries to escape the oppression of militarism. We in America have sometimes failed to give the soldier and the sailor their due, and it has hurt us. But we have always jealously guarded the constitutional provision that prevents the military from taking over the government from the authorities, elected by the people, in whom the power resides.

It has often been pointed out that the American people have a tendency to choose military heroes for the highest office in the land, but I think the statement is misleading. True, we have chosen men like George Washington and Andrew Jackson, and even Ulysses S. Grant, as our chief executives. But only Grant among these three had been raised to be a professional soldier, and he had abandoned that career and been brought back into service, like thousands of other civilians, when war broke out. We have chosen men who, in time of war, had made their mark, but until 1952 we had never elevated to the White House any man whose entire life had been dedicated to the military.

One reason that we have been so careful to keep the military within its own preserve is that the very nature of the service hierarchy gives military commanders little if any opportunity to learn the humility that is needed for good public service. The elected official will never forget—unless he is a fool—that others as well or better qualified might have been chosen and that millions remained unconvinced that the last choice made was the best one possible. Any man who has come up through the process of political selection, as it functions in our country, knows that success is a mixture of principles steadfastly maintained and adjustments made at the proper time and place—adjustments to conditions, not adjustment of principles.

These are things a military officer is not likely to learn in the course of his profession. The words that dominate his thinking are "command" and "obedience," and the military definitions of these words are not definitions for use in a republic.

That is why our Constitution embodies the principle of civilian control of the military. This was the principle that General MacArthur threatened. I do not believe that he purposefully decided to challenge civilian control of the military, but the result of his behavior was that this fundamental principle of free government was in danger.

It was my duty to act. . . .

I backed General Bradley completely in this matter, for it involved far more than just Harry Truman talking to Omar Bradley. It was a basic question of the meaning of the separation of powers in our government.

The men who wrote our Constitution knew what they were doing when they provided for three clearly separate branches of the government. They were mostly men trained in the law, and they were all well informed on the history of government from Babylon to Britain. They were convinced that the government of the new nation should be one that would protect individual freedom and allow it to flourish. They knew that arbitrary and even tyrannical government had come about where the powers of government were united in the hands of one man. The system they set up was designed to prevent a demagogue or "a man on horseback" from taking over the powers of government.

As a young man, I had read Montesquieu's *Spirit of the Laws* and the *Federalist Papers*, that collection of essays by Hamilton, Madison, and Jay that explains so much of what the Constitution was intended to mean. Later, during my evening studies of the law, I had read some of Blackstone and Coke and the *Commentaries* of Judge Story. This reading and the study of history and of our government have been the foundation of my thinking about the Constitution. It is a document of remarkable qualities, and every American owes it to his country to absorb not only its words but also the great ideas for which it stands.

The greatest of these, in my opinion, is the idea of a fair trial. We inherited from the British this idea that no man shall be considered guilty until a fair, judicial process shall have found him so.

Next to this, the most important thought expressed in our Constitution is that the power of government shall always remain limited, through the separation of powers. This means that each of the three branches of the government—the legislative, the judicial, and the executive—must jealously guard its position. This jealous concern is a good thing. When I was a senator, I was always anxious to see the rights and the prerogatives of the Congress preserved. If I had ever held judicial office, I would have considered it my duty to keep alert to any possible interferences with the independence of the judiciary. As president, it was my duty to safeguard the constitutional position of the office I held—the presidency of the United States.

There is no office quite like the presidency anywhere else in the world. It has great powers. But these powers must be safeguarded against inroads, just as Congress must look after its powers and prerogatives.

Now the running of government is, of course, a highly practical matter. You do not operate somewhere in a theoretical heaven, but with a tough set of tough situations that have to be met—and met without hesitation. It takes practical men to run a government. But they should be practical men with a deep sense of appreciation for the higher values that the government should serve.

As a practical proposition, the executive branch of the government can no more operate by itself than can the Congress. There have always been a few congressmen who act as if they would like to control everything on the executive side, but they find out differently when the responsibility of administration is on their shoulders. But no president has ever attempted to govern alone. Every president knows and must know that the congressional control of the purse has to be reckoned with. And so presidents, as a practical proposition, have usually leaned over backward in providing the Congress with information about the operations of the executive departments.

There is a point, however, when the executive must decline to supply Congress with information, and that is when he feels the Congress encroaches upon the executive prerogatives. Congress, of course, is anxious to obtain as many facts as it can; most of the time this is for legitimate reasons of legislation, but sometimes it is for the sole purpose of embarrassing and hamstringing the president—in other words, for partisan political reasons. When that happens, it is the president's solemn duty to resist the demands for fishing expeditions into his private files. Not even the so-called weak presidents would stand for it.

I always tried to take care of and preserve the position of the high office I held. The president cannot function without advisers or without advice, written or oral. But just as soon as he is required to show what kind of advice he has had, who said what to him, or what kind of records he has, the advice he receives will become worthless. Advisers, to be of value, must feel that what they say or write will be held in confidence, that the man or the office they advise will appreciate the fact that they are expressing opinions, and that probably they are not the only ones asked for opinions and advice. The minute an effort is made to challenge that decision after it has been made and to determine whether the opinions or the advice on which it was made was "right" (with retribution and criticism for those who were not "right"), independent thought, which alone produces sound decisions, will be stymied or killed. . . .

* * *

My decision not to be candidate for reelection in 1952 goes back to the day of my inauguration in 1949. On this day, facing four more years of the presidency, I kept reviewing the many grave problems that confronted the nation and the world. And I found myself thinking about my own future, and how long a man ought to stay in the presidency, and a nation's need for constant renewal of leadership. I now was certain that I would not run again. But I could not share this decision with anyone. By the very nature of his office, this is one secret a president must keep to himself to the last possible moment.

More than a year later, on 16 April 1950, I wrote out my thoughts and my intentions in a memorandum, which I locked away:

I am not a candidate for nomination by the Democratic Convention.

My first election to public office took place in November 1922. I served two years in the armed forces in World War I, ten years in the Senate, two months and twenty days as vice president and president of the Senate. I have been in public office well over thirty years, having been president of the United States almost two complete terms.

Washington, Jefferson, Monroe, Madison, Andrew Jackson, and Woodrow Wilson, as well as Calvin Coolidge, stood by the precedent of two terms. Only Grant, Theodore Roosevelt, and F.D.R. made the attempt to break that precedent. F.D.R. succeeded.

In my opinion eight years as president is enough and sometimes too much for any man to serve in that capacity.

There is a lure in power. It can get into a man's blood just as gambling and lust for money have been known to do.

This is a Republic. The greatest in the history of the world. I want this country to continue as a Republic. Cincinnatus and Washington pointed the way. When Rome forgot Cincinnatus, its downfall began. When we forget the examples of such men as Washington, Jefferson, and Andrew Jackson, all of whom could have had a continuation in the office, then will we start down the road to dictatorship and ruin. I know I could be elected again and continue to break the old precedent as it was broken by F.D.R. It should not be done. That precedent should continue not by a constitutional amendment but by custom based on the honor of the man in the office.

Therefore, to reestablish that custom, although by a quibble I could say I've only had one term, I am not a candidate and will not accept the nomination for another term.

In March of the same year, 1951, I took the memorandum out at the Little White House in Key West and read it to my White House staff. The reaction was to be expected. The staff responded with deep emotion and expressions of protest and disappointment. They pleaded with me not to make public any such announcement. But I had no intention of doing this until the proper time.

My mind was made up irrevocably against running in 1952, and I was concerned with the problem of suggesting the right man to present to the people as the standard-bearer for the Democratic party. The most logical and qualified candidate, it appeared to me, was the chief justice of the United States, Fred M. Vinson. . . .

Reference

Truman, Harry S., *Memoirs: Years of Trial and Hope,* Volume II (Garden City, NY: Doubleday, 1956).

DWIGHT D. EISENHOWER

FULL NAME:

Dwight David Eisenhower

BORN:

14 October 1890, Dennison, Texas

DIED:

28 March 1969, Washington, D.C.

Thirty-fourth President of the United States. Head of American troops in Europe in 1942. Supreme Commander of Allied Forces in Europe, 1943. Chief of Staff of Armed Forces. President of Columbia University. First military commander of North Atlantic Treaty Organization. Republican President from 1952 to 1960.

His major writings are his memoirs: *Crusade in Europe* (Garden City, NY: Doubleday, 1948); *The White House Years: Mandate for Change, 1953–1956* (Garden City, NY: Doubleday, 1963); and *Waging Peace: 1957–1961* (Garden City, NY: Doubleday, 1965). Writings about him include: Fred I. Greenstein, *The Hidden-Hand Presidency: Eisenhower As Leader* (Baltimore, MD: The Johns Hopkins Press, 1982); and Emmet Hughes, *The Ordeal of Power* (New York: Atheneum, 1963).

The White House Years: Mandate for Change, 1953–1956

. . . No individual can be completely or fully prepared for undertaking the responsibilities of the presidency; possibly no one can even be fully aware of their weight and difficulty, except one who has borne them. It is generally assumed, I think, that any person seriously considered by the public as a possible nominee for the office will be the possessor of a satisfactory education and competence in rather traditional fields. Certainly his ability in handling and understanding people would be of interest to the average voter, as would his training and experience in making significant decisions. The basic features of his political philosophy should be fully exposed to the public and his lively interest in fundamental issues of his time should be obvious.

I was, of course, a political novice. Of certain characteristics and beliefs that would engage public interest about me as a possible candidate, little was known. Even though I had long been reading about national and world movements and trends, military life, while it had by no means precluded my concern with public matters, had assured that my opinions respecting them would be almost wholly personal and private. Only while I was at Columbia had I ventured to speak publicly about anything of a political nature.

But because of special experiences in my past life, I was probably more acutely aware than the average citizen of the complexities, anxieties, and burdens of the life led by a head of government.

In varying assignments, over a period of many years, I had had a chance to observe and work with, among others, Prime Minister Winston Churchill; President Franklin Delano Roosevelt; and the chief executives of the Philippines, an "emerging nation" (the term was not used then), and of France, an old nation.

My education, which gave me at least a fringe familiarity with decisions affecting high officials of the executive branch, began relatively early in my military career. In 1929 I was assigned, as a major, to the assistant secretary of war (Patrick J. Hurley and, succeeding him, Frederick Payne) and later to the Chief of Staff of the Army, Douglas MacArthur. In Washington and elsewhere, as a personal assistant to these men, I had an opportunity to observe high-level activity in not only the executive, but in the legislative branch, particularly in matters pertaining to military budgets, public relations, and relations between the executive branch and the Congress.

While it is never possible for a staff officer to feel the full weight of responsibility that rests on the shoulders of his chief, it is feasible for him to gain a degree of insight into the magnitude and intricacies of those of his chief's problems that come before him for study. He learns to live with the frustrating fact that many issues on which he is required to work have no immediate, and sometimes not even a satisfactory future, solution. . . .

One of my first responsibilities was to organize the White House for efficiency.

There were many things that a good personal staff could and should do for a president—especially those things falling outside the responsibilities of major departments of the federal government. For such a group the name "White House Staff" seemed suitable; it could just as appropriately have been called "The President's Staff"; such a name, in fact, might have the additional advantage of setting this small group apart from the much larger "Executive Office of the President," which includes the staffs of the National Security Council, the Bureau of the Budget, the Council of Economic Advisers, and the Office of Defense Mobilization.

Organization cannot make a genius out of an incompetent; even less can it, of itself, make the decisions that are required to trigger necessary action. On the other hand, disorganization can scarcely fail to result in inefficiency and can easily lead to disaster. Organization makes more efficient the gathering and analysis of facts, and the arranging of the findings of experts in logical fashion. Therefore organization helps the responsible individual make the necessary decision, and helps assure that it is satisfactorily carried out.

I have been astonished to read some contentions that seem to suggest that smooth organization guarantees that nothing is happening, whereas ferment and disorder indicate progress.

There are men and women who seem to be born with a feeling for organization, just as others are born with a talent for art. But even the gifted natural artist needs training and experience, and so too anyone trying to find solutions to organizational problems must study them long and carefully. If he has not been so fortunate as to have personal experience, he must draw upon and trust the counsel of advisers who have.

I have often wondered, with occasional amusement, why so many who write on politics and public affairs apparently feel themselves experts on organization. Normally a writer is an individualistic rather than an organizational worker, and rarely has he gone deeply into the problems of organizing people into a great business or a large road gang, a vast military formation or a squad, a university or a governmental agency. Yet there are more than a few who seem to feel a compulsion, at times, to pontificate about organization.

I have read about "staff decisions" but I have never understood exactly what was meant by the expression, unless it is the assumption that decisions are sometimes made by group voting, as in a congressional committee, where a majority of votes controls the action. In my own experience—extending over half a century in various types of group mechanisms, large and small—I have never known any successful executive who has depended upon the taking of a vote in any gathering to make a decision for him. The habit of depending upon an "Aulic Council"—or for that matter, a cabinet—to direct the affairs of a great nation, or of calling a "council of war" by generals to make decisions that were properly their own, went out of fashion long before most of us were born.

On a crucial question during the Civil War, Abraham Lincoln is said to have called for a vote around the cabinet table. Every member voted no. "The ayes have it," Lincoln announced.

The presidency still works the same way today.

Nonetheless, the president needs an efficient staff, and now more than ever before. . . .

Of course, the matter of patronage is always present. I was scarcely nominated at Chicago when I was besieged by people seeking, conditional upon my future election, promises for appointments for themselves or for their friends. Arthur Krock, a veteran of the press corps whom I admire, wrote a story in the first few days of my administration about President Lincoln's troubles with patronage. Lincoln, thinking of the constant importunities for special favors with which he was constantly bombarded while in the presidency, once remarked, when told by the doctors that he had a mild form of smallpox, "Now I have something I can give everybody."

Faced with patronage problems, I recalled the pressures of the early New Deal days. They had been so pervasive that they had reached me when I was acting as an assistant to General MacArthur, who as chief of staff had the job of organizing the Civilian Conservation Corps in 1933. While the work was going on, the War Department was charged with a fault that seems ironic now: New Deal Democrats protested that all the reserve officers being called to duty were Republicans. The charge was ridiculous; our records showed nothing about an officer's political affiliation. But it did indicate how seriously these questions concern a politician. . . .

"Life in the White House—Tricycles in the Corridor"

The White House is not only the seat of authority in the nation, it is the home of the president and his family. It is the place where he greets and entertains a constant stream of guests, foreign and domestic, most of whom bring him a variety and richness of knowledge and understanding that can scarcely be obtained in any other post in the world. Among the great free nations of the North Atlantic we, except for modern France, are the only one with a form of government that makes its head of government also the chief of state. While this fact increases the volume of duties devolving upon the man occupying the presidency, it does provide opportunity for exercising an influence in a way that is almost uniquely personal and powerful.

The English sovereign "reigns but does not rule." The king or queen is the center of many occasions of solemn pageantry and ceremony, and is the symbol of Britain's traditions, history, and might. But the sovereign interferes in no way with the workings of the government itself, headed by the prime minister. I once read an account of the development of government among the English-speaking peoples in which a statement appeared—I cannot vouch for its accuracy—that the sovereign is required to sign any governmental decree placed before him by the British government, even his own death warrant.

Whether or not this is literally true, it does illustrate the complete separation of the duties and responsibilities between the chief of state and the head of government under the British parliamentary system.

The American system places all this responsibility and authority in the hands of the president, and the White House has for us the significance of Buckingham Palace and 10 Downing Street combined. Consequently we accord to the words "White House" a respect that amounts almost to veneration. Architecturally, such structures as Buckingham Palace and Windsor Castle in England, the Elysée Palace in Paris, Rome's Quirinal Palace, and the Rashtrapati Bhavan in New Delhi make the White House appear, by comparison, a simple and modest cottage. But I am quite sure that no American would like to see the White House revised materially in its general lines and appearance, or replaced by the most magnificent structure ever devised by the hand of man. . . .

I have heard people who in the past had been familiar with the White House characterize it as a cold, unlivable "institution." My family and I felt none of this. On the contrary, we liked the place and all it stood for. First occupied by John Adams—whose prayer of dedication is carved in the mantelpiece in the State Dining Room—it conveyed to us much of the dignity, the simple greatness of America. Because of this feeling, we never felt that we had any right to make major changes in the structure itself or in its principal furnishings.

The White House had been occupied fourteen years when it was burned by the British in 1814. By 1817 it was rebuilt. Then, in the early twentieth century it was enlarged. And it was completely rebuilt, save for the outside walls, in 1949–50. Growing and developing with the decades, the mansion itself has always remained largely the same.

In the rebuilding of 1949, architects took careful notes to ensure that the new structure within the old walls would be a faithful reproduction of the old.

My conviction is that the White House has been and should always remain a place to be venerated by its occupants as well as by all Americans. I believe that because of the White House's meaning for America—and assuming its stability in structure and surroundings—a visitor of the generation of 2050 or 3050 should be able to gain from it the same sense of humility, pride, reverence, and history that my wife and I felt every day of the years we were privileged to live in it. For the White House is not just a well-run home for the chief executive; it is a living story of past pioneering, struggles, wars, innovations, and a growing America. I like to think of it as a symbol of freedom and of the hopes and future accomplishments of her people. . . .

Reference

Eisenhower, Dwight D., *The White House Years: Mandate for Change, 1953–1956* (Garden City, NY: Doubleday, 1963).

JOHN F. KENNEDY

FULL NAME:

John Fitzgerald Kennedy

BORN:

29 May 1917, Brookline, Massachusetts

DIED:

22 November 1963, Dallas, Texas

Thirty-fifth President of the United States. Congressman and Senator from Massachusetts from 1952 until 1960 when he was elected President. Assassination victim before the end of his first term.

His own books include: *The Burden and the Glory* (New York: Harper, 1964) and *Profiles in Courage* (New York: Harper, 1956). Books about Kennedy include: Theodore C. Sorensen, *Kennedy* (New York: Harper, 1965) and Arthur M. Schlesinger, Jr., *A Thousand Days: John F. Kennedy in the White House* (Boston: Houghton Mifflin, 1965).

To Turn the Tide

Speech to the Massachusetts State Legislature,
9 January 1961

I have welcomed the opportunity to address this historic body, and, through you, the people of Massachusetts, to whom I am so deeply indebted for a lifetime of friendship and trust. For fourteen years I have placed my confidence in the voters of this state, and they have generously responded by placing their confidence in me.

Now, on the Friday after next, I am to assume new and broader responsibilities. But I am not here to bid farewell to Massachusetts. For forty-three years, whether I was in London, Washington, the South Pacific, or elsewhere, this has been my home; and, God willing, wherever I serve, it will always remain my home.

It was here my grandparents were born; it is here I hope my grandchildren will be born.

I speak neither from false provincial pride nor artful political flattery. For no man about to enter high public office in this country can ever be unmindful of the contributions this state has made to our national greatness. Its leaders have shaped our destiny since long before the great Republic was born. Its principles have guided our footsteps in times of crisis as well as calm. Its democratic institutions, including this historic body, have served as beacon lights for other nations as well as your sister states. For what Pericles said of the Athenians has long been true of this Commonwealth: "We do not imitate, but are a model to others."

And so it is that I carry with me from this state to that high and lonely office to which I now succeed more than fond memories and fast friendships. The enduring qualities of Massachusetts—the common threads woven by the Pilgrim and the Puritan, the fisherman and the farmer, the Yankee and the immigrant—will not be and could not be forgotten in the nation's Executive Mansion. They are an indelible part of my life, my convictions, my view of the past, my hopes for the future.

Allow me to illustrate: During the last sixty days, I have been engaged in the task of constructing an administration. It has been a long and deliberate process. Some have counseled greater speed. Others have counseled more expedient tests. But I have been guided by the standard John Winthrop set before his shipmates on the flagship *Arbella* 331 years ago, as they, too, faced the task of building a government on a new and perilous frontier. "We must always consider," he said, "that we shall be as a city upon a hill—the eyes of all people are upon us."

Today, the eyes of all people are truly upon us, and our governments, in every branch, at every level, national, state, and local, must be as a city upon a hill, constructed and inhabited by men aware of their grave trust and their great responsibilities. For we are setting out upon a voyage in 1961 no less hazardous than that undertaken by the *Arbella* in 1630. We are committing ourselves to tasks of statecraft no less awesome than that of governing the Massachusetts Bay Colony, beset as it then was by terror without and disorder within.

History will not judge our endeavors, and a government cannot be selected, merely on the basis of color or creed or even party affiliation. Neither will competence and loyalty and stature, while essential to the utmost, suffice in times such as these.

For of those to whom much is given, much is required. And when at some future date the high court of history sits in judgment on each of us, recording whether in our brief span of service we fulfilled our responsibilities to the state, our success or failure, in whatever office we hold, will be measured by the answers to four questions:

First, were we truly men of courage, with the courage to stand up to one's enemies, and the courage to stand up, when necessary, to one's associates, the courage to resist public pressure as well as private greed?

Second, were we truly men of judgment, with perceptive judgment of the future as well as the past, of our own mistakes as well as the mistakes of others, with enough wisdom to know what we did not know, and enough candor to admit it?

Third, were we truly men of integrity, men who never ran out on either the principles in which we believed or the people who believed in us, men whom neither financial gain nor political ambition could ever divert from the fulfillment of our sacred trust?

Finally, were we truly men of dedication, with an honor mortgaged to no single individual or group, and compromised by no private obligation or aim, but devoted solely to serving the public good and the national interest?

Courage, judgment, integrity, dedication—these are the historic qualities of the Bay Colony and the Bay State, the qualities that this state has consistently sent to Beacon Hill here in Boston and to Capitol Hill back in Washington. And these are the qualities that, with God's help, this son of Massachusetts hopes will characterize our government's conduct in the four stormy years that lie ahead. Humbly I ask His help in this undertaking; but aware that on earth His will is worked by men, I ask for your help and your prayers as I embark on this new and solemn journey.

Inaugural address, Washington, D.C., 20 January 1961

We observe today not a victory of party but a celebration of freedom, symbolizing an end as well as a beginning, signifying renewal as well as change. For I have sworn before you and Almighty God the same solemn oath our forebears prescribed nearly a century and three-quarters ago.

The world is very different now. For man holds in his mortal hands the power to abolish all forms of human poverty and all forms of human life. And yet the same revolutionary belief for which our forebears fought is still at issue around the globe, the belief that the rights of man come not from the generosity of the state but from the hand of God.

We dare not forget today that we are the heirs of that first revolution. Let the word go forth from this time and place, to friend and foe alike, that the torch has been passed to a new generation of Americans, born in this century, tempered by war, disciplined by a hard and bitter peace, proud of our ancient heritage, and unwilling to witness or permit the slow undoing of those human rights to which this nation has always been committed, and to which we are committed today at home and around the world.

Let every nation know, whether it wishes us well or ill, that we shall pay any price, bear any burden, meet any hardship, support any friend, oppose any foe to assure the survival and the success of liberty.

This much we pledge—and more.

To those old allies whose cultural and spiritual origins we share, we pledge the loyalty of faithful friends. United, there is little we cannot do in a host of cooperative ventures. Divided, there is little we can do, for we dare not meet a powerful challenge at odds and split asunder.

To those new states whom we welcome to the ranks of the free, we pledge our word that one form of colonial control shall not have passed away merely to be replaced by a far more iron tyranny. We shall not always expect to find them supporting our view. But we shall always hope to find them strongly supporting their own freedom, and to remember that, in the past, those who foolishly sought power by riding the back of the tiger ended up inside.

To those peoples in the huts and villages of half the globe struggling to break the bonds of mass misery, we pledge our best efforts to help them help themselves, for whatever period is required, not because the Communists may be doing it, not because we seek their votes, but because it is right. If a free society cannot help the many who are poor, it cannot save the few who are rich.

To our sister republics south of our border, we offer a special pledge: to convert our good words into good deeds, in a new alliance for progress, to assist free men and free governments in casting off the chains of poverty. But this peaceful revolution of hope cannot become the prey of hostile powers. Let all our neighbors know that we shall join with them to oppose aggression or subversion anywhere in the Americas. And let every other power know that this hemisphere intends to remain the master of its own house.

To that world assembly of sovereign states, the United Nations, our last best hope in an age where the instruments of war have far outpaced the instruments of peace, we renew our pledge of support: to prevent it from becoming merely a forum for invective, to strengthen its shield of the new and the weak, and to enlarge the area in which its writ may run.

Finally, to those nations who would make themselves our adversary, we offer not a pledge but a request: that both sides begin anew the quest for peace, before the dark powers of destruction unleashed by science engulf all humanity in planned or accidental self-destruction.

We dare not tempt them with weakness. For only when our arms are sufficient beyond doubt can we be certain beyond doubt that they will never be employed.

But neither can two great and powerful groups of nations take comfort from our present course—both sides overburdened by the cost of modern weapons, both rightly alarmed by the steady spread of the deadly atom, yet both racing to alter that uncertain balance of terror that stays the hand of mankind's final war.

So let us begin anew, remembering on both sides that civility is not a sign of weakness, and sincerity is always subject to proof. Let us never negotiate out of fear, but let us never fear to negotiate.

Let both sides explore what problems unite us instead of belaboring those problems that divide us.

Let both sides, for the first time, formulate serious and precise proposals for the inspection and control of arms, and bring the absolute power to destroy other nations under the absolute control of all nations.

Let both sides seek to invoke the wonders of science instead of its terrors. Together let us explore the stars, conquer the deserts, eradicate disease, tap the ocean depths, and encourage the arts and commerce.

Let both sides unite to heed in all corners of the earth the command of Isaiah to "undo the heavy burdens . . . [and] let the oppressed go free."

And if a beachhead of cooperation may push back the jungle of suspicion, let both sides join in creating a new endeavor, not a new balance of power, but a new world of law, where the strong are just and the weak secure and the peace preserved.

All this will not be finished in the first one hundred days. Nor will it be finished in the first one thousand days, nor in the life of this administration, nor even perhaps in our lifetime on this planet. But let us begin.

In your hands, my fellow citizens, more than mine, will rest the final success or failure of our course. Since this country was founded, each generation of Americans has been summoned to give testimony to its national loyalty. The graves of young Americans who answered the call to service surround the globe.

Now the trumpet summons us again—not as a call to bear arms, though arms we need; not as a call to battle, though embattled we are; but a call to bear the burden of a long twilight struggle, year in and year out, "rejoicing in hope, patient in tribulation," a struggle against the common enemies of man: tyranny, poverty, disease, and war itself.

Can we forge against these enemies a grand and global alliance, North and South, East and West, that can assure a more fruitful life for all mankind? Will you join in that historic effort?

In the long history of the world, only a few generations have been granted the role of defending freedom in its hour of maximum danger. I do not shrink from this responsibility; I welcome it. I do not believe that any of us would exchange places with any other people or any other generation. The energy, the faith, the devotion that we bring to this endeavor will light our country and all who serve it, and the glow from that fire can truly light the world.

And so, my fellow Americans, ask not what your country can do for you; ask what you can do for your country.

My fellow citizens of the world, ask not what America will do for you, but what together we can do for the freedom of man.

Finally, whether you are citizens of America or citizens of the world, ask of us here the same high standards of strength and sacrifice that we ask of you. With a good conscience our only sure reward, with history the final judge of our deeds, let us go forth to lead the land we love, asking His blessing and His help, but knowing that here on earth God's work must truly be our own.

State of the Union Message, U.S. Congress, 29 January 1961

. . . It is a pleasure to return from whence I came. You are my oldest friends in Washington, and this House is my oldest home. It was here, more than fourteen years ago, that I first took the oath of federal office. It was here, for fourteen years, that I gained both knowledge and inspiration from members of both parties in both Houses, from your wise and generous leaders, and from the pronouncements that I can vividly recall, sitting where you now sit, including the programs of two great presidents, the undimmed eloquence of Churchill, the soaring idealism of Nehru, the steadfast words of General de Gaulle. To speak from this same historic rostrum is a sobering experience. To be back among so many friends is a happy one.

I am confident that that friendship will continue. Our Constitution wisely assigns both joint and separate roles to each branch of the government; and a president and a Congress who hold each other in mutual respect will neither permit nor attempt any trespass. For my part, I shall withhold from neither the Congress nor the people any fact or report, past, present, or future, which is necessary for an informed judgment of our conduct and hazards. I shall neither shift the burden of executive decisions to the Congress, nor avoid responsibility for the outcome of those decisions.

I speak today in an hour of national peril and national opportunity. Before my term has ended, we shall have to test anew whether a nation organized and governed such as ours can endure. The outcome is by no means certain. The answers are by no means clear. All of us together—this administration, this Congress, this nation—must forge those answers.

But today, were I to offer, after little more than a week in office, detailed legislation to remedy every national ill, the Congress would rightly wonder whether the desire for speed had replaced the duty of responsibility.

My remarks, therefore, will be limited. But they will also be candid. To state the facts frankly is not to despair the future nor indict the past. The prudent heir takes careful inventory of his legacies, and gives a faithful accounting to those whom he owes an obligation of trust. And, while the occasion does not call for another recital of our blessings and assets, we do have no greater asset than the willingness of a free and determined people, through its elected officials, to face all problems frankly and meet all dangers free from panic or fear.

The present state of our economy is disturbing. We take office in the wake of seven months of recession, three and one-half years of slack, seven years of diminished economic growth, and nine years of falling farm income.

Business bankruptcies have reached their highest level since the Great Depression. Since 1951 farm income has been squeezed down by 25 percent. Save for a brief period in 1958, ensured unemployment is at the highest peak in our history. Of some five and one-half million Americans who are without jobs, more than one million have been searching for work for more than four months. And during each month some 150,000 workers are exhausting their already meager jobless benefit rights.

Nearly one-eighth of those who are without jobs live almost without hope in nearly one hundred depressed and troubled areas. The rest include new school graduates unable to use their talents, farmers forced to give up their part-time jobs that helped balance their family budgets, skilled and unskilled workers laid off in such important industries as metals, machinery, automobiles, and apparel.

Our recovery from the 1958 recession, moreover, was anemic and incomplete. Our gross national product never regained its full potential. Unemployment never returned to normal levels. Maximum use of our national industrial capacity was never restored.

In short, the American economy is in trouble. The most resourceful industrialized country on earth ranks among the last in the rate of economic growth. Since last spring our economic growth rate has actually receded. Business investment is in a decline. Profits have fallen below predicted levels. Construction is off. A million unsold automobiles are in inventory. Fewer people are working, and the average workweek has shrunk well below forty hours. Yet prices have continued to rise, so that now too many Americans have less to spend for items that cost more to buy.

Economic prophecy is at best an uncertain art, as demonstrated by the prediction one year ago from this same podium that 1960 would be, and I quote, "the most prosperous year in our history." Nevertheless, forecasts of continued slack and only slightly reduced unemployment through 1961 and 1962 have been made with alarming unanimity, and this administration does not intend to stand helplessly by.

We cannot afford to waste idle hours and empty plants while awaiting the end of the recession. We must show the world what a free economy can do, to reduce unemployment, to put unused capacity to work, to spur new productivity, and to foster higher economic growth within a range of sound fiscal policies and relative price stability.

I will propose to the Congress within the next fourteen days measures to improve unemployment compensation through temporary increases in duration on a self-supporting basis; to provide more food for the families of the unemployed, and to aid their needy children; to redevelop our areas of chronic labor surplus; to expand the services of the U.S. Employment Offices; to stimulate housing and construction; to secure more purchasing power for our lowest-paid workers by raising and expanding the minimum wage; to offer tax incentives for sound plant investment; to increase the development of natural resources; to encourage price stability; and to take other steps aimed at ensuring a prompt recovery and paving the way for increased long-range growth. This is not a partisan program concentrating on our weaknesses; it is, I hope, a national program to realize our national strength. . . .

I have commented on the state of the domestic economy, our balance of payments, our federal and social budget, and the state of the world. I would like to conclude with a few remarks about the state of the executive branch. We have found it full of honest and useful public servants, but their capacity to act decisively at the exact time action is needed has too often been muffled in the morass of committees, timidities, and fictitious theories that have created a growing gap between decision and execution, between planning and reality. In a time of rapidly deteriorating situations at home and abroad, this is bad for the public service and particularly bad for the country; and we mean to make a change.

I have pledged myself and my colleagues in the cabinet to a continuous encouragement of initiative, responsibility, and energy in serving the public interest. Let every public servant know, whether his post is high or low, that a man's rank and reputation in this administration will be determined by the size of the job he does, and not by the size of his staff, his office, or his budget. Let it be clear that this administration recognizes the value of dissent and daring, that we greet healthy controversy as the hallmark of healthy change. Let the public service be a proud and lively career. And let every man and woman who works in any area of our national government, in any branch, at any level, be able to say with pride and with honor in future years: "I served the United States Government in that hour of our nation's need."

For only with complete dedication by us all to the national interest can we bring our country through the troubled years that lie ahead. Our problems are critical. The tide is unfavorable. The news will be worse before it is better. And while hoping and working for the best, we should prepare ourselves now for the worst.

We cannot escape our dangers; neither must we let them drive us into panic or narrow isolation. In many areas of the world where the balance of power already rests with our adversaries, the forces of freedom are sharply divided. It is one of the ironies of our time that the techniques of a harsh and repressive system should be able to instill discipline and ardor in its servants, while the blessings of liberty have too often stood for privilege, materialism, and a life of ease.

But I have a different view of liberty.

Life in 1961 will not be easy. Wishing it, predicting it, even asking for it, will not make it so. There will be further setbacks before the tide is turned. But turn it we must. The hopes of all mankind rest upon us; not simply upon those of us in this chamber, but upon the peasant in Laos, the fisherman in Nigeria, the exile from Cuba, the spirit that moves every man and nation who shares our hopes for freedom and the future. And in the final analysis, they rest most of all upon the pride and perseverance of our fellow citizens of the great Republic.

In the words of a great president, whose birthday we honor today, closing his final State of the Union Message sixteen years ago, "We pray that we may be worthy of the unlimited opportunities that God has given us."

Reference

Kennedy, John F., *To Turn the Tide*, edited by John W. Gardner, (New York: Harper, 1962).

LYNDON B. JOHNSON

FULL NAME:

Lyndon Baines Johnson

BORN:

27 August 1908, Stonewall, Texas

DIED:

22 January 1973, on his ranch in Texas

Thirty-sixth President of the United States. United States Congressman and Senator. Majority Leader of the Senate from 1956 to 1960. Vice President under John F. Kennedy and became President on 22 November 1963. Reelected in 1964 and served until 1969.

Johnson's memoirs are: *The Vantage Point: Perspectives on the Presidency, 1963–1969* (New York: Holt, Rinehart and Winston, 1971). Studies about him abound: Doris Kearns, *Lyndon Johnson and the American Dream* (New York: New American Library, 1976); and Robert Caro, *The Years of Lyndon Johnson* (New York: Knopf, 1982).

The Vantage Point

It has been said that the presidency is the loneliest office in the world. I did not find it so. Even during the darkest hours of my administration, I always knew that I could draw on the strength, support, and love of my family and my friends.

But if I was seldom lonely, I was often alone. No one can experience with the president of the United States the glory and agony of his office. No one can share the majestic view from his pinnacle of power. No one can share the burden of his decisions or the scope of his duties. A cabinet officer, no matter how broad his mandate, has a limited responsibility. A senator, no matter how varied his interests, has a limited constituency. But the president represents all the people and must face up to all the problems. He must be responsible, as he sees it, for the welfare of every citizen and must be sensitive to the will of every group. He cannot pick and choose his issues. They all come with the job. So his experience is unique among his fellow Americans.

For better or worse, then, this is a book that only a president could have written. That is the sole excuse for its existence. I make no pretense of having written a complete and definitive history of my presidency. I have tried, rather, to review that period from a president's point of view—reflecting a president's personal and political philosophy, a president's experience and knowledge, a president's aspirations, and a president's response to the demands that were made on him.

I have not written these chapters to say, "This is how it was," but to say, "This is how I saw it from my vantage point." Neither have I attempted to cover all the events of my administration. I have selected what I consider to be the most important problems, the most pressing goals, and the most historic accomplishments of my years as president.

Finally, I have tried to avoid engaging in historical pamphleteering. I did not set out to write a propaganda piece in support of my decisions. My purpose has been to state the problems that I faced as president, to record the facts as they came to me, to list the alternatives available, and to review what I did and why I did it. Others will have to judge the results on their merits. The struggle in Vietnam, for example, inspired one of the most passionate and deeply felt debates in our nation's life. That debate will go on, no matter what is written in these pages. History will make its judgments on the decisions made and the actions taken. . . .

"The Beginning"

I knew from the moment President Kennedy died that I must assume the awesome responsibility of uniting the country and moving toward the goals that he had set for us. Like everyone else, I continued to be stunned. My president—the man with whom I had worked and had been proud to serve—had been killed, and killed in my own state. It was almost unbearable.

But in spite of the enormity of the tragedy, in spite of my sense of personal loss and deep shock, I knew I could not allow the tide of grief to overwhelm me. The consequences of all my actions were too great for me to become immobilized now with emotion. I was a man in trouble, in a world that is never more than minutes away from catastrophe.

I had not yet seen Mrs. Kennedy. I wondered with what inadequate words I could try to console her.

I had a staff—and a government—that would be plunged in the depths of despair, and I had to mobilize both for action. I had many decisions to make. No one was certain yet whether a widespread assassination plot might be involved.

Most of all I realized that, ready or not, new and immeasurable duties had been thrust upon me. There were tasks to perform that only I had the authority to perform. A nation stunned, shaken to its very heart, had to be reassured that the government was not in a state of paralysis. I had to convince everyone everywhere that the country would go forward, that the business of the United States would proceed. I knew that not only the nation but the whole world would be anxiously following every move I made—watching, judging, weighing, balancing.

I was catapulted without preparation into the most difficult job any mortal man can hold. My duties would not wait a week, or a day, or even an hour.

On the way to the airport, Agent Youngblood was in communication with *Air Force One*, to make sure it was secured and ready for us. When we arrived, we dashed up the ramp. Secret Service men rushed through the interior ahead of us, pulling down the shades and closing both doors behind us. The air-conditioning was off and it was extremely hot inside the plane.

I realized that the staff and Secret Service had been right in insisting that I go to *Air Force One* immediately. That plane is the closest thing to a traveling White House that man can devise. It affords the personnel, the security, and the communications equipment a president must have to do his job.

At first, Mrs. Johnson and I were ushered into the private quarters of the plane, which contained a bedroom and bathroom for the use of the president and his family. I told one of the agents that we preferred that these quarters be held for Mrs. Kennedy's use and we went forward to the crowded stateroom, which serves as the presidential office and sitting room aboard the plane.

When I walked in, everyone stood up. I still recall the deep emotion I felt. Here were close friends like Homer Thornberry and Jack Brooks; here were aides who were like members of my family; here were Secret Service agents who had covered every movement I had made, twenty-four hours a day, for three years. All of them were on their feet. It was at that moment that I realized nothing would ever be the same again. A wall—high, forbidding, historic—separated us now, a wall that derives from the office of the presidency of the United States. No one but my family would ever penetrate it, as long as I held the office. To old friends who had never called me anything but Lyndon, I would now be "Mr. President." It was a frightening, disturbing prospect. I instinctively reached for Lady Bird's hand for reassurance. I believe it was Congressman Thomas who broke the silence. "We are ready to carry out any orders you have, Mr. President," he said. . . .

"I feel like I have already been here a year"

Every president has to establish with the various sectors of the country what I call "the right to govern." Just being elected to the office does not guarantee him that right. Every president has to inspire the confidence of the people. Every president has to become a leader, and to be a leader he must attract people who are willing to follow him. Every president has to develop a moral underpinning to his power, or he soon discovers that he has no power at all.

For me, that presented special problems. In spite of more than three decades of public service, I knew I was an unknown quantity to many of my countrymen and to much of the world when I assumed office. I suffered another handicap, since I had come to the presidency not through the collective will of the people but in the wake of tragedy. I had no mandate from the voters.

A few people were openly bitter about my becoming president. They found it impossible to transfer their intense loyalties from one president to another. I could understand this, although it complicated my task. Others were apprehensive. This was particularly true within the black community. Just when the blacks had had their hopes for equality and justice raised, after centuries of misery and despair, they awoke one morning to discover that their future was in the hands of a president born in the South.

Yet in spite of these yearnings for a fallen leader, in spite of some bitterness, in spite of apprehensions, I knew it was imperative that I grasp the reins of power and do so without delay. Any hesitation or wavering, any false step, any sign of self-doubt, could have been disastrous. The nation was in a state of shock and grief. The times cried out for leadership.

There was doubt and bewilderment about what had actually happened in Dallas on 22 November 1963, and the uncertainty was compounded two days later when Lee Harvey Oswald was shot to death while in the custody of the Dallas police. A horror-struck, outraged nation wanted the truth and no one could immediately provide it. The entire world was watching us through a magnifying glass. Any signs of weakness or indecision could have had grave international consequences—in Berlin, in Southeast Asia, in Latin America. Friend and foe alike had to be convinced that the policies of our country were going to be continued and that we were one nation undivided in our resolve to maintain international order.

Months later Washington columnists would be writing that I had accomplished a political masterstroke in convincing most of the Kennedy appointees to continue serving in my administration. I saw it neither as political nor as a masterstroke.

It is true that I asked the top Kennedy-appointed officials to stay on, not just for a while, but for as long as I was president. It is true that by remaining on the job they helped give the government and the nation a sense of continuity during critical times—a sense of continuity that in turn strengthened my hand as chief executive. It is also true that I benefited from the experience that these officials had gained during the nearly three years of the Kennedy administration. But in the final analysis, when I asked those appointees to stay on I did so out of a deep-rooted sense of responsibility to John F. Kennedy. Rightly or wrongly, I felt from the very first day in office that I had to carry on for President Kennedy. I considered myself the caretaker of both his people and his policies. He knew when he selected me as his running mate that I would be the man required to carry on if anything happened to him. I did what I believed he would have wanted me to do. I never wavered from that sense of responsibility, even after I was elected in my own right, up to my last day in office.

I eventually developed my own programs and policies, but I never lost sight of the fact that I was the trustee and custodian of the Kennedy administration. Although it was my prerogative to do so, I would no more have considered changing the name of the Honey Fitz—the name Jack Kennedy had given one of the presidential yachts—than I would have thought of changing the name of the Washington Monument. I did everything I could to enhance the memory of John Kennedy, beginning with honoring Mrs. Kennedy's request to rename Cape Canaveral for her late husband. . . .

Teddy Roosevelt used to call the presidency a "bully pulpit." During my first thirty days in office I preached many sermons from that pulpit. I knew I had to secure the cooperation of the people who were the natural leaders of the nation. I talked with those leaders, from every walk of life.

I talked with the cabinet members and impressed on them the fact that even though John Kennedy was dead, it was the responsibility of every one of us to keep the business of the country moving ahead. I asked them to remain in their posts and to speak frankly and candidly with me always. I spoke before a Joint Session of Congress, and in pleading for a continuation of President Kennedy's programs I asked the Congress to pledge its help in enacting these programs into law. I spoke with black groups and with individual leaders of the black community and told them that John Kennedy's dream of equality had not died with him. I assured them that I was going to press for the civil rights bill with every ounce of energy I possessed.

I talked regularly with the congressional leaders from both sides of the aisle and urged them to start the legislative machinery moving forward. I particularly remember a telephone conversation with Senator Everett Dirksen of Illinois. I asked him to convey to his Republican colleagues, in the Senate and throughout the nation, that it was essential to forget partisan politics, so that we could weather the national crisis in which we were involved and unite our people. There was a long pause on the other end of the line and I could hear him breathing heavily. When he finally spoke, he expressed obvious disappointment that I would even raise the question of marshaling his party behind the president.

"Well, Mr. President," he said, "you know I will." And he did.

I spoke with such captains of industry as Roger Blough of U.S. Steel, Frederick Kappel of AT & T, Henry Ford II of the Ford Motor Company, W. B. Murphy of Campbell Soup, Frank Stanton of CBS, George R. Brown of Brown & Root, and Thomas J. Watson, Jr., of IBM. I made it clear that the days of labor-management feuds should end, and that the economic pie was big enough for everyone—and growing much faster than our population. I pointed out that the more people who were employed and working at good wages, the more people there would be to buy their products. I asked them to help me persuade Congress to pass the tax reduction legislation, so that we could infuse new vitality into the economy and put more people to work.

I spoke with the nation's leaders, including George Meany of the AFL-CIO, Walter Reuther of the United Auto Workers, Joseph A. Beirne of the Communications Workers, and A. Philip Randolph of the Brotherhood of Sleeping Car Porters. I told them we needed their help in passing such urgently required measures as Medicare, higher minimum wages, and civil rights. I praised them for opening their ranks to black workers, but I told them they would have to do even better in the months and years ahead.

I spoke with government workers and warned them that we must not let the nation falter or hesitate. I told them that even in an hour of tragedy we must move ahead with assurance. I spoke with foreign ambassadors and emphasized that we coveted no territory and sought to dominate no nation. "We want nothing that anyone else has, but we do want peace in the world."

I brought people together who under ordinary circumstances would have fled at the sight of each other. But these were not ordinary times and most Americans were ready to rise above past differences. I spoke with some of the nation's leading newspeople, including Merriman Smith, James Reston, William S. White, Walter Lippmann, Joseph Alsop, Ben McKelway, Gene Pulliam, Russ Wiggins, Kay Graham, and many others. I spoke to former presidents, to religious leaders, to old friends, and to old adversaries.

But I didn't just talk; I listened carefully to what my visitors had to say. After I had listened, I always returned to my basic theme: People must put aside their selfish aims in the larger cause of the nation's interest. They must start trusting each other; they must start communicating with each other; and they must start working together.

I pleaded. I reasoned. I argued. I urged. I warned.

There were a few—former high government officials, elder statesmen, and longtime advisers to presidents—who needed no convincing; who only wanted to offer their services. Among them were three former presidents, two of whom belonged to another party. Each pledged his loyalty, his support, and his help in any way he could give it. Herbert Hoover, although ailing, sent word to me through our mutual friend Richard Berlin of Hearst newspapers: "I am ready to serve our country in any capacity from office boy up."

President Truman gave me many good suggestions and wise counsel from his own experience of being suddenly thrust into the presidency. He pledged his support for our efforts in Vietnam. He told me he had faced the same problems of aggression—in Greece and Turkey and Korea. He said that if we didn't stand up to aggression when it occurred, it would multiply the costs many times later. He said that his confrontation of those international challenges—particularly in Korea—had been horrors for him politically, bringing his popularity down from a high of 87 percent to a low of 23 percent. But he said they represented his proudest achievements in office. He told me always to bear in mind that I was the voice of *all* the people. A few of the big voices, he said, would try to drown me out from time to time, but the duty of the president was to lead and champion the people's causes.

President Eisenhower drove down to Washington from Gettysburg on 23 November, the day after President Kennedy's assassination. After spending the better part of an hour with me in my office in the Executive Office Building, he went to my outer office, picked up a yellow tablet, and began writing in longhand the things he would do if he were in my place. He then asked if General Andrew Goodpaster's former secretary, Alice Boyce, was still working in the White House. He knew her and he trusted her. I told him that she was working for McGeorge Bundy, and he asked if she could come over to work with him. After dictating from his notes to Miss Boyce, he told her to make only two copies of the memorandum—"one for the president and one for me." . . .

"The Making of a Decision: Vietnam 1967–1968"

My biggest worry was not Vietnam itself; it was the divisiveness and pessimism at home. I knew the American people were deeply worried. I had seen the effects of Tet on some of the Wise Men. I looked on my approaching speech as an opportunity to help right the balance and provide better perspective. For the collapse of the home front, I knew well, was just what Hanoi was counting on. The enemy had failed in Vietnam; would Hanoi succeed in the United States? I did not think so, but I was deeply concerned.

Every president in this century has had to assume that there would be opposition to any war in which we became involved. That was true not only during the Korean War but also, though to a lesser extent, during World Wars I and II. It is never easy to accept the idea that fighting, with all its horrors and pain and loss, is preferable to the alternatives. I sensed that another idea was now influencing many Americans, including men who had played a major part in our critical decisions since 1965. They seemed to feel that the bitter debate and noisy dissension at home about Vietnam were too high a price to pay for honoring our commitment in Southeast Asia. They deplored the demonstrations and turbulent arguments about Vietnam. So did I. They wanted money poured into the deteriorating cities and into other public programs that would improve the life of our disadvantaged citizens. So did I, though I knew there was no guarantee Congress would vote those additional funds even if the war ended. They seemed to be saying that anything that happened in Asia or the rest of the world was less important than the strains we were suffering at home.

I could never agree with this argument. My own assessment in 1965 and in 1968 (and today) was that abandoning our pledges and our commitment in Vietnam would generate more and worse controversy at home, not less. Such abandonment would bring vastly greater dangers—in Laos, Cambodia, Thailand, and elsewhere, including India and Pakistan—than would a policy of seeing our commitment through in Southeast Asia. In 1947 the British were able to pass on to us their responsibilities in Greece and Turkey. In 1954 the French knew they could transfer the problem of Southeast Asia's security to our shoulders. But if the United States abandoned its responsibilities, who would pick them up? The answer, in the short run, was: No one. As I had said in 1965, we did not ask to be the guardians at the gate, but there was no one else. There was no question in my mind that the vacuum created by our abdication would be filled inevitably by the Communist powers.

As I reflected on the situation in Vietnam and the forces gathering strength in Asia, I felt that there was another answer—if this nation of ours had the stubborn patience to see it through. That answer was that we could shift an increasing share of responsibility to the Vietnamese and the other peoples of Asia. It was not inevitable that we would continue carrying the major burden year after year. The South Vietnamese army and populace had withstood the heaviest blows the enemy could launch during Tet, and we had seen them move forward, not fall back. During my trip through Asia in 1966 I had seen one country after another moving forward with great energy in economic and social reform. In addition to that, every national leader with whom I spoke said that in the future Asians would have to work more closely together and take more responsibility for their own security and development.

Looking ahead, I could not see a time when the United States could, with safety, withdraw totally from Asia and the Pacific, for we were a Pacific power with a profound interest in the stability, peace, and progress of that vital part of the world. But I could see a time when our share of the burden for that stability, that peace, and that progress would diminish greatly. If we failed to act in that patient, measured way, I believed that we would be risking far greater casualties, far more danger, than we faced in Vietnam. I feared that many Americans did not understand the real choices facing us in Asia. I knew that some people had changed their stand on Vietnam completely because of discouragement, and others for purely political reasons.

At the beginning of March 1968 I was concerned that we might have to contribute considerably more to Vietnam—more men, more equipment, more money. I have described the various influences that eased my concern and shaped my final decision. For me, the key influence was the change in the situation in Vietnam. But other matters, especially our financial problems, played an important part in that final decision.

Early in March I was convinced that I should make some sort of peace offer along the lines Rusk had suggested on 27 February. I considered several other proposals during the month, and I considered doing nothing, but the weight of evidence favored a move in this direction and I regarded Rusk's proposal as the best.

I wanted the South Vietnamese to carry a heavier share of the burden of fighting for their country. At the beginning of March I had serious doubts that they could do much more. As each day passed I became increasingly confident that these people whom we had pledged to help were not only willing but able to do more. Their performance represented a remarkable transformation, one that all too few Americans were aware of, then or even now.

Finally, I had decided not to run for another term in the White House. That decision was intimately linked with the others, especially with the plan to stop most of the bombing.

I had made these four decisions, but I could have unmade any one or all of them right down to the time I sat behind my desk and began to speak on television on the night of 31 March. If the enemy in Vietnam had suddenly launched a large and devastating new series of attacks, our reaction would have been strong. If I had then become convinced withdrawing from politics would have undermined our men in Vietnam or harmed our country, I would have changed my mind. Hanoi's actions or statements could have caused us to call off or alter the bombing proposal at the last moment. War or a serious incident could have erupted elsewhere in the world. Any one of dozens of things could have happened, and in each case I would have reconsidered my decisions and changed my course if necessary. But those things, thank God, did not happen. I went forward with the decisions that had taken shape in my mind years, months, and days earlier.

I repeat: No president, at least not this president, makes a decision until he publicly announces that decision and acts upon it. When did I make the decisions that I announced the evening of 31 March 1968? The answer is: 9:01 P.M. on 31 March 1968, and they are the same decisions I would make in retrospect. Time alone will reveal whether they were wise decisions—but good or bad I made them, and the full responsibility is mine.

"A Beginning and an End: March 31, 1968"

When I took the oath as president in January 1965 to begin my first full term in office, I felt that it would be my last, and this feeling grew stronger with every passing week in the White House. I have already described the conviction I had, after the 1964 election, that I would have to get my program through quickly. At the end of the first year of my administration, I was reasonably certain that by the time my term was over I would have gone as far as I could.

Two hospitalizations for surgery while I was in the White House had sharpened my apprehensions about my health. My heart attack of 1955 seemed well behind me, but I was conscious that it was part of the background of my life—just as I was conscious of my family's history of stroke and heart disease. I did not fear death so much as I feared disability. Whenever I walked through the Red Room and saw the portrait of Woodrow Wilson hanging there, I thought of him stretched out upstairs in the White House, powerless to move, with the machinery of the American government in disarray around him. And I remembered Grandmother Johnson, who had had a stroke and stayed in a wheelchair throughout my childhood, unable even to move her hands or to speak so that she could be understood.

I have very strong feelings about work. When it is there to be done, I do it. And the work of the presidency is demanding and unrelenting. It is always there to be done. Of all the 1,886 nights I was president, there were not many when I got to sleep before 1 or 2 A.M., and there were few mornings when I didn't wake up by 6 or 6:30. It became a question of how much the physical constitution could take. I frankly did not believe in 1968 that I could survive another four years of the long hours and unremitting tensions I had just gone through.

These were considerations I had lived with from the beginning. Others had developed in the course of events. On that last morning in March, as I moved toward one of the most significant hours of my life, several factors relating to the state of the nation fed into the decisions I was preparing to announce. First, we faced the absolute necessity of an increase in taxes. For two years the chairman of the Council of Economic Advisers had been stressing the need for a tax increase in the strongest terms. I knew that the stability of the dollar and the economic health of the nation and the world demanded an increase at the earliest possible time. I also knew that the likelihood of obtaining the necessary Republican votes to propel a tax bill through Congress, particularly in an election year, would be close to zero if I were a candidate for reelection. Second, we faced the possibility of new riots and turmoil in the cities in the summer of 1968. We had experienced widespread disturbances the previous summer, many of them exploited, I believe, by men who took advantage of distressed people to advance their own political causes. There were strong indications that rioting might be repeated or increased. FBI Director J. Edgar Hoover had reported to me on 31 May:

> The racial violence that has already erupted this spring clearly indicates
> that the United States faces the probability of riots and disturbances on
> an even more massive scale in the months ahead. Ever present in every
> urban area in the land are the sparks of violence that could detonate ri-
> ots. Although some cities have heretofore enjoyed seemingly harmoni-
> ous race relations and racial peace, no city is immune from possible vi-
> olence today.

The principal responsibility for dealing with such disorders rests with the nation's mayors and governors, but in a few cities in 1967 I had been asked to invoke presidential authority and send in federal troops. It seemed likely that I might face the same decisions again. I did not want the slightest suspicion to arise—in Congress, the media, or any segment of the public—that I had responded with too little or too much, too soon or too late, with one eye on the safety of our citizens and the other on election day.

Finally, there was the question of Vietnam. I had been preparing a speech on this subject to deliver to the American people late in March. In that speech I wanted to restate our position in Vietnam as clearly as possible—why we were there, what we hoped to achieve. I wanted to put the enemy's Tet offensive in proper perspective, and now that the offensive had been blunted and there was a chance that the enemy might respond favorably, I wanted to announce our new initiative for peace. If we were going to take the risk of a bombing pause, I felt I should make it clear that my decision had been made without political considerations. I wanted that decision to be understood by the enemy and by everyone everywhere as a serious and sincere effort to find a road to peace. The most persuasive way to get this across, I believed, would be to couple my announcement of a bombing halt with the statement that I would not be a candidate for reelection.

I also hoped that the combined announcement would accomplish something else. The issue of Vietnam had created divisions and hostilities among Americans, as I had feared. I wanted to heal some of those wounds and restore unity to the nation. This speech might help to do that. I deeply hoped so.

For several years Lady Bird and I had spoken many times about our plans to leave the White House at the end of my first full term. Her position had remained perfectly clear and consistent since she had first expressed it to me in the spring of 1964: She did not want me to be a candidate in 1968. We discussed often how to select the proper time and the right occasion to make the announcement.

As the months wore on, we talked it over with our daughters and their husbands. The girls' reactions were divided. Luci did not want me to run. She insisted that she wanted a living father. Lynda's response was more complex. As a daughter, she said, she would prefer that I not run, but as a citizen she hoped I would. Later, when her husband, Marine Captain Charles Robb, was under orders to go to Vietnam, her reaction as a citizen superseded her reaction as a daughter. . . .

In those final months, as the announcement of my decision neared, I believe only one thing could have changed my mind—an indication that the men in Vietnam would regard it as unfair or unwise. I asked General Westmoreland to come home in November 1967, and I put the question directly to him. As we sat in the family living room on the second floor of the White House one evening after dinner, I asked him what the effect on troop morale would be if I announced that I would not run for another term. Would the men think the commander in chief who had sent them to the battlefield had let them down?

General Westmoreland looked for a few moments at the windows facing out on the Rose Garden. Then he turned to me. "Mr. President," he said, "I do not believe so." . . .

I used the power of the presidency proudly, and I used every ounce of it I had. I used it to establish programs that gave thousands of youngsters a head start in school, that enabled thousands of old folks to live in clean nursing homes, that brought justice to the Negro and hope to the poor, that forced the nation to face the growing problems of pollution. In this exercise of power, I knew a satisfaction that only a limited number of men have ever known and that I could have had in no other way. Men, myself included, do not lightly give up the opportunity to achieve so much lasting good, but a man who uses power effectively must also be a realist. He must understand that by spending power he dissipates it. Because I had not hesitated to spend the presidential power in the pursuit of my beliefs or in the interests of my country, I was under no illusion that I had as much power in 1968 as I had had in 1964. . . .

At 1 A.M. I went to my bedroom. I was tired. It had been a long day, a day marking an end but also, I earnestly hoped, a beginning. I prayed silently that the action I had taken would bear the fruit I devoutly hoped for. By renouncing my candidacy, I expressed a fervent wish that problems that had resisted solution would now yield to resolution. I wanted Hanoi to know that Lyndon Johnson was not using this new move toward peace as a bid for personal political gain. Maybe now, with this clearest possible evidence of our sincerity thrown into the balance, North Vietnam would come forward and agree to a dialogue—a genuine communication dedicated to peace. Those who doubted me and disliked me, those who had fought my struggle to achieve justice for men and women who had for so long suffered injustice, might now be willing to adjust their rigid views and seek to fashion a workable formula for peace in the streets. Members of Congress who had believed that my crusade for the tax bill was linked to personal politics rather than an attempt to defeat inflation might reassess their motives, soften their antagonism, and turn this urgent piece of legislation—so vital to the nation's and the world's needs—into law.

Perhaps now that I was not a candidate commentators in the press and television might regard issues and efforts more objectively, instead of concentrating on criticism and cynical speculation. For a while the nation and the world would reflect on my words.

Just before I drifted off to sleep that night, I prayed that Hanoi had listened and would respond. The chance for peace, the opportunity to stop death and destruction, the opening toward a new decade of hope—all these were enfolded in the words I had spoken. There was nothing more I could do that day. All that I could do I had done. . . .

" 'It's the right thing to do': Vietnam 1968–1969"

As I left the presidency, I was aware that not everything I had done about Vietnam, not every decision I had made, had been correct. Should we have sent as many men to Southeast Asia as we did? Or should we have sent more and sent them sooner? Was I right in refusing to risk expanding the war by using ground forces to attack the enemy's supply lines and sanctuaries in neighboring countries or to mine the port of Haiphong? Did I make a mistake in stopping most of the bombing of the North on 31 March? And all the bombing on 31 October? Did I do all I could have done to make clear to our people the vital interests that I believed were at stake in our efforts to help protect Southeast Asia?

History will judge these questions and will render its verdict long after current passions have subsided and the noise in the streets has died away. History will judge on the basis of facts we cannot now know, and of events some of which have not yet happened.

Every president I have known has drawn heavily on past history—for lessons, for ideas, and for principles. But none of us can know what future history's conclusions will be regarding our time and our actions. Every president must act on problems as they come to him. He must search out the best information available. He can seek the counsel of men whose wisdom and experience and judgment he values. But in the end the president must decide, and he must do so on the basis of his judgment of what is best—for his nation and for the world. Throughout those years of crucial decisions I was sustained by the memory of my predecessors who had also borne the most painful duty of a president—to lead our country in a time of war. I recalled often the words of one of those men, Woodrow Wilson, who in the dark days of 1917 said: "It is a fearful thing to lead this great peaceful people into war. . . . But the right is more precious than peace."

That belief—that peace is precious but that there are values even more precious to free men—has strengthened us from the earliest days of our nation. It has given us the courage to do what had to be done in times of great danger. We will be a poorer and a weaker people if we ever abandon that belief. And the world will be a much more dangerous place for all mankind.

Reference

Johnson, Lyndon Baines, The Vantage Point: Perspectives on the Presidency, 1963–1969 (New York: Holt, Rinehart and Winston, 1971).

RICHARD NIXON

FULL NAME:

Richard Milhous Nixon

BORN:

9 January 1913, Yorba Linda, California

DIED:

22 April 1994, New York, New York

Thirty-seventh President of the United States. United States Member of the House of Representatives and United States Senator from California, 1950–1953. Vice President for two terms under Eisenhower, 1953–1961. Unsuccessful bid for presidency in 1960. President in 1968; reelected in 1972; resigned during Watergate scandal on 9 August 1974.

A prolific writer, his works include: RN: *The Memoirs of Richard Nixon* (New York: Grosset & Dunlap, 1978); *In the Arena: A Memoir of Victory, Defeat, and Renewal* (New York: Simon and Schuster, 1990); and *Leaders* (New York: Warner Brooks, 1982). Works about Nixon include: William Safire, *Before the Fall* (Garden City, NY: Doubleday, 1975); Henry Kissinger, *The White House Years* (Boston: Little Brown, 1979); Henry Kissinger, *Years of Upheaval* (Boston: Little Brown, 1982); and H.R. Haldeman, *The Haldeman Diaries* (New York: G.P. Putnam's Sons, 1994).

RN: The Memoirs of Richard Nixon

"1968 Campaign and Election"

. . . When Johnson and I returned to the Oval Office after the briefing, he talked with a sense of urgency. "There may be times when we disagree, and, if such time comes, I will let you know privately," he said. "But you can be sure that I won't criticize you publicly. Eisenhower did the same for me. I know what an enormous burden you will be carrying." He said that he wanted to do everything he could to help me succeed. "The problems at home and abroad are probably greater than any president has ever confronted since the time of Lincoln," he said. Johnson and I had been adversaries for many years, but on that day our political and personal differences melted away. As we stood together in the Oval Office, he welcomed me into a club of very exclusive membership, and he made a promise to adhere to the cardinal rule of that membership: stand behind those who succeed you. . . .

I had strong opinions, many of them derived from my experiences and observations during the Eisenhower years, about the way a president should work. In my view, then and now, the key to a successful presidency is in the decision-making process. I felt that the matters brought before a president for decisions should be only those that cannot or should not be made at a lower level on the White House staff, or by the cabinet member responsible for them. This was a lesson I had learned directly from Eisenhower, whose staff had too often cluttered his schedule with unimportant events and bothered him with minor problems that drained his time and energy. I knew that I could absorb far more material by reading it than by talking about it, and I have invariably found that staff members will present problems more concisely and incisively in writing than they will in meetings.

I had attended hundreds of cabinet meetings as vice president, and I felt that most of them were unnecessary and boring. On the few issues that cut across all departments, such as the economy, group discussions would sometimes be informative. But the day had long since passed when it was useful to take an hour and a half to have the secretary of defense and the secretary of state discuss the secretary of transportation's new highway proposal. Therefore I wanted to keep the cabinet meetings in my administration to a minimum. I felt that the better each cabinet member performed his job, the less time I should have to spend discussing it with him except for major questions of politics or policy. If we were going to run government with a clear eye for efficiency and a tough approach to wastefulness, we would have to have good managers who could immerse themselves in detail and learn the job. I was willing to trade flamboyance for competence. I had also seen the hazards of appointing cabinet members who were too strong-willed to act as part of a team. I wanted people who would fight to the finish in private for what they thought was right but would support my decision once it was made. . . .

In 1961 John Kennedy had challenged people to "ask not what your country can do for you—ask what you can do for your country." By the end of the decade, however, many people were asking why the federal government had not done all the things it had promised and undertaken to do for them.

Perhaps most demoralizing of all, the working poor watched while the nonworking poor made as much money—and in some cases even more money—by collecting welfare payments and other unemployment benefits. This began a bitter cycle of frustration, anger, and hostility.

I wanted to be an activist president in domestic policy, but I wanted to be certain that the things we did had a chance of working. "Don't promise more than we can do," I told the cabinet. "But do more than we can promise."

I had watched the sixties from outside the arena of leadership, but I had strong feelings about what I had seen happen. I saw the mass demonstrations grow remote from the wellsprings of sensitivity and feeling that had originally prompted them, and become a cultural fad. And the new sensitivity to social inequities that was awakened at the beginning of the decade had, by the middle of the sixties, spawned an intolerance for the rights and opinions of those who disagreed with the vocal minority. I had no patience with the mindless rioters and professional malcontents, and I was appalled by the response of most of the nation's political and academic leaders to them. The political leadership seemed unable to make the distinction between a wrong that needed to be set right and the use of such a wrong as a justification for violating the privileges of democracy. The young demonstrators held firmly to their beliefs, while the adults seemed stricken with ambivalence about their own guilt and doubts about their own values. By proving themselves vulnerable to mob rule, the political and academic leaders encouraged its spread. Contemptuous of most of their professors, encouraged by others on the faculty and in the political arena, and spotlighted by the rapt gaze of television cameras, the demonstrators and their demonstrations continued and grew, and so did the often rationalized or romanticized violence connected with them.

I was ready to take a stand on these social and cultural issues; I was anxious to defend the "square" virtues. In some cases—such as opposing the legalization of marijuana and the provision of federal funds for abortions, and in identifying myself with unabashed patriotism— I knew I would be standing against the prevailing social winds, and that would cause tension. But I thought that at least someone in high office would be standing up for what he believed.

Since the advent of television as our primary means of communication and source of information modern presidents must have specialized talents at once more superficial and more complicated than those of their predecessors. They must try to master the art of manipulating the media not only to win in politics but in order to further the programs and causes they believe in; at the same time they must avoid at all costs the charge of trying to manipulate the media. In the modern presidency, concern for image must rank with concern for substance—there is no guarantee that good programs will automatically triumph. "Elections are not won or lost by programs," I once reminded Haldeman in a memo. "They are won or lost by how these programs are presented to the country and how the political and public relations considerations are handled." I do not like this situation; I can remember a time in American politics when it was not the case. But today it is a fact of life, and anyone who seeks a position of influence in politics must cope with it; anyone who seeks a position of leadership must master it. . . .

As I anticipated becoming president, I found that I was awed by the prospect but not fearful of it. I felt prepared. I had the advantage of experience and of the detachment that comes from being out of office. The "wilderness years" had been years of education and growth.

I had no illusions about either the difficulty of the challenge or about my ability to meet it. I felt I knew what would not work. On the other hand, I was less sure what would work. I did not have all the answers. But I did have definite ideas about the changes I felt were needed.

As 1968 came to a close, I was a happy man. . . .

"The Presidency 1974"

On the night of 30 July I could not get to sleep. After tossing and turning for a few hours, I finally put on the light and took a pad of notepaper from the bed table. I wrote the time and date at the top—3:50 A.M., 31 July—and I began to outline the choices left to me. There were really only three: I could resign right away; I could stay on until the House had voted on the articles of impeachment and then resign if impeached; or I could fight all the way through the Senate.

For almost three hours I listed the pros and cons: what would be the best for me, for my family, for my friends and supporters? What would be the best for the country?

There were strong arguments against resigning. First and foremost, I was not and never had been a quitter. The idea that I would be running away from the job and ending my career as a weak man was repugnant to me. Resignation would be taken by many, and interpreted by the press, as a blanket admission of guilt. Resignation would set a dangerous precedent of short-circuiting the constitutional machinery that provides for impeachment. I also had to consider that my family and many of my supporters would want me to fight and would be hurt and disillusioned if I gave up before the battle was over.

The arguments in favor of resignation were equally compelling. I knew that after two years of being distracted and divided by Watergate, the nation badly needed a unity of spirit and purpose to face the tough domestic and international problems that would not wait through the six months of a Senate trial. Besides, I would be crippled politically as soon as the House voted to impeach, and I did not know whether I could subject the country to the ordeal of a weakened presidency during such troubled and important times. From a practical point of view, I also had to face the fact that if I decided to stay and fight, the outcome of the fight was all but settled: I would be defeated and dishonored, the first President in history to be impeached and convicted on criminal charges.

Another positive effect of resignation, one I knew to be uppermost in the minds of many Republicans, was that it would free the party from having to defend me. The 1974 elections would not become a referendum on Nixon and Watergate, and their campaigns and their congressional seats would not be held hostage to my political fortunes.

It was almost morning by the time I finished making these notes. My natural instincts welled up and I turned the paper over and wrote on the back: "End career as a fighter." . . .

I sat alone in the Lincoln Sitting Room that night for several hours, trying to decide the best course of action.

My family's courage moved me deeply. They had been through so much already, and still they wanted to see the struggle through to the end. Pat, who had let the others do most of the talking in our meeting, told me that now, as always before, she was for fighting to the finish.

I decided that instead of resigning on Monday night, I would release the 23 June tape and see the reaction to it. If it was as bad as I expected, then we could resume the countdown toward resignation. If by some miracle the reaction was not so bad and there was any chance that I could actually govern during a six-month trial in the Senate, then we could examine that forlorn option one more time. In a subconscious way I knew that resignation was inevitable. But more than once over the next days I would yield to my desire to fight, and I would bridle as the inexorable end drew near.

I called Haig and told him that Ray Price should stop working on the resignation speech for Monday night and instead begin work on a statement to accompany the release of the 23 June tape.

On Saturday afternoon I decided that we should get out of Washington and go to Camp David. Even up there in the mountains it was hot and humid, so as soon as we could change our clothes we all went for a swim. Then we dressed and sat on the terrace, looking out across the wide valleys. On evenings like this it was easy to see why Franklin Roosevelt had named this place Shangri-la, and I think that each of us had a sense of the mystery and the beauty as well as the history and the tragedy that lay behind our weekend together in this setting. . . .

Ziegler came over to discuss the arrangements for the speech. As we talked about the tremendous swings of fortune we had known over the past two years and about how tragic it was that everything should end so suddenly and so sadly, he recalled a famous quotation from Teddy Roosevelt I had used often in my campaign speeches. It was the one in which TR had described the "man in the arena,"

> whose face is marred by dust and sweat and blood, who strives valiantly, who errs and comes short again and again because there is no effort without error and shortcoming, but who does actually strive to do the deed, who knows the great enthusiasms, the great devotions, who spends himself in a worthy cause, who at the best knows in the end the triumphs of high achievement and who at worst, if he fails, at least fails while daring greatly.

I decided that I would use this quotation in my resignation speech. . . .

A president's power begins slipping away the moment it is known that he is going to leave: I had seen that in 1952, in 1960, in 1968. On the eve of my resignation I knew that my role was already a symbolic one, and that Gerald Ford's was now the constructive one. My telephone calls and meetings and decisions were now parts of a prescribed ritual aimed at making peace with the past; his calls, his meetings, and his decisions were already the ones that would shape America's future.

Ziegler arrived and described the technical arrangements for the resignation speech and the departure ceremony.

As we walked out of the Lincoln Sitting Room, I asked Manolo to go ahead of us and turn on all the lights. From the outside the second floor of the White House must have looked like the scene of a festive party.

Ziegler and I went into each room: the Queen's Bedroom, the Treaty Room, the Yellow Oval Room that Pat had just redecorated and that we had scarcely had a chance to enjoy.

"It's a beautiful house, Ron," I said, as we walked down the long hallway under the glow of the crystal chandeliers.

I asked Manolo to wake me at nine in the morning, and I started toward my room.

"Mr. President," Ziegler called, "it's the right decision."

I nodded. I knew.

"You've had a great presidency, sir," he said as he turned away.

Thursday, 8 August 1974, was the last full day I served as president. . . .

Reference

Nixon, Richard, RN: The Memoirs of Richard Nixon (New York: Grosset & Dunlap, 1978).

JIMMY CARTER

FULL NAME:

James Earl Carter, Jr.

BORN:

1 October 1924, Plains, Georgia

Thirty-ninth President of the United States. Governor of Georgia, 1970–1974. President in 1976, but defeated when ran for second term in 1980. Became one of the most active presidents after leaving office, involving himself in foreign policy and social and human rights issues.

His own writings include: *Keeping the Faith: Memoirs of a President* (New York: Bantam Books, 1982). For works about Carter, see: Haynes Johnson, *In the Absence of Power: Governing America* (New York: Viking Press, 1980); and Betty Glad, *Jimmy Carter: In Search of the Great White House* (New York: W. W. Norton, 1980).

Keeping the Faith

"A Graduate Course in America"

. . . As an American, I had been embarrassed by the Watergate scandal and the forced resignation of the president. I realized that my own election had been aided by a deep desire among the people for open government, based on a new and fresh commitment to changing some of the Washington habits that had made it possible for the American people to be misled. Because of President Ford's pardon of Nixon, Watergate had been a largely unspoken though ever-present campaign issue, and the bitter divisions and personal tragedies of those recent events could not quickly be forgotten. So, in spite of Ford's healing service, the ghosts of Watergate still haunted the White House. We wanted to exorcise them and welcome friendlier spirits.

However, in reducing the imperial presidency, I overreacted at first. We began to receive many complaints that I had gone too far in cutting back the pomp and ceremony, so after a few months I authorized the band to play "Hail to the Chief" on special occasions. I found it to be impressive and enjoyed it. . . .

"My One-Week Honeymoon with Congress"

From that cold morning in January 1975, when I left Plains on my first campaign trip across the United States, until the early morning hours almost two years later, when the final election returns from the state of Mississippi told me that I would be the next president, my confidence never wavered. In fact, what they called the overconfidence of an unknown candidate was the only theme I could stir up among the few news reporters who wrote about my first venture into the national political arena.

This unshakable faith in a final victory affected me in two important ways. It was of great benefit, in that it sustained me many times during weeks when I had every reason for despair. When others around me were discouraged because of our slow progress or lack of funds, their feelings had little adverse effect on me. But my freedom to act and speak during the campaign was severely restrained by the same confidence. I ran as though I would have to govern—always careful about what I promised, and determined not to betray those who gave me their support. Sometimes I irritated my opponents and the news reporters by firmly refusing to respond to questions to which I did not know the answers. And repeatedly I told supporters, "If I ever lie to you, if I ever make a misleading statement, don't vote for me. I would not deserve to be your president." Even during the earliest days I was always thinking about what would have to be done in the Oval Office after the inauguration ceremonies were over.

Of the presidents who had served during my lifetime, I admired Harry Truman most, and had studied his career more than any other. He was direct and honest, somewhat old-fashioned in his attitudes, bound close to his small hometown roots, courageous in facing serious challenges, and willing to be unpopular if he believed his actions were best for the country. Over the years the American people had come to realize how often his most controversial decisions were, in fact, right. To a surprising degree, many of his problems were still my problems—the Middle East, China, oil and natural gas, Poland, nuclear weapons, Soviet adventurism, human rights, fights with the Democratic party's liberal wing—and I was to see ever more clearly that the judgments he made, or did not make, had a great impact on my own administration.

It was my dream not only to be elected president, but to be a good president. However, I did not wish to go down in the history books as a "great" leader of America who had finally won a war I myself had started. I wanted to maintain peace and meet successfully the challenges our nation would have to face, so the major thrust of my transition effort was toward inventorying the country's problems and determining what should be done about as many of them as possible. At least for me, it was natural to move on many fronts at once.

I took serious the commitments I had made as a candidate. Peace, human rights, nuclear arms control, and the Middle East had been my major foreign policy concerns. I had also spoken out on issues closer to home: achieving maximum bureaucratic efficiency, reorganizing the government, creating jobs, deregulating major industries, addressing the energy problem, canceling wasteful water projects, welfare and tax reform, environmental quality, restoring the moral fiber of the government, and openness and honesty in dealing with the press and public. It was obvious that our nation would have to resolve many such serious questions, which had long been ignored or deliberately avoided because of the incompatibility of the White House and Congress, fear of special-interest lobbies, or concern about the next election. . . .

Why Not the Best?

"Presidential Plans"

I have always looked on the presidency of the United States with reverence and awe, and I still do. But recently I have begun to realize that the president is just a human being. I can almost remember when I began to change my mind and form this opinion.

Before becoming governor I had never met a president, although I once saw Harry Truman at a distance. He was present when we laid the keel of the first atomic submarine *Nautilus* in New London, Connecticut, in 1952. Great presidents like Washington, Jefferson, Lincoln, and Roosevelt have always been historical figures to me, and even the intimate biographical information published about them has never made them seem quite human.

Then during 1971 and 1972 I met Richard Nixon, Spiro Agnew, George McGovern, Henry Jackson, Hubert Humphrey, Ed Muskie, George Wallace, Ronald Reagan, Nelson Rockefeller, and other presidential hopefuls, and I lost my feeling of awe about presidents. This is not meant as a criticism of them, but it is merely a simple statement of fact.

After the 1972 convention I began with the help of those close to me to think seriously about a presidential campaign, and to assess my own strengths and weaknesses. In fact, the frank assessment of my shortcomings became one of the most enjoyable experiences of my staff, my friends, and my family, and was a time-consuming process. We talked about politics, geography, character, education, experience, appearance, age, mannerisms, and lack of fame. In spite of these critical assessments, I decided to run. . . .

"Those Two Questions Again"

For too long political leaders have been isolated from the people. They have made decisions from an ivory tower. Few have ever seen personally the direct impact of government programs involving welfare, prisons, mental institutions, unemployment, school busing, or public housing. Our people feel that they have little access to the core of government and little influence with elected officials. . . .

Our nation now has no understandable national purpose, no clearly defined goals, and no organizational mechanism to develop or achieve such purposes or goals. We move from one crisis to the next as if they were fads, even though the previous one hasn't been solved.

The Bible says: "If the trumpet give an uncertain sound, who shall prepare himself to the battle?" As a planner and a businessman, and a chief executive, I know from experience that uncertainty is also a devastating affliction in private life and in government. Coordination of different programs is impossible. There is no clear vision of what is to be accomplished, everyone struggles for temporary advantage, and there is no way to monitor how effectively services are delivered. . . .

The Wit and Wisdom of Jimmy Carter

. . . As Christ became my friend, other lives began meaning more to me. I became less proud and stopped judging others all the time. I ran once again for governor and knew that whether I won or lost, I could approach the result with complete equanimity. And though my term as governor was tough and combative and contentious, the day we drove from the Governor's Mansion I told my wife I'd never gotten up on a single morning without looking forward to the day with great anticipation. For unlike Lyndon Johnson . . . I feel sure about myself deep inside. Johnson never felt secure inside, especially around the Eastern Establishment—the professors, experts, writers, and media people—and that's why they got him in the end. But I don't feel ill at ease in a Harvard professor's house, or when I'm talking with experts on foreign policy or on economics, or when I'm with the leader of any group.

The point is that I'm not comparing myself with any of them. To judge our own goodness or sinfulness by comparison with other men is wrong. We all fall short in comparison with the glory of Christ. The Bible says, "Thou shalt not commit adultery." But I'm never proud of simply not sleeping with someone else. For if you've ever looked with lust upon another woman, you're equally guilty. Pride comes only when such sinful thoughts can be abolished. . . .

References

Carter, Jimmy, *Keeping the Faith: Memoirs of a President* (New York: Bantam Books, 1982).

Carter, Jimmy, *Why Not the Best?* (Nashville, TN: Broadman Press, 1975).

Carter, Jimmy, *The Wit and Wisdom of Jimmy Carter*, edited by Bill Adler (Secaucus, NJ: Citadel Press, 1977).

Acknowledgements

Every effort has been made to contact copyright holders; in the event of an inadvertent omission or error, the editor should be notified.

From *The Wit and Wisdom of Jimmy Carter* by Bill Adler. Copyright © by Jimmy Carter. Published by arrangement with Carol Publishing Group.

From *Keeping Faith: Memoirs of a President* by Jimmy Carter. (New York: Bantam Books, 1982). Reprinted by permission of Jimmy Carter.

From *Why Not the Best?* by Jimmy Carter. (Nashville: Broadman Press, 1975). Reprinted by permission of Jimmy Carter.

From *Fidel Castro Speaks* by Fidel Castro. Copyright 1969 by Grove Press. Reprinted by permission of Grove / Atlantic, Inc.

From *Revolutionary Struggle* by Fidel Castro. Reprinted by permission of the MIT Press.

From *Great Destiny* by Winston Churchill, ed. by F.W. Heath. G.P. Putnam's Sons, 1965.

From *The Second World War: Triumph and Tragedy* by Winston Churchill. Houghton Mifflin Company / The Riverside Press, 1953.

Excerpts from *The Edge of the Sword* by Charles de Gaulle. Copyright © 1960 by Criterion Books, Inc. and Faber & Faber, Ltd. Reprinted by permission of HarperCollins Publishers, Inc.

From *Mandate for Change* by Dwight D. Eisenhower. Copyright © 1963 by Dwight D. Eisenhower. Used by permission of Doubleday, a division of Bantam Doubleday Dell Publishing Group, Inc.

From *The Years of Challenge: Selected Speeches of Indira Gandhi* (1966-1969). Copyright © 1971. Reprinted by permission of Sonia Gandhi, Nehru Memorial Fund.

From *All Men Are Brothers* by Mahatma Gandhi. Copyright © UNESCO, 1958. Reproduced by permission of UNESCO.

Pages 25-27 from *Perestroika: New Thinking for Our Country and the World* by Mikhail Gorbachev. Copyright © 1987 by Mikhail Gorbachev. Reprinted by permission of HarperCollins Publishers, Inc.

From *Political Report of the CPSU Central Committee to the 27th Congress of the Communist Party of the Soviet Union*. Delivered by Mikhail Gorbachev, General Secretary of the CPSU Central Committee, February 25, 1986.

From *Mein Kampf* by Adolf Hitler. Reynal & Hitchcock, 1941.

From *The Speeches of Adolf Hitler*, ed. Norman H. Baynes., Oxford University Press, 1942.

From *Houphouët Speaks*. Offset-Auburn, 1985.

From *The Vantage Point* by Lyndon Baines Johnson. Copyright © 1971 by Hec Public Affairs Foundation. Reprinted by permission of Henry Holt & Co., Inc.

Excerpts form pages 3-11, 15-18, 31-33 from *To Turn the Tide* by John F.

Kennedy and edited by John W. Gardner. Copyright © 1962 by Harper & Row Publishers, Inc. Reprinted by permission of HarperCollins Publishers, Inc.

From *Suffering Without Bitterness* by Jomo Kenyatta. East African Publishing House, 1968.

From *Harambee! The Prime Minister of Kenya's Speeches 1963-1964* by Jomo Kenyatta. Oxford University Press, 1964.

From *Imam Khomeini, Islam and Revolution: Writings and Declarations* transl. by Hamid Algar. KPI, 1985.

From *Khrushchev Speaks: Selected Speeches, Articles and Press Conferences, 1949-61*, edited by Thomas Whitney. Copyright © by the University of Michigan, 1963; renewed in the editor's name, 1991. Reprinted by permission of the University of Michigan Press.

From *Lenin Anthology*, ed. Robert Tucker. W.W. Norton, 1975.

From "Mandela and de Klerk: Words on a Transition" *New York Times*, May 3, 1994.

Reprinted by permission of the Putnam Publishing Group from *My Life* by Golda Meir. Copyright © 1975 by Golda Meir.

From *Benito Mussolini: My Autobiography* transl. Richard Washburn Child. Hutchinson & Co. Limited, 1928.

From *President Gamal Abdel Nasser's Speeches and Press Interviews*, The Information Department of Cairo, 1961.

From *Nehru: The First Sixty Years*, vl. 2, ed. by Dorothy Norman. The John Day Company, 1965.

From *Jawaharlal Nehru, An Autobiography* by Jawaharlal Nehru. John Lane, The Bodley Head, 1937.

Reprinted by permission of Warner Books/New York from *The Memoirs* Richard Nixon. Copyright © 1978.

From *Freedom and Unity* by Julius K. Nyerere. Oxford University Press, 1966.

From *Freedom and Socialism* by Julius K. Nyerere. Oxford University Press, 1968.

From *Freedom and Development* by Julius K. Nyerere. Oxford University Press.

From *Eva Perón, the Myths of a Woman* by J.M. Taylor. Reprinted by permission of The University of Chicago Press.

From *The Voice of Perón* by Juan Domingo Perón. Subsecretaria de La Presidencía de la Nacíon Argentina, 1950.

From *Franklin Roosevelt: Selected Speeches, Messages, Press Conferences, and Letters*, Rinehart and Company, Inc., 1957.

From *Nothing to Fear* ed. by Harry Hopkins. Reprinted by permission of Ayer Publishers.

From *American Ideals* by Theodore Roosevelt. Copyright © 1926 Charles Scribners' Sons.

Reprinted with the permission of Scribner's, an imprint of Simon & Schuster from *Theodore Roosevelt: An Autobiography* by Theodore Roosevelt. Copyright 1913 Charles Scribner's Sons; copyright renewed 1941 Edith K. Carow Roosevelt.

From *Mao Tse-Tung On Revolution and War* by Mostafa Rejai. Copyright © 1969, 1970 by Mostafa Rejai. Used by permission of Doubleday, a division of Bantam Doubleday Dell Publishing Group, Inc.

From *Stalin's Kampf*, ed. M. Werner. Howell, Soskin & Company, 1940.

"Talk with the German Author Emil Ludwig" from *J. V. Stalin, Works*, vl. 14. Foreign Languages Publishing House, 1955.

From *The History of the Russian Revolution* by Leon Trotsky. Reprinted by permission of Natalia Sedov-Trotsky.

From *Years of Trial and Hope*, vl. 2, by Harry S. Truman. Copyright © 1956 by Doubleday and Company. Reprinted by permission of Margaret Truman Daniel.

From *Mao Tse-Tung Unrehearsed, Talks and Letters: 1956-71*, ed. Stuart Schram. Reprinted by permission of Simon and Schuster.

From *Selected Works of Mao Tse-Tung* by Mao Tse-Tung, Lawrence and Wishart Ltd., London 1954.

From *Selected Readings from the Works of Mao Tse-Tung* by Mao Tse-Tung.

From *The Papers of Woodrow Wilson*, ed. Arthur S. Lind. Reprinted by permission of Princeton University Press.